The Biden Logs

(1/10/21 - 6/30/24)

M.J. Paolercio

ISBN
Paperback: 979-8-218-48014-1
Ebook: 979-8-218-48015-8

This is a work of fiction ... really.

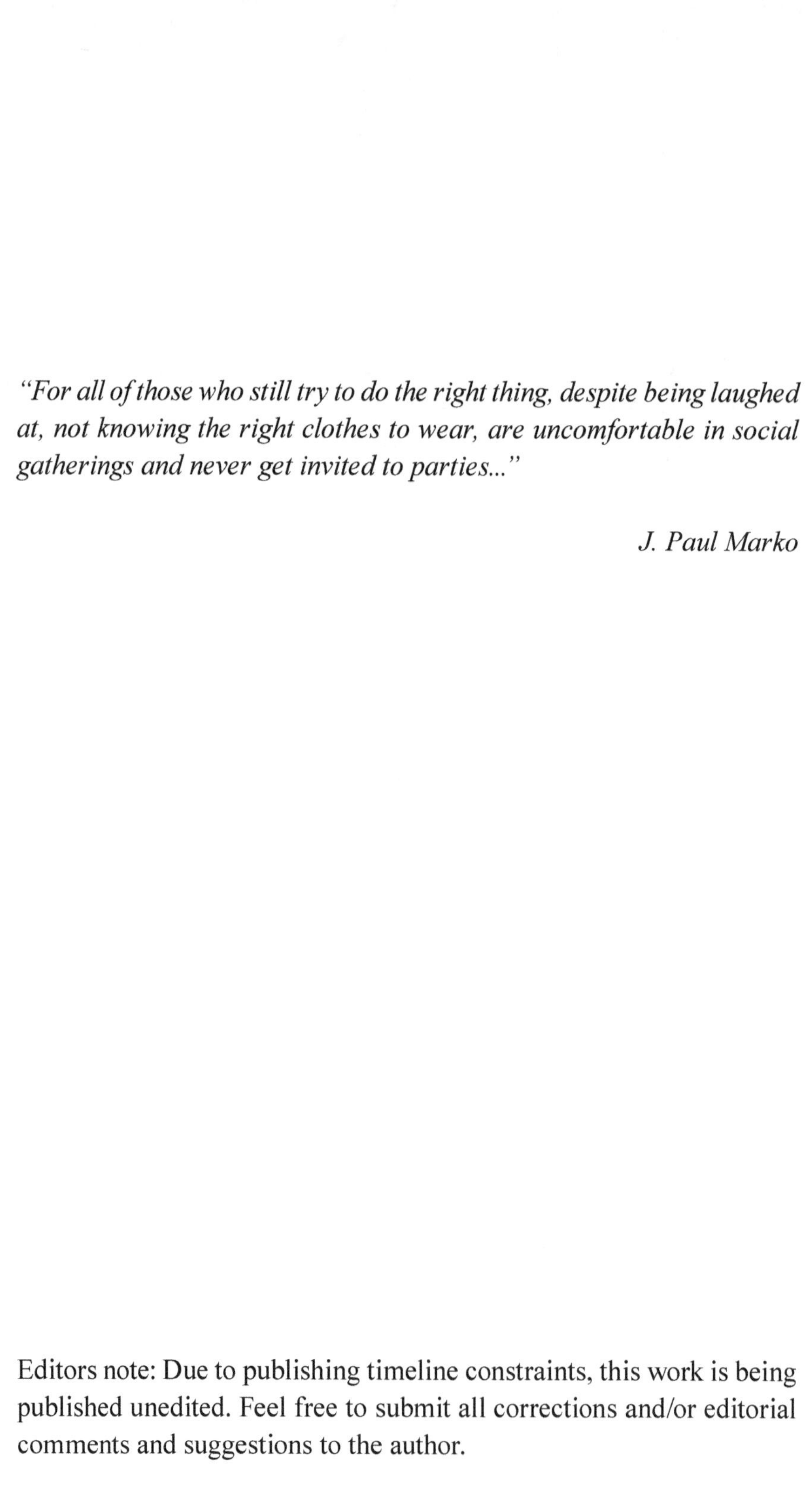

"For all of those who still try to do the right thing, despite being laughed at, not knowing the right clothes to wear, are uncomfortable in social gatherings and never get invited to parties..."

J. Paul Marko

An Introduction

This is an almost-daily account of Bidens' presidency since he took office in January of 2021. This work documents his attempt, like his mentor Obama, to reshape America into their vision of some kind of Marxist/Socialist utopia. Once accomplished, the dream of men like these is to rule like kings using only, as Obama famously said, "a pen and a phone". In this dream world they bypass the Constitution, Congress, the courts and, most dangerously, the wishes of the American people. If realized, this dream would be a death blow to this Republic.

This book also contains, with some editorial comment and dark humor, a daily recounting of some of Bidens' gaffes; his mangling of the English language, his stumbles when confronted by small obstacles, his creepy, incessant groping of women and girls of all ages and even his attempts to shake hands with either invisible or dead people only he sees. This by no means is a complete list: A website somewhere has tried to compile such a list and to date has recorded over 200 such incidents. To try to keep track of all of them would be exhausting and beyond the scope of this book.

Perhaps surprising to some, the genesis of this work was not strictly political. The germ of the idea for it started in 2016, right after Trump beat Clinton like a drum to win the presidency. During the race Clinton, with the help of many government agencies, fabricated her famous "Russian Collusion Hoax". This was the documentation she created out of whole cloth that "proved" Russia was aiding Trump with his campaign. In the end her lies were not enough to derail Trump, thus her humiliation on election day. A veritable legend for her bitter, petty outbursts when things don't go her way, Clinton continued to push her 'Russian Collusion' story, claiming that it was the only reason she lost. She demanded the FBI investigate and they complied, becoming a full partner with her in this shenanigan. An inquest called the "Muellar Investigation" was launched. Headed by former FBI chief Robert Muellar, it was one of the ugliest, unconstitutional, unnecessary and unnerving persecutions of an entire American family, just for political revenge and posturing.

It was what happened during Muellars' "investigation" of the Trump family that spurred the writing of this book. Nowhere in American history has this country witnessed such a boorishly unsuccessful attempt to smear an entire family, one member of that family in particular. All of the head-hunting participants involved in this witch hunt - roughly 30 investigators, mostly Clinton sycophants - spent two years combing through the entirety of the Trump family lives at a reported cost of $30 million to taxpayers, They went back decades, delving into every aspect of the familys' business, social and, some said, even their personal sex lives.* In the end, after two years this group of well-paid witch hunters found nothing other than a few process violations. True to form, though, like snails they left their ooze smeared across the Trump family as they slinked away, saying that even though their $30 million paid vacation turned up nothing, this didn't mean that Trump and his family weren't guilty "of something": Yes, snails to the end.

All involved in this travesty claim that they did this in an effort to preserve "American democracy". To this day, how this overbearing assault on a single American family "preserved democracy" in America has not been answered by any of them – not Clinton, Muellar, Rothstein, the FBI, et al. - none of them. What they did do in those two years is take every one of their perceived, calamitous injustices, from global wars and global warming, from their concocted "institutionalized" racism to white supremacy and privilege, from their dismay at not being allowed to have minors cut off their genitals and old men take showers with young girls in locker rooms, all the way down to parking and jaywalking tickets anywhere in America, and then try to hang the blame for all of them around the necks of Trump and his family.

The genesis of this book, then, was justice: I thought someone should return the favor.

MJP

* Considering the Muellar Investigations' pruriently perverse interest in the Trump family sex lives and the FBIs' disappointment when ravaging through Melania Trumps' underwear drawer during the Mar a Lago raid, it's clear that the ghost of J. Edgar Hoover still haunts the FBI, at least at it's higher echelons.

M

.

2021

1/10

Biden nominates Nira Tanden for the post of Office Management and Budget. Considered mediocre and facing an uphill approval from the Senate, she has had quite the career. She served as an attack dog for the Clintons, punched one of her employees and in 2011 she advised the Clintons to steal Syrian oil to offset economic troubles they had caused in the U.S. Often called ' bitch' by both parties, she shows she deserves the moniker by publicly naming - and thereby exposing - the victim in a sex harassment suit who had been promised anonymity. As his first nomination of his term, it seems Biden could've done better. Hopefully this is not prescient of his presidency.

1/15

Biden announces that on his first day in office he will reverse all of Trumps' executive orders, put the US back into both the Kyoto and Paris accords and insist that all new motorized vehicles in the US get a minimum of 54 mile per gallon. In his new COVID relief package Biden pledges to extend the moratorium on the non-payment of rent and provide legal help, free of charge, to any deadbeat renter that want to sue their landlords once the moratorium is lifted and the payment of rent is mandated.

1/19

Politico, a far-left rag, publishes a story on what they claim is Bidens' dementia dating back a year. It is rumored by some that this is the first nail in Bidens' political coffin for those who wish to move Biden out, replacing him with Harris, another far-left extremist.

1/21

Biden signs 10 executive orders one day after being sworn in. The EOs reverse much of what Trump accomplished. Among other things, Bidens' orders open the door for unfettered immigration, destroy women's' sports by allowing men who gender-identify as women to compete against women and ends Trumps 1776 commission which attempted to document the real story of the founding of the United States. In turn, Biden leaves in place the 1619 project which furthers a claim that Obama made in his presidency, that America has racism in its' DNA. How this furthers Bidens' promise to "...bring the country together..." is a mystery.

1/26

Biden signs a anti-Asian discrimination EO, purportedly to save Asians from the discrimination suffered since the COVID Virus outbreak. Biden claims Trump fomented this by calling the virus "the Chinese virus". Trump did this once and corrected himself the next day, calling it the China virus, or "...the Communist China virus". Biden ignores this and continues to blame Trump for any discrimination currently suffered by American Chinese.

1/27

Biden aides push for him to declare a 'Climate Emergency" in the country, thus allowing him to enact executive changes in all sorts of domestic policies while bypassing the normal legislative process, both Houses of Congress and the American voter.

1/31

China's top diplomat, Yang Jiechi, warns Biden not to cross Beijing's "red line" This "red line" constitutes any issues regarding Hong Kong, Tibet and Xinjiang. Jiechi warns Biden that any interference in the affairs of these three regions would undermine relations between China and the US. He also tells Biden that he should "strictly abide by the 'One China principle' with regards to Taiwan, the independent island that Beijing claims is part of its territory.

2/1

Biden signs his 40th executive order in the 10 days he's been president. Without asking, he is obviously following in the footsteps of his mentor, Obama, who once said he didn't have to consult Congress – and, tangentially, the American public – to rule because he had "...a pen and a phone." At the rate of four executive orders a day Biden should ask his mentor for a hefty supply of pens.

2/2

In one EO, Biden directs the secretary of homeland security to lead a task force to try to unite several hundred illega alien families he insists remain seperated because of Trump's "zero tolerance" policy. This policy sought to discourage migration across Americas' southern border. With two other orders, Biden authorizes a review of Trump's immigration policies that limited asylum, stopped funding to foreign countries unfriendly to the US and made it more difficult to get green cards or be naturalized. Apparently Biden wnats to undermine any Trump policy designed to keep America safer.

2/3

China again proclaims that dire consequences would result if Biden interferes with any of its' Communist goals, such as crushing Hong Kong and Taiwan. Their leaders direct warning for Biden was for him not "…dare cross the Red Line…" Seemingly chastised, Biden says nothing, leaving all to wonder if China would've ever spoken to Trump this way.

2/4

Biden reverses Trumps' programs that one, would bring all American troops home and, two, insist that NATO countries start paying their fair share for America protecting them from enemies such as Russia. Because of Biden, American troops in Germany are forced to remain there and American taxpayers are forced to continue to foot the majority of the bill for NATO.

2/9

It took Biden no more than a couple of weeks to break two of his most strenuous campaign promises: One, to do nothing to divide the country but instead unite it and, two, to seek bi-partisan agreement on all of his recommendations. So, in that vein, he endorses the show-trial impeachment of Trump, sharply dividing the country, and vetoed the GOP counter-offer to his COVID aid package without consulting or meeting with them. So much for Biden campaign promises.

2/12

It is reported that Biden has signed approximately 48 executive orders in his first 3 weeks of office. In defending Bidens seeming insatiable desire to rule by pen rather than the normal legislative process, – much like his mentor, Obama - his supporters hail Bidens' dictatorial moves as a salvation, since now they don't have to worry that their bills might languish "… in legislative limbo."

2/13

Biden calls for "common sense'" gun control. Bidens' definition common sense gun control is background checks on personal gun sales, strict liability for all gun manufacturers and a psychiatric exam of all family members when any member of a family purchases a gun. This last requirement borders on the ironic, since Biden appoints Beto O'Roarke, a person long suspected of serious mental problems of his own, as his gun czar.

2/14

Biden tells one of his nurses that he wants to send his wife a Valentine note today. The nurse reminds Biden that he sent a heartfelt message to his wife Jill on Valentines Day last year, which read "You're the love of my life and the life of my love.". Smiling and quite proud of his prose, Biden tells the nurse to send the same message this year... then asks the nurse who this 'Jill' is.

2/15

Biden announces that his new COVID relief package will target non-whites. Yes, instead of directing the funds to go according to need, he specifically targeted people of a certain race – this one being white – to not receive the bulk of relief dollars based on the color of their skin.

2/16

Biden claims his administration in not anti-Semitic, but he has been in office for almost a month and he has not called Ben Netanyahu, the leader of Israel, one of our allies. This, while he has called a myriad of other world leaders, many of whom in the past have shown much disdain for America.

2/17

Without any demonstrable evidence, Biden announces at a town hall gathering that White Supremacy is the greatest domestic threat to the country. Biden and if his DOJ wants to bring charges against Trump for anything he did while in office, he will not interfere. Then Biden whines that he is tired of people talking about Trump and only about Trump for the last four years. Biden promises that he will talk about Trump anymore and, during his term, the news "... will be (about) the American people" only. Bets are immediately taken on how soon he brings up Trumps' name again.

2/18

Biden announces an immigration policy overhaul, providing a pathway for citizenship "...for the 11 million illegals already living in the US" before 1/1/21. The lie is the 11 million number: Biden has held onto that lie for over two decades. The actual number of illegals in America that this "pathway" will benefit is closer to 25 million, if not more.

2/19

Under Biden the Department of Education released new guidelines for all public schools. They included having math departments move away from using numbers and discouraging any objection to the teaching that

2+2 doesn't have to equal 4. Biden and his DOE insist that the primacy of numbers or the logic of 2+2 equaling 4 were both examples of white privilege, white supremacy and racism. The question of when simple numbers became racially conscious comes up: Biden has no comment.

2/21

Biden wants to resume talks with Iran and lift all restrictions. For the restrictions to be lifted, Biden tells Iran they must stop enriching Uranium in an effort to build a nuclear weapon and let UN inspectors have access to their nuclear facilities. Iran gratefully accepts the billions Biden sends them, but continues enriching Uranium in order to build a bomb and limits access to UN inspectors. Despite this blatant defiance of his terms, Biden, glassy-eyed, gives Iran the money and announces that this is progress in American/Iranian relations.

2/22

Iran continues to tell Biden to pound sand in regard to his request for access to their facilities and they will continue to enrich Uranium and build their nuclear weapons. Biden capitulates and tells them he wants to open talks with them anyway. but then supposedly orders the US military to fires on Syrian/Iranian proxies.

2/23

Bidens' new COVID relief package contains funding for government employees to receive an extra 21k on top of their already full pay and benefits package. This is for government employees caring for their kids who aren't in school ... due to Biden and his CDC shutting down the schools. In his current mental state, it is unclear if Biden comprehends the irony of this absurdity, or just doesn't care.

2/25

Bidens' choice for assistant secretary of health, Rachel Levine, a rather unattractive man who put on a blond wig and now calls himself a woman. Rand Paul accuses Levine of supporting the injection of hormones and genital mutilation of minors in order to permanently alter and prevent secondary sexual characteristics. Levine, wig in place, refuses to answer the question, saying instead: "Senator, transgender medicine is a very complex and nuanced field. If confirmed to the position of assistant secretary of health, I would certainly be pleased to come to your office and talk with you and your staff about the standards of care and the complexity of this field." Perhaps his wig was too tight.

2/27

Biden overturns Trumps order to not buy technical equipment from China that might be used to spy on the US; Biden OKs this, probably helping his family who has done business with the Chinese Communists for over a decade.

3/1

It is revealed that 90% of Bidens' "COVID relief package" is in reality a massive pork bill, with most of the pork going to Marxist/blue states to bail them out of the massive deficits accumulated over the years due to their socialist, production-killing programs. Only 10% of the bill is targeted for actual COVID relief purposes.

3/3

Bidens' total number of Executive Orders has reached 55, but his supporters still claim that Biden does not intend to govern 'with a phone and a pen', a la Obama. Not only did 28 of the 55 EO s come in the first two days of Bidens' presidency, at this point in his presidency Trump, the supposed tyrant, had signed only 24.

3/5

It was revealed today that Bidens' entire staff and administrators - every one of them - are holdovers from the Obama administration. effectively making this Obamas' third term. Obamas' third term was supposed to be Hillary's' job, before Trump shellacked her, leaving Biden as Obamas' puppet.

3/8

Biden, getting involved where he has no business to be, announces his support of Meghan Markll, the ex-royal, after she did an Oprah interview where she accused the Royal family of bullying, racism and attempting to silence her. It is unclear why Biden considers this important in governing America. It is also unclear if Biden actually saw the interview since, if his wife wasn't there, there was no one to turn the TV on for him.

3/10

Biden releases excerpts from a speech he plans on giving tomorrow. In it he claims credit for solving the COVID crisis by ordering enough of the vaccine for everyone in the country, something Biden claimed the previous administration had failed to do. Either because he was lying, or no one told him, or his Politico-described dementia kicked in, Biden failed to mention that the Trump administration ordered between 550 and 800 million doses of the vaccine, three times the population of the US, and extra for emergencies and for helping our allies.

3/13

The number of young people detained at the southern border has swelled to 100% more than last year at this time, now in excess of 100, 000. The vast increase in numbers can be directly related to Bidens' stated objective of providing amnesty for any illegal that can make it into the US.

3/15

Biden released a statement announcing that he would insure that 100 million vaccines would be available by the first of May. Either again because he was lying or it was after 4:30 in the afternoon, Biden fails to mention that this was a process already put in place by Trump. Then Biden adds that he would "streamline" the delivery system responsible for delivering the vaccines … another system already put in place by Trump.

3/16

Following his 'taking-credit-for-something-I never-did' briefing from yesterday, Biden announces that he was committed to start re-opening all schools in America. Great idea, except that that almost all private schools and many public schools in the US and schools all over the world were already open, some for as long as seven months. It seems this information never made it to Bidens' basement.

3/17

It is reported that Biden went 43 days without making an appearance, holding a press conference or meeting with the press to answer questions. Yet it was Trump who was accused of being "non-transparent", even though he met with the media on almost a daily basis, whether behind a podium, on the White House lawn or even before boarding Air Force One, where he took on all comers and questions.

3/18

One of Bidens' staff repeats for reporters a synopsis of Bidens "American Rescue Plan". As part of his plan Biden announces a goal of safely reopening a majority of K-8 schools in his the first 100 days, evidently unaware that many schools across the nation have already re-opened, some of them for months before he took office. Bidens' plan also includes a promise to mount a national vaccination program (already put in place by Trump) in order to contain COVID19. In addition Biden vows to set up community vaccination sites nationwide (already set up by Trump), scale up testing and tracing (increasing programs already set up by Trump) and order enough vaccine doses for the US and its' allies (again, something Trump had already done). When admonished for presenting actions already taken by Trump as "new" actions taken by Biden, his spokesperson tells the reporters to wait, that he is saving the best for last: That is, come tomorrow Biden guarantees that the sun will rise and set in the same day.... unfortunately just another event already put in place by Trump.

3/19

North Korea unveils two new ICBM missiles capable of reaching the United States. While parading the missiles in their capital, Fat Little pajama Boy announces that his country is no longer subject, or will abide by, the anti-nuclear agreement he signed with Trump in 2018. at the same time a news report shows Bidens' trip and fall several times just trying to climb the stairs of Air Force One. Watching this display of Bidens' strength and health allows the Fat Boy another night of easy rest.

3/20

Biden is now detaining/housing/putting in cages/more than 13,000 illegals at the southern border. When Trump detained 3000 illegals, the media labeled him a racist, a Hitler, a dehumanizing monster that had created a "disaster" at the southern border. Now, instead of calling Bidens' 300% increase in detainees, including children, a disaster, the media labels it a "challenge".

3/21

Biden has now deployed FEMA, the group chartered with rescuing America from both natural and unnatural disasters, to the southern border. However, he re-iterates that they are not there to deal with any disaster his immigration policies – or the lack of them – have caused, but the "challenge" there.

3/22

With Bidens' acquiesce, the cancel culture activists have moved to force Disney to remove Pepe LePew, Speedy Gonzalez, Peter Pan and Dumbo from their world of f cartoons because of the "dilatory archetypes" they present to young children. The backlash is instantaneous as parents mock Bidens' complacency in this decision. They sarcastically point out that they are "ecstatic" about this decision regarding, Pepe, Speedy and the others. After all, their 8 year olds are now safe from the damaging effects of these culturally depraved cartoon role models: Now their kids are free to play Grand Theft Auto, where they set prostitutes on fire with a blow torch so they don't have to pay them:

3/23

The North Korean dictator, Pajama Boy, launches two more missiles into the Sea of Japan. That makes two missile launches since Biden became president. Biden is reminded that there was not a single missile fired during Trumps' presidency, once he threatened to blow Pajama Boy off the face of the earth. Bidens' reaction to this aggression? So far, nothing.

3/24

Even though Biden repeatedly stonewalls the media, denying access to film the "challenge" he created at the southern border, someone sneaks pictures out. They depict deplorable conditions there, far worse than at any time under Trump after he inherited a similar mess from Obama. Biden now reluctantly admits the situation there is a crisis. To solve this, he appoints Kamala Harris - a renowned open border and sanctuary city/state advocate - in charge of taking care of the problem. When asked if she planned to visit the border soon, Harris demonstrates her seriousness by laughing.

3/26

Biden invites the dictators from the largest Communist-suppressed countries, China and Russia, to join him in the world climate change summit he is hosting in April. When asked to defend why he invited Americas two most powerful enemies to his summit, Biden says he didn't really invite them directly but claims that "... they (Russia and China) know they are invited." How? Perhaps Biden believes his nurses when they keep telling him his telepathic thoughts really can travel through basement walls.

3/29

Continuing his "Taking Credit for the Accomplishments of Others" tour, Biden holds a press conference to take credit for the COVID19 vaccination progress across the country, Again he conveniently ignores the fact that almost all of these programs, including the manufacture and purchase of the vaccine, was set up by Trump long before Biden became president. What Biden does add is to implore all state and local leaders to re-invoke the mask mandate. This, despite conclusive evidence that, other than very specific situations, mask are not only useless but medically debilitating, especially to small children.

3/31

After imploring government leaders around the country and all US citizens to wear masks in an effort to 'thwart' the 'deadly' COVID19 virus, reporters point out that Biden, whether in the White House or at press briefings, often does not wears one. In addition it is pointed out that, for all of Bidens' claims of its' ferocity, the COVID virus has killed less than half of the average number of Americans who die because of the flu each year. For all of this, Biden has no comment.

4/2

In a confusing press release, Biden announces that he signed a memorandum that will "strengthen" US efforts to combat "...sexual violence as a weapon of war...". Stunned reporters ask a barrage of questions: What war or wars? What specific examples of sexual violence as a war weapon is Biden referring to? Is Biden talking about our military? If so, how long has the US military been using sexual violence as a weapon? If not our military, then whose? If Biden was referring to Americas' enemies, is he delusional enough to believe his "memorandum" is going to stop terrorists from raping their victims?

These and other questions go unanswered, leaving all once again to wonder what the hell Biden is talking about.

4/7

Bidens' position on abortion is questioned again today. Biden professes to be a devout Catholic and insists his faith guides him in all matters. However, Biden endorses aborting a baby even at 9 months. This usually involves removing the baby part way out of the womb before killing it, even if it's not endangering the mothers' health. Catholics around the world are wondering out loud what faith Biden believes he belongs to.

4/8

As part of Bidens' 2 trillion dollar infrastructure bill – separate from his 2 trillion COVID relief bill – Biden offers 5 billion dollars in financial incentives to local governments to change zoning laws that restrict middle and upper class neighborhoods to only single-family homes. This is an effort to allow federal low-income housing projects – better known as government ghetto apartment housing - to be built in the middle of these upscale neighborhoods. This would not only destroy property values in these areas, it would fan the embers of class warfare into a flame, a main goal of Biden and like-minded Marxists.

4/9

Biden announces he is authoring several EOs to combat the "epidemic" of gun violence in the US. The trouble is, his EOs have nothing to do with combating gun violence, but everything to do with restricting gun ownership for law-abiding Americans. When asked if this and some other actions hie is taking are in direct conflict with the Second amendment, Biden replies: "No amendment is absolute." Calling gun violence in America a "epidemic" rings hollow for Biden after last summer. It doesn't seem like violence was much of an issue for Biden then, since it took Biden 90 days to issue an extremely weak, tepid condemnation to the riots that burned down major portions of American cities and cost bullion in lost businesses and lives.

4/10

In the last weeks of Trumps' presidency, attempted border crossings averaged 100/day. On the day Biden was inaugurated the number jumped to 1000. Now, due to Bidens' immigration policies – or lack of them - the number of daily attempts is now 15000. Biden has caused the crisis to spread north to cities like Long Beach and Pomona in California, which have opened sites to house the illegals.

4/13

Iran again announces intentions to build intercontinental nuclear missiles specifically for the purpose of reaching the US. Biden responds by again taking a knee in his basement, saying he will still pursue the diplomatic route as "...there are no other options..." Does Biden mean options like boycotting Iran, freezing their assets, refusing to refine their oil, cutting them off from the rest of the world, causing such economic turmoil in their country that there were no threats or missile launches during the Trump administration ... does Biden mean those options?

4/14

Biden told a civil rights group that parts of the US were "...backsliding into the days of Jim Crow". Then his ambassador to the UN ripped the US in front of the rest of the world and the NAN, saying that she had seen how the "...original sin of slavery weaved white supremacy into our founding documents and principles." What Biden and his staff don't mention is that his own Human Rights Council has been accused of providing cover for dictators and human rights abusers like Russia, Cuba, China and Venezuela.'

4/18

Biden announces that he is no longer going to use the traditional ABA to vet his judicial choices, as it is "...not a diverse enough group...', meaning that the group is not liberal enough, not Marxist enough. This is the same ABA that has a history of taking liberal positions on issues including abortion, the death penalty, same-sex marriage, affirmative action and the Second Amendment. Claiming that this group is not Marxist enough for his judicial selections is an indication of just how far left Biden wants his nominees to be.

4/19

When he was running for president, Biden promised to "heal" America and bring people back together, though he was never clear from what. However, a main supporter of his, Maxine Waters, has promised to instigate further rioting and violence in the streets - reminiscent of the burning and looting that took place in the summer of 2020 - if a guilty verdict is not rendered against the cops in a Minneapolis court case. The 'great healer' Biden says nothing.

4/20

A la Maxine Waters, Biden furthers instigates possible violence by announcing that he is "praying the verdict is the right verdict" in the trial of a Minneapolis police officer. Biden has no problem in putting his thumb on the scales of justice, implying guilt on the officer's part, before any evidence is presented. However, Biden and his staff privately weigh how to handle the possible violent response if the verdict is an unpopular one. Laughably, Bidens' solution for the possible violence is to dispatch, not more police or National Guard, but specially trained "community facilitators" from the Justice Department. Yes, these "facilitators" should be a big help if the city is set on fire.

4/21

Biden praises the guilty verdict in the murder trial of a former police officer in Minneapolis. Not wasting a chance to throw gasoline on an already burning fire, Biden goes on to call the verdict a "too rare" step to deliver "basic accountability" for Black Americans and it "...ripped a scar." off America for the world to see. At the same time, Biden colleagues expressed gratitude to George Floyd for "sacrificing" his life "for justice". Not wishing to cool the fire, Biden doesn't mention that 93 percent of black homicide victims are killed by other blacks, or that in Chicago alone this year 127 blacks have already been killed, the vast majority of them killed by other blacks. Possibly Biden doesn't consider these facts scars because they are still open wounds that have been festering in Democratic-run cities all over America for decades.

4/22

With Bidens' approval, the House passes a bill attempting to make Washington DC - with an area footprint not much bigger than a large Costco and population that would have to stretch to fill a football stadium - the 51st state in America. With the Marxist swamp that is DC, the move is Bidens' not-so-subtle attempt to add two more Democratic seats to the Senate.

4/24

Bidden has made a number of false claims/lies/exaggerations in his first 100 days, many of them not exposed by the media. Two that are reported are his repeated claims that Georgia's GOP-led election law will end voting hours early – which it won't – and the lie that federal government contracts awarded to foreign companies went up by 30% under Trump. The medias' only defense of Bidens' lies is that Trump lied more.

4/25

Possibly the worst of Bidens' false claims that the Marxist media ignores is his claim that the Georgia voter-reform bill is a return to the Jim Crow era of the South. The bill does nothing to restrict voting rights and is, in fact, more liberal that Bidens' own state of Delaware. It requires valid IDs, a proof of residency and tightening up ID requirements for absentee ballots in an effort to end the mail-in fraud that happened in the last election. What apparently escapes Biden while hiding in his basement is that the Jim Crow era in the South was fomented, legalized, encouraged and maintained for decades almost entirely by Democrats.

4/26

Biden sends Harris to South America to meet with several corrupt, mostly cartel-run countries, to ask the leaders of these countries what the US can do to help them with their immigration and drug problems. As one, they agree to work on the internal problems of their respective countries that force so many to flee, but only if Biden will send more money. On her return Harris is asked why she spends so much time in other countries, offering to help them with their self-inflicted wounds, but she refuses to visit the southern border of her own country which hers and Bidens' immigration policies have turned into a type of war zone. She ignores the question, replying only that: "I don't play political games." A strange answer, since on her rise to the top there were many political 'games' Harris did not mind playing.

4/27

It comes to light that Bidens' address before Congress will actually be a fake-address because less than half of this august body will be present. Most notably Biden uninvited some of his harshest critics, citing 'COVID concerns'. This is a breakthrough in COVID science that only Biden is aware of: Apparently the virus, all on its' own, seeks out those that realize what a danger Bidens' decreased mental state presents to the nation.

4/28

Biden holds his fake-address before Congress where he announces his intention to spend 6.6 trillion on "infrastructure". As an example of Bidens' consistency, only 6% of the bill is slated for infrastructure, just like in his 1.9 trillion "COVID relief" bill where only 6% of that bill was to go to actual activities concerning the virus. The rest of the 11.8 trillion in Bidens' boondoggle bills are to go to Democrat/Marxist giveaway programs, including paying off the huge deficits run up by Marxist-controlled states like California, New York and Illinois.

4/29

While most of Bidens' speech is not understandable, one thing Biden emphasizes is that two states, California and New York, are models that all other states should be forced to follow. It is no surprise to anyone that Biden picks as his role models two states that have not only mismanaged their finances to the point of bankruptcy but also the COVID19 'crisis', needlessly killing thousands.

4/30

It took only a day for Internet sites to feature pundits that attempt to translate/interpret the portions of Bidens' speech that were so slurred they could not be understood in real time. Some sites even make a game of it, giving prizes to callers who can correctly identify what Bidens' slurred words actually were.

5/2

Despite Biens' efforts to stop it, parts of the southern border wall are continuing to be rebuilt, but only because it is to incorporate a flood barrier for a nearby town. Biden and his activists nevertheless insist that construction of the wall stop anyway, regardless of the possible loss of life and property that might result from ensuing floods.

5/3

Biden announces his plan to allow 400 families a day – yes, a day – to cross the border into the United states, starting in June. He also, again, reverses a promise that he made, to keep the Trump entry limit of 15000 asylum seekers a year in place. He promises now to allow 62500 of the same to enter the country in the next six months.

5/4

As predicted, on her return from her visit to the garbage scow countries in South America, Harris reports that these Marxist countries not only will work on their internal problems that have reduced their economies to shambles, but will also work on more global issues like climate change … if Biden sends them money. To this end, Biden pledges to send these gangster states 4 billion dollars.

5/5

Between 11/25//2020, and 4///19/2021, Biden's inaugural committee brought in over 60 million dollars from prominent billionaires and companies such as Lockheed Martin, Boeing, Uber, Comcast, AT&T, Bank of America, Pfizer and Qualcomm, all who donated at least one million dollars. Inaugural committees, unlike presidential and congressional campaigns, are not prohibited from accepting corporate donations. This is from a report Biden filed with the Federal Election Commission. For 60 million dollars that must've been some inauguration. Even when noticing the dates, no one questions how many of these 'inauguration donations' came in after the actual event.

5/6

Biden does an interview imploring the public to keep wearing masks and socially distance from each other, even if they're fully vaccinated. Biden claims that this will make other people "feel better" and "...it's the patriotic thing to do..." Then Biden and his wife pose for a picture with Jimmy and Roslyn Carter … indoors, not socially distanced, unmasked and all of them over the age of 65, the age group supposedly most at risk by the virus.

5/7

It is reported that at one of his press briefings Biden said that wearing a mask inside, even if fully vaccinated, is a good policy. Since this directly contradicts what the CDC and his Dr. Fauci advises, the question of where Biden received this 'policy' arises. Biden, glazed and confused look in place, has no comment.

5/8

A spokesperson for the Biden administration announces that Biden wants all illegal aliens to be referred to as "Unidentified Visitors" from now on. It is also rumored that in the future Biden will also want convicted rapists and child molesters to be referred to as "Over Eager Bad Dates" and "Over Committed Youth Counselors".

5/9

A terrible jobs report hits the news, with unemployment up and a full 30% fewer jobs created than last month. This despite Bidens' pumping trillions into the economy and promising to pump in trillions more. On hearing the news, Biden looks befuddled, perhaps not understanding that when you pay people more than they regularly earn to stay home, employment goes down and stays down. Then again, 'befuddled' is the normal look for this poor man.

5/10

A re-visited jobs report is even worse than expected. Biden had predicted over a million new jobs would be created in the month of April, but less than quarter of that number actually appear. Biden does not comment on this abysmal failure. In addition, Biden finds himself locked out of power in the Republican-run states that are enacting voter reform laws, mainly requiring stricter adherence to voter ID and mail-in requirements. To remedy this, Biden backs a plan put forward by Congressional allies that would allow him to 'Federalize' voting requirements. This would serve to override individual state voting laws and requirements, making all states submit only to voting laws enacted by Biden.

5/11

The recent poor unemployment figures are not so hard to understand as more parts of Bidens' giveaway legislation are made known; a $1,400 per-person check to households across America, a provision to provide direct housing and nutrition assistance t all who are "eligible", expanding access to childcare and affordable healthcare, increasing the minimum wage, extending unemployment insurance up to $1000/week and giving families with kids and childless workers an emergency boost of funds. When asked how he will pay for all this largesse, Biden has no comment.

5/12

As Bidens' giveaways from both his (supposed) COVID relief and (supposed) infrastructure package receive more scrutiny, all acknowledge that the funds are, one, boondoggles for those not inclined to ever return to gainful employment and, two, payoffs to Marxist organizations and Democratic controlled states. Through it all of the mess, one question Biden will not answer is, why do childless workers need economic help?

5/13

Although Biden claims his tax proposal would target only the wealthy, it is apparent that his call for a raise in capital gains tax will hit middle-class home sellers the hardest. In addition, his ending the step-up provision on inherited real estate will impact the middle class more than the supposed 'wealthy'. Finally, even his supporters admit that the Bidens' claim that these tax changes will not affect those making less than $400k is just more Biden hogwash.

5/14

As more and more states submit new voting laws to prevent the suspected wide-scale cheating that they engaged in the 2020 election, the Democrats ask Biden and the DOJ to act to prevent this. In addition, activist Democrat legislators encourage their supporters to "mobilize" and "make it personal" in advance of the 2022-midterm elections. This was the same call to arms by the Democrats that spurred Marxist groups like BLM and Antifa to burn and loot major US cities in the summer of 2020: Biden has no comment.

5/15

Russia hacks into a pipeline that is a major supplier of fuel to the East coast, bringing it to its' knees, causing fuel shortages and long gas lines. When asked what his response to this cyber attack will be, Biden answers only that he will invest more in education. His demented reasoning is that better educated students might grow up in future years to be better computer programmers and, thus, be better able to stop cyber hacking by our enemies. Biden blithely ignores the question about what he is going to do about the Russians and the present fuel shortages. Biden leaves the stage quickly, ignoring the shouted question of what Trump would've done in a similar situation.

5/16

At his last briefing Biden and Harris, though both vaccinated, show up socially distanced and masked, even though there is no one within 20 feet of them. Biden insists that even vaccinated, people should continue to wear masks, if only because it makes their neighbors "feel better". Now Biden and Harris show up at their next briefing, still socially distanced but unmasked, grinning stupidly and feigning no knowledge of their hard core mask-wearing stance of just a couple days prior. It's obvious that the clown show between the Biden administration and the CDC will continue.

5/17

The Palestinians start yet another conflict with Americas' fervent ally, Israel. In response, Biden orders 10 million dollars in aid to be sent to, yes, Palestine. Additionally, Biden assures Israels' sworn enemy that this is just the first installment of the 100 million dollars he promises to send to Israels' enemy in the very near future. Biden insists that the money will be used "to support exchange and reconciliation projects with Israeli" but refuses to identify the specific recipients who are to receive this money. If anyone believes the terrorist Palestinians will use the funds for "reconciliation" purposes, please rush to Brooklyn immediately, as there has to be a bridge for sale.

5/18

Definitely mumbling out of both sides of his mouth, Biden announces that Israel has every right to defend itself against the Palestinian and Hamas rocket attacks. No one asks Biden that, if this is true, why did he authorize sending this terrorist organization 100 million dollars recently. The fact that Biden authorized the funds while Hamas was in the middle of bombing Israel makes an answer to that question worth listening to, if Bidens' mumbles can be interpreted.

5/19

Despite the CDC new guidelines stipulating that vaccinated people no longer have to wear masks or socially distance, Biden is seen strolling the grounds of the White House, by himself, in daylight, fully masked. Later Biden does a photo opp at a Ford Motor plant where he climbs into a truck and shuts the doors with two people that are not in his personal social circle. Then, with rolled up windows, no social distancing and no masks, Biden waves gleefully at the cameras as he drives off. One can surmise that the guys with the nets can't be far behind.

5/20

In what is possibly a historical vote concerning one of Americas' staunchest allies, every Democrat in the House, with Bidens' approval, votes for a bill that effectively supports Hamas. This despite this terrorist groups' promise to wipe our ally Israel off the map. Biden has no comment.

5/21

For about the 10th time in his short stint as President, Biden issues an unintelligible statement that no one questions him about. It sounded like: 'The drivers of the state, here's what drives the drivers, these are the things you can do, don't panic....'' and then he drifts off. Instead of trying to figure out what Biden was trying to say, the media defended Bidens' mumbling by reminding everyone that at least twice in his four years, Trump mis-pronounced words also.

5/22

The Mayor of Chicago announces that she will not give any more interviews or press releases to white journalists. It is the first time in American history that a major American city blatantly issues a racist decree as policy, purposely stoking racial hatred. Biden, as leader of the country and self proclaims "healer of rifts', says nothing.

5/23

Members of Congress label the Chicago mayors' blatant anti-white racism as abhorrent and call on Biden and Harris to join them in calling for Mayor Lightfoot's resignation. They insist that Biden, as leaders of this country, he must condemn all racism, including anti-white. Biden is reminded again that he ran on the promise of being a 'unifire' of America. However, Biden says nothing, further promulgating racial hatred in the country.

5/24

Despite the incessant bad-mouthing in the press, the two clown impeachment attempts, the call for criminal indictments for his supposed role in the 1/6/21 White House brawl, and the Manhattan DA announcing a criminal probe into his business ventures, a new poll taken shows that if the 2024 election was held today, Trump would beat Biden, 49% to 45%. Biden does not comment on the poll.

5/25

 Biden supposedly issues a Twitter post - since it came from his basement it is unclear who really wrote it – saying that the recent attacks on the Jewish community are despicable and must stop. Biden wrote further that he condemns the anti-Semitic behavior both at home and abroad, but still ignores the question of why he recently sent the Palestinians, in the midst of their attacks on Israel, $100 million dollars, or whom he sent it to.

5/26

Over a year ago Trump proclaimed that the COVID virus originated in China, probably in a lab in Wuhan. He was denounced as a racist and a conspiracy theorist, among other things. Now as more information comes out proving that the virus was created in a lab in China, Biden is pressed to get more information out of China concerning their involvement in its' creation. Biden remains silent.

5/27

It is reported that even hardcore leftists in France, the left-wing wacko country of Europe, think that Americas' obsession for erasing gender identification has reached the point of insanity. The president of the country went so far to say that this obsession is 'an existential threat to the French Republic'. Apparently bureaucrats in France's education bureaucracy who agree with this assessment, even if there is not a single bureaucrat in the Department of Education in Washington, D.C., that does. Biden and his administration has no comment.

5/28

Biden still insists there is a COVID health emergency in America and that is why people can't open their businesses or attend weddings and funerals. However, every day Biden welcomes thousands of people across the southern border who test positive for COVID and yet are released into America and even sometimes are driven to a nice hotel and put up there at taxpayers' expense. Biden has no comment on this.

5/29

With Biden watching, Harris kicks off the Memorial Day weekend by posting an attempt at a glam picture of herself, coyly advising her followers to "enjoy the long weekend '. Apparently it is lost on the vapid VP that this "long weekend" is the one where true Americans remember their war dead. After receiving a torrent of criticism for her shallowness, she took the post down and replaced it with a canned 'appreciation speech' about memorializing this nations' war dead. Since her 'sincere' speech was made only after her public berating, her words ring hollow.

5/30

This was the 67th day that neither Harris or Biden has visited U.S. communities along the southern border. Harris, supposedly the "immigration czar", still has not held a news conference about what her border-related duties are. To add preposterous fuel to an already-preposterous fire, Bidens' Homeland Security Secretary announces: "The border is closed." This despite reports that there are as many as 10,000 encounters with illegals along the border daily and that Biden and his staff have been relocating many of them to destinations across the US at taxpayer expense. Bidens' Homeland Secretary night be forgiven this particular idiocy since on the same day he announced that bathers along the Eastern Seaboard no longer have to fear shark attacks since he has closed the ocean.

5/31

In a surprising change of pace from his mentor, Biden continued the tradition of US presidents – all except Obama - of visiting Arlington National Cemetery on Memorial Day to honor the nations' military dead. Then what was not surprising was Bidens' speech there. Rather than focusing on honoring the fallen heroes, Bidens' speech devolved into leftist drivel. Biden mentioned every liberal talking point, from minorities being denied the vote and equity under the law, to Bidens' self-aggrandizing efforts to rectify "...persistent economic and racial disparities...." All this pontificating, but hardly a word about Americas' fallen heroes. What Biden also doesn't mentions is why he stood stone-faced still while homeowners, landlords and small business folks suffered this same lack of "law equity" and "persistent economic disparity" when BLM, Antifa and other Biden-supported groups attacked, assaulted and burned down their businesses last year, with hardly an arrest being made. At the end of this latest embarrassing spectacle all that can be said is that, unlike Obama, at least Biden showed up.

6/1

Biden calls for countries around the world to raise their tax rates on their own businesses and corporations, in order discourage American companies to move abroad once he inflicts his tax increase on them. His hope seems to be that if foreign countries increase their tax rates enough, he will be able to raise taxes on American corporations even further while leaving them, in essence, no where to run.

6/2

Despite what Biden told the nation, Harris puts out a notice that she is not responsible for handlimg the border crisis. She and her team were quoted, saying: "'We do not own the issues at the border.'" Harris claims that this is because she is more concerned about the "root causes" of the Americas' immigration problem, crisis, things like "... climate change (and) **food** insecurity..." Someone soon should wake Biden from his afternoon nap and infromhim that there is a real crisis on the southern border of the US. The unwillingness of Biden to even pretend to care about the crisis - people dying, getting raped, killed or trafficked or being held in horrendous conditions. Just the economic and social harm being done to the US by this tsunami of migrants is unimaginable. Meanwhile Harris has scheduled visits to, not Anericas'' border, but to Mexico and Guatemala. There she hopes these countries accept the bags of cash bribes she is bringing them, but only if they promise to encourage their citizens to, well, just stay home.

6/3

It seems Biden never tires demonstrating that not only is he not the sharpest knife in the drawer, but in his present state, probably not even in the knife drawer. Biden announces that he is not raising taxes on anyone but corporations and then only by 7%. What dim-bulb Biden either fails to realize or is to dumb to comprehend, an increase in corporate taxes is an increase in everyone's loss of their own disposable income. This is because corporations usually just pass tax hikes onto their customers. In effect, Biden is staking the entire country to a 7% tax hike.

6/4

Biden lies again about Trumps' tax cuts benefiting only the top 1%. In the five tax brackets, going from the lower middle class to the top, Trump reduced taxes from 15%-12%, 25%-22%, 28%-24%, 33%-32% and 39%-37%. It is apparent that the middle class received greater tax cuts than the upper class. The lowest of the classes were left out because they owe no taxes. In fact, the top 10% of wage earners – the hated 'upper class' – pay approximately 90% of all taxes, with the other 90% of the country pretty much along for the ride, much like one of Bidens' biggest supporters, the LA Teachers Union, did during the COVID pandemic 'crisis'.

6/5

Economic analysts point out to Biden that with the increase in corporate taxes and him allowing the Trump tax cuts to expire, all Americans are going to effectively experience a 9 - 11% tax increase. Add to this that inflation has reached its highest rate in almost two generations. Even if inflation lands at the predicted 3.5% for the year, Americans will feel a real loss of income between 12.5 and 14.5%. Consider too that this is happening in the first half of the first year of the first term of a Biden presidency. Analysts are eager to see Bidens' reaction once his nurses reads this him.

6/6

Biden doesn't make any mention or acknowledge the 77th anniversary of D-Day on Sunday, the date of the invasion, angering many service members and veterans for the lack of tribute. This was the day, June 6, 1944, when in World War II Allied forces invaded northern France by means of beach landings in Normandy, resulting in roughly 4,500 Allied deaths, with 2,500 of those being American. Perhaps this was his effort to 'one-up' Obama, who snubbed the troops on Memorial Day when he was President. Then Biden makes an ass of himself by informing these battled-hardened troops that the greatest danger to America today is - not China, Russia, North Korea or any of the other dictator-led enemies of the US – global warming and climate change.

6/7

It is reported that a Rasmussen poll taken in the last couple of days shows that 39% of Americans believe that race relations have gotten worse since Biden became President, 28 percent believe they have improved under Biden, with the other 33% feeling they were about the same or were unsure. Quite a tumble from the campaign promises of Biden and Harris that, compared to Trump, race relations would improve dramatically with their election,

6/8

Biden gives another speech that was almost incoherent. Now new programs are launched across the Internet where people are encouraged to call in and guess what the President was trying to say. In this speech where Biden garbled words, mashed two different words together and made pronouncements like "COVID cases are down and COVID deaths are up..." all served to leave the audience dazed and confused, much like Biden himself.

6/9

A remark Biden made last week, where he stated that Blacks are just as talented as Whites, except "...they don't have lawyers and accountants..." comes back to haunt him. Biden supporters defend his semi-racist remarks by doubling down on them, particularly when it came to states enacting new voting laws. Besides "...not 'having lawyers and accountants..." Bidens' supporters claim that Blacks don't know where or how to use the DMV, cannot attain IDs of any kind and don't have the equipment, access and the skills to use the Internet. With his supporters using language expected at a white Supremacy rally, it seems Biden has kept one campaign promise, if partially: Perhaps not the whole of America, but Biden has definitely united the racist portion of the Democratic party.

6/10

In perhaps his dumbest proclamation to date, Biden claims that by taxing the entrepreneurs, the successful business men and all of the educated, high wage earners, then giving that money to the uneducated, the unsuccessful and minimum wage earners, he will be able to revitalize the economy from the "bottom up". As a great start for Bidens' "bottom up" rebuilding of the American economy, which he shattered, a new report shows that inflation during Bidens' short presidency had risen to its' highest level in 13 years.

6/11

After a legal challenge by white farmers who argue Bidens' latest policy is discriminatory, a federal judge in Wisconsin orders a temporary halt to Bidens' latest race-baiting plan. In it. Biden plans to establish a $4 billion federal loan relief program for "farmers of color". In an order issued recently, Judge William Griesbach found that the U.S. Department of Agriculture's "… use of race-based criteria in the administration of the program violates their (farmers of 'un-color) right to equal protection under the law …" For now, Bidens' latest race bait is left on dry land.

6/12

With Biden and Harris still ignoring the disaster at the southern border, Harris goes on Unavision to explain their immigration policy or, rather, their lack of one. The reporter asks Harris when she and/or Biden will visit the border. Instead of a border visit, Harris insists that Bidens' plan to line the pockets of Central and South American dictators with billions of American tax dollars is the better option. In Harris and Bidens' warped logic, the cash will enable these thugs to change their current suffering countries into economic paradises, thus removing the incentive for their citizens to leave. When the reporter still persists with his initial question, Harris says that she and Biden will visit the border in the future. When pressed for a date, Harris snaps: "I'll get back to you on that." and ends the interview.

6/13

For three months Biden has insisted that COVID relief funds will "… provide economic growth for the entire nation…" That might've been his plan, but it is brought to his attention that so far, as much as 400 billion dollars of Bidens' "COVID relief money" has ended up in the hands of the criminal elements in the country. Biden has no comment.

6/14

Biden embarrasses himself and the US at the G7 meeting by giving another almost-incoherent speech that lasts several minutes. It seems Biden was demanding more transparency from China, but he kept not only mispronouncing words but repeatedly confused words like 'pandemic' and 'transparency'. Later Biden interrupted the host while he was introducing the attending countries in order to reminds him to mention South Africa … which the speaker had already done. Embarrassed laughter from the crowd followed as Bidens' mental struggles were on full display.

6/15

Biden is almost three hours late for a scheduled G7 press conference. When he eventually shows up, Biden mumbles to reporters; "I didn't say anything." and wanders off, leaving them confused. He comes back later, answers a few questions semi-coherently and emphasizes that the main concern of he and all the other G7 leaders was combating what he and they consider the greatest threat to humanity, global warming and climate change. Ironically, a photo of the UK airport makes the rounds. It showed the airport crammed, fence to fence, with all the private jets - supposedly major polluters of the environment – that these concerned climate change dignitaries flew in on

6/16

Bidens' campaign promise to replace jobs in the fossil fuel industry with better paying jobs in Bidens' delusional "Green" industry, falls flat in South Dakota. There a solar turbine blade manufacturer announced it is shutting its doors permanently while being in business for less than two months. Biden had previously stated that there was no reason that the blades for wind turbines can't be built in Pittsburgh instead of Beijing. What Biden glosses over is that Beijing, which the Biden family has been doing business with for more than a decade, is getting virtually all of the solar turbine blade – building business.

6/17

It is reported that last month, in the spirit of Trumps' proposed tariffs on China to prohibit unfair market practices, a South Dakota senator proposed an amendment to Bidens' expansive energy tax credit bill. It would require Biden to certify that U.S. manufacturers would not be undercut by foreign suppliers who use low-cost-close-to-slave labor and create higher emissions. His amendment falls on deaf ears. With Biden also killing the Keystone pipeline project, which ran through the state of South Dakota, overnight Biden single-handily turned portions of one of the most prosperous states under Trump into a variable wasteland.

6/18

In maybe the worst optic from many Biden embarrassments at the G7, Putins' bodyguards muscle Bidens' guards and assistants away from Biden during their face-to-face, leaving Biden sitting alone with Putin and his staff. Biden seems unfocused and tired, allowing Putin to take over the question and answer period. When later questioned about his obvious lethargy, Biden snaps at the reporter, implying that she didn't know how to do her job. Later Biden apologizes, but the apology sounds as weak and frail as he is.

6/19

Biden calls for the all members of families of asylum seekers currently in the US to be re-united together at taxpayer expense. Biden also announces that any citizen in the world that is seeking asylum in the US because of criminal activity in their country – even low-level criminal activity - be automatically offered US citizenship. Not a green card, not a pathway, but full citizenship. The fact that this imbecilic proposal is unconstitutional, irresponsible, morally reprehensible and a direct threat to Americas' economy and way of life, bothers Biden not a wit; this is apparent because during his entire call, Bidens' unfocused watery eyes do not blink.

6/20

The White House physician under former Presidents Trump and Obama collects signatures for his petition this week, requesting Biden take a cognitive test like Trump did during his presidency. The physician cites that, in his opinion, "...[Biden] doesn't know what's going on, where he's at. He's very confused all the time..." Biden just grins, has no comment and still refuses to submit to this test.

6/21

The office of Ron Jackson, former physician to Obama and Trump, and now a Texas congressman, released this follow-up concerning Jacksons' request for a Biden cognitive test: He sent a letter Biden, Physician to the President Kevin O'Connor, D.O. and Chief Medical Advisor Anthony Fauci, M.D., calling on Biden to immediately undergo a cognitive test and share the results with the American people, His letter comes as a result of him observing a clear decline of Biden's cognitive ability, including embarrassing performances on the world stage.

6/22

Biden attempts to Federalize national elections with a piece of legislation he called a "voting rights bill". In response to many states enacting voter reform bills after the 2020 fiasco – mainly now requiring such 'radical' things as voter ID and ballot verification – Biden attempts to bring all voting in the country under his direct control, regardless of the unconstitutionality of it. Fortunately for the country, he fails.

6/23

In an attempt to avoid embarrassment, Biden and Harris announce that Harris will visit the border ahead of Trumps announced visit on 6/30. She's going to El Paso, however, where a minimum of the illegal immigration damage is being done. She is purposely avoiding the hot spots that put a spotlight on her and Bidens' epic fail in this matter. It's humorous to see that Trump, by his mere presence, at times, can still push the Marxists into doing the right thing.

6/24

Bidens' supporters claim that the use of the filibuster rule is the same as apartheid and insinuate that violence against Conservatives, as the violence in South Africa that erupted when that country opposed apartheid, may be the only solution. to oppose it. Biden, the great 'healer', who promised to bring the country together, says nothing about his supporter advocating violence against Conservatives.

6/25

With Bidens' approval, Harris goes to the border, finally, but picks El Paso where the immigration damage is minimal so her photo op wouldn't be embarrassing. She spends less than 5 hours there and barely leaves the airport. Then, because perhaps El Paso was too uncomfortable, and she didn't want to return to Washington for some reason, she orders the Secret Service to fly her to LA so she can spend a comfortable evening in her house there. The fact that her last-minute desire to spend a night at home would destroy the Friday evening commute home for Angelinos does not bother her at all.

6/26

In one of his most bizarre ramblings to date, Biden joked about people who say they need to own weapons to, perhaps one day, protect themselves from the government. In response Biden says that these 2nd Amendment advocates, if they really needed protection from the government, would need "...F-15s and maybe some nuclear weapons..." Though possibly fomented through a lack of Ensure, all Americans would do well to understand the veiled threat in Bidens' latest rant.

6/27

In another bizarre rambling – one-upping his bizarre behavior yesterday - Biden holds a presser where he whispers to the media some rambling collection of bits concerning the pandemic and, his relief bill, most of it unintelligible. He finishes by lecturing restaurant owners, who are complaining that they can't find workers because Biden is paying them so much to stay home, to "…just pay them (employees both current and prospective) more." Considering that Biden is paying some of these deadbeats as much as $50000/year to not work, the fast food industry would have to increase their average payroll by 70%, just to compete.

6/28

Biden reneges on his promise to sign a bi-partisan infrastructure bill. Since his original 6 trillion dollar proposal was rejected, Biden promised to sign a smaller compromised package. Biden said he would be happy to sign a one trillion-dollar deal worked out between Senate Republicans and Democrats … just as soon as the they approve the rest of his mufti-trillion dollar deal.

6/29

Biden is aghast as Republicans accuse him of lying and trying to blackmail them into signing his 6 trillion dollar "infrastructure" bill by refusing to sign their compromise deal. Biden claims they should've known he wouldn't sign one without the other. Then Biden attempts to stack the Federal Election Commission, but is rebuffed. Currently 3 Republicans and 3 Democrats staff the FEC. Biden wants two Republicans, two Democrats and one Independent on the committee … with the 'Independent' chosen by him; nice try.

6/30

Biden weaponizes the U.S. Department of Justice to sue Georgia in an attempt to overturn its' Election Integrity Act. The Governor of Georgia accuses Biden of villainizing his states' Election Integrity Act by pushing outrageous lies about it, all for political fodder. He believes Biden is doing this because Georgias'' EIA legislation makes it easier to vote in his state, but harder to cheat.

7/1

A large condominium structure collapses in Florida. In yet another of his ever-increasing semi-coherent ramblings, Biden infers that, rather than poor construction and lack of maintenance, "global warming" and "the rising seas" were contributing factors in the buildings' collapse.

7/2

It is reported that this past spring illegal immigration in the US hits its' highest level since the year 2000. Biden says nothing. It is reported that an average of 5000 illegals a day – up from 100 a day when Trump left office – are apprehended in March, April and May. Biden says nothing.

It is pointed out that all of this is happening since Biden suspended many of Trumps' border initiatives in his first month in office. Biden says – even incoherently – nothing.

7/3

Earlier this year Biden was advised that as the U.S. military vacates its Bagram air base in Afghanistan, thousands of Afghan interpreters who worked alongside American troops would be slaughtered by the Taliban. This immediate emergency does not seem to penetrate what is left of Bidens' mind because, in response to this immediate threat of death to the interpreters, Biden announces that he will gladly put these allies on a three-year plan to enter the US. After being awoken by his nurses and schooled on the word 'immediate', Biden mumbles that he is sure a plan is in place to evacuate these allies safely, but when questioned, admits he doesn't know of any specific details. This must be a great comfort to our friends sitting on a veritable 'Death Row' in Afghanistan.

7/4

Four months after Biden announced an unprecedented vaccination roll out plan to return American life to "normal", by Independence Day, he was back at a podium pleading with those in the US that decided long ago to ignore him. The nation has fallen short of Biden's dreams of 70 percent vaccinations for American adults by July 4. Undeterred, Biden announces a redoubling of efforts to convince millions of vaccine-hesitant people to get shots in arms, regardless of the apparent uselessness of the "vaccine".

7/5

Biden unveils his radical "30 by 30" land grab initiative. Basically Biden wants to grab 30 million acres of private property and turn it over to the

Federal Government bu 2030. Ostensibly for 'environment protection', it is nothing short of pure theft. Biden and Obama tried the same thing on their way out of office in 2016. At that time they grabbed 11 million acres of land in Utah by executive order. Trump reversed this in his first few days of office, using an executive order to give the land back to Utah. Ignoring this rebuke, Biden is once again bent on stealing land from American citizens.

7/6

Biden announces his plan to use federal money to get states to inject radical racist theories into childrens' history classes, imposing the most radical forms of Critical Race Theory on America's school children. Since CRT is mere window dressing for Socialist/Marxist/Communist dogma, Bidens' attempt to subvert Americas' Capitalist, free-market system becomes decidedly more obvious.

7/7

During the 2020 election, reportedly hundreds of people signed affidavits attesting to Democratic voter fraud. In addition, allegations were made of millions of illegal citizens voting and millions more of Biden ballots with no valid Ids or signatures. None of these allegations were seriously investigated. On the other hand, one voter in Arizona was caught illegally voting for Trump; he was arrested and faces 40 years in prison.

7/8

China rattles its' sabers again. They threaten open re-unification with Taiwan and open military retaliation if America tries to help its' ally. They follow this up with open threats against Japan and American military bases. Biden, apparently again asleep in his basement, says nothing.

7/9

Biden continues Trumps' plan to bring soldiers home from Afghanistan, but insists on leaving large caches of weapons and equipment behind, knowing that this will serve only to restock the Taliban with the latest in military supplies. Biden is asked if he trusts the Taliban: He says "no", but offers no explanation as to why, if he doesn't trust them, is he leaving so much equipment and firepower for them. Biden says nothing.

7/10

Biden, through his press secretary, announces there will we no 'Job well done' or congratulatory parade for the troops returning from Afghanistan after twenty years. His reason is that since there was no military victory, no parade is warranted. One with full mental capacities would realize this is spitting on the servicemen who gave so much, but in Bidens; condition it is a accomplishment if he even realizes what day of the week it is.

7/11

As predicted earlier, since the US pullout, allies and military personnel who fought along side American forces in Afghanistan are continuing to be assassinated by the Taliban, despite Bidens' promise of protection. A seventh Afghan pilot was assassinated recently. Biden again pledges to continue providing security assistance to the Afghan military, but, as more friends of the US are assassinated daily, the question remains, when?

7/12

Demonstrations erupt all over Cuba. Citizens there are demanding there freedom and the end to food and medical shortages. After 60-odd years of brutal dictatorship, Cuba asks for Americas' support. Biden is silent. This is to be expected since it was he and Obama who tried to normalize relations with this Communist enemy. Obama was seen holding hands, drinking beer and enjoying a baseball game with the dictator elite. The suffering Cubans may have to wait awhile for that phone call from Biden, since he and Obama have been their enemy for years.

7/13

Biden sends out Harris to attack the voter reform laws many states are implementing as "racist". She is particularly upset about the 'strict' requirement that, if the voter cannot present their ID in person, they can remotely submit a photocopy of some documentation – drivers license, utility bill, bank statement - proving who they are. Harris stupidly claims this requirement is racist because there are no Kinkos or Office Depots where "these people" - her words - live.

7/14

Biden makes a tepid, 10 second statement to the Cuban people along the lines of: 'America supports the Cubans demand for freedom.' but nothing more On the same day Biden, who promised to protect the Afghan allies from reprisals from the Taliban, is asked about the additional 22 Afghan allies executed by the same Taliban yesterday. Biden has no comment.

7/15

It is reported that some days ago Biden made a trip to Pennsylvania in order to encourage the state to shut down the embarrassing audit of the 2020 election results there. State officials, who initially said they had nothing to fear from a transparent audit, change course, comply with Biden and order that no election data – ballots, voting machines, poll worker information, etc. - be turned over for any audit purposes. Bidens' personal attention and the states' complicity in something they purportedly "had no fear of" is interesting.

7/16

Biden rescinds one of the last immigration policies Trump enacted, the one of not allowing children who cross the border alone to request – and granted by Biden - family members to join them in the US. Trump enacted this law after being informed that one of these 'children' requested that 147 'relatives' join him in America.

7/17

Biden revives memories of the Nazi Brown shirts, announcing that he is going to send government workers door-to-door to "encourage" people to be vaccinated against the COVID virus. After receiving considerable criticism, Biden defends his plan against comparisons to the Nazi youth who were sent door-to-door to 'encourage' adherence to various Hitler dictates. Biden insists that the difference is that his troops, unlike Hitlers, will not be government employees, but "trusted messengers". This is yet another example of Biden pissing down the backs of American citizens, but insisting it's just the rain.

7/18

Biden makes a speech where he compares voting reform laws being enacted in dozens of states – the ones that require in-person voting and Ids – as "…Jim Crow on steroids". According to Biden, requiring voters to show ID is just like the old Jim Crow laws enacted by Democrats, where Blacks were murdered if they tried to vote. His oft trips to Fantasy Land aside, this Biden hyperbolic tripe could lead to violence and even death to those merely trying to uphold the Constitution.

7/19

Biden, who said nothing several days ago when it was reported that the Taliban executed 22 Afghan allies, is silent again when a video surfaces that shows the actual execution of these allies. Bidens' silence seems to indicate that Biden is standing firm on his absurd plan to allow these allies safe passage to the US within three years, his fogged brain oblivious to the fact that they all will be executed long before this.

7/20

It is reported that when the Chancellor of Germany visited Biden last week, Biden asked her to stop buying energy supplies from Russia, as Trump had demanded. The Chancellor refused, saying that she prefers working with one of Americas' long-standing enemies. Biden spinelessly backs down and says that he and America will "remain friendly" with the German Chancellor anyway.

7/21

A summary of Bidens' first 6 months as president is shocking in its' virulent incompetence. Worse yet is Bidens' seeming intent to pile on his ineptitude by insisting on saddling future generations with trillions more in tax payer debt, money that Biden insists he needs to enforce his agenda. Worse still is his incessant insistence that every American be vaccinated against COVID. Biden continues to ignorantly blame the un-vaccinated for spreading the virus despite overwhelming evidence that the vaccinated are much more likely to catch COVID again before the vaccinated catch it once. Despite this evidence that these vaccines are really only pharmaceuticals and as many as 25000 American have either died or reported problems with them, Biden continues to insist that everyone in America take the shot.

722

Biden defends his order to Facebook to censor any posting that disagrees with his position on the COVID pandemic, saying it is his right to do this because he is saving the lives of innocent Americans. If his words produce a tiny echo of Mao, who slaughtered millions for 'the public good', or Stalin who murdered 30 million to protect the ' innocent common man from the proletariat ', or Hitler who killed millions in order to preserve the 'race purity' of Germany, or Pot, Castro, Noriega, Chavez, et al, who murdered, raped and pillaged at will for the "public good" … same words, same echo chamber.

7/23

Biden doubles down on his request for Face Book to de-platform anyone who disagrees with his position on COVID, calling for these disagreeable types to be de-platformed completely from all social media venues. On the same day Biden places a call to the leader of Afghanistan, asking him to lie about the true strength of the Afghan military. Biden implores him to lie so he can present a picture of Afghan military competency to Americans so they will support his plan for unconditional withdrawal of American troops from the country. Demanding censorship of his perceived enemies and lies form his perceived allies in order to maintain a false perception of himself, both at the same time, makes it quite day for Biden.

7/24

The UK, Australia, NATO, Canada and Japan issue a joint statement condemning China for it's persistent attempts to hack their respective IT infrastructures. They invite Biden to join them since the US suffered a major hack from the Chinese last spring. Biden refuses to join the rebuke or even threaten sanctions against the Chinese. This should come as no surprise since Biden and his family have been working with the Communists for over a decade in one form or another..

7/25

In Bidens' administrative guide for school re-openings, he promotes a radical activist group's handbook that advocates for educators to "…disrupt Whiteness and other forms of oppression." This is blatant racist Critical Race Theory in a nutshell, but in all of the pontificating concerning his guidelines, Biden won't say these particular words. Like a child, Biden seems to e believes that if he doesn't say them, they won't be true.

7/26

Bidens' inability to form coherent sentences is reaching new heights. In getting off (or on) Air Force One, Biden was asked a question about immigration. His answer was impossible to understand, sounding like: "My butts been wiped." or "The Trumps were right." A number of websites came online immediately, offering prizes for any who could figure out what Biden said. So far, no winners.

7/27

When asked about forcing the FDA to approve the as-yet unapproved COVID vaccines, Biden word-salads: "Whether or not we should be in a position where you are why can't the experts say we know that this virus is in fact it's going to be or excuse we know why all the drugs approved or not temporarily but permanently approved, that's underway too" While reporters try to hold onto minds blistered by Bidens' garbled nonsense, it is believed that what Biden was trying to say was that he is going to force the FDA to approve the vaccines far ahead of schedule so Biden can use their approval as a hammer to legally force all Americans to take it. Welcome China, Russia and Cuba, via the United States.

7/28

A new poll released yesterday reported that 72% of registered voters believe that Bidens' fiscal policies are responsible for the runaway inflation the country is seeing, even though just a few months old. Bidens' media sycophants downplay the poll. They say, unbelievably and hysterically at the same time, that looked at one way, fewer than 6 out of 10 voters blame Biden for the inflation problem. What this lunatic take on these poll numbers doesn't downplay is that Bidens' mental deterioration is contagious and spreading unvarnished to his acolytes.

7/29

It is brought to Bidens' attention that his 'immigration czar', Vice-Presidents Harris, has allowed a policy of letting COVID-ridden immigrants enter the country and be placed in various locations in the US. At the same time Biden announces that a mandatory masking of US citizens might be in the offing because of the recent surge of reported COVID infections. Since they are not US citizens, illegal aliens – or "'Undocumented Visitors" as Biden likes to call them now - are under no such mandate, even if infected with the virus.

7/31

In a surprise move, Biden announces his intention of levying additional sanctions on Cuba in wake of the recent protest marches of its' citizens against the Communist government there. It is a surprise because Bidens' family reportedly has done business with Communist countries around the world, particularly China. Then it is revealed that the 1.5 million Cubans who reside in Florida voted heavily for Trump in the last election. This raises the likelihood that Bidens' largess has more to do with appealing to those voters Biden will need to win back Florida in 2024 than any real concern he might have for their relatives back in Cuba.

8/1

Some in the Democratic party appeal to Biden, saying they are losing credibility as they try to ramp up more fake fear mongering concerning the COVID19 virus. This is because, while Biden is advocating masks mandates, lock downs and forced vaccinations in order to "keep Americans safe", he is allowing thousands of COVID-ridden illegal immigrants to cross the border each day. So far, Biden has turned a deaf ear to their pleas.

8/2

In responding to the poll from several days ago that, in just 6 months, Bidens' fiscal policies have produced the worst inflation in years, Biden claims that his plans to flood the American economy with even more funny money would ease inflation. His reason is that then Americans would have more money in their pockets to buy necessities … which is a main reason why inflation skyrockets. Bidens' unbridled ignorance of simple economic principles causes jaw dropping looks from competent economists alive today and forces those long dead to turn over in their graves.

8/3

In addition to all of the adults, it is reported that the increase in unaccompanied minors crossing the border might've reached an all-time high in July. So far it is reported that in his first 6 months in office, Biden has allowed 1 million illegal aliens into the country. Biden and his immigration czar, Harris, say nothing.

8/4

Biden calls out the governor of Florida, a Republican, blaming him for the current rise in COVID cases. He swears it's not political, but conveniently fails to mention that between 20 and 30 states, most of them run by Democrats, currently have COVID infection rates higher than Florida.

8/5

A string of legal defeats for Bidens' proposal to forgive the debts of minority farmers is presenting the Biden administration with a choice: Already three different judges have issued preliminary injunctions blocking the program because the debt relief effort unconstitutionally discriminates on the basis of race. Continuing to fight further might provoke an embarrassing Supreme Court ruling against him. Biden, so far, is silent on what he plans to do next.

8/6

The escalation of violence in Afghanistan has forced tens of thousands of people to flee the country in search of safety. Biden promised to make it easier for Afghan refugees access to the US, but first they must get themselves to a location where they can be declared official refugees. Refugee organizations are aghast at this stipulation. In order to get to a location where they can be declared refugees, those fleeing would have to cross Taliban-controlled checkpoints, where the Taliban has promised to slaughter them. Biden, either unaware or uncaring, has no comment.

8/7

Iran issues a formal denial that it was behind the major drone attack on the Mercer Street oil tanker off Oman. Managed by an Israeli firm, the attack left two crew members dead. On the same day both the United States and Israel charged that Tehran was without doubt behind the attack, which the US Navy said involved multiple explosive drones targeting the vessel. Iran's Press TV subsequently responded by vowing a "strong and crushing" military response to any hostile moves against the country: Biden says nothing.

8/8

In answer to the growing refugee crisis in Afghanistan, Biden has his Secretary of State release a statement, commiserating that the refugee situation there "... is hard on so many levels." He lists that it's hard for refugees to pick up and leave everything, hard to get to a place where one "...can take advantage of what opportunities exist...", hard to apply for refugee status, etc. True, perhaps, but probably not as hard as getting shot down in the street like dogs while waiting for Biden to do something.

8/9

Biden defends his proposed mufti-trillion dollar spending bill, saying that it will decrease inflation, rather than increase it as all economists predict it will. As proof, he says that his increased investment in education will make it possible to graduate more future citizens in the field of computer security, which should help in cracking down on the cyber hacking that recently paralyzed a domestic oil company. This, he assured his audience, will help lower prices at the pump. Apparently his 'solution' of future computer experts traveling back in time to solve a current problem eludes his fading mental capacity.

8/10

A group of high-ranking Democratic operatives hold what is supposed to be a secret meeting to discuss Bidens' growing unpopularity and failing mental health. The meeting concludes with them accepting they are wedded to Biden because the alternative – Harris – is even more despised by both Republicans and Democrats.

8/11

Biden again is confronted with the disaster at the southern border. Biden does not deny that he has allowed possibly as many as 1.5 million to cross the border in his first 6 months as president, but does deny he has done nothing in response. As an example, he points out that just the other day he ordered border patrol agents to round up a number of illegals being housed at one section of the border … and move them to another section of the border. The vacant stare in his eyes when responding makes it impossible to know if Biden thought this was a valid response to the disaster.

8/12

Biden calls out the governor of Florida as the reason the COVID virus is again spiking. Biden blames it on the governors' lax controls on mitigation efforts concerning COVID. This, while failing to mention that at least two dozen other states, most of the Democratically controlled and following Bidens' guidelines, have far worse COVID infection rates than Florida.

8/13

Biden, in what can be described as hilarious if not so mind-boggling inept, asks the Taliban – yes, 'asks the Taliban – not to burn down the US embassy there when they take over Kabul. So far, on a almost daily basis, Biden demonstrates his diminished mental capacity, only to exceed it the following day.

8/14

In a apparent response to his apparent weakness in confronting Americas' enemies, Biden issues a "strong warning" to the Taliban in Afghanistan. In it, Biden warns these murderers that their place in the world community could be jeopardized by their current actions. Only someone as brain-deprived as Biden could think that these semi-literate, cave dwelling, women and child beating animals are concerned about their appearance to the "world community" at large.

8/15

Bidens request to the Taliban to not burn the US embassy seems to have fallen on deaf ears. The U.S. military has started to evacuate the embassy in Kabul on fears that a Taliban assault on the capital may come within days. It is reported that yesterday Biden boosted the U.S. troop deployment in an attempt to ensure an "orderly and safe draw down." The rapid, domino-like fall of Afghanistan's cities to the fundamentalist forces has ramped up both Republican and Democrat criticism of Bidens' apparent lack of a coherent plan for Americans and their allies to safely evacuate from Afghanistan.

8/16

The government of Afghanistan collapses into the hands of the Taliban. Apparently Bidens' seeming lack of attention to the travails there is because he is on vacation. Biden returns to the White House briefly, makes a brief statement to the nation where he blames everyone but himself for the collapse, takes no questions, then goes back on vacation. It is reminiscent of Obamas' handling of a crisis in his administration. Not aware that the cameras were rolling, Obama came off a golf course, put on a jacket, addressed the American people, assuring them that whatever the current crisis was, it had his full attention. Then thinking the cameras were off, Obama laughs, takes off his jacket and jumps back into a golf cart, resuming his game. Obviously these two patriots have their priorities in order.

8/17

Bidens' careless pull-out of Afghanistan leaves the majority of American weaponry in the hands of the Taliban, resulting in now arming this murderous cult to the teeth. Biden defends his decision to move slowly in evacuating American Afghan allies by claiming they did not want to leave the country, bizarrely intimating that they and their families preferred to stay and be murdered while waiting for the conflict to be resolved. Biden then doubles down on his stupidity by claiming Americans should not defend a country that refuses to defend itself, pissing on the graves of the 50000 Afghans that perished fighting alongside American troops.

8/18

While still on vacation, Bidens' nurses post a picture of him, alone at a table, supposedly conferring virtually with his advisers about his concern for the 15000 US citizens Biden left cornered in Afghanistan. Instead of demonstrating strong reassurance, the scene shows a frail, weak old man looking confused at the array of screens before him. Instead of the leader of a great free country, Biden looks more like a resident of an old folks home, staring blankly at a TV screen, befuddled as to why Jeopardy no longer comes on at this time.

8/19

While still insisting he had a plan all along for evacuating Americans and Afghan allies – a plan no one has seen yet – Biden tells the American citizens and our allies to "…make it to the airport in Kabul…', the same airport now controlled by the Taliban. Even if by some miracle they make it there alive, Bidens' Defense chief admits the US has no means of evacuating "…a large number of people." A reporter questions Bidens' claim about no one getting hurt during the evacuation when there are pictures of Afghans falling from the wheel wells of departing planes in an effort to escape. Biden cuts him off, snapping: "That was four or five days ago." It seems Biden feels the passage of time renders death and carnage irrelevant, again begging questions of his possible senility.

8/20

At yet another press briefing where he refused to take questions, Biden does not address the issuer of the US citizens stranded in Afghanistan, the illegal immigration disaster he has caused at the southern border, or the inflation caused by Bidens' spending packages that are starting to wreak havoc in the American economy. Instead he goes on a rant, declaring all students across the nation must mask-up before returning to school, regardless of what individual state, local jurisdictions or even parents feel about the matter.

8/21

What most people missed in Bidens' mask-rant is that he threatened to use the power of his DOE to force compliance to his whims. This dictatorial bypassing of the Constitution and states' rights sets the stage for Biden to Federalize the public school system. Since Biden has already attempted to Federalize private property, health care and voting rights, this gets Biden even closer to his goal of re-making America in the image and likeness of China.

8/22

While the disaster in Afghanistan has for the moment distracted peoples' attention from other distressing national issues, it comes out that a short while ago Biden implored both Russia and OPEC to step up oil production to make up for the shortfall in American supplies. This from Biden, the man who in his first days in office canceled the Keystone pipeline project. It seems the only accomplishment of Bidens' first six months in office is to take America from standing tall as energy independent to back on its' knees, begging countries who hate the US to supply it with our energy needs.

8/23

Biden keeps prattling on, saying that it was 'unlikely' that a Taliban takeover of Afghanistan and a rapid collapse of the Afghan military would happen. However, this is exactly what happened. According to classified assessments by US agencies over the summer, current and former U.S. government officials warned Biden that this is exactly what would happen. Biden has no answer for why he repeatedly ignored these warnings and now, embarrassing even for Biden, claims that no one warned him. This is possible because if these same government officials did not have the secret knock for Bidens' basement door, it is possible they could not reach him. Still, any of Bidens' nurses could've relayed the message.

8/24

In another press briefing Biden is caught lying at least 5 times in less than two minutes about his role in the situation in Afghanistan. The best came when, during his last lie about no one dying or being beaten there, reporters in the room were receiving real-time texts from those stranded there that claimed at least 12 people had been killed and hundreds were being beaten in the streets: It's obvious Biden didn't get the memo, or at least no one read it for him.

8/25

Senior aides to Biden and Harris are trying to avoid any potential comparisons between the falls of Kabul and Saigon as Harris prepares for her upcoming diplomatic trip to Southeast Asia. Claiming that the comparison was unwarranted because Vietnam was "a different war", Biden is hard-pressed to demonstrate the differences, particularly with the iconic image of a helicopter rescuing people from the U.S. Embassy in Saigon in 1975 being shown side by side with a similar photo taken recently in Kabul.

8/26

A tape is played back for Biden where on July 8 he said that the Afghan government was unlikely to fall and that there would be no chaotic evacuations of Americans similar to the end of the Vietnam War. With all the warnings he received contrary to this, the question was raised about why he, his administration officials and military planners in Afghanistan seemed ill-prepared to deal with the Taliban's takeover of Kabul, including a failure to ensure security at the main airport and rushing thousands more troops back to the country to protect the United States' final exit.

8/27

A couple of days ago, with the promise of full transparency, Biden released a transcript of a meeting he had with the the President of France. The French released a copy of the same meeting also. The French version contained a scolding of sorts Biden received from France, insisting that Biden was failing his moral obligation to do whatever is necessary for the US citizens he left behind in Afghanistan. Interestingly, Biden edited out that portion of the transcript he released.

8/28

Bidens' disastrous withdrawal from Afghanistan escalates to deadly levels. First, Biden does not see that the proper paperwork is issued for targeted Afghans, the ones that were the friends and allies of the US, to leave to country. This leaves our co-patriots open to certain execution, which does not seem to bother Biden. Additionally it is reported that. Biden capitulated to every one of the Talibans' demands, despite these murderous outlaws violating Trumps' entire peace agreement. As a final insult, upon finally exiting Afghanistan, Biden furnishes the Taliban with guns and money.

8/29

Because of Bidens' decision to abandon the Bagrum airbase in Afghanistan, the Prime Ministers from Italy, France and Denmark announced they were ending attempts to evacuate their citizens as it was no longer safe. Biden defends his decision to abandon the airfield, saying he could not protect the airfield and the US embassy in Kabul at the same time. In addition to being a coward, Bidens' declining mental capacity convinces him that people will buy the story that the strongest military in the world could not accomplish these two things simultaneously. For a final insult, all of the countries involved sent "heartfelt" apologies to their citizens they abandoned in Afghanistan

8/30

It is pointed out to Biden that his claim of the inability of the US military to simultaneously protect both the airport and embassy in Afghanistan, then issuing apologies to those citizens and allies abandoned, is a textbook case of Biden pissing down the backs of those he abandoned and telling them it's just rain. The case of the stranded becomes more unforgivable as Biden decides to leave Afghanistan a day early, forgoing another day and another chance to evacuate the stranded safely. The loved ones of those left behind are left to ponder if Bidens' thousand – mile-stare as answer to their concerns as him not caring, or if he is really this stupid.

8/31

Bidens' cowardly early withdrawal from Afghanistan has an ugly side effect; other countries allied with the US who had citizens in Afghanistan are forced to strand their citizens because they were depending on the US military to help them get out. Biden does not apologize for this and, instead, gives a speech where he touts the success of his surrender to the Taliban. In response to his abandoning US citizens, other allies and arming the Taliban with billions in military equipment, Biden proudly announces that, if history repeats itself on his watch, he will handle the next withdrawal in an identical, gutless manner.

9/1

It is reported that Biden met the plane carrying the bodies of the soldiers killed a few days ago during his disastrous surrender to the Taliban. Unbelievably, he seems distracted, constantly checking his watch as each body is unloaded from the aircraft in front of him. It must be some important meeting Biden is concerned about missing if the fear of it keeps him from paying the proper respect to the13 young people he helped kill in Afghanistan with his moronic evacuation scheme.

9/2

Bidens' constant watch-checking during the deplaning of the servicemen murdered because of his botched evacuation plan did not go unnoticed by the parents of the soldiers. One of them interviewed following the incident said that if Biden checked his watch just one more time during the ceremony, he would've beat him right there on the spot. Others in the crowd supposedly yelled "Murderer!" and "Killer" at him. Biden looked nonplussed, but that might've been because he didn't have his hearing aid tuned properly.

9/3

Back in July Biden demanded, that the FDA approve the COVID vaccines far ahead of schedule so that he could legally force all Americans to take it. Since then Biden has demanded that they at least approve the third 'booster shot' Big Pharma is pedaling. The two top officials at the FDA refuse and resign, saying that Biden is 'messing with the science' and, consequently, peoples' lives. The third whore up, however, has no problem issuing an approval for this as-yet not fully tested shot, giving Biden the dictator what he wants.

9/4

A personal plea is made to Biden to aid in evacuating one of Ameicas' Afghan allies, an interpreter that actually saved Bidens' life on one of his visits to the country. In addition, am American mother and her three children are also trapped, not being able to pass the Taliban checkpoints for weeks due largely to Bidens' removal of all military personnel. However, Biden stridently maintains that the only people abandoned in Afghanistan were those that wanted to stay, or those through their own fault, not his, never made it it to a place where they could be rescued.

9/5

Because of Biden's' refusal to retrieve those citizens and allies he abandoned in Afghanistan, private parties in America, made up mostly of ex-servicemen and volunteers who have access to planes, have for some time now organized their own expeditions to go in and rescue those stranded. Biden has no comment on whether these private rescuers have his permission or not. At the same time a speech he gave on antisemitism some days ago came under critique because in it he claimed to have visited the the site of the Pittsburgh synagogue shooting, when he didn't. Whether another demented rambling or another lie, Biden seems to be bothered by it not at all.

9/7

In an effort to rescue Americans and allies abandoned by Biden in Afghanistan, private parties in America organized and financed private planes to rescue them. Biden didn't try to stop them from arriving in Afghanistan, but once there he alerted the Taliban that he did not give these planes permission to fly these rescue missions. As a result, the Taliban have seized all of the planes, refusing to let them take off, basically holding them all as hostages.

9/8

The mother and her three children that Biden abandoned weeks ago in Afghanistan are ferried out of that country to safety by a private party. Even though Biden had nothing to do with it and was actually obstructive, he takes credit for their rescue. In another of his ever-increasing delusional moments, Biden giggles that more important than the rescue was that ' his employees ' working at the embassy of the country that provided safe haven, were there to greet them. His giggling during these type of announcements is getting more pronounced, to the consternation of his nurses.

9/9

A recent poll shows that over 60% of Americans, both Democrat and Republican, believe Biden botched Trumps' plan on leaving Afghanistan. Despite this, Bidens' record-setting inflation and the disaster at the southern border – 1.5 million illegals allowed to enter the country since the start of Bidens' term – his approval raring stays in the high 30% to low 40% range, an indication of the number of left – leaning, Marxist sycophants still in the United States.

9/10

Biden says he is helpless in getting the Americans and allies he stranded out of Afghanistan because he can't vet them properly. Biden claims he wants to be sure that no scurrilous people sneak, into America, even though the abandoned are holding passports and green cards. At the same time Biden announces that all Afghan non-citizens seeking refuge in the US will be allowed in un-vetted, with no health testing required. In addition, they will be immediately authorized to receive free welfare, health care and a promise of US citizenship within a year. To Biden, sickly, possible terrorist non-citizens, yes, but healthy, peaceful citizens and allies – no.

9/11

On this anniversary of the worst terrorist attack on Americans and American soil, a highly decorated British Army officer, Special Operations Staff Sgt. Trevor Coult, said he is "absolutely shocked" at Biden's Afghanistan withdrawal, rendering the 20-year war, in his words, "a total waste." He points out that not only were 3,000 people killed in the Twin Towers and not a single thing was achieved, but Biden also "... destroyed 20 years' work in less than 24 hours."

9/12

Following up on his statement from yesterday Coult told the Washington Examiner "Biden is the most incompetent president in the history of the United States. He has befriended terrorists. The White House is not a friend to the West. It's a danger while he is president." Coult said he has spoken to numerous British generals and Special Operations officers about Biden, and they all agree that Biden is more of a threat to the West than the Taliban ever was. To this, Coult added: "Without a shadow of a doubt: He betrayed us."

9/13

Former British Prime Minister Tony Blair issues a statement, saying that Europe and NATO should prepare to act when the U.S. is unwilling. He points out that one of the most alarming developments recently has been the sense that Biden lacks the capacity to formulate strategy, that his short-term political imperatives have squeezed the space for long-term thinking. Blair is just one of several British politicians who have criticized Biden's handling of the Afghanistan withdrawal, being most upset that calls to Biden by the UK Prime Minister were ignored for 36 hours during the initial Afghanistan chaos. Because of this, the UK Parliament, for the first time possibly ever, votes to hold an American president, Biden, in contempt: Biden has no comment.

9/14

In a striking consequence to Biden turning his back on the UK, that country and other former allies say that any military cooperation with the US is likely finished until a new president is elected. These countries reason, besides not knowing what Biden is going to do next, why would they trust someone who would so easily turn his back on them? According to these former allies, Biden "...has nailed that door closed...." on future co-operation. Incredibly, Bidens' only response is to announce that he is sending 70 million dollars in aid to the new Taliban government in Afghanistan.

9/15

It is reported that Biden furnished the Taliban with a list of Americans and their allies he stranded in Afghanistan, right down to their personal description and current known addresses. Biden claims he did this in order to facilitate the Taliban in finding these people and evacuating them from the country. Now, thanks to Biden, the Taliban now know where these people are hiding and the question of whether these savage killers will use the information as an "evacuation list" or a hit list is left to speculation.

9/16

Biden drones the wrong people on a tip from the Taliban. Senator Rand Paul scorches Bidens' Secretary of State Blinken at a Senate hearing for the drone strike that killed a U.S. Aid worker and nine other civilians in Afghanistan. As more proof of the addled-ness his addled brain, Biden actually believed the Taliban would tip him off where he could kill their ISIS friends. The killing of innocent civilians is a major victory for the Taliban because this "savage attack".by the U.S. will surely birth more terrorists who hate America.

9/17

The transcript of Pauls' scorching of Bidens' Secretary of State is made public. He not only criticizes Biden for possibly killing the wrong people, but states that Obama did the same thing. Paul claims that Obama also droned hundreds of people without verifying that they were enemy combatants. He warns that, if the pictures "…of these beautiful children that were killed in the attack (are) true and not propaganda…" maybe Obama and Biden have created hundreds of thousands of new terrorists because of bombing the wrong people. Biden, his SoS - and even Obama – have no comment.

9/18

Bidens continues to embrace Critical Race Theory, a Marxist theory that pits all races against each other, particularly against the white race. Biden embraces the fact that it is being taught at all levels of American education. As if this racist, race-baiting of the country is not enough, now Biden gives a class-bating speech pitting the successful against everyone else. The example Biden uses is that 55 corporations did not pay any taxes last year, ignoring the facts that, one, "the rich" or "the top 1%" as Biden likes to call them, already pay over 40% of the entire tax burden, while the bottom 50% - the victims in Bidens' world – pay almost nothing.

9/19

It turns out that when Biden delivered his clownish 'tax-the-wealthy-give -tax- break-to-the-poor' speech, economists in the audience point out the great fallacies in his plan. The enormous tax increase Biden plans on subjecting corporations to will simply be passed down to the consumer. Thus, any minimal amount of money the lower classes receive back because of lower taxes will be consumed almost completely by the increase in their everyday cost of living. Thus, with one proposed stroke of his pen Biden will condemn the lower classes to even more poverty than they are in now. The economists never get a chance to question Biden during his speech because Biden, once again, leaves the stage without taking questions, his nurses leading him to a safe place.

9/20

Biden and Harris are made aware that approximately 14,000 migrants, many originally from Haiti, are now in Del Rio, Texas, a city of only 35,000. These illegals are overwhelming the resources of local, state and federal authorities and all are expected to try to claim asylum in the U.S. City leaders of Del Rio were told by the Border Patrol they are processing 3,000 migrants a day. Some of these illegals will be allowed to await the results of their asylum claims in the U.S., a process that can take years. Encouraged by Bidens' open-border policies, residents of Del Rio say immigrants cross into their city on a daily basis, with no attempt to stop them, Both Biden and Harris, his "Border Czar", have no comment.

9/21

Biden makes a speech in front of the UN where he pledges over 11 billion dollars in US aid to foreign countries, many of them enemies of the the US. Biden claims the funds are to help American enemies fight such calamities as climate change. Biden also sells Israel out, calling for a two-state solution for the Palestinians and promises to send this terrorist-backed country more foreign aid, even as it continues to lob missiles into Israel.

9/22

Biden and his staff admit to members of the House Foreign Affairs Committee that there were still roughly 100 American citizens stranded in Afghanistan, but that the number was a "snapshot" and there might be even more that are stranded. It appears Biden is waiting for those stranded to let him know that "…they wish to leave the country…." before he rescues them. When asked if he really believes that there are Americans who wish to remain in Afghanistan to be murdered, Biden has no comment. As for the number of U.S. green card holders, legal permanent residents who are still in Afghanistan, Biden admits there were several thousand of these people still stranded, but also admitted that the fate of these people is "… something that we don't track directly,"

9/23

Biden again defends his handling of the Afghanistan evacuation, including the number of lives lost and abandoned, against criticism from both Democrats and Republicans. Biden claims that the deal Trump left him with tied his hands. This is another Biden lie. Trumps' 'deal' contained conditions that no Americans were to be hurt, no cities were to be invaded and all American equipment – down to the last nut and bolt - was to be returned or the agreement could be voided. Since the Taliban reneged on all of these conditions, Biden was free to cancel the withdrawal. Instead, Biden abandoned crucial airfields, stranded thousands of citizens and their allies and left the murderous savages over $80 billion dollars of military equipment, making them the best-armed terrorists in the world.

9/24

It is revealed that several days ago that the apology Biden issued for killing innocent civilians, many of them children, with his ill-planned but much-bragged about drone strike in Afghanistan, was never issued directly to the families affected. One family itself lost ten members. Among them were children and young adults ranging from the ages of 6 to 20. Biden claims he has apologized, but to exactly whom is unclear. Biden also admits that 85% of the people re-located to the US from Afghanistan are of unknown origin, with no vetting for possible terrorist connections. Biden reassures Americans, however, now they are already in the US, their security vetting will begin.

9/25

It didn't take long for the lack of vetting to bear results: In just a matter of days several Afghan refugees housed at an Air Force base, were brought up on charges of child rape and domestic abuse. Their sick defenders say that Americans have to get used to the behaviors of "..different cultures.", one of them obviously being child rape. Biden has no comment. On the same day Biden and Harris are accused of purposely not visiting the border because cameras would follow and Americans would see firsthand the extent of the illegal immigration disaster Biden and Harris have caused. Again, Biden, possibly still asleep because it is not yet noon, has no comment.

9/26

Biden is reminded of his mid-August promise to make COVID booster shots available this week, contingent on FDA approval. Bidens' promise stokes concerns of political meddling in a matter that required the unhindered evaluation of scientists, the vast majority whose research showed that a third vaccine shot would not be effective or necessary. Besides Big Pharma, who is making billions selling the vaccine to Biden, the only other person of note to come out in favor of the booster shots is, as expected, is Dr. Fauci, the reliable government troll.

9/27

It is reported that Bidens' son Hunter tried to shake down Democrat donors in 2015 for $2 million in annual retainer and "success" fees to help persuade the Obama-Biden administration to unfreeze up to $15 billion in Libyan assets. The release of yet another fraud scheme cooked up by Biden and his son came from the trade magazine, Business Insider. In it it details the Bidens' scheme to use the retainer to aid in the recovery of Libyan assets frozen by Obama while Biden was vice president, proving once again the media has lied to the American public and covered up more sordid details about the Biden family business.

9/28

Biden condemns the images of mounted officers aggressively blocking Haitian migrants from crossing the border and has promised that there will be consequences for the Border Patrol officers involved. The governor of Texas, defying Biden assures them that any agents fired by Biden will be hired immediately by the state of Texas to help him control the border in his state since Biden is unwilling to do so.

9/29

The governor of Texas is asked to respond to Bidens accusation that he is exceeding his authority in handling the situation at the U.S.- Mexico border, noting that Biden has asked his AG to sue the governor over this. The Governor responds that, since Biden is refusing to enforce the laws of the United States, he is left him with no choice other than to step up and do what he has to do as Governor to make sure that the people of Del Rio are protected as well as all these other communities in the state of Texas that Biden, in his incompetence, has failed.

9/30

Almost comically, Biden asserts that the Taliban would have to convince the world it was serious about becoming part of the world community by altering its' former savage method of governing. If they do, Biden promises to send these butchers more American tax-payer funded money. In answer to Bidens' generous, heart felt offer, one of the Taliban's founders interviewed said that the his followers would once again carry out executions and amputations of hands in order to enforce its' interpretation of Muslim law. Biden responds by announcing that this activity by the Taliban would constitute clear, gross abuses of human rights... and nothing else. The possibility of these savages receiving American aid is still on the table.

10/1

Biden and Harris assure the American people that the crisis brought on by the 14000 Haitians who illegally invaded Del Rio, Texas, has been handled and the invaders are being deported back to Haiti. It turns out that this is another Biden lie, as in less than a week over 10,000 of these illegals have been "processed" and placed in various locations in the US, with the other 4000 "pending processing". In actuality, almost none of the illegals are actually being sent back to Haiti.

10/2

Biden and Harris receive criticism from an unexpected source – the few illegal Haitians being deported back to Haiti. What Biden and Harris are too dense or refuse to realize is that these Haitians originally fled the impoverished hell-hole that Haiti is for a better life in various South American countries. They came to the US only because of Bidens' and Harris' tacit invitation. Now, thanks to Biden, they find themselves in the ironic position of being deported, not back to their new homes in South America, but to the impoverished hell-hole Haiti has become, to start over again

10/3

Biden refuses to respond to criticism that, while Trump kept up regular communication with Border Patrol personnel, he and Harris have yet to speak to a single agent on the front lines, have not visited any of the hot spots along the border and still refuse to call what is going on there a crisis. Harris feebly defends her incompetence by reminding reporters that she did visit El Paso, but then is asked, when compared to the rest of the border, what the hell was there to see in El Paso? Harris, like Biden, has no comment.

10/4

Under pressure from Biden, a U.S. district judge blocked the expulsion of migrant families caught crossing the U.S.-Mexico border under Title 42. This was an order put in place by Trump, issued in 3/20, its' purpose to limit the spread of COVID19. The judge wrote that expelling asylum seekers denies them the "opportunity to seek humanitarian benefits", benefits they are apparently entitled to under Bidens' illegal immigration policies. The judge, apparently pressured by Biden, ignores the fact that the law was put into place not just to stop illegal immigration, but also curb the spread of the virus brought in by the hordes of untested and un-vaccinated illegals, the number now in the millions.

10/5

At a NASCAR event and a NFL football game, stadium crowds spontaneously broke into a "F..k Joe Biden" chant and kept it going for quite awhile. It was interesting to watch crowds of between 60000 and 100000 chant their respect for their bumbling President. It is rumored that if the public display of derision bothered him, Bidens' sleepy gaze did not change..

10/6

Biden refuses to condemn activists who illegally trespassed and confronted a Democratic Senator who has been critical of Bidens' handling of, in order, the border, his boondoggle 3.5.trillion spending package and, particularly, the upsurge in crime sweeping America. As for the crime wave, the Senator remarked: "... it happens to everybody (in America), the only people it doesn't happen to are people (like Biden) who have Secret Service standing around them."

10/7

Biden directs his Attorney General to have the DOJ and FBI co-ordinate with local officials to begin targeting and investigating any parents who show up at local school board meetings to criticize and/or protest the teaching of the Marxist Critical Race Theory in their schools, Biden marking them as "domestic terrorists"

10/8

Bidens' battle with the teleprompter continues in Michigan. Biden tries to compliment the lieutenant governor there, saying the LG "... covers her (the governor) in every way, both in terms of physically, and mentally, and every other way." While Biden does not detail how the male Michigan LG "physically" covers the female governor, Bidens' verbal miscues and gaffes in his speeches continue. It now comes to light that some time ago White House staffers resorted to muting Biden on TV or turning it off completely during newscasts of his public appearances in order to avoid confusion and possible embarrassment.

10/9

Biden reiterates his direction to his AG to go after any parents – whom he still calls domestic terrorists - who object to the public school curriculum he endorses. This curriculum includes gender nullification and the teaching of CRT. All of this while Biden ignores – or it cannot dent his rapidly-deteriorating gray matter - the apparent conflict of interest with his Attorney Generals' son-in-law making money peddling CRT curriculums across the country.

10/10

With his ever-decreasing gray matter showing no signs of slowing, Biden announces that he has created several hundred thousand "new jobs" recently. Biden blatantly ignores – and hopes no else notices – is that the majority of these "new jobs" are the same old jobs, lost because of pandemic restrictions, that people are now returning to after these same restrictions were lifted. When these not-newly created jobs are added to the looking at the actual "new" jobs Biden has created, the number is minimal.

10/11

Bidens' penchant for creating a problem, then expecting gratitude when he fixes the 'problem' he created, is not new behavior for Biden. In a previous political life it is rumored that he ordered an entire section of a city to evacuate their houses because of a gas leak. When it turned out to be a false alarm and the citizens were allowed to return, Biden held a news conference to announce that the leaking gas threat was over and all the citizens were back in the 'new houses' he provided for them. While sounding exactly like a 'Biden-ism', this story is heatedly challenged by Biden supporters.

10/12

In the ever-increasing crisis at the southern border, it is reported that now Mexican cartel members, dressed in military-like outfits and toting AK-47 rifles, have been taunting U.S. soldiers assigned to the southern border. It is estimated that the cartels are making more than $40 million each month from smuggling people over the border. As for this latest report on this new aggression at the border, Biden and "Border Czar" Harris, have no comment.

10/13

It is confirmed that a chant previously thought to be "Let's go Brandon!" that broke out at a NASCAR event over the weekend was actually the tens of thousands fans present, in unison, screaming "F..k Joe Biden". Rather than anecdotal, it is also revealed that similar chants have been breaking out at sporting events all across the country.

10/14

Biden gives yet another rambling, incoherent speech in Ohio … maybe. It's hard to tell where the speech took place because Biden confuses the states of Ohio and Pennsylvania, confuses the names and political positions of the local representatives and has trouble completing even one coherent sentence. Biden confounds the confusion even more at the end of this speech by asking: "Where's Tim?", looking forlornly around the audience. There is some speculation that 'Tim" might be one of his nurses, but no one is sure.

10/15

To help find funds for his enormous "infrastructure" boondoggle, Biden wants banks to give the IRS new details on their customers and provide data for accounts with total annual deposits or withdrawals worth more than $600. This has sparked an uproar among banks and Republican lawmakers, who say giving the IRS such power would be an enormous breach of privacy and also government overreach. Banks and their trade groups are running advertising and letter-writing campaigns to raise awareness and concern about the proposal.

10/16

As national concern about Bidens' competence continue to grow, a new poll shows that his senility/ineptitude is dragging his party down with him. The poll shows that on security matters, 54% prefer the Republican Party while only 39% prefer the Democratic Party, the largest GOP advantage since 2015. On 'prosperity', 50% prefer the Republican Party and 41% prefer the Democratic Party, the largest GOP advantage in this category since 2014.

10/17

It is revealed that, under Biden's direction, at least 94,570 illegal immigrants have been released into the U.S. since March, given only something called 'Notice to Report'. Those who receive such a notice are required only to check in with an ICE office when they get to their final destination, which could be anywhere across the country. Those who check in are not deported or detained as their immigration proceedings move forward. These "official" numbers are highly suspect as it has been reported that a minimum of 1.5 million illegals have crossed the border since Biden took office.

10/18

It is reported that in the last two months alone Biden and his administration has released roughly 32,000 immigrants into the U.S. via "parole", a form of legal status that allows these illegals to obtain work permits. It seems Biden is abusing this 'Parole Authority' since under Federal law it is to be used on a case-by-case basis and only for "urgent humanitarian purposes" or "significant public benefit." Typically only a handful of parole cases are granted by officials each year, but Biden has been using it more broadly. Even a former Border Patrol Chief who served under Biden said that that he believes Biden and his administration are abusing this statute because, when he was in charge, he never approved more than 5 or 10 paroles in a year, compared to the horrific number of thousands Biden is approving.

10/19

As the number of illegal immigration cases skyrocket, Bidens former Border Chief Scott is asked again about the "parole" policy Biden is flagrantly abusing. He reiterates that by law and regulation a parole of an illegal immigrant should only be granted on a case by case basis and only for significant humanitarian reasons or significant public benefit. In his opinion, neither of these appear to apply to the current situation that Biden and Harris are exacerbating.

10/20

More reports are leaked that, in addition to the 32000 immigrants Biden and Harris have released since August on "parole", they have also released an additional 40,000 illegal immigrants into the US on their own recognizance. The report also show that on one single day in the Del Rio sector alone, 128 single adult illegal immigrants were released into the U.S. without any tracking or monitoring required. If their current rate of paroles for illegals continues, Biden and Harris will release and additional 40,000 plus illegals on parole in the US by the end of the year.

10/21

Biden holds a 'town hall meeting to answer questions from supposed Trump supporters and independent voters. It turns out that the hall was filled with Marxist and Democratic activists. On top of this fraud, the questions and answers are scripted in advance. Sadly, even with the script Biden fumbles his way through the answers, mostly looking befuddled. One statement he does make is that he has no short-term answer for the skyrocketing gas prices besetting the nation. It's possible that Bidens' increasing senility is making him forget that his canceling of the Keystone pipeline when he first got into office is largely to blame for these bloated prices.

10/22

Bidens' supporters rush to deflect criticism of his recent 'town hall' sham performance where he used a planted audience and responded, still badly, to only scripted questions. Critics claim that it shows Biden's' contempt for the American public, while Bidens' supporters claim that this is not a new ploy. They remind the critics that when Obama was president, he held a news conference where he was joined on stage by a dozen or more "doctors", all in white coats and all supporting his Obamacare plan. Later it was revealed that there were few, if any, doctors on that stage. In fact some were laymen Obama found wandering the halls whom he put white coats on. Supporters claim Bidens' supposed 'town hall' shenanigans was nothing more than harmless political theater. Harmless? To whom? Biden and his supporters have no comment.

10/23

In answer to demands that he visit the border, Biden claims he has already, that he and his wife had a wonderful time visiting Niagara Falls. Politely ignoring Bidens' mental denseness, the reporter explains that he meant the southern, not the northern border. Biden claims he has already been there, too, but no one can find any documentation of this supposed trip. Biden brushes off this apparent lie, claiming he's been too busy attending to presidential duties to take time to visit the disaster at Americas' southern border, largely of his creation. His claim of 'attention to presidential duties' is also suspect since it is well-documented that he has spent almost half of his time as president in his Delaware basement, unless napping is considered a integral part of 'presidential duties'.

10/24

Reporters question Bidens' claim of recent visits to the southern border since they can't find any record of him visiting the border since 2008. Not denying this, Biden however defends his claim by having his press secretary remind reporters that he and his wife have visited Mexico and South America many times in the past. With the 'sun-downer' effect clearly taking hold, Biden claims these trips are valid substitutes for current southern border visits, since most illegal aliens trespassing in the US come from Mexico and South America. The shock of Bidens' vapid response causes even seasoned reporters to pause, allowing Biden, aided by his wife and nurses, to escape.

10/25

It is reported that, according to those affected, Biden has directed his AG to employ the FBI and DOJ to target parents who show up at board meetings to protest their school board's agenda. In particular the parents are protesting the teaching of genderism which allows boys access to girls' restrooms and locker rooms and the teaching of the Marxist Critical Race Theory. Biden and his AG now brand these concerned parents "domestic terrorists".

10/26

With his approval, Bidens' AG pens a letter directing the DOJ and FBI to target parents who threaten violence against school board members. It I supposedly in response to a letter Biden supposedly received from these board members. He particularly picks out a father who threatened violence against his school after his teen daughter was assaulted in a girls' locker room by a boy who claimed he was a 'girl' that day. Biden has no comment.

10/27

With publicity escalating as more outraged parents accost their school; boards over their crude Marxist curriculum, Biden doubles down, backing his FBI and DOJ going after these supposed "domestic terrorists".This, even after a report that the one parent targeted specifically by Biden's shock troops, was there not to protest the left-wing agenda, but that his daughter was raped in a gender-neutral bathroom, a crime made possible by this same agenda. His anger boiled over after the school board, rather than accepting responsibility for the rape, still maintained that the boy had every right to be in that bathroom with the girl he raped. Biden, his DOJ and his FBI, have no comment.

10/28

Bidens' AG is called before Congress to answer for his proposed crack down on concerned parents because of this supposed letter he held describing acts of violence towards school boards. After intense grilling and several denials, Bidens' AG admits he had no such letter describing acts of violence. When asked about an apology on behalf of Biden to the father who was targeted when he expressed outrage at his daughters rape in a "gender-neutral" bathroom – another Biden initiative - Bidens' AG mumbles incoherently. He finished by acknowledging, graciously, that rape is reprehensible and parents still had First Amendment rights.

Seemingly as brain dead as Biden, his AG doesn't realize that his first point is patronizingly obvious, the second of little comfort to the the rape victim or her father.

10/29

It comes to light that it was after the National School Boards Association asked Biden to utilize tools, including the terrorism-related Patriot Act, to deal with concerned "domestic terrorist" parents that Biden and his AG issued the 'Target Parents' memo to the DOJ and FBI. Now the NSBA admits that the disruptions by the parents were non-violent and no board member was threatened. However, they still want Biden to target the parents as "domestic terrorists" anyway because of their protesting the NSBA teaching of CRT and genderism to their kids. Biden has no comment.

10/30

As parents continue to protest Bidens' Marxist school agenda, seventeen states sign a petition asking Biden to stop using his FBI and DOJ to intimidate parents into silence at school board meetings. It turns out that two days ago a Congressman from Ohio attempted to show a video of parents at school board meetings to prove Biden and his AG lied about the violence involved. However, in order to protect Biden, the Democratic chairman of the committee refused to show the video, claiming he needed at least a 48 hour advance notice to do so. The Democratic chair is informed that there is no official rule requiring such a ridiculous notice, but he still doesn't allow the video to be shown. Biden, saved from embarrassment again, has no comment.

10/31

Biden proposes to pay every illegal alien who was allegedly separated from his or her family last year $450,000 apiece to settle a lawsuit filed by the illegals. It does not occur to Biden, glassy grin in place, that if his latest idiotic proposal it enacted, it would result in a taxpayer bill that would surpass the entire amount of money in the US Treasury. Again dismayed Americans have to be wondering, what color is the sky in Bidens' mentally-depleted world?

11/1

Biden holds a press conference touting the "framework" of his proposed "infrastructure" boondoggle. He fails to mention that a key part of his plan included the canceling of the Keystone pipeline, which helped cause the price of a barrel of oil to rise from the $38/barrel price it was under Trump to the almost $90/barrel it is now, fueling a historic inflation rate and a dismal 2.3% quarterly GDP growth rate. Biden has accomplished all of this economic disaster in just the first nine months of his presidency. Instead of answering concerns about these dismal economic figures, Biden blathers on for a short time about investing more money into 'head start' programs for children. This was followed by Biden wandering off the stage without taking a single question..

11/2

It is reported that dozens of House Republicans sent a letter to Biden regarding rumors that his AG and his DHS are in talks regarding Bidens' proposal to give money to illegal immigrant families who were separated at the border. In the letter, the Republicans outline their concerns about the AG and other government agencies seriously considering paying the $450,000 Biden asked for to these illegals who have already broken an American law at least once. Reporters attempt to question Biden about his questionable plan, but Biden s' only response is to look away in the distance, scratching his forehead.

11/3

It is reported that the letter the Republicans sent to Biden regarding his proposed 'separated-at-the-border' compensation plan contained several accusations. One was that Bidens' plan would in effect reward criminal behavior. Another was that Bidens' plan would send a message to the world that the US borders are open and US rule of law will not be enforced. Finally the Republicans also accuse Biden of incentivising illegal border crossings since his first day in office. It was then he struck down several Trump-era border policies which has led to to what many have called "… the worst self-inflicted border crisis in American history." Biden, whether asleep or in an Ensure-induced daze, has no comment.

11/4

In keeping up the pressure on Bidens' "urgent travesty" to recompense criminal illegal alien behavior, members of Congress point out that the average median American household annual income and the maximum payout from a SGLI life insurance policy for military members in 2019 was $68,703 and $400,000, respectively. These both pale in comparison to the $450,000 Biden is proposing to pay to each member of an illegal alien family separated at the border. Evidently confused bu actual financial numbers, Biden has no comment.

11/5

At the G7 summit Biden apologizes to the rest of the world leaders for the supposed sins of America. These include either pulling out of or not living up to various agreements 'world agreements' Obama committed

America to. It all-too painfully reminded Americans of Obama bowing and grovelling to these same leaders during the 'apology tour' he took around the world when he was president. On that infamous tour, Obama reassured the various dictators and Marxist leaders worldwide that Americas' glory days were behind her. Now Biden caps off his similar, feckless ma culpa at this years' G7 by taking his seat in the audience and then promptly falling asleep.

11/6

A group picture of the participants in this years' G7 meeting was released. It was compared to the picture taken of the same group when Trump was President. In his picture, Trump is front and center, with most of the participants in dark suits and ties, all looking serious and professional. In Bidens' picture the participants were arrayed in a cacophony of clownish colors, looking for all the world like a bad Sesame Street audition. For his part, Biden was standing last at the left-most part of the picture, almost off the stage. In nine months America has gone from being perceived as having a capable leader of the free world to Biden, almost an afterthought, looking lost and confused.

11/7

Biden issues a emergency rule that makes COVID vaccines mandatory for every U.S. private business that employs 100 workers or more. This affects everyone from grocery clerks to meat packing plant employees, impacting some 80 million Americans. It would be the first time Washington has set a federal standard that regards a respiratory virus as an occupational hazard outside of the health care sector. This essentially puts it under the auspices of OSHA, giving Bidens' rule a monstrous, intrusive, legal backing.

11/8

A federal judge issues a stay blocking Bidens' nationwide vaccine mandate. Biden promises to go to court to fight the injunction. Meanwhile a new poll shows Bidens favorable/unfavorable numbers to be at a new low, 38% to 62%. If Biden doesn't want to feel bad and is sentient enough to feel anything he can take comfort in the fact that the numbers for his VP Harris are 27% favorable to 73% unfavorable.

11/9

It is projected to Biden that by rescinding and dismantling Trumps' "Third Safe Country" and "Stay in Mexico" immigration policies, an estimated 2 million illegal immigrant border crossings – an historical record - will happen in his first year in office. Trumps' first order forced immigrants to remain in the first safe country they reached, the second deterring illegal immigrants from roaming the US while waiting for their cases to be adjudicated. By rescinding these in his first few days in office, Biden precipitated the current border disaster. Biden has no answer.

11/10

Biden has a tense exchange with reporters who press Biden over his comments disputing reports that the he is considering issuing $450,000 payments to illegal immigrants who were separated from their families at the southern border. Biden doesn't deny payments will be made, but he does take issue with the dollar amount. Biden, while angrily pointing a finger at reporters, maintains that while the final figure has not been decided, the illegal immigrants "...deserve some kind of compensation.".

11/11

Biden and his spokesmen double down on his 'compensate the illegals' policy, saying that it will save taxpayer dollars and put "... the disastrous history of the previous administration's use of zero tolerance family separation behind us". While Biden orders his Department of Justice to settle with the illegal individuals and families who are currently in litigation with the US government, he fails to explain how non-citizens involved in criminal activity have any standing to sue the US government and its' taxpayers in the first place.

11/12

Biden is asked by a reporter if his proposed illegal alien payments could serve as an incentive for more illegal immigrants to try to enter the U.S. Biden responds by blaming any "incentive" illegals might have on reporters who keep reporting "that garbage" that each illegal will be paid $450,000. Bidens' "garbage" claims stem from, yes, the illegals will be financially compensated, but Biden has not settled on the final amount. Regardless of the final amount Biden settles on, it is expected that payouts to the illegals will cost the American taxpayer several billion dollars.

11/13

Bidens' Secretary of the US Treasury, a Russian Marxist immigrant, states that she hopes Bidens' climate and environment programs will bankrupt all the mid-to-small size oil companies because she believes this will be good for the environment, regardless what it does to the economy: Biden has no comment.

11/14

Biden is asked about his failing poll numbers occurring so soon in his tenure. Biden expresses surprise by this, saying that his numbers are comparable to Obamas and Clintons at the same time in their presidencies. When reminded that, at this time in their stints in the White House, Obama and Clintons' numbers were in the 50% to 60% popularity range - not 38% like Bidens – he replies that he has his own poll showing him at a 48% popularity, much closer to the Obama/ Clinton range. When asked about the rumor that the only people polled in Bidens' were his chief of staff, his cabinet, his wife and other members of his family still working for the Chinese, Biden replies: "Hey, man. a poll is a poll."

11/15

Biden sends Harris overseas for a conference with other nations. Even though it is supposed to be about climate concerns, Harris is asked about the historical inflation rate Bidens' polices have caused in the US in just the first few months of his presidency. Before she can answer, the reporter asks how more trillions of dollars Biden and Harris are demanding to be spent would not exacerbate this historical inflation problem. In her best intellectual response, Harris lectures the reporter that, one, inflation is when 'things cost more than they did before' and, two, this causes many Americans to have to "stretch" their budgets. After this intellectual response, fit for elementary school children, Harris moves on to the next reporter, leaving the first one speechless.

11/16

Biden's' has a virtual, on line meeting with Chairman Xiping of China. The range of topics Americans hoped Biden would discuss with the Communist leader range from the murderous Chairmans' abusive takeover of Hong Kong, his threatened takeover of Taiwan, the current genocide of the Uyghurs by the thousands, his Wuhan lab currently working on a new virus that, unlike the 1% kill rate of the COVID 19 virus he released upon the world, has a kill rate of 80%, or why the lab was still operating at all. If Americans expected these topics to be broached, they were sadly disappointed. Biden declared the number one problem he and the Communist Chairman would work on is … climate change.

11/17

Harris' embarrassing evasive non-answer at the climate conference a few days ago makes the news cycle, eliciting defensive silence from her supporters and derisive laughter at both her and Biden from their detractors. One wag points out that if one thought that answer was humorous, just think how shamefully funny Harris would have sounded if she actually tried to answer the question.

11/18

Biden claims that not a single economist in the world believes that his 1.7 billion infrastructure boondoggler will add a penny/dollar/peso to his historical inflation rate. Biden might be forgiven this view since it comes from him peering out of his basement window. First – and perhaps tomorrow after todays' sun-downer effect eases – someone should explain to Biden that you can't add a money figure to a statistic; you can only raise or lower the statistic. Secondly there are dozens of economists that predict pouring this much money into a labyrinth of undefined welfare projects will do much more harm than good to the current economy, not to mention devastate future ones. Now, if someone could just get some of these economists to wander by Bidens' basement window.

11/19

Biden heatedly denies that he is at war with the productive members of and businesses in the American economy. Biden claims his infrastructure boondoggle is completely paid for and won't cost taxpayers a cent. Then two seconds later (or to him, a half hour in his current mental condition) Biden claims that his plan won't cost anything because the first part would be paid for by increasing taxes on US businesses, the second part by increasing taxes on "the wealthy" in the country. It is apparent that, along with his ongoing battle with the teleprompter, Biden is battling with such difficult concepts as 'free' and 'paid for'.

11/20

On his tour across America -which, like his other tours, seem seldom to cross West of the Mississippi - Biden stops on a bridge somewhere that needs repair. There Biden babbles disconnectedly about people worrying about crossing such a bridge, and if there was a fire on the other side, and then maybe "the extra 10 miles" it would take to reach such a fire. Biden claims these are "real" and "ordinary" and "profound" concerns that Americans sit around their dinner tables at night discussing. Biden finishes by claiming his 1.7 trillion infrastructure boondoggle will alleviate these "real" fears for Americans. Bidens' nurses look uncomfortable around him, too embarrassed to tell Biden that these American bridge fears are "real" nowhere except maybe in his basement.

11/21

Amid demands for a boycott of the Olympic games scheduled this year in China because of the countrys' extreme human rights abuses in Hong Kong, their slave labor camps, their genocide of the Uyghurs and various other crimes, Biden "mulls" a possible "diplomatic boycott" of China where no US officials will attend the games. China, the country Bidens family has been working for and with for years, is understandably miffed.

11/22

Biden is reminded that during his campaign he referred to Kyle Rittenhouse as a white supremacist before trial, without looking at the video evidence or hearing from witnesses. Now acquitted and clearly shown that he was defending his life, the young man urges Biden to get all the facts before defaming him and making a criminal trial into a political one: Biden has no comment.

11/23

It is reported to Biden and his administration that illegal immigration crossings now average approximately 6500 a day, over a 6000% increase over the daily crossings under Trump once he got a handle on the disastrous border situation that Obama and Biden had left him to fix in 2016. Biden has no comment.

1124

Biden once again asks OPEC and Russia to increase their oil output to help America with its' new-since-Trump-left-office energy shortages. Both comply, but only if they can sell oil to the US at a 300% increase over what the lowest price of a barrel of crude was during Trumps' time in office. Incredibly in just a few months Biden has taken America from a proud, energy-independent country (so energy independent it was actually exporting energy to other countries) led by a strong leader to a vision of a feeble, demented old man on his knees, begging Americas' enemies for help.

11/25

Biden will eat his Thanksgiving feast at the Nantucket mansion of private equity billionaire David Rubenstein. This move seems seems out of touch to most Americans who face an all-time-high bill for their own dinners due to the rampant inflation Biden has caused. An American Farm Bureau Federation survey found that the average cost of a Thanksgiving meal for 10 people increased 14% since last year to an all-time high of $53.31, thanks mainly to Bidens' economic policies.

11/26

In an effort to relieve the countrys' current energy woes, most clearly manifested by gas now costing $8/gallon in some areas, Biden proudly announces he has ordered the release of some of Americas' gas reserves. Frightening because this is the gas held in case of calamities like war or natural disaster. How much this will help is questionable since the amount Biden ordered released equates to two-and-one- half days of fuel use in this country. This means that by noon Wednesday America will be in the same fuel predicament it awoke to on Monday, only now its' ability to help itself in case of a disaster seriously depleted..

11/27

It is reported that Russia has amassed more than 100,000 troops near eastern Ukraine and may be preparing to launch a major military incursion. Satellite imagery show Russian armored units and artillery moving to the area. Ukraine's military has warned Biden that Russian forces could attack in late January or early February, a stunt they never dared when Trump was in office. Biden says nothing, which is not surprising: When the Ukraine asked Obama and Biden for help with a similar incident a few years ago, they sent them blankets; on his watch, Trump sent them guns.

11/28

Biden assures Americans that he is keeping a 'watchful eye' on Russian troop buildup on the Ukraine border. Biden bristles on being accused that in response to this aggression he has spent an inordinate amount of time browsing household goods sites, looking for blanket sales. However, Biden lets slip that, if one is so disposed, at this moment Pendleton is offering its' Camp Blankets at a killer price.

11/29

Biden called on all nations expected to meet at the World Trade Organization next week to agree to waive intellectual property protections for COVID-19 vaccines. This is in the wake of the identification of a new coronavirus variant in South Africa. Apparently the news hadn't reached Bidens' basement that the meeting he was referring to was postponed after the new variant led to travel restrictions preventing many participants from attending the WTO. Hopefully Bidens' nurses nurses inform him of this before Biden boards a plane to Geneva.

11/30

In a fumbling, semi-coherent press conference, Biden slurs out the boast that he, as a result of the detection of the new COVID variant, immediately called for a ban of all travel to and from South Africa. Biden does this even though the doctor who discovered the variant says there is no need to panic as it is an extremely mild form of the virus. Biden is then reminded that when Trump banned travel to and from China when there was a real serious viral threat, Biden called Trump racist and xenophobic. For an answer, Biden leaves the stage with no comment.

12/1

Biden is called on the carpet again for instituting a travel ban on South Africa after he called Trunps' China travel ban racist and xenophobic. Biden tries to explain that he did not call Trumps' ban all those bad names, but it was a tweet Trump sent out concerning the virus that he considered racist and xenophobic. The problem with this is that his defaming remark about Trump came out quite a few days, if not weeks, before Trumps' infamous tweet. Since it was late in the day it's possible that something like a 'sun-downer syndrome' caused Biden to confuse these dates: Otherwise, it would mean Biden was just outright lying, again.

12/2

Biden is asked why he and Harris did not go to Waukesha, Wisconsin after a BLM follower murdered 6 people there, including children. Biden and Harris did go to Kenosha to support BLM members protesting the "white supremacists and racist police" who, in their minds, unnecessarily took down an armed criminal who refused to surrender. In answer, Biden and his press secretary cite the 'exorbitant' cost of a trip to Waukesha as the reason for Biden and Harris not going there.

12/3

Biden is reminded of his campaign statement that "Anyone (Trump) who allows 220000 people to die (due to COVID) doesn't belong in the White House." and is asked if the same standard applies now. This because since Bidens' remark an additional 560000 people have died from the virus, many of them under his watch. Biden, through his PS, claims the standard is different now because he is trying to "help solve this crisis" and get the "pandemic under control.", insinuating, amazingly, that Trump was not.

12/4

Reporters note that Bidens' excuse of 'cost' being the reason for him not going to Waukesha to support the parents and families of those murdered by a BLM follower, is a bit strange. Strange, that a man who recently forced a multi trillion expenditure package through Congress, loaded mostly with pork for his friends and such groups as BLM, would suddenly become cost - conscious and chafe at the extra $15 dollars a round trip ticket to Waukesha would cost him.

12/5

Biden sheepishly announces that a Trump immigration policy he dismantled when he was first inaugurated – where asylum seekers looking to enter the US from Mexico would be sent back to Mexico while their claims are assessed – is being re-instated. It is hoped that this will curtail he 5000/day border crossing attempts, up from the 100/ day total it was when Trump was president.

12/6

Bidens' braggadocio because of re-instating the effective Trump-era immigration policy is shot down quickly upon revelation that it was the Supreme Court that ordered Biden to do so. Any attempt by Biden to take credit for the sudden drop in attempted border crossings is nothing short of hypocritical. What Biden can take credit for adding a new twist to the old adage: "If you're being run out of town, turn around and make it look like you're leading a parade."

12/7

For months Biden has been accused of deliberately re-locating thousands of unvaccinated COVID immigrants into the border states of Texas,

Arizona and Florida, states Biden views as political 'enemy states'. His purposeful in-fluxing of these immigrants is seen as a way to not only tip future elections, but also to impact these states' very favorable COVID reduction rates. These three states have remained relatively open in defiance of Bidens' mandates and have prospered as few other Democratic-run states have. As such, they have been a constant embarrassment Biden, thus his naked attempt at sabotage.

12/8

Biden denounces all officials who have blocked efforts to mandate vaccines. In an attempt to appear tough and virile, the president called out Republican governors specifically who have banned businesses and universities from requiring vaccines and/or masking guidance from the Centers for Disease Control and Prevention. However, instead of virile, Biden looks frail and confused; instead of tough, he sounds and gestures like an old man railing against the 'gosh darn' wind that blew his hat off his head, a hat he apparently wasn't even wearing.

12/9

Biden and his administration are questioned why, if the Supreme Court ruling for re-instating the Trump-era immigration policy was issued in August, it took Biden three months to enact it. Bidens' answer is that it took some time to negotiate with Mexico how the reinstatement would be implemented. While all details of this negotiation were not released, one glaringly hypocritical Biden detail was: All illegal immigrants would be offered a COVID vaccine before being returned to Mexico, an immunization not required of the thousands of un-vaccinated immigrants Biden forced-relocated to his enemy conservative states.

12/10

Despite being ruled unconstitutional by a Federal judge, Biden states that he will continue to push his mandatory vaccine program. Some leeway is necessary here: Once his nurse wakes him from his afternoon nap, lets him take a straw-sip from his can of Ensure, then explain to him - slowly – what the Constitution and a Federal Court judge is, Biden might relent.

12/11

In one of his greatest shows of chutzpah to date, Biden includes monoclonal antibody treatment sites as part of "his" plan to further combat the COVID "pandemic". This, though the governor of Florida - whom Biden has repeatedly decried as anti-science, anti-patriotic, anti vaccine and any number of other 'antis' - has had as many as 25 of these sites operational in his state for months, with much success. One wonders how many lives would've been saved if Biden hadn't refused to acknowledge the governors' success purely for political reasons; that is, until he could lie and claim them as his own.

12/12

Reports indicate Biden takes umbrage at being accused of lying about the Florida Governors' success at implementing monoclonal treatment centers being Bidens' idea first. Biden might have a point: Since he is renowned for plagiarizing papers in college and plagiarizing others speeches throughout his political career, Bidens' claimed ownership of the monoclonal treatment centers ideas is not so much a lie as it is theft of intellectual property, something Biden has shown consistently in his career he is comfortable with.

12/13

A short time ago Biden had a face-to-face meeting with Putin, the Russian Premier. In it, Biden supposedly warned Putin about his troop build-up along the Crimea border. Biden reported to the media that he and Putin left the meeting with a mutual respect for each others' views. It turns out that Putin has so much respect for Bidens' "views" that, upon returning to Russia, he ordered an additional 10,000 troops to the Crimea border in preparation for an eventual invasion.

12/14

After his 'respectful' meeting with Putin. Biden has no comment concerning the massive Russian build-up of troops along the Crimea border. This does follow a pattern of sorts: Before his meeting with Putin, Biden met with Xi Jinping of China where Biden claimed he "... stared into the soul..." of this dictator, thus engendering a mutual respect between both men. That meeting was so 'respectful' that upon his return to China, Xi ordered increased war plane flyovers of Taiwan in further attempts to intimidate that nation state. Perhaps while Biden is taking that straw-sip from his Ensure and having what the Constitution and a Federal Court judge are, one of Bidens' nurses might hold a dictionary open for Biden so he can learn what the word 'respect' means.

12/15

In regards to Bidens' penchant for stealing others ideas, a reporter brings up an incident involving Biden in 1987. Then Biden not only lifted entire lines of his stock stump speech from Britain's then-Labor Party leader, Neil Kinnock – complete with with phrases, gestures and lyrical Welsh syntax intact - for his own closing speech, Biden appropriated Kinnocks' life story too, including a coal mining grandfather. What makes this really embarrassing is that it was so easy to check: While Kinnocks' grandfather did work in the mines, Bidens' sold cars. One might be tempted to blame something like pre- dementia for Biden confusing another life with his, but this was 1987 when Biden was only 45 years old.

12/16

Biden blames the 'Meat Conglomerate' – whatever that is – for inflation. Yes, not his trillions of pork dollars he has flooded into the economy, the tax hikes or policies like shutting down oil and gas pipeline construction, causing the price of oil to triple since Trump was in office … no, for Biden it's a 'Meat Conglomerate' conspiracy. fault. A reporter asks how, if this so-called Conglomerate has been in existence for decades, can it be responsible for the sudden inflation explosion during Bidens' short time in office? Instead of answering, Biden first makes a chopping motion as if his mike has gone dead, then waves his hands frantically on the sides of his head, as if he suddenly can't hear. Fortunately two of his nurses move quickly to grab his arms and lead him safely off the stage, before he accidentally pokes himself or some other innocent in the eye.

12/17

A federal appeals court reinstates Bidens' vaccine and testing mandate for private businesses that covers about 80 million American workers. The ruling by the 6th U.S. Court of Appeals in Cincinnati lifted a November injunction that had blocked this rule from OSHA which applies to businesses with at least 100 workers. In the decision Friday, the 6th Circuit noted that OSHA demonstrated the pervasive danger that COVID-19 poses to workers, whether vaccinated or not, in their workplaces. It's unclear what research OSHA used for its' 'demonstration', particularly since there have been few hospitalizations and no deaths reported worldwide concerning the latest COVID variant.

12/18

Bidens' "Build Back Better" plan is stalled when Democrat Joe Manchin refuses to support it because of some of the overwhelming costs the plan will levy on American tax payers, particularly future generations. Biden claims he is working closely with Manchin to forge some kind of agreement. This led reporters to ask Harris who the real president of the US was, Biden or Manchin. In a fiery retort, Harris barks: "It's Joe Biden … and I'm vice president and my name is Kamala Harris." Thank goodness she cleared that much since many people wondered if she was still alive, disappearing as she did after butchering her job as 'Immigration and Border Czar' some months back.

12/19

Harris is asked to defend Bidens' accomplishments so far, such as allowing hundreds of thousands illegal border crossings, an inflation rate of historical proportions and allowing war-mongering by China, Russia, North Korea and Palestine. It is pointed out to Harris that none of these "Biden accomplishments" were present in any great degree while Trump was in office. Harris counters by advising critics to focus on Bidens' accomplishments like the child tax credit and his plans to replace every lead water pipe in the country. Yes, with imminent war with our enemies, an asphyxiating inflation rate, drugs, human trafficking, rape and murder occurring daily at our southern border, thank goodness Biden is focused on the absolute terror Americans face when confronted by a deadly lead water pipe.

12/20

Bidens' penchant for stealing other people' work and calling it his own is becoming legendary. Even Bidens' supposed trademark slogan "Build Back Better" is neither his or original. It turns out that Biden lifted it from U.K. Prime Minister Boris Johnson who was using the same slogan long before Biden stole it. At that same time the United Nations launched a climate change initiative in April, 2020 with the same title, 'Build Back Better'. before Biden and his campaign plagiarized the title from them. Sad that the only question now for Biden to answer is not if he plagiarized the slogan, but from whom

12/21

One of Bidens' campaign promises was that he would to do a better job of handling the pandemic than Trump. If this is the case, Biden is asked then how is it that more people have died from the virus in his first 10 months in office than in Trumps' last 10? This is particularly galling since Biden has had access to research, case studies, pharmaceuticals, a host of vaccines, including 'booster' vaccines', and a greater distribution network than Trump ever did. Considering his campaign promise, Biden has no answer for this epic failure.

12/22

A reporter claims to have a document listing 94 examples of Biden lying and plagiarizing other peoples' work during his career. Biden feigns no knowledge of such a list. The reporter points out that Biden said publicly that he marched during the civil rights movement but later admitted he didn't, that he claimed he finished in the top half of his law school class when records showed he finished in the bottom 5%, barely graduating. Biden also bragged about attending law school on a full scholarship, but records show this isn't true, either. Biden has been asked to explain these lies for years. Back in 4/20, when asked to explain these lies, for an answer Biden angrily snapped at the reporter: "I think I probably have a much higher IQ than you do." and nothing more.

12/23

Biden claims that a Democratic Senator went back on his word when he announced that he will not support Bidens' mammoth "Build Back Better" spending package. The Senator disagrees with this, saying that Biden and his "...Democratic colleagues in Washington..." are determined to dramatically reshape American society in a way that leaves the country more vulnerable to outside threats. Because of this the Senator maintains that voting for Bdiens' boondoggle would not be in the best genuine interest of his constituents or the country. Genuine? Best interest? Constituents? Country? These words, foreign to Biden, are sure to be added to the growing list that Biden might look up one day when his nurses show him how to use a dictionary.

12/24

Biden, still smarting over the failure of his mammoth pork proposal, 'Build Back Better', signed off on a published statement which read, in part, that he will continue to press the reluctant Senators to reverse his position to honor, according to Biden, "... his prior commitments and be true to his word." It is laughable that a congenital liar and plagiarist like Biden would insist that someone else be "true to his word". In the meantime Biden insists that this Senator will have to explain to those families paying $1,000 instead of $35 a month for insulin why they have to keep paying that price, a sophomoric and shallow threat, at best.

12/25

In one of Bidens' press conferences, he claimed that he 'saved Christmas' because the supply chain problems have been solved and now people were receiving their Christmas gifts on time Bidens' press secretary reiterated the same claim, saying that "we" (apparently meaning she and Biden) had "saved Christmas". The reporters in the room wonder aloud, saved exactly what? Many store shelves are still depleted and those that weren't featured prices at record levels due to Bidens' record inflation. On top of this, Biden used COVID to recommended people give up their Christmas gatherings for no substantial medical reason. Along with crime rampaging across major American cities because of Biden acquiescing to the 'Defund the Police' demands of his constituents and the war mongering among Americas' enemies all over the world, exactly what did Biden "save"/Biden and his little elf have no answer.

12/26

Biden urges people to take the COVID vaccines and boosters. Then uncharacteristically Biden praises his predecessor, saying that Trump and his administration made it possible for the United States to be "… one of the first countries to get the vaccine." Before the shock of this curtsy to Trump wears off, c, Biden followed his flattery with a call for nationwide vaccine mandates, revealing Bidens' cynical motivation. It is obvious to Biden that the major opposition and push back to his unconstitutional vaccine mandate will come mainly from Trump supporters.

12/27

Biden tries to take credit for some stores not having bare shelves during the holiday season, claiming that his economic policies must be working; far from it. It turns out that major companies like Walmart, Target, Home Depot, Best Buy, etc., anticipating Bidens' business-busting policies, loaded up early with products to ensure items were available for the holidays. Smaller companies, assuming supply-chain problems would only worsen under Biden, did the same, increasing orders by double or triple their usual volume. Biden is like the fire chief, showing up only after volunteers have put out the blaze and then turning to the cameras with thumbs up, saying: "Look what a good job I did!"

12/28

Biden does a radio interview about his plans for battling the COVID "pandemic" in 2022. In an embarrassing few minutes he confuses the difference between 'pills' and 'test kits', corrects himself, then continues to confuse the two until his response is incoherent. Biden then promises that more test kits will be ready soon. The reporter reminds Biden that he also promised that there would be more test kits available in January, 2021, then February, then March, then finally in July, with no appreciable results. Biden garbles a response, then there is some noise in the background. It is hard to tell, but it sounds like one of Bidens' nurses, leading him out of the interview room.

12/29

Russian President Putin informs Biden that if NATO does not provide binding guarantees to curtail military deployments in Eastern Europe and bars Ukraine from membership, he will be forced to consider a variety of options, including a military response. Besides threatening sanctions, Biden has no response to this new threat. One is reminded that when Ukrainians were being slaughtered and asked for US help, Obama and Biden sent them blankets; Trump sent them guns.

12/30

A news outlet reports that Bidens' poll numbers that Bidens' poll numbers are at a historical low when compared to the poll numbers of Carter, Obama and Trump at the same time in their terms. Added to Bidens' historical bungling of the US withdrawal from Afghanistan and the historical level of inflation caused mainly by his economic policies, it is safe to say Biden is ending the year on a historical note in America, if for the wrong reasons.

12/31

A news agency admits that Bidens' policies, both domestic and abroad, have largely been failures on a grand scale. It is further pointed out that it's evident Biden has no plan for getting inflation under control, does not exhibit a sense of competency, appears frail and doddery in public and is shielded by his nurses from prolonged exposure to the media. However, the same agency defends Biden, pointing out that his negative poll numbers have held steady for weeks at between 38% and 41% and are nowhere near as bad as Vice-President Harris, whose numbers hover around 28%. While true, it's not much of a defense and little comfort to Biden.

2022

1/1

Despite it being challenged on constitutional grounds in the courts, Biden starts the new year off by trying to sell his proposed nation-wide vaccine mandate. Now calling COVID the "pandemic of the unvaccinated" Biden accuses this group of not being "patriotic" and risking the lives of fellow citizens. If it was anyone else but Biden this would be considered criminal dissemination of dangerous information. Every health organization around the world, including imminent virologists and his own CDC, have published dozens of papers maintaining that even the vaccinated can still infect others with the virus. Biden puts the entire country at a unnecessary risk by insisting it follow his ignorant view of the effectiveness of the COVID vaccine. Once again calls go out for Biden to please, please leave his basement once in awhile, with or without his nurses.

1/2

The liberal media has another mental melt down over the father who, on a Christmas Eve call with Biden, got the president to agree with him on the now-famous "Let's go Brandon!" chant, the euphemism for the original "Fuck Joe Biden!" made famous at numerous outdoor events in the fall. The media is outraged at someone who could be so disrespectful to a president. This is the same media that cheered the crowds that shouted: "Fuck you!" at Trump on every occasion. They even lauded a D-level comic who decapitated a Trump doll and showcased the bloody head on social media, an event Biden let go unnoticed.

1/3

In a telephone call Russian president Putin warns Biden that any substantive moves against Russia because of his imminent threat to invade the Ukraine could lead to a "...complete breakdown in ties between out countries...". When there was no immediate response,

Bidens' nurses entered his basement to find him talking into a tin can tied to a string. Once they put a real phone in his hand, Biden warned Putin that there would be "substantive measures" taken if he continued to escalate tensions in the Ukraine. If Biden innumerated what those "substantive measures" would be, he did so only once back on his tin can.

1/4

Biden apologists are asked why, if Bidens' mental acuity should not be questioned, why Biden has referred to his vice president as "President Harris" three times in the last few months. His defenders claim this is not a sign of mental deterioration, but just a man prone to gaffes. If true, then Biden didn't disappoint them recently. He gave an interview, just four days into the year 2022, where he insisted that the future for America is bright, saying that "There is a lot of reason to be hopeful in 2020..." Before this people wondered, rightfully, what world Biden exists in: Now they have to worry about what year in what world Biden lives.

1/5

Biden holds a presser with American farmers, reminding them that he has signed an EO designed to break up large farm conglomerates, thereby "...increasing competition". Biden then starts to mumble about the chicken farms in Delaware, repeating "...chickens ...chickens ...chickens..." over and over, until his voice starts to fade. His nurses immediately escort him out of the room, still mumbling, while reporters are left again shouting ignored, unanswered questions and wondering why "chicken" is so important to Biden.

1/6

Biden is reminded of a federal ruling, issued in August of 2021, to re-instate Trumps' 'Stay in Mexico' policy which mandated that all immigrants illegally crossing the border and requesting asylum remain in Mexico until their cases are heard. Since his inauguration, Biden has overseen between 1.5 and 2 million illegals cross the border, of which only 600,000 or so were processed for deportation. For his part, Biden mocks the judge, insisting that he is complying with the judges' order since, out of these hundreds of thousands, Biden has forced a total of 203 illegals to remain in Mexico.

1/7

Biden is confronted again with his statement from a week ago, about the supposed COVID crisis being a "pandemic of the un-vaccinated" because of medical reports coming from all over the world. These report that a sizable number of re-infections are occurring to many that have been fully vaccinated, including booster shots. Even Bidens' own CDC admits that in some parts of the US a full 43% of new COVID cases are individuals that have been vaccinated. Biden is unmoved. Petulantly, he still rests the blame for the COVID crisis solely on the shoulders of the vaccinated. This leaves all to wonder if Biden is not listening or, considering his other physical and mental problems, Biden just can't hear.

1/8

Biden announces a plan to buy 500 million at-home COVID testing kits to mail to Americans who request them. Floridas' governor dismisses the idea, saying that rather than sending test kits to everyone, vulnerable communities should be the first priority for the kits, as he has done in Florida. This rebuke adds to the embarrassment the Florida governor has caused Biden during COVID. Florida did not shut down its schools or business, did not follow Bidens unconstitutional vaccine mandates and prospered better than almost all the rest of America that followed Bidens' policies and guidelines. All Biden can do is grumble and pout.

1/9

Biden confuses reporters again. He announces that he signed an EO requiring insurance companies to pay the $7 to $15 dollar cost of each COVID self test, the test that just a day ago Biden said would be free to anyone requesting them. Biden sees no discrepancy, insisting that the tests are free since he has ordered insurance companies to reimburse anyone who has to pay for them. Obviously another word Biden is in constant struggle with is 'free' and what it means to the rational.

1/12

Georgia's' Governor takes exception to Bidens' charges concerning his states voting reform bill. He claims that Biden is lying about about his state's 2021 new voting law, insisting the legislation actually makes it easier to vote and harder to cheat. He points out that Bidens' lies about Georgia's new election law being "...designed to suppress your vote and subvert our elections..." was truly ironic. It turns out that with their new voting rules, it is much easier, safer and more convenient to vote there than in other states that have much more oppressive rules, like Delaware for example... Bidens' home state. Embarrassed into silence, Biden does not answer the Governor.

1/13

Perhaps it's memory loss that prevents Biden from realizing what a hypocrite he appears to be now, demanding the Senate filibuster rule be eliminated. This, after Biden defended it as far back as 2005 and as recently as 2021. Bidens' comments now stand in stark contrast with remarks he made six months ago. Then he said that he did not want to get "wrapped up" in arguments about a move (getting rid of the filibuster rule) that would "…throw the entire Congress into chaos." One might be angry at Bidens' apparent two-face stance, but it is possible that Biden just does not remember.

1/14

While Biden continues to harangue the Senate to kill the filibuster, it comes to light that Bidens' former boss Obama argued in defense of the filibuster on the Senate floor in 2005. Not a stranger to hypocrisy himself, Obama now calls the very rule he once defended a "Jim Crow relic", a comment parroted by Biden many times since the filibuster works against him and Obama. In defending the now-despised rule back in 20005, then Senator Obama declared: "If the majority chooses to end the filibuster, if they choose to change the rules and put an end to Democratic debate, then the fighting and the bitterness and the gridlock will only get worse," Perhaps Bidens' reluctance to see himself as two-faced is not so much a character flaw as it is homage to a trick he learned at the feet of the Master.

1/15

The Supreme Court rules that Bidens' unconstitutional demand for a vaccine mandate is, amazing only to Biden, unconstitutional. Biden throws a tantrum, insisting that he will appeal the ruling in the 6th Circuit Court. At the same time Biden uses a juvenile ruse in an attempt to get his demand that all elections – state, county, city, etc. – be put under his and his DOJs control. Biden takes a bill already under consideration, cuts a section out of it and replaces it with his "Federalizing all Elections" law. Then Biden places the bill back under consideration, hoping no one notices; juvenile and cynical, yes, but pure Biden.

1/16

Bidens' attack on the Constitution seems relentless. Following his tantrum over the Supreme Court disallowing one of his unconstitutional demands, Biden now asks all Big Tech companies to censure the free speech of anyone using their various platforms that disagree with him. Biden defends this blatant attack on the First Amendment by insinuating that those that disagree with him are disseminating "false information" and must be stopped, First Amendment rights be damned.

1/17

Biden throws another tantrum when it appears that his "Voting Rights Law", which includes mail-in ballots for everyone and no requirement for voter ID, will not be passed by Congress. Despite the fact that a law of this kind will invite massive amounts of voter fraud, Biden likens anyone who disagrees with with him to people like George Wallace, Bull Connor and Jefferson Davis. So much for the man who promised, if elected, he would heal the political and intellectual rifts that currently divide the country: Just another day, just another lie.

1/18

In yet again another in a stream of unending lies (or as Biden supporters like to call them, "unfulfilled promises") Biden waives sanctions on a company building a gas pipeline between Russia and Germany. This was the same pipeline that Biden promised, once he became president, to "... do whatever we can to prevent that completion" Now Biden insists that the completion of that pipeline from Russia to Germany is in the best national interest of Americans. This flummoxes most Americans in light of Biden canceling the Keystone pipeline project here. How can a pipeline built by Americas' enemy to service a lukewarm ally, while canceling an identical project here that cost thousands of jobs, weakens the US economically, politically and puts it at the mercy of such enemies, be in Americas "best interests"? Biden has no comment.

1/19

In another head-shaking bout of hypocrisy, Biden uses the filibuster rule in the Senate – the same rule he tried to scuttle a few days ago when it didn't serve his purposes - to protect Russia from any sanctions Congress might pass concerning their gas pipeline to Germany. Biden said he wanted "...a predictable, stable relationship with Russia". Wait, a predictable relationship with a Communist dictatorship? All Biden has to do is look out of his basement window at China, North Korea, Cuba, and most of South America to see what is "predictable".

1/21

What is left out of most of the analysis of Bidens' first year in office is his buffoonery on the world stage. When Trump left office, he had an agreement with the Taliban for a peaceful withdrawal from Afghanistan and a signed peace accord between five Arab nations and Israel. He brought North Korea, Russia and China to heel, stopping their Obama - and - Biden era aggression almost completely. In just one short year Biden ignored Trumps' agreement with the Taliban, causing a disastrous withdrawal from Afghanistan which left 13 servicemen dead and thousands of Americans and Afghan allies stranded in the country to face almost certain torture and death. In addition, missiles are once again being launched into Israel, Russia has massed troops at the Ukraine border, China is moving aggressively against Taiwan and North Korea has begun their missile testing again, something that was stopped completely under Trump. Combined with Bidens' economy-busting domestic policies, it's hard to conceive that one man could do so much damage in so short a time.

1/22

Biden holds a rare news conference where he actually takes questions. For the first half of it Biden sticks to an scripted plan, calling only on reporters that are on a list list approved by his nurses. Then an unscripted question was asked about the aftermath of Bidens' disastrous Afghanistan withdrawal. Instead of answering the question, Biden lose control and starts ranting "You guys have been trying to convince me that I'm Bernie Sanders. I'm not like him. I'm not Bernie Sanders. I'm not a socialist. I'm a mainstream Democrat!" With Bidens' excess social spending, race-bating and constant attacks on the American private sector, this statement is true, Biden is a mainstream Democrat.

1/23

Even though Biden never answered the original question put to him in his presser about Afghanistan, to his credit Biden did take questions on his mental health and why many Americans have real concerns about his cognitive fitness. Biden assures all in attendance that he is fit as a fiddle, even though Biden still refuses to take a cognitive health test with his yearly physical. Biden was also asked if his reluctance to press the Chinese president for more transparency in the hunt for the origins of COVID had anything to do with his son's involvement with an investment firm controlled by the Communist Chinese. Biden answers that he had brought up the issue of transparency with the Chinese but he ignores the question about his son; so much for transparency.

1/24

Days after his press conference Biden finds himself still playing defense. One remark Biden made stunned the Ukraine. In it Biden acknowledges that there is disagreement within NATO on how to respond if Russia invades Ukraine. Biden claims that Russia would face harsh sanctions if it launches a full-blown military invasion, but suggests that Moscow might see lesser consequences if it undertakes a more limited invasion. Bidens' 'little bit pregnant' approach to warfare could be seen as a green light by Putin to invade since Putin has never bought into the 'partially pregnant' approach for any of his invasions in the past.

1/25

Biden states twice that the failure of his attempt to Federalize all national elections, running them from his basement, might call into question the legitimacy of the midterm elections. The questioning of election legitimacy, as opposed to fairness, puts Biden on the same election-results-canceling track that he has been accusing Trump of. The hypocrisy of Bidens' remark seems to escape reporters. Besides, running all national elections from his basement in Delaware is probably more than Dr. Jill bargained for.

1/26

Latest reports show that Biden is keeping on track of allowing 5000 illegal border crossings a day in the US, up from Trumps' low of 100/day. In December alone 179,000 border crossings were reported. ICE agents insist that Biden must be aware of this since daily reports are sent to the White House. This might be the reason why Biden is not aware of the border problem: During his short reign, Biden has spent over a quarter of his time in his basement in Delaware rather than the White House, where Biden was absent for 40 of 52 weekends.

1/27

Almost impossible to believe, Biden cancels all Monoclonal Antibody COVID treatments for Florida citizens, 2000 of which were already scheduled to receive them. This seems a blatant political move as Florida and its' governor have routinely embarrassed Biden for over a year by ignoring most of his ridiculous and unscientific COVID mandates and, yet, the state thrived. A highlight of Floridas' success was using this particular antibody to effectively treat COVID patients. Bidens' decision, without any major clinical data or peer review to support it, will mean possible deaths of hundreds of Floridians.

1/28

It is revealed that Bidens' decision to cancel monoclonal treatments for Floridas' COVID patients was not based on any legitimate, peer-reviewed medical study but on a "study" published by a company competing with the one supplying the antibodies to Florida. It was with only this flimsy, compromised documentation that Biden used to possibly send Floridian COVID patients to death.

1/29

The Governor of Texas assails Biden over the crime wave Biden has caused at the southern border. Besides the usual rapes, assaults and child sex-trafficking, now there is an overwhelming amount of drug trafficking. It is estimated that enough Fentanyl has been seized at the border to kill 200 million adults in the US. No mention is made of possibly how much of the drug has made its' way into the country. Biden and his "immigration czar", Harris, have no comment.

1/30

With deportations of illegals at a all-time low, Biden changes yet another immigration policy Trump initiated in an effort to keep America safe. This one made sure that all illegal alien criminals, once released, were deported back to their country of origin. Incredibly Biden vetoes this, saying that these illegal alien criminals will not be deported as long as they, one, have family members in the US and, two, can demonstrate that they have made 'significant contributions' to their community. As expected, Biden and Harris have no answer when asked what constitutes a 'community' and a 'significant contribution' for a convicted illegal alien criminal.

1/31

A pilot is caught on video landing an unmarked Boeing airliner in the middle of the night and unloading a planeload of illegal aliens fresh from the southern border. When asked, he says that he is acting on direct orders from Biden and his administration. When asked why the surreptitious use of an unmarked plane and of landing in the dead of night, he replies: "Because they don't want you to know that they are betraying America." It is unclear by "they" if the pilot meant Biden, Harris, the Biden administration, or all of the above.

2/1

Biden again calls on Big Tech to censor any information on social platforms that Biden does not consider true or accurate. The prospect of someone as mentally challenged as Biden deciding what is 'true' and 'accurate' aside, this is yet again another attack by Biden on the Constitution, particularly the First Amendment. Biden and his press secretary defend his positron, claiming that Bidens' request to shut down opposing opinions is 'only' censorship and not an unconstitutional attack on free speech. Once again all in the room are left shaking their heads, wondering if these two ever listen to themselves as they jabber.

2/2

Biden responds to Trumps' latest assertion that the 2020 election was stolen by saying that the 2020 presidential election was the most safe and accurate in American history. Unfortunately Biden makes this claim on the same day that the Pennsylvania AG publicly admits that Trumps' assertion that the wide use of mail-in voting in that state was indeed unconstitutional and therefore illegal. In addition two other states currently continue to investigate alleged voter fraud in those states. Apparently the words 'fair' and 'accurate' mean something different in Bidens' basement than they do in the real world.

2/3

Bidens' alternate universe continues to collapse in flames. In another interview Biden claims that the economy under his direction is now more robust that before the pandemic, before Trumps' economic record breaking years. It seems few outside of Bidens' basement bubble share his belief. A new poll shows that only 1% of the American public believe that the economy is excellent, while a full 75% believe his performance in terms of the economy is poor and/or failing. Apparently, along with the words 'fair' and 'accurate', 'robust' must also must morph into a different meaning in Bidens' basement.

2/4

Despite the polls that show most Americans believe Biden has failed the US economy, Biden stubbornly sticks to his claim that the economy is doing better now than any time under Trump. It is hard to fathom what numbers are being shown to Biden by his nurses. Before the pandemic, under Trump more Americans – 160 million - were employed than ever before, the unemployment rate fell to a 50-year low and unemployment rates for minorities, women and Americans without a high-school diploma all hit record lows. On the other hand, Bidens' contribution to the economy is his spiking inflation to a 40 year high with his irresponsible spending programs, forcing the economy to sputter and in some places, quit. Maybe in the reports Bidens' nurses are showing him they should use real big numbers in crayon; it might help.

2/5

Biden continues to be indignant and is curt to those who remind him that, before COVID spread from China across the globe, Trump helped America build its' strongest economy in recent history. Under Trump, it was reported that median household incomes rose to their highest level ever in 2019 and the poverty rate hit an all-time low. Additionally, Trumps' "Blue-Collar Boom" saw wages grow faster for workers than for managers and supervisors. Biden has reversed all of this. Median incomes have stalled, unemployment for minorities and women has begun to rise and incomes for business mangers again are outstripping those of workers … and Biden did this all of this damage in less than a year.

2/6

Further evidence if Bidens' delusional view of his 'vibrant' economy is Bidens' insistence that he is relying on current economic reports to justify his position. It is unclear which reports Biden is referring to, but one for sure he is ignoring is the National Employment report for January. Biden had predicted that 200 thousand new jobs would be created in that month, but in actuality over 400 thousand jobs were actually lost in the non-farm, private and small business sectors of the economy in January. It is hard to see where the country is better off under Bidens' economy than Trumps, but then few have the same view Biden has, peering out of his basement windows.

2/7

It has been a year since Biden issued new marching orders for ICE, basically disbanding the organization without disbanding it. ICE agents state that the changes Biden insisted on took away their ability to arrest and deport illegal alien criminals. Now any agents seeking to arrest illegal alien fugitives need prior approval from their director in

Washington under Biden, justifying their decision. Biden has single-handily changed ICE from an organization which could fully enforce immigration laws to a shell organization that can enforce nothing.

2/8

Biden plays his Occams' Razor to the hilt while explaining why he refuses to obey the federal judges' order to keep all illegal aliens in Mexico while they await their hearings. Biden explains that the judges' ruling applies only to immigrants seeking asylum, not to the millions of others Biden has let cross because, well, they want to. Biden also proposes giving amnesty to any and all immigrants separated from family members at the southern border, shifting away from his earlier plans to pay them money. Also, if Biden gets his way, hundreds of thousands of relatives of illegal alien children could be granted amnesty and instantly become full citizens of the US, exacerbating the illegal immigration crisis even further.

2/9

Calling it "...a relic from the Jim Crow era..." Biden demands that the filibuster rule in the Senate be abolished in order to insure that his 'black-woman-only' candidate to the Supreme Court be approved. The hypocrisy of this latest Biden demand is astounding because Biden used this same rule when he was a senator to deny a black female candidate submitted by Bush a place on the Supreme Court. Only someone with a failing mental capacity – or hopelessly dense – could fail to see the irony: Biden calling for an end to a "Jim Crow era" law that he used to blackball a qualified black woman who actually lived through the Jim Crow era.

2/10

Biden defends his racist pledge to appoint only a black woman to the Supreme Court, claiming it is no different than what past presidents have done. This is Biden attempting to re-write history to cover his bias. Nowhere in American history has any President bragged about making his judge recommendations based solely on one race to the exclusion of all others. Perhaps once Biden comes down from his daily Ensure high, one of his nurses can explain this difference to him.

2/11

Now that his 'Build Back Better' crony-rewarding spending boondoggle has little chance of passing, Biden grouses that America is missing out because, if his proposed environmental plans are followed, there will be no more use for fossil fuels by 2035. One shocked scientist quickly responds, insisting that this is the most stupid, irresponsible and uneducated statement Biden could ever make. His fellow scientists quickly quiet him down, afraid that Biden might take his remark as a challenge.

2/12

Biden again rants that all who oppose his fraudulent 'Voting Rights' bill, which seeks to put all elections under his auspices, are on the side of George Wallace, Bull Connor, Jefferson Davis and other perceived racists. Biden doesn't seem to realize that his rant that Biden has thrown Alveda King, the niece of Martin Luther King, on the side of Bull Connor, a man who would often sic attack dogs and use fire hoses on the people who marched with her uncle. Biden included her in his perceived group of "racists" because she supports voter ID laws. In her own words, Alveda King accuses Biden, by vilifying voter ID laws, of attempting to instill fear in people, which is the polar opposite of what her uncle strived and died for. Biden has no comment.

2/13

Biden warns Putin that any further escalation of hostilities towards Ukraine will bring swift reaction with attendant consequences from America and its' allies. However, military experts feel that once Putin takes a good look at Biden allowing NATO to maintain minimum defenses, Bidens' minimum support of Americas' military and the less-than-lukewarm support Biden has shown two of Americas' staunchest allies, Israel and Taiwan, Putin will likely feel he can invade Ukraine at his leisure.

12/14

Bidens' claim that Americas' economy is stronger than any time under Trump is met with derision when the inflation rate just for January is reported to be 7.5%, the highest since 1982 when Reagan was wrestling with the inflation debacle that Carter left him. Biden is asked how can America have a healthy economy with a historically high inflation rate? hen Biden is asked why he still refuse to call the problems at the southern border a crisis when ICE reported that they are now averaging 9000 confrontations/arrests/detainings a day, 63000 a week. For both questions, Biden has no answer.

12/15

Biden announces that he will not be evacuating any Us citizens from Ukraine since they've had "plenty of time" to leave on their own. Biden claims the situation in Ukraine is different than Afghanistan so they had no reason to expect the same type of 'successful effort' Biden engineered there. The stranded Americans ask, which "successful effort" was Biden referring to? The one that resulted in 13 American servicemen being slaughtered and thousands of American and Afghan allies stranded? Or was he referring to the detailed list of Afghan allies that Biden gave to the Taiban, which this murderous group turned into a revenge hit list? Or maybe Biden was referring to his "successful effort" in leaving billions of dollars of munitions for the Taliban, making these animals one of the best-armed terrorist groups in the world? On second though maybe the Americans stranded in Ukraine are better off being "left on their own".

2/16

In an interview Biden is expected to take questions on subjects like illegal immigration, the crisis at, now, both borders, Russia' imminent invasion of the Ukraine, the record setting inflation he's responsible for, but instead Biden stumbles off script and decides to regale the crowd with a tale from his youth. When Biden was a commissioner or supervisor somewhere early in his political career, one of Bidens' constituents called him to remove a dead dog from her front yard. After first refusing her, Biden is reminded by his constituent that it was part of his job and that Biden worked for her. Feigning chastisement, Biden promises he will take care of it immediately. Then displaying the grace and class that would hallmark his future career, Biden promptly removes the dog from the front yard and dumps it on the constituents porch.

2/17

Some reporters take exception to Bidens' 'dead dog' story from yesterday. Not only was Biden crude, belligerent and sarcastic, they thought it poor taste that Biden extended his arms as if encouraging applause when he finished. It seemed to dawn on some in the room that this was perhaps a not-too-subtle warning for the country. With Bidens' seeming indifference to a historic mess of record setting illegal immigration and inflation, Russia's imminent invasion of the Ukraine and crime sweeping the nation, what Biden has created very much resembles that dead dog on the lawn. The fear now is if Biden is asked to fix his personally created debacle, the only place that dead dog is going to end up is on Americas' front porch.

2/18

Biden is asked why his 30 million dollar grant to HHS to reduce the risk of infection and disease among drug users includes "safe smoking kits", one piece of equipment HHS outlined that seems to include crack pipes. Biden insists that these smoking kits contain only materials like lip balm to promote hygiene among drug users. Biden is asked, if this is the case, why then are they called "safe smoking kits"? Biden turns the question over to his PS, who claims the name 'smoking kits' is a misnomer.

2/19

Biden is asked about the claim made now by Mexicos' drug cartels that they now "own" the US territory near the southern border. Biden attempts to deflect the question by changing the subject to the Child Tax Credit, pretending to commiserate about the problems facing taxpayers trying to use the credit. Biden claims his father had similar problems, the main one being that he did not have enough income to take advantage of the credit when he was working. A tear-jerking story, to be sure … except the Child Tax Credit didn't exist until 1997, when Bidens' father was 82 years old and Biden was 54. Perhaps, just perhaps, the lack of income wasn't the main reason Biden senior had trouble using the Child Tax Credit for his son.

2/20

Bidens' recollection of his father trying to use the Child Tax Credit just a few years before he died displays a disturbing pattern: Biden also claimed to having a heart-to-heart talk with a Amtrak worker who had been dead for over a year and also bragged about negotiating the Paris climate deal with Deng Xiaoping, who had been dead for almost two decades. So maybe it's true, that right before their final breakdown, the demented really do see dead people.

2/21

Biden is apprised that the number of illegal immigrant attempted crossings at the border for January has been revised, from 90000 to 154000, a 400% increase over the number when Trump was president. It is hard to tell if the numbers register at all, as Bidens' only response is to look at the audience with his famous 1000- yard, vacant stare, as if trying to remember where he parked his car at the senior center.

2/22

Biden brags that he has all of NATO, particularly Germany, united in sanctioning/criticizing/boycotting Russia and providing support for Ukraine if Russia invades. This raises eyebrows because Germany and much of NATO and the EU gets much of their energy supplies from Russia. What Biden doesn't mention is that Germanys' total support of the forty million Ukrainians, to counteract Russias' 190000 troops, thousands of tanks at their border consists of 5000 helmets; no food, water, money, nothing but the helmets. There is a rumor that Germany actually sent only 4999 helmets, the other one going to Biden so he could start protecting that soft spot on the top of his head.

2/23

During a press conference, Biden announces that he has offered Putin "a path to diplomacy" in regards to his intention of invading the Ukraine. Biden stresses the "pathway to diplomacy", phrase using it repeatedly during his speech, showcasing what Biden considers his generous nature to the Russian leader. It seems that Putin heard Bidens' speech about his 'generous offer' and would to think about it. Then after thinking about it long and hard, sizing up both Biden and the offer, Putin decides to invade Ukraine.

2/24

To Bidens' great chagrin, a truck convoy organized to protest Bidens' vaccine mandates, much like the one in Canada protesting that countrys' similar Marxist, ham-fisted vaccine policies, rolls out of Barstow California, scheduled to arrive in Washington DC in time for Bidens' State of the Union speech.

2/25

Ukraine's' president Zelensky asks for help from Biden and other countries, fearing that he will be captured and possibly executed with in a day or so. Biden responds by promising more sanction and more meetings with the members of NATO in a month or so to see if the sanctions are working. In Bidens' mentally fluid state, apparently 'one day' and '30 to 60 days' register about the same.

2/26

It is revealed that almost all of the so-called "sanctions" the EU, NATO and the US issue against Russia are not worth the paper they're written on. This was not unexpected since most of the NATO countries involved with imposing these 'sanctions' rely on Russia for 40% of their energy supplies. Even Biden, while supposedly chastising Russia, is buying as much as 7 million barrels of oil daily from this sworn enemy of the US. Biden claims he is making this sacrifice so that the daily lives of Americans will be unaffected by the Russian invasion of Ukraine, What is lost on Biden is that in this same time frame dozens of Ukrainians are affected by being murdered.

2/27

Biden is confronted with the fact that because of his energy policies, like canceling the Keystone pipeline and drilling in Anwar, America, once energy independent under Trump, now kneels before some of its' worst enemies, begging for energy supplies. Biden mumbles something about keeping America green, then stumbles off the stage with his trademark watery, thousand-mile stare and goofy grin. Then VP Harris takes the stage to defend the Russian sanctions, saying they will have an immediate effect. When she is reminded that Biden has said that it will be months before anyone can tell if the sanctions are working, Harris mumbles something about keeping America green and leaves the stage, now grinning with a familiar watery, thousand - mile stare: It must be contagious.

2/28

It is reported that the citizens of the Ukraine are rhetorically asking: "Where is America?" They are referring to the pact they signed in 1994 in which America promised them that they would support the Ukrainians in case of an attack in the future as long as the Ukrainians agreed to give up their nuclear arms. In his reply, Biden reminds the Ukrainians that the agreement stipulated that the US would only "support" them, not "defend" them in case of an attack. So in his usual smarmy manner Biden mocks the Ukrainians for not reading the agreement carefully before signing.

3/1

Careful work by reporters exposes the that Biden took office a little more than a year ago, he has insisted that all the branches of the US military undergo as much as 60 million dollars in training, not for military strategy or techniques in defending the nation, but for climate change and Critical Race Theory. Biden seems to believe that knowledge in these two hoax studies will be adequate defenses against Chinas' nuclear build-up and Russias' ongoing cyber attacks.

3/2

Biden gives his first State of the Union address and even though it is full of his usual gaffs and unintelligible mumblings, Biden is wide-eyed and yelling. He shouts that the American economy is the strongest economy in US history. Yes, Biden is speaking of the current US economy, the one with historical inflation, the one impacted by Biden allowing 2 million illegal aliens to infiltrate in just the last year, the one with major parts of the business sector destroyed and 2 years of education for the young lost because of Bidens' COVID policies – yes, that economy. Perhaps Bidens' nurses should re-consider hopping Biden up on Ensure before his next SOTU.

3/3

Bidens' State of the Union address invokes a strong response from the Governor of Florida. He points out that most of the domestic issues the country is facing now are of Biden's own creation. The Governor goes on to say that Bidens' policies, like shutting down the Keystone pipeline and blocking oil exploration in Anwar has caused a 40 to 50 percent increase in the price of gas and Biden is now importing more energy from countries like Russia which threatens Americas' national security. The Governor finishes by pointing out, as many other have, that America was energy independent under Trump, but no longer so since Biden took office.

3/4

With brazen audacity, Biden attempts to divert the countrys' attention by focusing on the problems in the Ukraine while he tries to sneak a pro-abortion bill through the Senate. Bidens' bill would would federalize all abortion laws and strip the sates of their Constitutional sovereignty in this matter. The bill is defeated by a single vote and Biden is left seething when it turns out that vote was cast by a Democrat.

3/5

Biden angrily denounces a new Texas law that categorizes parents' per-pubescent mutilation of their children's genitalia as child abuse. Bidens' stridency is considered surprising until it is uncovered that the 'Equity' bill Biden mentioned in his recent SOTU speech is in direct opposition to the Texas law. Bidens' equity bill would not only allow prepubescent children to 'transition' without their parents' knowledge, the children can be taken away from the parents if they object. The children will then be turned over to Bidens' state where they can presumably 'transition' in peace.

3/6

Some media pundits remind Biden that under Trump America was a net exporter of energy for the first time in 75 years and, in less than a year, Biden has completely dismantled this feat. It is because of Bidens' inept handling of Americas' energy resources that he is now faced with begging Russia, a mortal enemy of the US, for energy supplies to the tune of as much as 800,000 barrels a month at a cost of 2.2. billion dollars. Biden has no comment.

3/7

Bidens' schizophrenic dealing with Russia is throwing the American public for a loop. First Biden insists that the sanctions he placed on Russia because of their incursion into the Ukraine are intact and effective. Then Biden announces that he will still purchase oil from Prussia at a cost of billions of American taxpayers of dollars daily. Then, for a final head-spinner, Russia uses these American dollars to continue the war that Biden is sanctioning them for. In an effort to ward off criticism of this bout of schizophrenia, Biden opens talks with Iran, another mortal enemy of America, as another potential supplier for the shortfall in American oil that he caused. The final irony is that Iran is willing to talk about supplying Biden with oil, but only if Biden conducts the talks through a Russian intermediary. In this case perhaps 'pathological' rather than 'schizophrenic' is a better descriptor for Biden.

3/8

Bidens' schizophrenic tendencies are on display again as he attacks American oil companies. Biden starts by warning these 'evil' companies' that he will not stand for their greed, taking advantage of the war in Ukraine to price gouge American consumers at the pumps. Not one minute later Biden laments that these same greedy oil executives s are not making as much money as they could because they are not developing all the drilling leases they have. The reporters are confused: Are these oil executives greedy, price-gouging profiteers or are they businessmen content with the amount of money they're making now and see no reason to exert themselves?.Biden takes no questions and stumbles from the stage, stumbles from the stage, looking as confused as his audience.

3/9

Biden suspends oil shipments from Russia right before being presented with a bi-partisan bill demanding he do it. Biden tries to hide the fact that his canceling the Keystone pipeline and all future oil leases on his first day in office had gas prices spiking before the war in the Ukraine. One wag points out that Trump predicted that if Biden was elected, America would see gas prices in excess of $7 and $8 dollars a gallon, either through his domestic "green" policies or Bidens' bungling foreign policy. On this date, in many places in the country, gas prices have exceeded $7 a gallon. Biden has no comment.

3/10

Either Bidens' detachment from reality is becoming chronic or he is receiving bad information – really bad information – from his nurses. Biden now claims that more oil is being pumped in the US now than when Trump was president; this is patently not true. Biden then claims that more oil rigs are in operation today than under Trump, when in reality there are 40% less rigs in operation today. Biden finishes by defending his decision to keep America energy dependent on foreign enemies, claiming that making America energy independent now is a long-range solution and doesn't help him with the current crisis. Perhaps Biden was in his basement and missed this, but America was virtually energy independent just a little more than a year ago, before he took office.

3/11

Biden again deflects criticism from critics calling on him to do more to make America energy independent again, saying that focusing on 'long range' solutions 1 energy independence only serves to distract from solving short range problems using sanctions. This, even though Biden admits it could take months for sanctions to become effective. Maybe because Bidens' mind is Ensure-deprived, it is unclear what Biden considers 'long range'. After all, it was not much more than a year ago that America was well on it's way to being energy independent, so much so that it was actually exporting energy, a capability Biden dismantled his first day in office.

3/12

Biden declines to attend a European press briefing, likely because the questions and answers would not be scripted and there would be no teleprompter for him to fumble through. Biden instead sends Harris, who promptly embarrasses herself and the US with incomprehensible, word-salad answers. She giggles in answer to simple questions concerning Americas' commitment to Ukraine and its' European allies, Poland in particular. Biden has no comment on this snafu, but it's likely he didn't see the press conference. Because of the time difference, the European briefing took place at the same time Biden is usually in his basement, watching re-runs of 'Fantasy Island'.

3/13

Bidens' so-called sanctions against Russia are not working, but Biden insists that more r sanctions might cause Russia to escalate its' war mongering. In response, Russia moves even further into the Ukraine. Biden then reiterates that he will not commit troops to this battle because this might cause the Russians to escalate; Putin responds by launching air strikes on citizen populations. Poland offers to send fighter planes to the Ukraine to even the playing field, but Biden objects, saying again that a move like this might serve as an excuse for Russia to escalate. Russia responds by bombing hospitals and orphanages. At this pace, a few more of Bidens 'de-escalate' concessions and Russia will wipe Ukraine d off the map.

3/14

Biden, angrily flailing his arms like those inflatable tire store dummies, says he's tired being criticized for his domestic economic policies. Amazingly and, a bit sad, Biden bitterly insists that his flooding the American economy with trillions of mostly unfunded dollars has no affect on inflation. There is an old adage that when you have the law on your side, pound the law, if you have facts on your side, pound the facts and, if you have neither, pound the table. It is fitting that this mentally challenged old man, in yet another fit of pique, has nothing to pound but thin air.

3/15

In response to the thousands dying from Russian missiles and bombs in the suburbs of Ukraine, Biden and his climate-change, private-jet-owning envoy, John Kerry, lament that Putin might no longer remain their partner in reducing global warming. Biden and Kerry fret that the current war and all the civilian deaths will divert attention from the "real" problems facing the world, like "going green" and battling climate change. Perhaps one of Bidens' nurses will whisper in both of these idiots ears that, yes, the war might divert attention from their supposed important environmental initiatives, but launching hundreds of missiles and watching thousands die unnecessarily will sometimes do that.

3/16

Biden is asked about the 'laptop controversy' concerning his son Hunter. This story broke in the fall of 2020 before the presidential election. However, it was buried by a partisan media and internet social platform giants to protect Biden election chances. It turns out that the emails on Hunters' laptop insinuated that 10% of the bribe money he received from the Ukraine went to Biden. Instead of commenting on the investigation, Biden and his press secretary advise anyone curious about the matter contact the DOJ since Hunter "… is not a government employee.".

3/17

Biden labels Putin a "war criminal" and a "murderous dictator" after reviewing the Russian leaders' recent bombing of citizens in the Ukraine. Putin considers Bidens' remarks "personal insults" and said Biden's remarks appeared to have been fueled by irritation, fatigue and forgetfulness ... or what Americans have, when it comes to Biden lately, call 'Tuesday'.

3/18

In another appearance Biden laments that the First Lady's husband has COVID. Biden screws his face downward in an attempt to look sorrowful, until one of his nurses whispers that he, Biden, is the First Lady's husband and he is not the one with the virus. Biden attempts to pass the gaff off, but leaves his audience wondering, exactly how many Tuesdays could there be in one week?

3/19

As Bidens' mental acuity comes under more scrutiny, a video surfaces from back in August of 2021 where Biden was asked to defend his plan for evacuating Afghanistan that got 13 Americans and at least 90 Afghans killed. Instead of answering, Biden bows his head, grasps a notebook to his chest and refuses to look up for several seconds, leaving reporters to wonder if he was having some kind of breakdown. This bowed image of the supposed leader of the free world did nothing but whet the appetites of dictators the world over, in anticipation of an unobstructed future.

3/20

It is revealed that a few days ago Biden invited a number of what he called 'Tik Tok influencers' to the White House. Since Bidens' persistent blaming the current problems of rising gas prices and inflation on Putin continues to elicit howls of laughter from the American public, he thought these 'influencers' might help. Biden instructed this group to use their presence on social media to propagandize their social media followers that it is indeed Putin and not Biden who is responsible for these current problems in America. In Bidens' graying mind, nothing can be more convincing than a group of basement-dwelling nerds lecturing the American public on the causes of inflation.

3/21

The product of Biden meeting with the Tik Tok avengers hits the social media airwaves. Comical and pathetic at the same time, these basement zombies regurgitate, word for word, Bidens' talking points on gas prices and inflation, the same ones that have mostly fallen on the deaf ears of the American public. Perhaps by using this group of marginally educated, hugely inexperienced young, Biden is hoping to relate to a group more in line with his sagging mental acuity. If true, Biden probably won't feel fully at ease until he can recruit the audience of Sesame Street as social media influencers also. In fact, the rumor is that Biden and his PS are in negotiations with Big Bird at this very moment.

3/22

Bidens' pick for the Supreme Court runs into trouble. What concerns lawmakers is her record of light sentences for child rapist and molesters and her belief that CRT should be molded into the Constitution. Additionally, though one of Bidens' requirements for his nominee is that she be a woman, in an insane moment his nominee professes that she cannot define what she, a woman, is. Despite Bidens' promise of transparency in her nomination process, as more questions about her judicial radicalism arise, Biden orders that as many as 48000 pages of her past proceedings, sentencings and opinions are sealed.

3/23

In another of his pathetic political moves, Biden requests that two members of the President's Council on Sports, Fitness & Nutrition – Dr. Oz and Hershel Walker - either step down or face termination because they are running for other political offices. Biden insists that the fact that both Oz and Walker are Republicans and oppose him on almost every important matter, has nothing to do with his demand. There might be some truth in this. In his current mental condition it probably seems impossible to Biden that anyone can do two things – like walk and chew gum – at the same time.

3/24

Biden embarrasses himself – and America -on a trip to Brussels. Expected to speak on matters concerning the current war in Ukraine, he instead begins to ramble about "...when he said there were good people on both sides, I had to..." While not positive, it seems Biden was having a flashback moment to years ago, when he lied about Trump supporting white racists. Regardless, the audience in Brussels was there to discuss such matters as sanctions and Putins' threat of using chemical weapons. Bidens' trip down a fog-bound memory lane leaves everyone looking as befuddled as he.

3/25

At a news conference in Brussels Biden declares that if Putin uses chemical weapons in Ukraine the US would respond. When asked if this means the US would then also use chemical weapons, Biden says only that the nature of the US response would "…depend on the nature of the (Russian) use.", not ruling out the possibility of the US engaging in a chemical war with Russia. Additionally Biden announces that America will accept 100000 Ukrainian refugees, but insists that refugees of the LGBTQ community be favored over others. In Bidens' mind, this group – not the injured, crying, starving babies and other youth – are the most at risk.

3/27

Biden afforded the world a glance at his confused, schizophrenic mental state when on his recent trip he took the opportunity to visit NATO. First Biden assures the audience of mostly American soldiers that he will not deploy them in the Ukraine. However, then he lauds the Ukrainians for having the "backbone" and "guts" to resist the Russians and assures the American soldiers that they will witness this bravery for themselves when "you're there". Biden then dilutes his compliment to the Ukrainians by saying "... they (the Ukrainian soldiers) take a lot on inspiration from us." Not yet finished, in speaking about Putin Biden bravado-ly roars: "This man cannot stay in power!" but then assures the audience he is not seeking regime change in Russia. This whirlwind of schizophrenic babble leaves the young soldiers bewildered, exhausted and wondering what the hell is going on with their Commander in Chief.

3/28

Bidens' staff and nurses attempt to walk back his rhetoric about Putin being removed from power, but Biden countermands them, declaring he is not walking back anything. As an explanation, Biden claims that what he meant is not a regime change for Putin but "... bad people shouldn't continue to do bad things." While Biden is comfortable speaking in this pre-elementary school manner, his charges are manic in their attempts to one, convince the world that Biden is not calling for Putins' ouster, even though time and time again it seems that is exactly what Biden is calling for and, two, despite outward appearances, Biden is actually mentally competent.

3/29

Even though denying he is seeking regime change, Biden still bellows that a man like Putin "...cannot stay in power." While the world media is distracted by trying to decipher Bidens' indecipherable ramblings, Russia uses this 'no-one is-looking' moment to drop phosphorous bombs, the kind that burn flesh, on Ukrainians in Avdiivka, take over the city of Slavutych and murder civilians in Mariupol. The world media is still not looking as it is focused on the demented mumbling of Biden, concerned on how he might escalate the war that they are, at least for the moment, no longer reporting on.

3/30

Biden finds it necessary to hold a press conference in order to walk back what he said he wouldn't walk back, that is, his remark that "This man (Putin) can no longer stay in power." What Biden is unaware of is that a camera zooms in on his podium while he is speaking. It shows that Biden is holding a card that has not only the scripted answers to any questions about his remarks concerning Putin, but also the questions he will be asked. Biden has now reached the point where his nurses type out both questions and answers before they allow him to speak to the media.

3/31

Biden announces that he is creating a new government bureaucracy called FAVE in order to eliminate racism in real estate housing appraisals. Biden claims that low-income areas unfairly and routinely receive lower property appraisals than more affluent neighborhoods.

This brings derisive howls of laughter from the appraisal community. One, they have been under government control since the last housing crisis and, two, how can it be racism if they, the appraisers, rarely meet either the buyer or the seller during the appraisal process? Biden has no answer.

4/1

Biden announces his intention to let Title 42, an order Trump initiated, expire next month, something he promised to do when inaugurated. Even though this will add to the disaster at the southern border, Biden adds this to his left-wing policies that have resulted in unsustainable inflation, unaffordable energy, war, humiliation abroad, spiraling crime and racial hostility. Add to this Bidens' arrogant defiance while enacting these disastrous policies, this would be the perfect day for Biden to say: "Hey these last two years, I was just kidding! Honest!" Sadly, Biden wasn't and, instead, the joke is on this once great country.

4/2

Biden again touts his proposed FAVE group as the means to end racism in the appraisals of real estate, citing as proof the low appraisals that ghetto, government and Section 8 home dwellers receive compared to more affluent neighborhoods. What doesn't seem to reach Bidens' ever-decreasing brainwaves is that it is precisely Biden and his party's' Marxist policies of rent control, subsidized housing, welfare dependency, etc. that are fundamental in creating poor neighborhoods. Rather than admit that these abhorrent policies have failed (and have failed for decades) and produced the misery these neighborhoods are enduring today, Biden insists that it is instead racism and not his polices that is responsible for creating this barren landscape.

4/3

Biden announces a new plan to get America out of debt and pay for his 'Green New deal' proposal: that is, slap a 20% increase on "billionaires" on their unrealized income, a concept that would be laughable if not so dangerous and incredibly stupid, even for Biden. What he is proposing is that when property, stocks and other investments increase in value, the holders of these instruments should be taxed 20% immediately on their increased value, even if this value is just on paper. His brain-deadness becoming more apparent every day, Biden now advocates taxing people on money they don't have.

4/4

Biden doubles down on his intent to repeal Title 42 even though many of his own party warn him that it would expand the already disastrous illegal immigration problem on the southern border In voicing their opposition, many Democrats point out that Biden allowed two million illegals into the country his first year and the repeal of Title 42 could mean as many as three million more in his second year. Bidens' only answer is to this real, possible disaster is to agree to delay the repeal until May 23, but no further.

4/5

Biden continues to be berated by members of his own party on the foolishness of eliminating title 42. Even the Democrats cannot imagine Biden allowing millions more illegals surge across the border while having no plan on how to accommodate them. Instead of addressing his critics, Biden pivots instead and orders that shipping the monoclonal antibody treatment know as 'sotrovimab', used for successfully treating some COVID patients, be suspended in 22 states. Biden is again roundly criticized because monoclonal antibodies have been used world wide to successfully treat many COVID patients. Biden again ignores his critics, saying only that HHS and the FDA, two organizations knee-deep in political mud, approve of his plan.

4/6

It is brought up by reporters that Bidens' canceling the use of monoclonal antibody medication seems to be a continuation of his attacks on his political enemies, most particularly the Governor of Florida. He has continually embarrassed Biden throughout last year repeatedly using the antibodies to successfully treat thousands of COVID patients in his state, this over Bidens' strenuous objections. Watching this defiance by a possible 2024 opponent whose poll numbers continue to rise as Bidens' continue to fall aggravates Biden to no end. Rather than admit he is wrong, Bidens' pathetic and morbid political recourse is to order shipments of the life-saving drug that is the source of his embarrassment be stopped in all states, the needless suffering and death his order will bring to thousands troubling Biden not at all.

4/7

Bidens' canceling shipments of the monoclonal antibodies appears to be little more than brutal political posturing and, dangerously, he is not done. Biden orders 14 additional states to stop using another COVID-19 treatment made by GSK and VIR Biotechnology. Biden claims he is relying on science for his decision, citing a new FDA report. Laughably - unless one is dying from COVID - the FDA report finds only a small problem with the treatments concerning only a sub variant of a sub variant, three levels down, of the COVID virus. Biden uses this almost non-existing problem as a flimsy excuse for stopping all shipments of the potentially life saving medicine. How many more lives will suffer and even die from Bidens' decision is anyone's guess.

4/8

In a press conference Biden proclaims that America can be summed up in one word, then stammers a unintelligible multi-syllable word salad. Neither stopping nor coming up with the word, Biden then mentions Xi Pings' name and that when he was vice-president he thinks he traveled somewhere for 17000 miles with the Communist leader … maybe. Bidens' nurses can't rescue him fast enough, leaving Biden exposed to the jackals that are the enemies of America, licking their chops again at the advantages they might take of once strong America while this confused, fumbling old man is at the helm.

4/9

Biden is presented with the incredible statistic that as many as 18000The incredible statistic, presented to Biden, is that as many as 18000 illegals will cross the border daily once he Title 42 to expire. In response, Biden reaffirms his pledge send his DOJ after any parents or legislative body that seeks to prevent underage children from., or being manipulated by their teachers into accessing, gender changing drugs. When done, Biden boobs his head up and down, his mouth loosed in a sagging grin, apparently unaware he answered a question no one asked.

4/10

Biden responds to the criticism that his canceling of the monoclonal antibody treatment to Republican controlled states is an embarrassingly blatant political move by assuring all that he is canceling shipments of the drug to all 50 states. The tens of thousands of COVID patients Biden sentences to suffering and possible death should surprise no one. After all, when a mental and moral deficient is ordered to put down the hammer he is causing so much damage with. his next move is always to pick up a sledge.

4/11

Biden oversteps his authority again by ordering a ban on ghost guns, or non-serialized kit guns. Bidens' critics point out that, one, nowhere in the Constitution is it stipulated that citizens cannot make their own weapons and, two, Congress – and not the president - has the Constitutional authority to make laws concerning the day-to-day lives of American citizens. As he has done in his short tenure as president, Biden again ignores a basic tenet of the Constitution, again with the same vapid look on his face.

4/12

Details of an Obama visit to the White House a few days ago surface now and prove to be more humiliation for Biden. Obama routinely entered rooms in front of Biden, greeting and glad-handing all while Biden huddled in the background. Obama adds to the humiliation by reminding all he meets – including Biden - that Biden is still his vice-president and, Bidens' presidency, is really his, Obamas' s' "… third term in office." Harris enters the room and also ignores Biden, who is left at the rear of the room. Bidens' back is to the audience, as he stares blankly at a huge curtain, looking like an old man searching for an exit so he can sneak through and use a restroom. This sad scene now borders on elder abuse, but in his current condition Biden probably doesn't suffer much.

4/13

Aware that Bidens' canceling of Title 42 might mean as much as 18000 illegals crossing the southern border every day, many of them in Texas. The governor of the state demands that Biden start enforcing Federal immigration laws. Biden refuses and reminds the governor that, as governor, he can't enforce immigration laws because enforcing these laws – or in Bidens' case, not enforcing them – is the province of the

Federal government. The governor then threatens to send busloads of illegals to Washington DC. Biden warns him to do so would be breaking several laws which he would be held accountable for. Undeterred, the governor delivered the first busload of illegals near the nations' capital: For the moment, Biden is speechless.

4/14

Biden and his press secretary mock the Texas governors' deliverance of the illegals to Bidens' doorstep, but in doing so incriminates themselves in a bigger scandal. For over a year Biden has denied spiriting illegals away from the border and busing or flying them to locations around the US, most times under the cover of darkness. By mockingly thanking the Texas governor for 'doing his job for him', Biden tacitly admits this is what he has been doing all along.

4/15

On this most wonderful day of the year for American taxpayers, Biden supporters remind him of his pledge to tax the wealthy for their "fair share". Economists have pointed out repeatedly to Biden that he could confiscate 100% of all those Biden considers 'wealthy' and it would not pay for even a small portion of his bloated, pork-laden "Build Back Better" boondoggle. Instead, economists warn what Bidens' 'tax the wealthy' plan would do is destroy the business base in America, send unemployment through the roof and bankrupt the economy. To this Biden reportedly remarks: "Yes, but it would be a good start."

4/16

Saudi Arabia TV channel MBC airs a skit depicting Biden and Harris holding a press conferrer. In it Biden continually screws up his speech, forgets what and who he is talking about, confuses China with Russia, repeats his famous faux pas where he calls Harris his "first lady" and falls asleep. While the impressions are adequate and the material funny, it is distressing to imagine that this is the way the rest of the world sees America now thanks to Biden, a buffoonish caricature of its' former self. good only for the laughs it provides for the rest of the world.

4/17

Biden extends the mask mandate for all air travel in the US, citing CDC "science" as his reason. This CDC "science" is humorous at best. After 60 straight days of enormous declines in COVID cases, there is only a small uptick in the last seven days from the bottom of this crater, but this is what the CDC uses to convince Biden. Yes, Biden believes that masking, not people attending restaurants, bars, churches, schools, concerts and other mega events, but air travelers will curb this latest wave of infections. This is proof positive that, regardless of others, Biden has been breathing in his mask far too long.

4/18

Fallout from the Saudi Arabia skit continues. Critics of Biden point out that Russia, China, North Korea and even Hamas would be pulling the crap they're pulling now if Trump was still in office. The fact these despots are having belly laughs while doing it makes this embarrassment hard to watch. As if to emphasize Americas' neutering, when finishing his latest press briefing, Biden turns to shake hands with … no one. There is no one standing there, leaving Biden again looking lost and befuddled, for all the world to see. It is astonishing to see that, in just a little over a year into his presidency, Biden has taken America from royalty to clown prince in the eyes of the world.

4/19

Only days after Biden initiated it, a federal judge rules his mask mandate for air travel to be unconstitutional. Biden acquiesces quietly, but in a face saving attempt to distract from another failure of his to circumvent the Constitution, Biden re-announces his plans to tax "billionaires" a minim of 20% on their earnings to the great applause of his sycophants. Yet again displaying his loosening grip on reality, Biden assures the public that his tax would affect "...only those making in excess of 100 million...", a far cry from Bidens' supposed target of billionaires. However, before accusing Biden of being confused or lying, consider that in his current mental state Biden probably has trouble working with numbers this large on his abacus.

4/20

A video comes to light showing Biden officiating at the annual Easter Egg Roll at the White House with a giant costumed Easter Bunny. A reporter asks Biden a question about Afghanistan and Pakistan, but as Biden starts to answer the Easter Bunny rushes up, waves off the reporter and escorts Biden away before he can finish answering. Another great moment for the world to witness, the leader of what once was the most powerful, most free country on the world, be led to the safety of not answering questions by none other than the Easter Bunny.

4/21

Perhaps bolstered by the reassurance that his protection detail now includes the Easter Bunny, Biden continues his attacks on the American taxpayer. He now insists that working class peoples' capital gains, now taxed at 23%, be taxed at normal tax rates which can be as high as 40%. This almost- doubling of the tax burden would, as it always does, result in a drastic shrinkage in the economy, including investments, job hiring, disposable income, et al., a disaster obviously obtuse to Biden. Perhaps if the Easter Bunny whispered in Bidens' ear, alerting him to these dangers his newest policy would create, Biden would have a change of heart... perhaps.

4/22

Bidens' befuddlement continues apace, demonstrating why his nurses shouldn't leave him alone to answer questions. Two current issues facing Biden are some courts declaring his mask mandate unconstitutional and his allowing Title 42, the measure that allowed the deportation of illegals for health reasons, to elapse. Biden is challenging the mask mandate decision in court, but when asked why he is allowing Title 42 to elapse, Biden confuses the two issues, saying that he has to wait for a decision on his mask mandate before he can deport illegals for health reasons. At this stage of Bidens' fading mental capacity reporters would probably get more coherent answers from the Easter Bunny.

4/23

Biden attempts to reassure the American people that his mental capacity is just fine, that his confusing the two issues the day before was merely a mistake, not an indication of any lack of mental prowess on his part. Yet the question arises that with just his most recent gaffes, like confusing millionairess with billionaires, turning to shake hands with invisible people, calling VP Harris his First Lady, wandering helplessly along a backstage curtain, his unintelligible word-salad answers to simple questions, his assertion that taxing Americans on money they don't have is a viable economy-saving option ... does Biden mean "mistakes" like these? Biden has no answer.

4/24

More Democrats distance themselves from Biden as he insists on letting Title 42 lapse. Even Senators in his own party call the decision "frightening", pointing out that America is already facing an unprecedented increase in migrants this year, and that will only get worse if Biden ends the Title 42 policy, which allows border agents to immediately expel illegals attempting to cross the border. They also publicly worry that it is evident that Biden has no plan on how to deal with the expected influx and, until he does, these Democrat Senators believe Title 42 should stay in place. For his part, Biden gives no indication he is listening to even his own supporters.

4/25

Biden underwent a medical checkup some days ago and the final report is out. It is long and detailed, but what is obviously missing is the report on his mental cognition. While the test is supposed to include both a physical and mental evaluation, Bidens' nurses admit that this was only a physical test and promise that a mental evaluation of Biden will follow shortly: Americans are advised not to hold their collective breath.

4/26

One of Bidens' ardent supporters, Senator Elizabeth Warren, she of the 'stolen Indian heritage' fame, claims that she knows first-hand that Biden is planning on granting amnesty and full citizenship to as many as thirty million illegal aliens before Bidens' term expires in 2024. Biden has no comment

4/27

Biden is still silent on Warrens' announcement of his plan to grant large-scale amnesty and citizenship to illegal aliens before 2024. A grain of salt might be taken with Warrens' claim. After all, she advanced her entire career by claiming she was Native American when in truth she is 1/1024 Indian and the DNA test that 'proved' this was questionable. This means she probably has more Dunkin' Donuts ancestry in her blood than Native American. However, so far the doughnut chain has not granted her sovereignty, but with Biden the doughnut ancestry might be enough.

4/28

The numbers on the economy came out and show that, instead of growing at all, the economy is actually going backwards at a 1.4% clip. Biden was expected to address this, but instead to the press gives a rambling semi-coherent statement about Ukraine. In it he talks about seizing the ill gotten (which he mispronounces) gains of the oligarchs (which he mispronounces) who are part of the Russian aristocracy, which he also mispronounces. Biden finishes with a demented giggle, saying that he is going to "accommodate" the oligarchs by confiscating their yachts. Bidens' nurses must've been on break, as no one tries to save or stop him this time.

4/29

In a frantic attempt to one, bolster his sagging approval ratings and, two, stave off the possible disaster looming ahead for the Democrats in the 2022 midterms, Biden throws a hail Mary pass, this one combining the promise of a massive tax hike and the forgiving of all student loan debt. The major portion of this student debt is held by a large section of his voting base, i.e., entitled, lazy, spoiled young grifters. Biden feels this 'Hail Mary' will lock in this part of his base for the upcoming elections, unconcerned about passing this massive debt onto the shoulders of, unlike his constituents, the hard working and responsible citizens of America.

4/30

Bidens' panic over his perceived debacle looming for him this coming November escalates. Unbelievably, even for Biden, he sets up a Communist-style censorship group called the Disinformation Governance Board. Run by the DHS, Biden will have the Board target anyone who has an opinion different than his on such subjects as COVID lock downs and vaccines, election fraud, and the January 6 insurrection hoax, just to mention a few. Also included as intended targets are parents who want more control over their childrens' education, whom Biden labels, again unbelievably, "domestic terrorists".

5/1

Critics suggest that Bidens' setting up the Communist/Nazi - style DGB is in direct response to Elon Musk buying Twitter and vowing to make it a true free speech platform. In response, a Biden friend and supporter, Apple CEO Tim Cook, promises Biden that once Musk assumes control of Twitter, he will look into deleting the service from his App Store, making it no longer available to his subscribers. The question arises, why does opening up and supporting a true free speech platform scare Biden and his yokel supporters so much? Biden has no comment.

5/2

Biden continues to take slap shots from all sides for the new DGB board he set up for it's resemblance to similar 'Ministry of Truth'" departments set up under Nazi and Communist regimes. Biden responds by claiming Trump set up this department first and he was just continuing that work.

This is counter to what his head of DHS and his press secretary say, as both claim this new Ministry of Truth' is Biden's own brand and brand new. This is just the latest example of Biden and and his staff reporting different stories to the press. To keep everyone on the same page, maybe the PS and DHS head should slip a note to Bidens' nurses so they can slip it to him, or maybe Biden should slip his nurses a note so they cal slip it to … never mind.

5/3

Biden is asked to comment on the US economy going in reverse, according to the latest negative numbers. Biden remonstrates the reporter, telling him that what he is seeing with this negative 1.4 percent is an economy that is actually growing, which leaves the audience once again dumbfounded. Biden does not notice the groans from the audience, even when informed that many Congressional Democrats and other of his supporters are distancing themselves from Biden because of his insistence of letting Title 42 expire later this month. Bidens' face remains blank and he seems nonplussed, but really these days, how does one tell?

5/4

In a historical moment in American history, a brief being reviewed by the Supreme Court is leaked to the press, ostensibly by one of the radical liberals on the court. It is hoped that a preview of the ruling, which Biden doesn't like, will stir up enough of a public outcry so to influence the Court before it makes its' final ruling. Nothing like this has ever happened in American history, yet Biden still will not criticize this black day in American judicial prudence nor call for an investigation of how it happened, though anyone with a warm brain knows exactly who is responsible for the leak. By his lack of action it is apparent that Biden hopes the leak does sway the court into changing their minds and rules the way that Biden favors.

5/5

Biden holds fast to his outlawing the use of Ivermectin, monochronal antibodies and other pharmaceuticals proven effective in treating the various COVID viruses. Biden insists that only the vaccines and their booster shots should be used. In an ironic twist, many of the attendees at Bidens' White House Correspondence Dinner, despite the requirement that all attendees heed Bidens' plan to be vaccinated and show evidence of a negative COVID test that day, many test positive for the virus; Biden has no comment.

5/6

It is revealed that Biden has chosen a new press secretary. Regardless of credentials - of which she has few - a concern is raised about her transparency and objectivity when it is revealed that she is dating a reporter for CNN, the same organization Bidens' previous press secretary is joining. This seems like a glaring conflict of interest: Biden has no comment.

5/7

Biden declares that the supporters of Trump are the worst domestic terrorists in the history of the United States. Not the Klu Klux Klan, not the Weather Underground, not the Black Panthers, not BLM, Antifa or even the Oklahoma bomber, who actually killed and maimed people; no, it's those people wearing the MAGA hats. Biden has made stupid statements in the past, but his nurses parading him around to make such idiotic proclamations now really is getting close to elder abuse.

5/8

Bidens Treasury Secretary finally, reluctantly, admits that Bidens' $1.9 trillion "American Rescue Plan" has contributed mightily to inflation., but said Bidens' irresponsible spending spree was "justified" because of the various economic risks of not super-inflating the economy, risks she did not clarify. She also chose to ignore and/or not defend Bidens' claim that his enormous pork-laden spending plan would not increase inflation at all and would actually lower it. The fact that the exact opposite happened bothers the Secretary and Biden not a wit. Apparently the color of the sky in her world is the same as Bidens.

5/9

Biden continues to receive hardcore criticism from all sides for his insistence on forgiving student loan debts across the US. What he pretends to forget – and hopes everyone else has – is that two of the people most responsible for this 'crisis' are he and Obama, the two most responsible for permanently saddling so many young Americans with a debt they will have, for some, until they die. The only ones in favor of Bidens' plan are a large part of his constituency, the deadbeats reveling in their theft and amoral irresponsibility.

5/10

Biden feigns no knowledge of his complicity in the Student Loan crisis. His critics remind him that serving as a member and sometime chairman of the Senate Judiciary Committee from 1981 to 1997, Biden was instrumental in removing bankruptcy protection from both government-backed and privately-made student loans. Bidens' action then is the main cause of these problems now. Of course, since it's rumored that Biden cannot even remember when he had his last can of Ensure, it's to much to hope that Biden will remember his complicity decades ago in the current Student Loan fiasco.

5/11

Biden is called out for labeling all people wearing MAGA hats as the worst domestic terrorists in US history. Biden is asked how this possibly helps his pledge for bi-partisan cooperation. Biden replies that he can do both, but then insists his remarks about domestic terrorists was meant for only the "ultra MAGA" crowd. What's next? The 'Real Big' MAGA crowd? The 'Colossal MAGA crowd'? The 'Super-Duper MAGA crowd'? Then Biden sends his press secretary out to echo his "ultra MAGA" comments. Though she doesn't need the help, she sounds as dumb as her boss.

5/12

Bidens' lies, which he has foisted on the American public throughout his long, rude and plagiarized career, are well know. However Biden may have reached his apex in lying today with him insisting that before he took office there were no COVID vaccines available. This is truly mind-bending because before he was inaugurated Biden himself received as many as two vaccine shots. If there were none available, where did Biden get this secret stash? Inquiring minds want to know, but one of these minds won't be Bidens.

5/13

Biden is the host for the US - Asian Special Summit this year. His remarks contain references to Bidens' wish for better relations with the Indo-Pacific community, pledging more funds to the organization in order to provide growth and stability to the region as well as nonstaining a respect for the "...rule of law and for human rights" Conspicuously absent in Bidens' remarks is any references to China's' encroaching influence in the area, its' catastrophic record of human rights abuses and it's continuing threats towards Taiwan, one of our – supposedly - closet allies.

5/14

Of all the shortages that Bidens' fiscal policy has created since he took office, one of the more egregious is the lack of baby formula for Americas' mothers and their offspring. It is more distressing because of the reports that Biden has aggravated this shortage by stockpiling an excess of this commodity at the southern border for use by illegal alien mothers and their children. Biden feigns no knowledge of this and promises to "crack down" on the baby formula manufactures in order to spur production.

5/15

Photographic evidence shows that indeed pallets of baby formula have been stockpiled at the southern border for use by illegal alien mothers, at the expense of legal American mothers. Biden promises again to crack down on baby formula manufactures, blaming them for this problem. However, one of the CEOs of these companies snaps back at Biden, claiming production at his plant has come to a standstill because of the lack of FDA inspectors which Biden himself, in another pique of stupidity, has insisted remain home and off the job due to COVID.

5/16

Bidens' proposed "two-pronged attack's' on inflation would be comical, if it wasn't so dangerous. First Biden is going to impose a huge new tax on the "wealthy" and "greedy corporations". This is only going to curtail production, meaning fewer goods available, until these companies can absorb or pass on the taxes to consumers in the form of higher prices. His other prong, the infusing of trillions of dollars into the economy, will only have the effect of weakening the purchasing power of the dollar because it sends a boatload of more money after fewer goods, causing hyper-inflation and/or a recession. Looking at both of these two "prongs", there are only two explanations: One, Biden is truly evil and is doing everything he can to bring this country to its' knees or, two, what's left of his mind has truly fermented into the consistency of an Egg McMuffin.

5/17

Unable to hide his ignorance, Biden again states that the cure for inflation is to "make sure" the largest corporations in America pay their "fair share". Bidens' new press secretary tries to gaslight Bidens' statement, but being only a diversity hire finds this task beyond her. Hiking corporate taxes doesn't bring inflation down, but it does annoy Bidens' corporate CEO supporters. They point out it's not their tax bills that are the problem, Bidens' penchant for printing money and issuing checks in the trillions of dollars for his 'American Rescue' and 'COVID-19' relief plans that are the main causes of inflation. Biden, as dense as ever, still refuses to acknowledge his bone-headed economic policies are responsible for Americas' economy being stalled in a whimper today.

5/18

A tragic mass shooting occurs in Buffalo and Biden uses it to deliver a hate-filled speech where he implies that the shooting is the fault of conservatives, them all being white supremacists. Then Biden calls for openly censoring all and anything Biden considers hate speech, from all social platforms that 'dangerous' conservatives use.

5/19

Instead of acknowledging the economic travesty his two-pronged 'solution' for combating inflation will cause, Biden doubles down with a proposed 'solution' for the gas and fuel shortage the US is currently suffering from. Incredible and unbelievable at the same time, Bidens' so-called 'solution' is to cancel – yes, cancel – all future oil and gas leases in the country. How this will help Americas' current energy shortage is cosmically uncertain, but one thing that is, is that with any more 'help' like this in fighting inflation and fuel shortages from Biden, America will shortly be in a recession.

5/20

Economists start to weigh in on Bidens' recent proposals to solve the current economic doldrums the US economy finds itself in. None of the economists are complimentary, one of them going so far as to say that regardless if Biden is tossed out of office or not in two years, the damage he has done already or is going to do with his policies in the future, could easily send the American economy into a black hole for at least a decade.

5/21

Biden sends Harris in his place to address the SEAN conference. She delivers another one of her now-becoming-famous 'word salad' speeches. In this one she garbles the phrase 'work together' incoherently at least five times. More frightening, she is actually reading the speech from prepared notes she is holding, causing one wonder if this was the actual way the speech was written and by whom. More frightening still, it is apparent that Bidens' mental deterioration may be infectious.

5/22

Biden continues to be criticized from both parties for letting Title 42 expire in a couple of days. Biden belligerently insists that even if Title 42 goes away, the border is secure and no substantial influx of illegals is expected. Bidens' claims run counter to ICE officials and even Mexican authorities, who estimate that when Title 42 expires tomorrow, the US can immediately expect a surge of no less than 180000 illegals.

5/23

Heeding the dire warnings of ICE officials and the pending lawsuits from various border state governors, a judge orders a stay on Bidens' attempt to cancel Title 42. Biden has no comment, but members of the media report seeing Biden shuffling around the White House in furry bedroom slippers, full pouty face on.

5/24

Biden again irks the Chinese by declaring that the US would immediately intervene in any conflict they start with Taiwan. Biden made the same remarks last October, which his nurses had to walk back the next day. Now after making the remark, Biden schizophrenic - ly signs a new trade deal with Asian countries, but pointedly leaves Taiwan out of the agreement at the behest of China. So, Biden is not afraid of possibly starting WW lll with a nuclear giant of a couple of billion people, but trembles when this same giant asks him not to receive bicycles and computer chips from a nation of 23 million people. Once again, Biden has the whole world laughing.

5/25

Bidens' nurses, as they did last fall, again walk back Bidens', to them, strident remarks concerning his willingness to involve the US in a China/ Taiwan conflict. Biden himself maintains that, despite his remarks, he still honors China's' One China' policy, which claims the countrys' ownership of Taiwan. When asked about his apparent conflicting statements, his nurses maintain that Biden does this on purpose, that this is a negotiating tactic called "diplomatic ambiguity". Through all of this Biden has no comment but smiles blissfully, probably the result of him just finishing his morning can of Ensure.

5/26

Biden rushes to Texas to deliver what most thought would be words of comfort to the families of the murdered schoolchildren and adults. Instead Biden launches into a prepared Marxist rant, demanding more power be given to him to enact more gun control laws. If the scene smacks of deja vu, Obama did the same thing when he stood on the graves of children at Sandy Hook, lamenting he did not have more power to curb gun violence. At least Obama had the good grace to wait until some of the children dead were buried. Biden, learning only a part of the Obama strategy of "Don't waste a crisis for political gain', did not even have the class or dignity to let the parents collect and bury their dead before using them for a political prop.

5/27

Biden, supposedly tired of not getting bi-partisan support for what he callas 'police reform', instead signs an executive order to do so. Bidens' EO is quite comical in its' reading. It requires police to stop the use of excessive force when they see it and render medical assistance to anyone injured .... which every police force in America is already required to do. In the order Biden admits he has no direct control over any police agency, but hopes that the AGs of various states will acknowledge Bidens' order and institute this reform ... which is already a standard practice in these states. What does Biden have with an order that duplicates what already exists and can't be enforced if it didn't? Another one of his empty political shows.

5/28

A remark that Biden made a couple of days ago after meeting with Japans' Prime Minister now receives national attention. A boasting Biden declares that the suffering Americans are feeling because skyrocketing fuel prices are "...an incredible transition..."' that Americans must bare so that the US can move towards his vision of a 'green future'. Biden goes further, insisting that his canceling of all oil and gas leases, the shutting down of the Keystone pipeline and turning the supplying of oil and gas over to Americas' most hated enemies has been instrumental in keeping skyrocketing fuel prices from going even higher. Americans are used to Bidens' unhinged-from-reality proclamations, but now Japans' PM is forced to peak into Bidens' basement window and leaves America a frightened man.

5/29

Biden is criticized for his choices of who and where he will visit to to extend the nations' support after a tragic loss. His critics point out that Biden rushes quickly to places like Buffalo and Uvalde because the killings there fit his political narrative. However, when it is a black racist who is killing whites, like in Waukesha last year, suddenly the logistics for the trip are too difficult and expensive. Two problems here: one, the blatant hypocrisy of it and, two, if the logistics for a trip must not be confusing to Biden, the only gatherings he will be attending in the future will be his grandchildren' birthday parties, if they deign to hold them in his basement.

5/30

Biden, unlike his mentor Obama, honors Americas war dead by placing a wreath at Arlington cemetery, This ignoring of Americas' war dead is one of Bidens' mentors' nastier lessons that, thankfully, didn't take.

5/31

In addressing the aftermath of a mass shooting, Biden makes a tasteless joke about why hunters fell the need for semi-automatic weapons since deer don't wear Kevlar. Not the time or place for one-liners, Biden continues by promising to raze the entire school where the shooting took place. In its' place Biden promises to build a brand new school so future students won't be traumatized by this tragic incident. Like a space-walking astronaut that has had his tether cut, Biden floats farther and farther away from reality really believing that a new building will make people forget what happened there.

6/1

In a attempt to prove that he and his family are not Communist Chinese puppets, in 2021 issued an Executive Order demanding that US companies divest themselves of investments in 59 Chinese military-leaning companies by 6/3/22. However today, two days before the deadline, Biden quietly issues new guidelines, informing these U.S. investors in Chinese military operations that they would not be punished for holding on to their investments after the divestment period. making Biden and his famiys' Communist puppet masters very happy.

6/2

Lost in the tumult of the shooting in Texas a week or so ago, Biden quietly submitted amendments to the WHO which would give the WHO over-riding authority over the US and other member nations whenever the WHO declares a worldwide 'pandemic'. This is another first for Biden, giving up American sovereignty to foreign entities under the fake cover of 'medical emergency'. So far Bidens' amendments have not been approved as many of the worlds' smaller countries are reluctant to give up their sovereignty. This was reported a week ago, but in the anguish over the Uvalde massacre, few noticed Bidens' sell-out of America until today

6/3

Biden declares it is time to put an end to the "carnage" and loss of American lives in mass shootings across the country. He pleads with Congress to pass "rational, common-sense measures" to curb gun violence. Reporters wonder where Biden has been since his inauguration while criminals in cities like Chicago and Detroit have been slaughtering innocents by the hundreds. It is pointed out to Biden that the states and cities he ignores are political allies while the states he is focusing his 'Grab all Guns' policy on, like Texas and Oklahoma, are two states with populations diametrically opposed to him. Biden has no comment.

6/4

Apparently feeling like he is not being heard, Biden stridently reiterates that his economic policies, like pouring trillions of dollars into an already over-heated economy and canceling projects like the Keystone pipeline and numerous gas and fuel leases, is actually good for the economy. What seems to have escaped Bidens' attention is a series of new polls showing that close to 40% of his support among Black Americans has waned because Bidens' economic policies, rather than helping, have left many minority communities suffering. Maybe Biden feels he's not being heard because, fearing a heart attack, his nurses make sure these polls never make their way to Bidens' basement, where he peacefully naps.

6/5

Unable to stem the criticism for his failing economic policies, sends his Commerce and Treasury Secretaries out to the media to defend him. In separate interviews they both admit that Biden had "...gotten it wrong..." on how painful inflation would be, but continue they blame Bidens' economic debacle on COVID, supply chain problems, greedy oil companies, and Russias' invasion of the Ukraine for Bidens' inflation problems. Parroting Biden, the two Secretary say that Bidens' canceling of all oil and gas leases, his shutting down the Keystone pipeline and turning the supplying of fuel over to some of Americas' hated enemies have nothing to do with Americas' record high inflation. If they truly believe this, it's apparent that Bidens' mental delusions have made their way to his Cabinet.

6/6

In what will undoubtedly lend more credibility to the charge of his mental instability, Biden invokes the Defense Production Act (DPA) to advance his clean energy and climate change agenda. The DPA was passed into law in 1950 to streamline production of necessary products in the time of war for Americas' the national defense. Biden feels he is within his constitutional rights to invoke the DPA in order to produce solar panels. Yes, within his addled brain, Biden believes America is at war with, no, not Russia, North Korea, or China, but with climate change.

6/7

Biden is warned by defense analysts that his insistence that all the branches Americas military Bidens' concepts of diversity and inclusion over combat readiness undermines both combat training and readiness. Bidens' persistence in making diversity, inclusion, equity and hiring of diverse applicants be the primary criteria in developing Americas' military is seriously affecting Americas' ability to defend it self against its' enemies. Biden has no comment.

6/8

Biden appears on TV, claiming that, under him, the US has the fastest growing economy in the world, actually repeating the phrase "in the world" three times and would've continued if one of his nurses hadn't shaken him. Perhaps it was because he had just awaken in his basement, but Biden made this statement right after the latest economic numbers were released. They show that the American economy has shrunk by over 1%. since the last time numbers were published. Unaware of his latest gaffe, Biden makes the next priority seizing the lunch money the Federal government usually sends to Florida for its' school children. This is Bidens' childish response to the governor there blocking Bidens' attempt to force a gender identity and realignment curriculum on Florida children as young as five.

6/9

Biden economic policies, so hurtful to American bushiness, are forcing these same businesses and corporations to reorganize in order to move to other countries. Rather than amend his policies, Biden asks all other countries to set their corporate and business tax rates equal or greater to those in America as a disincentive for US companies planning to relocate. Like a demented little boy whose pricking of a dam causes it to leak, Biden uses his political extremities to try to plug each and every new hole his ineptitude creates. This presents a clear and present danger to this country, because eventually Biden will run out of fingers and toes.

6/10

As if mocking Bidens' claim of a few days ago of a robust America, several newspapers and financial journals report that Biden has broken his old 3/20 inflation record by posting – again – a historical yearly inflation increase in 5/22, greater than what this country has seen in the last 40 years. Instead of answering for this, Biden returns to his basement and hides.

6/11

Biden still has not commented on the attempted assassination of a Supreme Court Justice that happened days ago. Some on Bidens' staff have commented, some in Congress, but not Biden, His critics suggest that is probably due to Bidens' loyalty to his radical Democratic/Marxist base who would like nothing better than to see a Constitution-based Justice murdered. Still, having the perceived leader of the free world pretend murdering a judge from the highest court in the land is no big deal, is a monumental embarrassment worldwide.

6/12

Biden still will not comment on the assassination attempt on a Supreme Court Justice. Kavanaugh. Biden is now in California for something called 'The Summit of the Americas'. Biden spoke on crime, climate change and even took time at one of LA's ports to rail against something he called "Putin's' Tax" that he claimed was really responsible for Americas' economic ills. Still, through it all, not one word on the attempt on the life of a Supreme Court Justice.

6/13

New polls shows that almost 60% of Americans believe that Biden is purposely allowing fuel prices to skyrocket. They believe Biden is doing this in an effort to force people to stop using fossil fuels and and align wit his stated 'green goals' for the future American society. The humorous side of the poll is that the other 40% thought inflation was caused by Bidens' inept policies, meaning the choices for those poll takers were that Biden is either malicious or incompetent; quite a choice.

6/14

In another class-baiting speech, Biden appears before a AFL-CIO group and rants about the unfairness of the American tax system and the unevenness of wealth in the country. Like a broken record Biden blames the current ills of the country on corporations being taxed differently than individuals – which is prescribed by law – and CEOs being taxed at rates different than individuals, which is an outright lie. Everyone is subject to the same tax code, but what they are taxed on can differ greatly. By the end of his rant, Biden is yelling and waving his arms like a third-world despot, trying to exhort the crowd into a frenzy. Biden seems to be seeking their violent help in order to help him fight these imaginary injustices. Bidens' only hope to accomplish this is if his audience is as ignorant and uneducated as he is in the field of economics, which is just not possible.

6/15

In Bidens' AFL-CIO speech he mocks Trump, saying he was one of only two presidents who left office with higher unemployment numbers than when he entered. Biden does not mention that before the pandemic, Trump had ushered in one of the greatest American economies in years, complete with historic lows in unemployment for all minorities and women. Trump handed Biden vaccines, pharmaceuticals, a distribution network and a economy poised for resurrection, which Biden promptly turned into a dumpster fire from his first day in office. Bidens' only chance for the audience to accept his re-write of current political history is if his audience is as ignorant and uneducated as he is on current political history, which is just not possible.

6/16

Biden delivers another speech where he talks about his first day in office. Biden boasts that on that day he signed an executive order barring discrimination against members of the LGBTQ community. Sadly, this is another of Bidens' infamous political dog-and-pony shows since all of his proposed "laws" were already on the books in one form or another. Bidens' braggadocio loses all effect and elicits giggles from the audience when he tries to use the LGBTQ acronym, gets lost halfway through, incoherently mumbles the rest, then continues his speech hoping his babbling is not noticed. This is possible only if his audience is as mentally disjointed and confused as Biden is, which is just not possible.

6/17

Biden sends a scathing letter to the executives of several major oil companies, complaining that they weren't producing enough oil and then reaping windfall profits from the resulting higher gas prices. This leaves the oil execs shaking their collective heads. Is this the same Biden that as far back as 2/20 declared, if elected, he would get rid of all fossil fuels? The same Biden who canceled the Keystone pipeline and all new oil exploration leases? Now this is the same Biden blaming them for the lack of energy supplies? The oil executive shake their heads in disbelief momentarily, then go back to producing as much oil as Biden will allow.

6/18

Biden continues to blame doubles down on blaming oil executives and their "corporate greed" for Americas' current fuel crisis. It is revealed that his cynical letter, demanding that oil companies increase output to counter decreasing oil supplies, went to 7 major oil companies, who have yet to respond. They must be puzzled because this is the same Biden who as far back as late 2019 declared all fossil fuel executives should be put in jail and "...I'm not joking about this." These executives are also aware of Bidens' empathy for those his policies force onto the unemployment lines, like coal miners. Biden, when apprised of all the coal miners who could lose their jobs due to his policies, replied that they should "...learn to (software) code"

6/20

Bidens' famous, career-long hypocrisy is beginning to tie him in knots. First, while Biden demands that fossil fuel executives be prosecuted and jailed, Bidens' own son is one of those executives helping run the largest Ukrainian natural gas producer. Then Biden announces that he endorses a carbon tax on the American people, feeling that this will force them to accept his vision of a "green future" where they will use less of the fossil fuels … that he is currently exhorting oil companies to supply more of … so the American people can pay more taxes … for using the same resources Biden feels should be criminalized. It is no wonder that by the end of the announcement all minds are as confused as Bidens.

6/21

Biden continues his boorish criticism of Americas' oil companies executives, tiredly railing against them again for their exorbitant profits, using them as a example of what Biden calls "corporate greed". This is interesting because oil company' profits, on average, run at approximately 6% while their tax rate is 32%. What Biden ignores – and hopes no one else notices – is that a major supporter of Biden, Goldman Sachs, reported a profit of 32%, during this same period while paying only 15% in taxes. "Corporate greed" might be flourishing with GS and their pet Biden, but not so much inside the oil companies.

6/24

Oil companies continue to push back against Bidens' boorish attempt to blame them for the shortage of fuel in America. One company, Exxon Mobil, issued a statement informing Biden that not only had they been investing throughout his unnecessary pandemic shutdown, increasing refining capacity to process U.S. light crude by about 250,000 barrels per day, the equivalent of adding a new medium-sized refinery. In addition, EM kept investing even during the pandemic even though it lost more than $20 billion and had to borrow more than $30 billion in order to increase capacity to be ready for the expected post-pandemic demand. EM goes on to suggest that Biden could promote further investment by oil companies by consistently supporting U.S. resource development, issuing regular and predictable lease sales and streamline regulatory approval. To all of this, Biden has no comment.

6/25

Biden cannot help embarrassing himself. In another class-warfare speech Biden at first mumbles incoherently about Trumps' tax cut, but finishes by panning those he considers "the wealthy". Biden shows his ignorance again by claiming that if they are using their wealth buying yachts, that "... doesn't help the economy a whole lot." Interesting, since most of the yachts purchased are made here in America by an industry worth 3.2 billion dollars. In addition, it supports an estimated 690,000 jobs, either directly or indirectly and 35000 businesses nation wide. If a 3.2 billion industry and 690,000 jobs doesn't help an economy according to Biden, what in Bidens' world does?

6/26

Biden rolls out another attempt to silence his political foes. Since his proposed Communist-style censorship group called the Disinformation Governance Board was put on pause because of public backlash, Biden signs a memorandum creating something he is calling the 'Task Force for Combating online Abuse'. Like his failed DGB, this group will monitor the Internet for what Biden calls "misinformation"' However, Biden immediately assures the American people that his new censorship project will be an abject failure by putting by putting VP Harris in charge of it.

6/27

Biden inadvertently shows reporters a "cheat sheet" his nurses have provided for him, detailing everything from how and when to enter and leave a room, when to stand and sit and what questions to ask and to whom. Biden proudly sees no harm in showing reporters the sheet, much like an elderly patient near his end in a rest home, showing pictures of his grandchildren, whose names he has long forgotten, to anyone who will look and listen.

6/28

A truck that imprisoned and killed over 50 illegal immigrants was not checked at one of the southern border checkpoints because the checkpoint was unmanned. According to the governor of Texas, incidents like this happen regularly because this checkpoint and many others have not been manned for awhile due to Bidens' budget cuts to the Border Patrol agency. Biden has no comment.

6/29

Biden refuses to comment on the illegal aliens dying in a van while trying to cross the border at one of his unmanned checkpoints. Biden has his press secretary attempt to beguile the American public by claiming that these 50 deaths prove the border is closed. In what can only be called a Herculean, cynical twist of logic, Bidens' PS asserts that many illegal aliens die all the time at the border because there is no place for them to cross. Meanwhile, the head of Homeland Security, in speaking to Border Patrol agents, admits that border security is "...worse now than... at least in twenty years, if not ever." Biden has no comment.

6/30

While Biden spends more time in his basement, his approval ratings stay mired in the 35% - 39% range. A recent poll shows that 85% of those polled believe the country is moving in the wrong direction, including for the first time 8 out 10 Democrats. Biden has no comment.

7/1

Biden attends the G7 summit in Germany and is asked to speak; big mistake. Biden falters through the intro to his speech, mispronouncing and misusing words with glaring alacrity. Then Biden tries a joke, saying: "Putin wanted the "Finlandization" of NATO, instead he got the "NATOlization"of Finland. Embarrassing for Biden, no one laughs. Even though it's an international meeting, Biden calls almost exclusively on only US reporters for questions, but this does not go well. Biden is asked both about some comments world leaders made about him and about the 85% of Americans believing America is going in the wrong direction. Biden replies bluntly that, despite the polls, no one in the U.S. believes it is heading in the wrong direction and, further, the only comments he's received from world leaders are ones thanking him for his great leadership. This is true, but what Biden leaves out is that he was wearing a 'Donald Trump' name tag.

7/2

Bidens' continued bumbling performance at the G7 is alarming, even to his most ardent supporters. At one point, Biden does not take his seat at a table and, looking confused, remains standing long after the other members have sat down. Apparently Biden was lost without the 'cheat sheet' his nurses usually prepare, telling him when and where to sit. Eventually someone notices the embarrassment and helps Biden to his seat.

7/3

While Bidens' on again, off again forays into senility continue at the G7, polls back home continue to be unkind to him. Besides the one showing that 85% of Americans, both Democrat and Republican, believe Biden is taking America in the wrong direction, another poll shows Trump easily defeating him if the election was held today. To make matters worse, another poll showed that 71% of Americans do not want to see Biden seek a second term and a full 30% of Democrats would not even vote for him in a Democratic primary. With data like this awaiting him, Biden may find stumbling around the G7, not knowing what chair to sit in or when, more enjoyable than a return to the States.

7/4

A video of Biden yelling at the top of his lungs at a past union meeting resurfaces. In it Biden demands that union members not hear the "lies" anymore about his reckless spending because he, Biden, is "changing peoples' lives". For once his critics have to agree. With historic inflation and fuel prices strangling most American households, with everyday necessities like baby formula disappearing from shelves, with the millions of illegals allowed by Biden to cross the southern border, wreaking havoc there and in other areas of the country, with the DEA reporting that 90% of the Fentanyl overdose deaths reported this year in the U.S. were from this drug coming across these same borders Biden has murderously opened, no one can deny that on this day that celebrates Americas' former greatness, Biden is indeed "changing peoples' lives".

7/5

In another display of his low IQ level when it comes to economics, Biden claims the energy crisis would be fixed if gas companies would simply lower the prices they are charging "... at the pump." To its' credit, the US Oil & Gas Association replied by suggesting that Biden send 'whoever' made this remark to "... register for Econ 101 for the fall semester." A head of one of Americas' largest companys chimed in, saying that d Bidens' remarks show "... a deep misunderstanding of market dynamics." Meanwhile Biden is overseas and is criticizing the US Supreme Court to anyone in Europe who will listen. As some might be dismayed that Biden can get so much so wrong so consistently, all should be reminded of Bidens' famous claim that he always, always prefers "truth over facts".

7/6

White House Correspondents from multiple outlets rip Biden over what they call a "historic" lack of access to him and using excuses like the pandemic to keep Biden out of areas that Trump freely gave them access to. Even the corporate-controlled media, like NBC and CNN, usually flagellant supporters of Biden, sent a letter to his press secretary demanding more access to the president, a request they have made often in the recent past. While Bidens' nurses scramble to spin their attempts to hide Biden from the media, he has no comment.

7/7

With Bidens' increasing unpopularity dragging the entire Democratic party down on his suspender-ed coattails, projections for Democratic losses in both houses come November seem a real possibility. Biden, seeming unaware or uncaring about this, instead decides to put the American people in greater jeopardy in regards to illegal immigration. Biden orders immigration laws be changed immediately so that immigrants with terrorist ties be allowed to immigrate into the US, as long as their ties to terrorist organizations and terrorist activities are 'limited'. Biden does not define what "limited" means as he establishes this first U.S. history,

7/8

Afraid that a lame duck presidency seems likely, Biden appears determined to do as much damage to the country before November rolls around and the list is ominous. Along with Biden demanding that terrorists with 'limited' activity" be allowed into the US., he continues to allow illegal immigrants, with all of their attendant problems, to flood the nation. In addition, Biden has decided to deplete American emergency oil reserves, the reserves that are supposed to be kept on hand to insure American safety and security, and send them to other countries like China. Understanding that this is just a partial list for Biden, perhaps "terrifying" is more appropriate than "ominous".

7/9

One of Bidens' first acts as president was to reverse Trumps order that the Chinese social media giant, TikTok, be sold off from ByteDanceIt, another Chinese tech giant with close ties to the Communist party. Trumps' concern then and since proven, was that this unholy alliance would allow the Chinese Communists to have access to all data collected by TikTok. This includes Americans' search histories, web browser data and bio metric information like their voice and face "prints".By reversing Trumps' order, Biden has now granted the Chinese Communists access to a treasure trove of US citizens' private information. Apparently Bidens' goal of damaging America as much as possible started long ago.

7/10

Biden puts his plan of damaging America as much as possible before the midterms on steroids. Reuters reports that in a political stunt to ease gas prices at the pump, Biden plans to release 1 million barrels from the U.S. Strategic Petroleum Reserve each day until October. This despite being advised by experts that this move is too small to have an effect on gas prices in America, but will continue to drain Americas' emergency fuel supply, which has already dropped to its lowest since 1986. Rubbing slat in the wound, Biden plans to send 20 million of these 90 million barrels to countries like Germany and China. Bidens' idiocy continues unabated.

7/11

Biden, shaken awake by his nurses, turns his watery gaze towards Arizona, a state that a passed a law requiring every voter there to show proof of American citizenship before voting in Presidential elections. The requirement was signed into law earlier this year after it was discovered that 11,600 voters in Arizona cast ballots in 2020 without showing proof of citizenship; Biden won that state in that election by 10,457 votes. In response to Arizona's new law, Biden orders his Justice Department to sue Arizona to eliminate the citizenship requirement, claiming that it would impose unlawful requirements on eligible voters. One of his nurses cautions Biden that under federal law, it is illegal for non-citizens to vote in federal elections, but by this time it seems Biden had fallen back asleep.

7/12

In reading his speech as usual off a teleprompter, Biden, without hesitating, reads an instruction on the screen which says "repeat the line" as part of his speech. So much of Bidens' speech is bumbled incoherence this gaffe is not easy to pick up, but it's there. From this point on his nurses will have to put the instructions for the speech in bright; cheerful colors so Biden can differentiate between those and the actual lines he is supposed to robotically read.

7/13

Bidens' penchant for incoherent speaking seems to be infectious. His Secretary of the Interior was asked a question on infrastructure. His answer, a two-minute word salad, was not only semi-coherent and not an answer, but was delivered with the smiling pride of an elementary school student, beaming not because he understands a single word of his answer, but because of all the big words he is using. Then Harris gave an answer to a question on the economy where she used the word 'seriously' three times in one sentence, bringing guffaws from the audience. At this rate Biden will be the first president that requires an English translator to be present when Biden or his staff gives a speech.

7/14

Several days ago Biden went on a rant about a10 year-old rape victim who couldn't get am abortion because of the Supreme Courts' recent decision to overturn Roe v. Wade. It turns out that the story is false, but Biden refuses to retract or correct his statement, making it another of his infamous lies. The media, particularly the Washington Post, is complicit, incredulously claiming that, while the story is a fake, it has been repeated so often and now has Bidens' approval, it can be considered true. Bidens mental derangement, once thought to be infectious only to those close to him, now can be officially considered a contagion as it has obviously leaked into the media.

7/15

There is a theory that Bidens' staff members really can speak more coherently, but don't so as to minimize the difference between this and the incoherence of Biden. In effect, they speak like intellectually challenged buffoons in an effort to protect their boss, trying to convince the public that Bidens' inarticulate mumbling are actually a new norm; interesting theory.

7/16

Frustrated by the American people and their Representatives unwillingness to approve of his radical "Green" agenda, Biden threatens to take executive action to to force his economy-killing climate change initiatives down Americans' throats. This is not an empty threat because Biden regularly, like Obama, uses EOs to circumvent the wishes of American voters, much like any third-world dictator.

7/17

Under Trump, America was energy independent. In only a year and a half Bidens' energy policies have so crippled America that he is forced to make a embarrassing, 'on-his-knees' trip to the Middle East to beg the Saudis to produce more oil to help alleviate the fuel shortages in America that Biden created in America. Bidens' 'on your knees, head bowed' picture is reminiscent of a similar posture his mentor, Obama, assumed on his humiliating world wide apology tour' when he was president. In both case, quite a humiliating picture of two men thought to be leaders of the free world, for all the world to see.

7/18

Biden continues to be embarrassed by his trip to the Middle East even after returning. Bidens' claim of a productive meeting and renewing close relations with Americas' Saudi "allies" is not quite true. Not only did the Saudis pay only lip service to Bidens' request to produce more oil, almost immediately after Biden left the UAE, the Saudis sentenced an American citizen to three years in prison on nebulous charges. It is clear that since Biden took office, our supposed allies around the world feel like they can disrespect and embarrass the United States at will, laughing all the way.

7/19

On his return from the Middle East, Biden is greeted by a new poll that shows his approval rating is at a new all-time low. So low, in fact, even his most ardent supporters question whether he should seek a second term and are starting to worry about what impact Bidens' flagging popularity will have on the upcoming midterm elections.

7/20

Whether due to jet lag caused by his recent trip to the Middle East or it's after 4:30 in the afternoon, Biden implies again that there is no crisis at the southern border. To reaffirm this Biden sends his HSS secretary out to announce like he did in 2021, that the southern border is "safe' and "secure". He and Biden don't go as far as they did in 2021 when they announced that the border was 'closed', despite the millions of illegals that have crossed into the U.S. illegally, the tripling of illicit drugs since Trump left office, and that Biden is now quietly continuing to build the wall Trump started and Biden openly criticized; strange going-ons along a border that is supposedly closed, safe and secure.

7/21

Biden, who is fully vaccinated, fully masked and twice boosted, has nevertheless contracted COVID19 again. This only continuing to build the case for the uselessness of vaccinating, masking and boosting except in specific cases involving a co-morbidity. Biden will not say where he contracted the virus and his staff says this information is unimportant since the new, "immune-evasive"virus is surging everywhere across the country. Bidens' nurses admit, reluctantly since it doesn't fit Bidens' fear-mongering agenda that, as is the case with each mutation of the virus, Biden is feeling few, in any, ill effects.

7/22

After reviewing Bidens' statements about his current COVID condition, many half truths and some outright lies are evident. Bidens' biggest lie about COVID remains calling vaccinated people 'immune' when the only truly immune people are the ones who healed naturally and did not receive the vaccine or any of the boosters.

7/23

Even though the country is now in a recession, Biden proposes yet another new spending package worth 250 billion dollars. This one is for subsidizing the computer chip industry. This brings back fearful memories of Obama and all the companies he Federally subsidized, with billions of American taxpayer dollars, that ultimately failed. Unfortunately, this is not the worst part of Bidens' proposed spending package. The worse part of it it is that Biden proposes to pay for this boondoggles by instituting large tax increases on both individuals and corporations, and Biden plans on doing this while in the middle of a recession.

7/24

In what is possibly the best comedic relief he has provided in awhile, Biden comes up with a unique, if somewhat insane, new name for his multi-billion dollar boondoggle subsidy for chip manufactures, green new deal and climate change hucksters: Biden calls it his his 'Inflation Reduction Bill'. Uncontrolled belly laughs roll across America, but probably don't penetrate Bidens' Delaware basement.

7/25

After previously claiming he can't control the price of gas, Biden tries to take credit for bringing gas prices down. Biden points to the national average price for a gallon of gas is $4.39, down from a high of $5.00 at its' peak. It's obvious that Biden is grasping for anything positive about the American economy he stalled, when he joyously points to a $.70 reduction in gas prices, leaving out that these same prices have jumped almost 100% since Biden took office.

7/26

An American basketball player who smuggled drugs into Russia and got caught now pleads with Biden to bring her home. What is somewhat ironic and wholly hypocritical, this is the same person who refuses to stand for the National Anthem before games to protest what she calls the "institutional racism" that is America. Yet. suddenly when compared to a Russian prison, the 'horrible' institutional racism she has to 'endure' in America doesn't seem so bad. Since she is one of Bidens' major constituents, a gay, tattooed, Marxist American hater, it is expected that Biden will comply.

7/27

As expected, Biden is prepared to release convicted Russian arms trafficker Viktor Bout in exchange for WNBA basketball player arrested in Russia for smuggling drugs. Biden and his staff feign remorse at this "painful choice" of exchanging a convicted arms dealer, responsible for thousands of deaths and attempts on American lives for a spoiled, rich athlete who routinely spits on the soul of America and sees no reason why she should be punished for drug smuggling. Yes, it is a "painful choice", as it painfully exposes Bidens' lack of any moral compass.

7/28

Biden refuses to accept any blame for Americas' failing economy. His pork-loaded "Inflation Reduction Act" spending package is approved by Congress. The package is just the disguised portion of Bidens' 'Build Back Better' plan that was voted down some months ago. This Biden bill raises taxes substantially on both individuals and businesses, making people have less money that will chase fewer products and make hiring harder. In lieu of this, a better name for this Biden boondoggle would be "Inflation Increasing Act", which it will surely do.

7/29

Ignoring all available science, Biden insists that all people 5 years and older are not only to get vaccinated and boosted against COVID, but must continue to wear masks indoors. Biden makes this demand despite that the majority of states no longer have masking requirements and, to date, there is no peer-reviewed scientific evidence that masking prevents the spread of COVID. As Biden has himself proven so eloquently a few days ago, the so-called "vaccines" are no more than temporary pharmaceuticals and curtail neither the spread or the contracting of the virus.

7/30

North Korean leader Kim Jong Un warns the world that he's ready to use his nuclear weapons in potential military conflicts with the United States and South Korea. The pajama-boy leader of this Communist country unleashed fiery rhetoric against rivals, saying they are pushing him to the brink of war. Biden has no response, but this may be because he is isolating himself again in his basement after testing positive for COVID yet again. A possible nuclear threat and a possible minor virus threat are the same in Bidens' eyes.

7//31

Biden announces a new plan to give valid IDs to illegal aliens. One of the insane reasons Biden gives for this is that the current documentation illegals receive is easily lost and degrade rapidly in real-world use The documents degradation probably comes from the illegals using them to wipe away tears of laughter as they partake in Bidens' further rape of America. Biden claims the program is a 'concept', with 'specifics' to follow later. It is unclear if the 600000 illegal immigrants Biden promised to release into the country last April will participate in this new program.

8/1

The result of Bidens' economic policies came with the announcement of the second quarter GDP numbers, a - 0.9% growth. This marks the beginning of the Biden recession, the historical definition being with two consecutive quarters of negative economic growth. Biden responds by comically attempting to change what the definition of a recession is. To this end Biden delivers a mealy-mouthed definition of a recession that claimed a recession, even replete with negative growth numbers, didn't really exist if there was a strong job market. To add to the comedy, the definition of a recession in Wikipedia was mysteriously changed to match Bidens'. If this bumbling, semi-coherent incompetent is going to be a source of economic definitions for the U.S., one should be afraid … very afraid.

8/2

Biden gleefully announces he signed the order to kill Zawahiri, noted terrorist and the head of the Taliban, claiming it as a major accomplishment. Counter terrorism experts object to Biden taking a victory lap so quickly. They point out that Bidens' disastrously executed withdrawal from Afghanistan allowed terrorist commanders like Al Zawahiri to continue to openly operate in cities like Kabul. In effect, Biden took a non-problem, blew it up into a huge problem, then wants a slap on the back for fixing the problem he created. Not an unusual sleazy political trick, but this one was paid for with hundreds dead lives, 13 American servicemen among them.

8/3

Biden wants to implement a centralized digital currency that would allow him and the government to monitor all financial transactions of all American citizens. Biden wants to call them "FED accounts" and puts his plan in the form of a bill and presents to the Senate for passage.

8/4

Now that Biden and his policies have forced the country into a recession, Biden tries to save what's left of his Presidency by re-defining what a recession is. Wikipedia joins in the attempt to protect Biden It locked the page where the previous definition of a recession two consecutive quarters of negative economic growth. In an obvious attempt to shield Biden, it replaced the long-held definition of a recession with the statement: "There is no global consensus on the definition of a recession.

The definition of a recession varies between different countries and scholars." Nice try., Wikipedia, nice try.

8/5

In response to Bidens' open southern border policies, since April states like Texas and Arizona have been busing illegals to these Democrat-controlled cities like Washington DC and New York to give them a taste of their own medicine. Though only a few thousand have been relocated so far, the Mayors of DC and New York have declared a "humanitarian crisis" and demanded that Biden send in the National Guard – and tens of millions of dollars - to bail them out of this crisis. So far Biden has refused both requests, infuriating key leaders of his own party.

8/6

Biden calls his hiring of his new press secretary "historical" because she is black, female and a lesbian. At the same time, though Biden implies that he doesn't believe she is up to the task because he orders a second person, a 'helper', to stand next to the new press secretary during her briefings. Biden seems unaware that making his new PS share the podium with a 'helper' humiliates both her and his "historic" selection.

8/7

Biden emerges from isolation after testing positive for the COVID virus for the second time in two weeks. Biden again instructs all Americans to get vaccinated, get boosted, wear a mask and stay away from large gatherings to avoid contracting the virus, then heads to Rehoboth beach for a day of relaxation

8/8

Biden sanctions an FBI raid on Trumps' personal residence in Florida, claiming that Trump has classified documents in his possession. Biden is hoping that a little known provision in the civil code that makes it unlawful for any unauthorized person holding documents deemed classified to hold any public office in America. It is the first documented case in American history where a sitting president permits federal assets to go after a private citizen perceived to be a political rival.

8/9

In a semi-coherent, rambling, bib-dribble-my-morning-Ensure moment, Biden vehemently denies he had anything to do with the raid on Trumps' private residence. He denies it three times: First, Biden claims he had no foreknowledge of the raid; second, he insists that no one in the White House authorized this activity and, third, Biden assures reporters that, even if he wanted to authorize such a raid, he has no control over the daily activities of the FBI and DOJ. This seems to mollify the audience, but they do report that after Bidens' third denial, a short distance away they distinctly heard the sound of a cock crowing.

8/10

Reporters claim they have caught Biden in yet another lie in his compulsive lying streak. Biden claims that he had no prior knowledge of the raid on Trumps personal residence, learning about the raid only when the rest of America learned about it, However, emails surface showing complete co-ordination and approval of the raid between Biden, the DOJ and FBI. Bidens' doctors and nurses come to his defense. To a man they maintain that, in his current mental condition Biden could've received the emails, participated in the co-ordination of the raid and even approved it, then forgot about it fifteen minutes later, particularly if it was after 4:30 in the afternoon.

8/11

In response to a barrage of questions hurled his way concerning the historical raid on Trumps' private residence, Biden, acting as always the responsible grown-up, leaves town. His two "partners in crime" in this matter, the heads of the FBI and DOJ, are also unavailable for comment. Considering that all might be hiding out in Bidens; basement, it might be awhile before the American public find out any information on the who, what, and why concerning this historical abuse of government power by Biden.

8/12

In his new spending plan Biden sets aside funding for the hiring of 87,000 new IRS agents, increasing the size of this agency by 100%. This makes the IRS, already the most onerous collection agency in the history of America, larger than the Pentagon, State Department, Border Patrol and FBI organizations combined. It is confirmed that, with Bidens' approval, the new IRS agents will target middle income Americans and small business owners. Coincidentally, throw in the school children demographic and this is the identical group that Biden and other government official tried – are are still trying – to crush with the pandemic lock down hoax of the last two years.

8/13

In another embarrassing performance, Biden proclaims that America was now at 0% inflation. Biden bases this statement because inflation ticked down to 8.9% from it's historical high rate of 9.1% last month. Seeing the reporters exchanging embarrassed glances and taking this to mean they were not understanding his brilliance, Biden continues by explaining that, see, sometimes prices go up, then other prices go down and that's how he, Biden, gets to the number 'zero'. Bidens' nurses immediately leap to the stage and hold a mirror in front of Biden. He giggles excitedly, clapping his hands and pointing at the mirror, saying: "I know that guy!" Holding the mirror steady as a prompt, his nurses lead Biden off the stage before he embarrasses himself further.

8/14

Reporters pepper Biden and his staff with questions about Biden weaponizing the FBI and the DOJ, then sending them to harass Bidens' political enemies. These agencies have arrested people, denied them bail, put them in handcuffs, among other techniques not usually applied to American citizens. An example of Bidens' over reach was his siccing the DOJ and FBI on journalists like James O'Keefe and parents who show up to school board meetings to protest the teaching f CRT and gentrification of their children. It is obvious to all that Trump must live rent-free in Bidens' head, since anyone in Trumps' orbit immediately become a persistent target of Biden and these agencies. Biden has no comment.

8/15

Bidens' promise that his 'Inflation Reduction" bill (actually an inflation increasing bill) contains tax increases only on those entities making more than $400K yearly turns out to be other lie, and a whopper of one at that. Not only will the IRS collect as much as $20 billion dollars more from citizens making less than $400K yearly, bill creates 87,000 new IRS agents who will conduct 710,863 new IRS audits for Americans making $75k or less yearly. To top this lie off, Biden lied about not giving ID cards to illegals who cross the border, giving them full access to American taxpayer-funded public benefits. In this phase of his life Biden, a career liar, seems to have accepted the notion that if you're going to lie now, go big.

8/16

A new video surfaces where Biden claims that he, like Obama, has put together "... the most extensive and inclusive voter fraud organization in the history of American politics." While it's probably safe to say this feeble old man meant to put the word 'prevention' or 'preventing or 'prevented' somewhere in his statement, Bidens' Freudian slip cannot be missed, even by Jungians.

8/17

Biden and his administration are being sued by a group of individuals who claim that recent publicly-released documents establish that Biden violated the First Amendment by directing social media companies to censor viewpoints that conflict with Bidens' messaging on COVID -19. Further, a federal judge in Louisiana ruled there was "good cause" for the attorney generals of Louisiana and Missouri to go through the legal process of discovery in their case against Biden. This gives the AGs the ability to fact-find in order to get to the bottom of this possible collusion between Biden and Big Tech to subvert free speech. Though directly involved, Biden has no comment.

8/18

In a hilarious attempt to make himself look less feeble, Bidens' nurses now have him sporting Aviator sunglasses whenever Biden is in public. While inducing laughter from most and sympathy from others, the media chooses to see this recent change differently. They report that the 'Top Gun' sunglasses make Biden look cool, strong, reinvigorated and "...on a roll." Sadly, the truth is that Biden now looks even less like a President and more like that aged, wrinkled elder on the beach in a speedo, thinking his Aviators are fooling anyone that he is doing anything other than checking out pre-pubescent girls.

8/19

The fallout of Biden hiring 87000 new IRS agents begins. It is already predicted that Americans making less than $75,000 a year will be hit with about 711,000 new IRS audits. It is obvious that there will be considerable incentive to shake down taxpayers. The advantage the IRS has is its' unlimited resources and no accountability, whereas an audited taxpayer has to weigh the cost of accountants, tax lawyers and whatever else it takes to fight an audit in tax court. Bidens' promise that his new tax proposal will not affect anyone making less that $400000 a year is another one of his never ending, career -long lies.

8/20

Biden is barraged with criticism, except from his Democrat supporters, for failing to respond to the Chinese Communist Party (CCP) aggression towards Taiwan, a supposed ally of the US. The criticism follows more than two weeks of large scale Chinese military exercise around Taiwan which raises fear on the island of an impending invasion of the island by the Communists. Biden, who with his family has worked with and for the CCP for years, says nothing, his Aviators and goofy grin firmly in place.

8/21

CEOs from some of the largest companies in the US complain that Bidens' economic policies and the rampant inflation he caused are affecting Americans in every walk of life. They point out to Biden that inflation alone is forcing Americans to change their lifestyles as the price of almost every product in existence has gone through the roof. Their reluctant conclusion is that, because of Bidens' massive, bloated funding bills, is that "…at some level inflation … (is) going to be with us basically forever," Bidens, still sporting his ridiculous Aviators and loose grin, says nothing.

8/22

To Bidens' chagrin, a U.S. District Court Judge ordered the discovery phase of a lawsuit filed by the states of Louisiana and Missouri against Biden to move forward. The lawsuit accuses Biden of pressuring tech companies to censor conservative voices critical of Biden. The lawsuit alleges that Biden, his DHS and other departments violated the Administrative Procedures Act by colluding with Facebook, Twitter, and YouTube to censor dissenting views as "misinformation." The judges' decision paves the way for these states to gather important documents to get to the bottom of this alleged Biden-led collusion.

8/23

A new poll shows that Biden is possibly the most unpopular president in US history. Even many of his Democratic supporters again are reluctant to have him run again in 2024. The big problem they have is that the natural choice to succeed him, Kamala Harris, is more unpopular than Biden, and by quite a few percentage points.

8/24

Bidens' lie about hiring of 87000 new IRS agents to take down mainly for taking down, for example, "... a billionaire who uses the corporate jet for private trips..." is exposed by none other than the IRS. The agency released a training video' that shows the new recruits practicing a take down of a landscape business owner who failed to properly report how he paid for his vehicles, without a billionaire in sight. Biden having the IRS using a phrases like "taking down" and "going after" - phrases usually used when dealing with the Mob or drug cartels - when talking about small business owners and middle class families is revealing look about this Aviator wearing, sputtering goof really views the American citizen.

8/25

Bidens' lack of respect for the Constitution, on display since his first day in office, is reflected in his broken policies on the economy, illegal immigration, vaccines and the like. Now, though, criticism of these policies is starting to come from places Biden never expected. One of these are American sports legends, ripping Biden for not getting American sports back to normal sooner, largely because of Bidens' vaccine requirements. These requirements, highly restrictive to athletes of all types, are still in place over a year after it has been proven conclusively that vaccines don't work. These athletes pointedly ask Biden why he is still prohibiting some un-vaccinated athletes to freely travel, but allows millions and millions of un-vaccinated illegals to enter and roam the country freely, Biden asserts that the two situation are completely different, but shuffles off the stage without explaining how.

8/26

Biden boasts again that his policies have led to the most robust American economy in recent years, which begs the question: What economy is Biden peeking at through his basement window? Certainly not the American economy which a recent Price/Waterhouse/Coopers' Pulse Survey found that half of the companies in America are preparing to begin cutting jobs, 46% of companies are eliminating or reducing signing bonuses and 44% of them are rescinding job offers. Apparently from his basement window nothing says 'prosperity' to Biden like 40% to 50% of American companies being forced to laying off their employees or not hiring employees at all due to his ignorant, misplaced economic policies.

8/27

A federal appeals court on strikes down a Biden statute that forced doctors to perform medical procedures, including gender-transition procedures, against their religious beliefs. The U.S. Court of Appeals for the Fifth Circuit unanimously upheld a lower court's ruling in Franciscan Alliance v. Becerra which protected around 19,000 health care professionals in the Franciscan Alliance, a Catholic health care network, from performing medical procedures against their conscience. Biden, ever the bully, is miffed that at least for now he can't.

8/28

The Ford Motor Company announces that it is backing Bidens' call for electric cars and will focus the majority of its' future efforts on phasing out gasoline and diesel power vehicles in favor of electric vehicles. Lost on Fords' senior management is the irony that the three-to-five thousand current employees that will be laid off because they do not have the requisite skills to work on electric cars are the rank and file members of the the union that helped elect Biden.

8/29

In what appears to be more evidence of Bidens' failing mental health, in short order Biden both announces that pro-Trump supporters are "semi-fascists" and warns Americans who think their guns will protect them and their country from the government are badly mistaken since, Biden brags, he has F-15s. It is another historical first for Biden, along with his soul-crushing manufactured inflation: No president in history has threatened the majority of the American population; the fact that Biden issues the F-15 threat while giggling should worry all, even his most ardent supporters.

8/30

In a letter to Republican lawmakers, the supposedly non-partisan CBO further refutes Bidens lie that his new IRS funding bill for 87000 new agents would not weaponize Bidens' IRS to go after Americans making less than $400k a year. In the letter the CBO projected that Bidens' bill will "certainly" lead to increased IRS audits of middle class Americans, so much so that over the next decade taxpayers making less than $400k will have an additional $4 billion of their income confiscated due to these audits.

8/31

A reporter appears on a news show to outline how bad the situation in Afghanistan is now, a year after Biden abandoned the country with his withdrawal plan that left13 American servicemen dead and thousands of Afghan allies stranded. The reporter believes that Biden swept his failure in Afghanistan under the rug in the hope the American public would forget all about it. He finishes by questioning why, after one of the most humiliating and deadly failures in American military history and under Bidens' watch, was neither Biden or a single member of his administration fired, or held accountable in any way for this debacle. Biden has no comment.

9/1

Biden announces that he is stepping out on the campaign trail help his Democratic allies in their upcoming elections. It seems, though that some don't want his help. Democratic candidates for Congress and governorship in two states snub Biden when he showed up for rallies, both preferring not to be seen with him. Another Democratic Congressman running for re-election openly joined his Republican rival in criticizing Bidens' recent student loan amnesty plan. At least these three from Bidens' own party see him as too politically toxic to be associated with ahead of November.

9/2

Biden delivers a 24-minute nationally televised rant where he paints his political foes as "MAGA forces" that need to be dealt with because they were a threat to the "soul of the nation." Ranting semi-coherently, Biden stands deliberately in front of a ominous red and black screen with the military at his side, looking forever like a dictator cut from the Stalin and Mussolini cloth. His delivery ranges from bellicose implied threats to whispered, pleading whining. Instead of a strongman, Biden comes across more like the weak, octogenarian bully at the local delicatessen, demanding his soup be replaced for a third time because it's cold.

9/3

Biden attempts to walk back his recent vitriolic rantings about Trump supporters being semi- fascists, saying he was referring only to those Republicans who embrace violence as a means to their political ends. Biden is asked rhetorically that if this is his belief, where was he when his ardent supporters BLM and ANTIFA were occupying and burning down major sections of major cities across the country? What did he have to say about the attempt on Republican softball players lives by a Democratic activist? Why did he have such a muted response to the attempted assassination of a conservative Supreme Court Justice? To this date Trump supporters have not burned down or occupied any major cities, have not shot any Democrats playing softball or attempted to assassinate a Supreme Court Justice. Biden has no comment.

9/4

Biden makes lame attempt to walk back his claim that all Republicans were enemies of the state. Now Biden says he meant only those Republicans that refuse to accept election results were the ones that had to be 'dealt with'. Biden claims this group is the real threat to American democracy, stumbling, literally, into another hypocrisy. Since

2016 Biden and all of his supporters have claimed that the 2016 election was rigged and Trump illegitimate. Even now they maintain that the last Georgia governors' race was stolen. To this day, Biden addresses the Democratic loser in that race as 'governor' and invite her to all Democratic governors meetings.

9/5

In what would surely surprise Biden, if he could feel surprised, is that his "student loan forgiveness" edict is popular with almost no one. Most Republican, Independents and even some Democrats say the plan is, besides being immoral and unfair, unconstitutional. Even the small segment of the population it portends to help are angry because they say the amount Biden is giving them is paltry considering the size of their debt. It seems Biden has stumbled and fumbled his way into a golden rule of negotiating: If you can't make everyone happy, make sure you make all parties equally unhappy.

9/6

Biden continues to try to walk back his remarks about fascist Republicans, explaining that he meant only MAGA supporters of Trump … which means Biden was referring to the 75 million who voted for Trump in the last election. How Bidens' new remarks about half of the voting population in America can be considered 'walking back' his original insults is unclear to everyone, save maybe Biden.

9/7

Biden receives bad news about his poll numbers. While Bidens' approval rating did 'surge' by three points after his red-and-black, Gestapo-like stage show rant against conservatives, in just three days his approval rating was back down to 38%. This means that all the hell-inspired staging, the insults, the bullying threats with the military at his side, all were for nothing, except to politically divide the country further. This, from the man who campaigned on the promise of bringing the country together is particularly galling.

9/8

Biden receives bad news from economists They point out that since taking office, Biden has been on an unprecedented socialist spending spree, starting with his catastrophic $2 trillion American Rescue Plan. Sold as a pandemic relief plan, it did little more than shower Bidens' left-wing special interests with cash. Then there is Bidens' student loan bailout plan which will cost the country another $500 billion dollars. Economists tell Biden that sustained inflation will always be the result of his massive expansion of the supply of money. That is why, unfortunately, the country not only has runaway inflation now, but will continue to have inflation through 2023 and probably into 2024. Biden has no comment.

9/9

On top of the bleak news Biden received from economists, it is now reported that fentanyl is now the leading cause of death for Americans between the ages of 18-45. Everyone, even Biden supporters for the most part, blame this tragedy on Bidens' open border policy at the southern border. This policy, which has led to millions crossing the southern border since his inauguration, is also responsible for the tenfold increase in fentanyl smuggling and overdose deaths in the U.S. Bidens' only response is to adjust his Aviators, probably to hide the vacant, confused look in his eyes.

9/10

Fallout over Bidens' "Red Curtain" speech continues as he defines 'good Republicans' as ones that agrees with him, while the other 70 million that don't need to be 'dealt with'. A direct result of Bidens' implied call to arms is the recent "SWAT-ting" of two of his biggest critics. In both cases Biden supporters called 911 to report armed violence was occurring at these critics' residences, hoping that a SWAT team would show up in force and kill them. h. When informed of this 'SWAT-ing' or 'Murder by Cop' initiated by his rhetoric and carried out by his supporters, Biden has no comment.

9/11

Biden welcomes Obama back to the White House. The two gush all over each other with such gust one wonders if a full on make-out session is going to break out shortly. Obama congratulates Biden because the country is "…in better shape…" since he took office. With historical inflation, food and fuel prices almost doubled from what they were under Trump, a weaponized FBI, IRS and DOJ being sent after American citizens, what country has Obama been living in where everything "is better"? Add to this a UN report that, due to immigration policies begun under Obama and continued by Biden, the US southern border is now the deadliest land crossing in the world. Everything is better? Obamas' delusions are second only to Bidens', but they're catching up fast.

9/12

It turns out that the attempt by Bidens' supporters to have two Biden critics murdered by cops, or 'SWAT-ed, was not their first attempt. It is reported that both critics have been targeted at least once before, but Biden still refuses to call off the dogs. Instead he delivers a speech lamenting all of the violence being fomented supposedly by the 70 million-plus Americans who don't agree with his socialist/Marxist policies. What he conveniently ignores – or in his diminished capacity, doesn't remember - is the terrible damage and carnage his supporters did in the summer of 2021 to major cities across the US. Perhaps an extra serving of Ensure will jog his memory.

9/13

In the same manner that Obama weaponized the IRS against Tea Party groups, Biden is accused of weaponizing the DOJ and FBI to take out Donald Trump and conservatives for standing in the way of his radical agenda. A example of each is Biden ordering the raid of Trumps' personal residence and having his hatchet man Garland label parents who showed up at school board meetings to protest the teaching of CRT and gentrification to their children, as "domestic terrorists." As for why he would OK the labeling of concerned parents as terrorists, Biden has no comment. As far as ordering the raid on Trump, Bidens' claim of "... no knowledge..." is repudiated by the judge who granted Trumps request that a Special Master be assigned to the case. On pages 2-3 of her ruling, Judge Cannon revealed that it was Biden who ordered the FBI access to the Mar A Lago documents and Trump's personal belongings. Once again, Biden has no comment about this apparent lie.

9/14

In Bidens' continued targeting of political opponents, his FBI confiscates the cell phone of Mike Lyndell, the famous 'My Pillow' guy and Trump supporter. This left Lyndell not only with no business contacts, but also with impaired hearing since the app that controls his hearing aids are on his phone. Instead of returning the phone to Lyndell for his hearing, the FBI triumphantly turns the phone over to Biden, so sure that it contains incriminating evidence of Lyndells' insistence that the 2020 presidential election was stolen, Biden, though, looks flummoxed and confused. He didn't want the FBI to harass the 'My Pillow' guy because of his assertion of election fraud, but because Bidens' order of white slide sandals and black quarter-hose socks from Lyndells' website still have not arrived.

9/15

After Biden orders the the DOJ to raid the house of his chief political opponent and at least 40 subpoenas to go after any of his supporters, then calling the 75 million-plus of his opponents' supporters semi-fascists, Biden announces that he is hosting a 'Unity Conference', the main goal of which is to 'Bring America Together'. There can be only one of three reasons that Biden would share this glaring example of his mental capacity: One, Biden is brain dead or, two, Biden has such contempt for this countrys' citizen that he thinks they won't remember all the chaos Biden created the last couple of weeks or, three, as a joke one of his nurses spiked his Ensure. This last one is possible, but it is no joke.

9/16

Bidens' claim that Republicans are a threat to Democracy, just because of their refusal to accept the 2020 presidential election results, elicits barely-restrained guffaws from his audience. Democrats haven't accepted the election of a Republican president since 1988 and that was only because Reagan's 1984 victory was such a landslide, with Reagan winning 49 of the 50 states. In just the last few years Democrats have claimed that all elections won by Republicans, from state governors down to municipal dog catchers, were stolen. As recently as last week a Texas Democrat claimed his Republican rival stole her last election, also. In light of this, Bidens' claim of "dangerous Republicans"'is just his latest episode of 'the pot calling the kettle black'. In Bidens' career, this amounts to a lots of pots and kettles.

9/17

Purposely blurring the difference between legal and illegal immigrants, Biden repeats his oft-mentioned defense of his open border policy, claiming that immigrants "enrich" American lives. This sentiment is echoed by his supporters in Democratic-controlled communities, most of which are situated far from the southern border where states there are inundated by thousands of illegal immigrants daily. The governor of Florida takes Biden at his word and ships 50 of the reported 4,000,000 illegals that have crossed into the US since Biden took office, up to Marthas Vineyard, allowing the uppity, mostly Biden-supporter there to be "enriched".

9/18

The residents of Marthas Vineyard are outraged by the 'invasion' of 50 illegal immigrants into their area, even though they profess to be a sanctuary haven for them. With Bidens' acquiescence they accuse the Florida governor of everything from kidnapping and human trafficking to political stunt-ism. The governor defends his actions, claiming that the illegals should be better treated in the Vineyard because the residents claim they are a sanctuary haven for illegals where his state is not. He further asserts that these measures would not be necessary if Biden "... would just do his damn job." Biden has no comment.

9/19

It seems that Bidens' 'enriching' experience afforded by allowing illegal immigration was short lived on Martha's' Vineyard. After less that 72 hours of being 'enriched', the residents there called for buses to expel the illegals off the island, claiming they had no resources to take care of them. This from a vacation spot that regularly takes care of 200,000 visitors a year with a plethora of hotels and rental houses that are empty for much of the year. Biden and this rich enclave turned their backs on these 50, when thousands of illegals invade small, much poorer towns along the southern border daily: So much for being enriched.

9/20

The residents of Marthas' Vineyard tired of the "enrichment" the 50 illegals brought to their and evicted them almost immediately. Reporters shout questions at Biden, asking why, if the Vineyard, where the residents are largely Biden supporters, is a supposed "sanctuary" for illegals, why were these 50 evicted so quickly? Why did sanctuary Martha, where the median house prices well in excess of a million dollars, refused to house the 50 but expect southern border towns with median house prices of less than $200,000 and are inundated by at least 500 illegals a day, to do so. They ask Biden why his mentor, Obama, who own a $13,000,000, thirty acre estate on the island, could find no room for even one illegal in all those acres. Biden has no comment.

9/21

Bidens' recent ill conceived remarks, calling the 70 million+ Trump supporter fascists who needed to be confronted and "dealt with", continuing to inspire violence. Even two of his Democratic leaders, Hirono of Hawaii and Ohio Senate candidate Ryan supposedly said that banning abortion was "...literally a call to arms in our country...." and the radical left (should) "kill and confront" Trump voters. Again Biden is painfully slow to grasp that burning down cities, attacking innocent bystanders with bricks, attempting to assassinate a Supreme Court Justice and other conservative politicians, almost 100% of the political violence that has occurred during Bidens' term in office is from his supporters, all violent and all seeming as as mentally deficient as he is.

9/22

Both Biden and Harris continue to assert that "the border is secure" However, their consternation and anger was evident when the Governor of Texas continue to unload busloads of illegals in Democratic sanctuary cities across the country. Blowing up Bidens' claim of a secure border even further, several of the illegals were interviewed after getting off the buses. When asked about Bidens' and Harris' claim that the border is "secure" the illegals said: "The border is open, everybody believes that the border is open. It's open because we enter. We come in, free, no problem…". When asked if these embarrassing remarks contradict their claims about a secure border, neither Biden nor Harris choose to answer.

9/23

A few days ago Biden held a press conference where he crowed, over and over again, that he "…beat (big) Pharma this year! We beat Pharma this year and it mattered! We're gonna change people's lives!" Now the numbers are in. Pfizer expects to make more than $50-billion off its COVID-19 medicines this year and that's after accruing $37billion last year. Add to that the record profits reported by Moderna and Johnson & Johnson in the same year, does that sound like. to anyone, that Biden beat Big Pharma?

9/24

Biden fumes to his allies in the media that Fox News is covering a story that Biden expected to be covered up, namely the staggering crisis of Bidens' illegal alien invasion. One report showed massive single groups crossing illegally at the border into Eagle Pass, Texas, the line of people going so far into the trees that it made it almost impossible to get a count. Hundreds upon hundreds of illegals, with Coyotes guiding them in water. Biden argues that there is an alarmist quality to this type of reporting, feeling that it feeds political narratives rather than illuminate the actual issues feeding the migrant flow. Biden fails to detail what these 'actual issues' are, but fumes anyway.

9/25

Bidens' Press Secretary admits that Biden was working with local authorities in Delaware to deal with the illegal aliens that were bussed there. Apparently Biden can deal with Delaware officials to deal with an illegal alien problem that is embarrassing to him, but won't lift a finger to deal with the immigration crisis he created in southern conservative states. According to Biden, flying or busing illegal aliens to a wealthy resort island that's home to multi-million dollar mansions is putting illegal aliens' lives "at risk". However, Biden sees no risk with the Biblical flood of illegal aliens he has encouraged to pour into southern states, across a border the United Nations now calls the deadliest land crossing in the world. Instead Biden continues to flail around, fuming about having the tables turned on him by Republican Governors

9/26

In his two years of office, Biden has used the DOJ and FBI in terrifying ways. Biden has weaponized both organizations and sicced them on conservative journalists, raiding their homes, seizing their property and electronic devices. Not content with this abridgment of constitutional rights, Biden then sicced these agencies on parents who showed up to school board meetings and had them labeled as domestic terrorists. Still not done, Biden had his heel hounds raid the home of a former president, another historical first for Biden.

9/27

Perhaps out of boredom or because he had a few minutes to kill before the next 'Matlock' rerun, Biden sends his shock troops after the Eagle

Forum, a very small non-profit in Alabama. The Forum filed a motion to quash the subpoena that Biden and his DOJ issued some time ago for documents they issued in support of Alabamas' attempt to criminalize the providing of transitory medical treatment to transgender youths. One of the issues the Eagle Forum is concerned about, along with parents and doctors in Alabama, is 'gender-altering medical treatment to minors' and the 'permanent, life-long adverse effects of such medical procedures. Biden weaponizing the DOJ to go after the Eagle Forum for opposing Bidens' "gender-affirming" initiatives is reminiscent of Obama sending Lois Lerner and the IRS after conservative 5013(c)s when he was president. Taking a page out of Obamas' playbook, Biden is trying to criminalize any opposition to his gender-mutilating agenda.

9/28

What might turn out to be the best example of Bidens' rapidly decreasing mental state occurred at a recent press conference. Biden wanted to give kudos to lawmakers who helped pass one of his bloated spending bills. He specifically calls on Jackie Walorski to stand up and take a bow for her tireless effort in support of the bill, except Walorski died a month ago in a car accident. Worse yet, Biden had sent condolences and flowers to her family at that time. Bidens' staff tried to pass off the gaff as "normal". Normal? Perhaps for someone suffering from a diminished mental capacity or Alzheimer's disease, maybe, but not for the supposed leader of the free world.

9/29

Bidens' remarks about the 70 million+ Trump supporters who needed to be confronted and "dealt with" continue to inspire more violence from his supporters. One of them ran over and killed an 18 year old boy. In a chilling echo of Bidens' exact words, the murderer said he had to kill the boy because he was a Republican and a "threat to democracy," Undeterred, Biden continues to fan the flames of political violence with his increasingly over -the -top attacks on generally anyone else who disagrees with him and Republicans specifically.

9/30

Biden has repeatedly claimed he is the only Democrat who can defeat Trump in a 2024. However, if the information could dent Bidens' oatmeal brain, he might be dismayed by a poll released today that showed if the election was held today Biden would lose to Trump by a substantial margin. Even more distressing for Biden, if he could feel distress, is that the same poll revealed that almost 70% of Americans believe he should not even run for President in 2024. Hopefully, mercifully, his nurse gave Biden this news after 4:30 pm, mitigating the chance of a heart attack.

10/1

In spite of Hurricane Ians' imminent landfall in Florida, Biden continues his vendetta against the Governor there. As the storm inched closer, the usual coordination between a President and a Governor facing a major disaster was nowhere to be seen. In fact Biden didn't contact the governor until a day after the hurricane made land fall. Biden did call the mayors of several of Floridas' major cities over the impending emergency, but chose not to call the governor Bidens' campaign promise to unite the country is not only absent, but demonstrates how petty Biden can be, even in the face of a natural disaster that affects all citizens, regardless of political party.

10/2

Harris makes a racists demand, that hurricane equity relief for the state of Florida be handed out based on skin color. Biden is asked if he approves of this scheme. Showing courage, Biden says he neither approves or disapproves of this racist plan: Courage, indeed.

10/3

Bidens' supposed allies do him no favors. First Harris declares that Biden must require that race be taken into account when divvying up federal relief aid to hurricane-battered Florida. Then Pelosi echos Bidens' criticism of the Florida governor sending illegals northward, Pelosi maintains that the Florida governor should keep the illegals local so they can help his state "pick the fruit" grown there. When asked if he supported these two overtly, blatant racist remarks, Biden has no comment.

10/4

Fallout continues from Harris' racist rant concerning the distribution of hurricane relief fund to Floridians based on race. Biden and his staff defend Harris, saying that her racist remarks were taken out of context. Her actual quote was: "It is our lowest-income communities and our communities of color that are most impacted by these extreme conditions. We have to address this in a way that is about giving resources based on equity, understanding that we fight for equality, but we also need to fight for equity.", equity being the code word Biden, Harris and all Marxists use for "race": Context, indeed.

10/5

Bidens' mental incapacity is becoming so obvious that nationally published cartoons are making fun of it. In one, as Biden is preparing to walk to the podium, his nurse warns him to try not to shake hands with invisible people or address anyone who is dead. Bidens' supporters are outraged, claiming this type of mockery borders on elder abuse; they may have a point.

10/6

Biden is asked to defend some incredible illegal immigration numbers. Reports claim that as many as 4.9 million illegal immigrants have crossed the southern border of the U.S. since Biden took office. Other reports claim that the 4.9 million is the number of incidents at the border, not actual crossings. Even so, under Biden border incidents average close to 8000 a day. Under Trump, once he got the immigration mess that Obama left him under control, border incidents averaged approximately 100 a day. This means that border incidents have increased over 7000%. to which Biden has no answer. To be fair, these numbers were presented to him after 4:30 in the afternoon. It is doubtful Biden would have come up with an answer, even if he understood the math.

10/7

Now that it is morning, Biden is asked to explain why, if roughly the equivalent of the entire population of Ireland has illegally entered the United States since he became president, he continues to maintain that the border is secure. Biden argues that the 4.9 million number is "incidents" at the border, that no more than 900,000 illegals have actually entered the country. Even if true, this means that by using Bidens' numbers, 18% of illegals detained at the border evade apprehension and disappear into American communities. More troubling for Biden, roughly 26000 terrorists or illegals with ties to terrorist organizations have been detained at the southern border. If Bidens' 18% number for all illegals detained holds, it's very possible that between 4000 and 5000 terrorists or terrorist affiliates have made their way into the US over Bidens' "secure" border. Biden, befuddles as usual by simple math, has no comment.

10/8

Bidens' behavior, until now mostly imbecilic, sinks to the level of a child when an open mic catches him mocking Floridas' Governor, intimating that he is a coward for not responding to the criticism Biden has leveled at him the last few days. Apparently lost on Biden is that for the last week or so the Governor been concentrating on returning services to his state of Florida in the aftermath of hurricane Ian. Over the mic Biden boasts that "No one f*cks with a Biden..." and "You can't argue with your brother outside the house." Though unclear as to exactly what Biden meant by this, one thing is clear: After almost two years of stumbling on and off stages, semi-coherent rambles, trying to shake hands with ghosts and extorting some dead people to rise, Bidens' sinking to the emotional level of a child should surprise no one.

10/9

A reporter points out that on the same day Biden proclaims his toughness with his "No one f*cks with a Biden," comment, leaders around the world thumbed their noses at him. In response to Bidens' demand that they increase their oil production to benefit America, OPEC cut production by two million barrels a day. Then in response to Biden sending an aircraft carrier to convince North Koreas' Kim Jong Un to stand down, the pajama wearing fat-boy dictator continued to fire ballistic missiles in the vicinity of Japan. Add to this Putins' continued encroachment in Ukraine and it's apparent that there are plenty of world leaders who are not afraid to "f*ck(s) with a Biden,"

10/10

Biden and Harris are again criticized because of their inattention to the southern border where death, rapes, drug and human smuggling chaos reigns every day, courtesy of the Mexican Cartels and Bidens' open border policy. In their defense, Biden claims that he has visited the border and Harris says she will be heading to ground zero for the border crisis shortly. It turns out that Biden did visit the border, but it was 14 years ago and in a motorcade that drove past sections of the border but did not stop. For her part, Harris is indeed going to Texas soon, but not to address any of the critical immigration issues there. She is going only to take part in a Democratic fund raiser. Rather than being angry, both supporters and critics of this pair see these half-truths, rather than the full-blown lies they usually engage in, as an improvement.

10/11

Biden, Aviators in place, threatens to stop providing military aid to Saudi Arabia unless they increase oil production to help the US, the country that was energy independent. This was before Biden and his energy-killing policies came to power, policies that not only curtailed current oil production but also killed long-range oil production plans like the Keystone Pipeline. Apparently Bidens' answer to the energy crisis in America is rather than enacting pro-production energy policies at home, hold the threat of national security support for our allies over their heads until they produce energy for America. Somewhere in the dark recesses of his graying mind, Biden calls this 'leadership'; others call it petulant, unnecessary bullying.

10/12

While Bidens' career-long lying jag is well documented, there is one that he seldom gets called on. He repeated it again recently in a speech in Colorado There Biden, with properly attenuated speech, came close to sobbing as he professed empathy with those in the crowd who lost loved ones in the service of their country. He said: "I say this as a father of a man and won the Bronze Star, the conspicuous service medal, and lost his life in Iraq," Sad indeed, the only problem being that his son died here, in America, of brain cancer in 2015. Perhaps it is out of respect for those who have lost loved ones, or the possibility that in his current mental state Biden cannot remember where his son died, that keeps people from calling him out on this lie. Until someone does Biden will continue to repeat it at every political opportunity.

10/13

Some time ago Biden engaged in destroying the careers of some Border Patrol agents based on a photo he received purportedly showing the agents whipping migrants at the border. He gave an over-acted speech, swearing retribution on these men that dare treat illegal immigrants this way. An email now surfaces that Biden and his staff were alerted some time before his speech that the report that accompanied the photo was faked, that there was no whipping of illegals taking place. Regardless, Biden went ahead, lied about what was taking place at the border and ruined these men's' career, all for what Biden saw as political profit.

10/14

Bidens' open border policy has led to the Mexican drug cartels turning human smuggling into a monstrously lucrative business. Bidens' own DHS has reported to him that the cartels have capitalized on Bidens' border policies, turning human smuggling into a billion-dollar enterprise. The DHS has warned Biden many times that human smuggling has overtaken drug trafficking as the main source of revenue for the cartels. Their income from this inhuman enterprise has grown from $500 million a year in 2018 to a staggering $13 billion this year, a 2,500% increase under Bidens' watch. Even with all this blood on his hands, Biden still has no comment.

10/15

It comes to light that, rather than being a result of his senility, Bidens' recent nascent bullying of the Saudis might just be an old tool in his repertoire. When Biden, then vice-president, threatened to withhold military support to Ukraine until the official investigating Bidens' family for corrupt business practices in that country was fired. It turns out that Bidens' bullying tactics are nothing new. When Biden was just starting his career as a lowly public official, he responded to a constituent that requested help for removing a dead dog from her lawn. Biden came to her house, picked up the dog, threw it on his constituents' porch and not only bragged about it then, but continues to boast about it even now. When looked at in a reflective light, that this feeble, brain-addled incompetent, a bully at heart and thug in practice, could rise to such a level of power, may be more a comment on the current soul of America than on the character of this shallow incompetent.

10/16

Recently Biden re-iterates his claim that high fuel prices are a necessary component of his intent of turning America into what he calls a "green energy" country. Actually, Bidens' energy policies and those of other Marxist countries have had the opposite effect of promoting 'green energy', almost all failing badly. Not only are poor nations like India, China, Indonesia, Philippines and Vietnam turning their coal plants back on, so too are supposedly rich nations like Germany, Netherlands and France as their need for a more reliable power source grows. It is possible that in his current mental state Biden does not realize that, once again, what he claims as an achievement not only proves his critics correct but underscores yet another of Bidens' abysmal failures.

10/17

Biden announces that he is opening a portal for people seeking relief from their student loan debts. Biden claims that 40 million Americans will get student loan forgiveness through the program. Once again initiating class warfare, Biden brags that ninety percent of that relief will go to the middle class, people making less than $75,000 per year and nothing will go to those in the top 5 percent of earners.

Bidens' ignorance is clearly on display when he claims that it is the "middle class" that will benefit from this, as it will be the middle class that will bear the brunt of this, Bidens' latest vote-grabbing boondoggle.

10/18

Biden tries to take credit for falling gas prices, claiming that gas has fallen below $3/gallon in some states. Unfortunately for him, at the same time AAA issues a report that states there is not a single state in the union where gas prices are less than $3/gallon. Biden further claims that he has issued more permits for gas and oil drilling than any other President has in a long time. Where he s doing this is unclear, as Biden has issued permits for oil and gas drilling on the smallest amount of federal land since the 1940s. Fabrications? Exaggerations? Lies? Whichever, Bidens nurses should do a better job of prepping him before letting Biden wander close to a microphone.

10/19

Mayra Flores, a House member representing the state of Texas, rips both Biden and Harris over their open-border policy and the irreparable harm it's done to her state. At one point Flores calls Harris "completely useless". She points out that Harris has yet to visit the border to see what Bidens' polices have done to her state. This is true: outside of a brief visit to El Paso, a city miles away from the front lines of the crisis. Yes Harris, Americas' "Border Czar" has yet to visit the southern border in any meaningful way. The Congresswoman rhetorically asks Biden and Harris how many more immigrants have to die before they visit the border even as a show that they actually care about Texas and its' immigration problems. Biden and Harris have no comment.

10/20

Biden acknowledges that his student loan forgiveness program is facing numerous legal challenges and blames Republicans for this. Biden says that the Republicans are attempting to "...deny relief to their own constituents," Biden also called Republicans "hypocritical" for opposing his plan while supporting a $2 trillion tax cut for "wealthy Americans and corporations", a tax cut that seems to exist nowhere but in the growing grayness of Bidens' mind.

10/21

In what seems desperate attempt to curtail rising gas prices right before the mid-term elections, Biden signs an order to release another 15 million barrels of oil from Americas' Strategic Oil Reserve, the reserve that is kept on hand in case of a drastic national emergency. Bidens' insistence that this is not a political move waxes hollow even to his die-hard supporters. Even more ridiculous, it is estimated that Bidens' order will provide, at best, a 3 cent reduction in the price of a gallon of gas. In Bidens' 'Sophies Choice' between keeping America safe from its' enemies and a low-brow, pandering political trick, Biden chooses the trick and the .005 saving at the gas pump for America.

10/22

Biden uses a press conference to insult all of the Republicans in Congress. Biden calls them hypocrites for attempting to block his student loan forgiveness program when they passed tax-cut legislation for the benefit of who Biden calls the wealthy 10% of Americans. What Bidens' nurses should do is take this feeble old man by the hand and gently explain to him that Bidens' 'wealthy 10% -ers pay between 70% - 75% of all income taxes collected each year. Therefore it only makes sense that any tax cuts would benefit those that actually pay the taxes more than those that don't. Hopefully, and if his nurse want to increase Bidens' chances of understanding this difficult math, they pass this information to him before 4:30 in the afternoon.

10/23

Biden announces support for providing confused minors with irreversible sex change treatments. These include puberty blockers, chemical castration and the removing of healthy sex organs, or what is often euphemistically called "gender affirming care." When asked if he thought states should have the right to ban this 'gender-affirming health care', Biden responds: "I don't think any state or anybody should have the right to do that, as a moral question and a legal question." Biden repeats this opinion later, saying that he opposes states restricting access to irreversible sex-change treatment for minors, calling these states "outrageous" and "immoral." Of course a state can't be either outrageous or immoral, which makes it a safe bet Biden doesn't know what these big words mean, either.

10/24

Bidens' prediction that there would be legal challenges to his 'Student Loan Forgiveness' program comes true. People ranging from State AGs to regular taxpayers file a myriad of lawsuits seeking to block the program, Biden at first admits he signed the an EO initiating the program, Then, under increasing criticism, Biden backtracks and claims that Congress passed the SLF program into law "... by a vote or two." Yet another interesting lie by Biden, since to date no legislation concerning Bidens' program has been presented to Congress to vote on.

10/25

Biden, almost painfully by now, publicly embarrasses himself again in a MSNBC interview. He informs a reporter that it is his intention to run for President again in 2024. When asked if his wife supports his decision, Biden leans back and closes his eyes, appearing to fall asleep. Startled, the interviewer gasps, which wakes Biden back up. The reporter asks again if Bidens' wife supports his decision to run again. Again Biden appears to fall asleep and many embarrassing seconds pass before he wakes up and with stumbling speech which includes a lot of "uh"s, finally mutters that, yes, his wife does support his decision because she believes "...that we're... that we're doing something very important..." and looks as if he's about to drift off again. Startled more than embarrassed, the reporter mercifully ends the interview.

10/26

The blow back from Bidens' consistent attacks on Americas' fuel and energy industries continue to haunt him. Now Americans are facing a painful winter because of Biden. A new report from the Consumer Energy Alliance (CEA) points to a report from Biden's own Energy Information Administration (EIA) about the skyrocketing cost of energy. The report shows that consumers will shell out over $14 billion more on electricity and heating this winter compared to last, another punch in the gut to Americans already struggling with the rising cost of living that Biden has caused.

10/27

As the dust begins to clear on Bidens' $2 trillion American Rescue Plan, which was sold as "pandemic relief", it is apparent that it was little more than a funnel to slide the majority of the money over to Bidens left-wing priorities. Even some Democrats are admitting that Bidens' reckless spending sprees unleashed devastating inflation on the country. One of them, a Congressman, admitted publicly that "...all of us knew this (hyper inflation) would be the case when (Biden) put in place his recovery program(s). Any time you put more money into the economy, prices tend to rise." Now that's a giant "Duh"for Biden to consider when he wakes up.

10/28

In more bad news for Biden, a watchdog group has been combing through his son Hunters' laptop emails. They even created a website that allows anyone to search through these emails. After a year of investigating the laptop, this watchdog group claims they've found evidence that Hunter Biden committed at least 459 violations of federal and state law in his career They've released a massive 630-page report that documents each of the crimes allegedly committed by Hunter. Even if they are off by a factor of two, this means that Bidens' son was involved in hundreds of crimes that, to this day, Biden swears he was unaware of.

10/29

No matter how often Biden is called on it – and there are dozens' examples of it – Bidens' congenital lying continues. Bidens' latest is his tear-tugging account of how he romanced his wife. Biden claims that, upon first meeting her, he was so enamored that Biden gave up his starting position on his high school varsity football team and a promising football career, just to spend more time with her. As most have come to expect, one, Biden never played varsity football, let alone start on his high school team and two, Biden barely made the freshman team and, three, Biden didn't quit the team for the love of his future bride, but because his father made him quit so Biden could spend more time on his academics, in which he was failing.

10/30

Bidens' other congenital trait, unapologetic hypocrisy, rises again. Recently Biden labeled an attack on the spouse of a Democratic Congresswoman a blatant example of political violence and the sole province of radical Republicans. However, when a volunteer working for a Republican Senate candidate is attacked by Biden supporters and beaten so badly that he will need facial reconstructive surgery, Biden is silent. To be fair, if the nurses who read the news to Biden each day left this particular story out, it is possible that Biden is honestly unaware of it.

10/31

With Biden sporting an approval rating deeply underwater in key battleground states, Democrats are hoping Obama will ride to their rescue in the midterms. Many states have imposed stricter voter identification laws, adding some restrictions to mail-in ballots Some of these same states also enacted laws that facilitate the de-listing of voters who should no longer be on the voting rolls. Biden, maintains that these efforts are nothing more than an attempt by Republicans to keep minorities from voting. This is another of Bidens' backhanded racist comments. Biden feels that minorities can never do difficult tasks, like acquiring a valid ID or pulling a lever in a voting booth with out help from the 'Chief Whitey' himself, Biden.

11/1

Biden has always refused to face reality, but he may not be able to dodge it much longer. No amount of spin will change the fact the economy has taken a nosedive from his disastrous policies. Mortgage rates have doubled in the last year, gas prices are still up as much as 70% from where they were before Biden took office and inflation is running at 8.3%, still a historical40-year highs. As if this wasn't enough, a new poll predicts that as many 40% of Hispanics and 21% of blacks, normally a lock for Democratic votes, might be voting Republican in the upcoming election.

11/2I

n another of his endless displays of hypocrisy, Biden and his staff rail against the Governor of Arizona for stacking large shipping containers along a hole in the border wall to stop illegal immigrants from crossing. Biden claims that placing the containers there constitutes trespassing by the Governor on federal land. Yet, for the reported 300,000 illegals that have crossed at that point and have actually trespassed on American soil, Biden adjusts his Aviators and has no comment.

11/3

At a national scare-people-to-vote-Democrat rally thinly disguised as a national press conference, Biden rants that "...overwhelming majority of Americans believe (their) democracy is at risk, that (their) democracy is under threat..." because Trump has refused to accept the results of the 2020 election. In yet another example of Bidens' blind hypocrisy, he sees no threat to American democracy from such notables as Stacy Abrams not accepting her loss in a Governors' race, or Hillary Clinton in her failed presidential campaign that she blames, to this day, on a Russian collusion hoax she actually created.

11/4

In an attempt to shore up support for Biden and other Democrats in the upcoming midterm elections, Hillary Clinton intimates that Republicans were poised for a big 2022 midterm success. This, according to Clinton, because the American people are too dumb to realize they are on the verge of losing their democracy unless they vote Democrat. Even Biden realizes, if it's earlier than 4:30 in the afternoon, that attacking the voters as not being intelligent enough to understand their own interests is not a winning campaign message. This is the kind of 'help' Biden, with his approval rating in the '30s, does not need.

11/5

Democrats are realizing that it might've been a mistake to have Biden campaign for them in this election cycle In the most recent embarrassment at a Florida -get-out-the-vote rally, Bidens' cognitive decline was on full display. First, he said that he has no "...greater friend in the United States Senate" than the woman who introduced him at the rally. Trouble is, the lady was a former Congresswoman who never served in the Senate and had not served in Congress for almost two decades. Biden then repeated his old lie that his late son Beau was killed in Iraq, even though he actually died in the U.S. of cancer six years after his deployment ended. To add to the humiliation that Biden evidently was not even aware of, the Governor of Florida joked that Biden's appearance in his state was an in-kind contribution to the Governors' own re-election campaign.

11/6

In what should be Bidens' most demoralizing defeat to date, two of his journalist supporters turn on him and ask that because of his increasing cognitive impairments Biden should not seek re-election in 2024. The first article appeared in the New York Post, the second in the Washington Post. The reporters wrote that Bidens' growing senility represented a problem for Democrats. Using the episode where Biden claimed his student loan forgiveness scheme was passed by Congress, forgetting that he actually rammed it through himself via a EO, the reporters called Biden' memory failure "frightening,". and due to his obvious mental decline, the reporters suggest Biden leave politics for good on inauguration day, Fair, but one has to ask, where were these reporters the last two years

11/7

Demonstrating that he cannot learn from his own history, Biden lashes out at American oil and gas companies again for the energy disaster he created. Biden is threatening oil and gas companies with a new "windfall profits tax" if they don't increase production and decrease prices at the pump. This is the same move Carter made during his failed presidency. Carter instituted a windfall profits tax on oil companies during the 1970s energy crisis. As expected, this only made oil and gasoline more expensive, reduced supplies and did not bring in the promised tax revenue. By Biden proposing this same disastrous tax in the middle of an energy crisis and inflationary period, Biden seems intent on upstaging Carter by bringing Carters' past historic failures up to the present.

11/8

Due mainly to Bidens' disastrous economic policies on all fronts and Americans dissatisfaction with them, Republicans take over control of the House. Also, across the country many states replace formerly Democrat-help positions with Republicans. However, the sweep was not as expansive as was predicted. Biden touts this as a victory and intimates that he has a "mandate" to double down on his past ruinous policies in the future.

11/9

Biden shoulders the main responsibility for losses that his Democrats took in the primaries. Not only unpopular due to disastrous foreign and domestic policies and viewed as seriously mentally diminished,

Biden seems oblivious to the damage his gaffes do to the reputation of the Democrat party. Bidens' latest was a last-minute 'get-out-the-vote ' rally in Southern California one day before the midterms. There, to the dismay of his nurses, Biden announced his intention to shut down coal plants "...all over the country..." To say this the day before elections, with Democrats running in coal-dependent states makes Bidens' nurses just drop their heads into their hands. They realize from now on Biden will have to be watched 24 hours a day.

11/10

Bidens' lying has become so pervasive even some of his supporters are calling him out. One of his former media friends apparently has had enough. He reported that just in his last speech alone Biden lied three times and they were whoppers. The first was about gas being \$5/gallon when he took office when it was \$2.39. Biden then lied about cutting the deficit in half. The deficit did fall in 2021 and 2022, but not because of anything Biden did. It fell mostly because Bidens' grotesque pandemic spending relief packages ended when Congress scheduled them to when making them a law. Finally and in the same speech, Biden lied about Trumps' 2017 tax cuts benefiting only the top one percent of Americans. Actually, 82% of middle class households saw a tax cut and 90% of Americans saw an increase in take home pay. Three more Biden lies, all in just one speech. Someone could have a full-time job, just trying to keep up.

11/11

In just one month the Border Patrol intercepted 46,000 illegal aliens at the Del Rio section of the border. Bidens' policy of turning illegals loose even if caught has created a magnet. for illegal aliens all over the world. Eye witnesses report that illegals are "...just walking in this single file line, willing to give themselves up and surrender to the Border Patrol..." because they know once they step foot across the border, Biden will have them released somewhere in the U.S. rather than deport them. It is estimated that between 2.000.000 and 3,000,000 illegals have been released into the US since Biden took office.

11/12

A report reveals that the fallout hasn't ended from Bidens' disastrous exit from Afghanistan which caused 13 American soldiers and thousands of Afghan citizens to die. The report reveals that Biden has given over $1 billion in humanitarian aid to Afghanistan's Taliban government since the 8/21 withdrawal, making America the single largest financial supporter of this murderous terrorist group. Biden is silent about how this American taxpayers $1 billion is/was spent. Biden's Afghanistan failure marks the lowest point for America abroad since Obama left the Situation Room in the middle of the 2012 attack on the American embassy in Benghazi, leaving Americans Ambassador Christopher Stephens and others to be raped and murdered by terrorists.

11/13

Biden is asked about the organization 'Doctors Without Borders' actively handing out road maps of common routes illegal aliens can take to enter the United States. These maps delineate safe routes and rest stops for the illegals on their way to entering the U.S. Biden claims that this organization has not received government funding in 20 years. This is true, but is asked if they do receive massive funding from Biden-supporting tech giants such as Google, Microsoft and Amazon. Biden has no comment.

11/14

While Bidens' apparent senility might be an excuse for his fumbling behavior, reporters are starting to lay into Harris who has no such excuse for hers, other than outright incompetence. One reporter released a column where he listed all the times the VP "...took verbal detours around coherent thoughts and complete sentences...". He continued by echoing another critic who said that Harris sounds like someone giving a book report on a book she has not read. Another wag states that Harris, lacking natural talent, needs to prepare but evidently doesn't, her "complacency and arrogance (making for her) a ruinous compound." He concludes by writing that while it's evident that Biden is far past his prime, Harris never had one.

11/15

During a late campaign stop at a black college, Biden stuns a crowd by patronizing the black student body, telling them that they were just as smart as students in other schools. Taken together with Bidens' remark that, unlike Hispanics, Black people all think alike and were incapable of independent thought, then admonishing them that anyone of them who voted for Trump was not authentically Black and then when Obama was running for president, Biden quipping that it was nice for a change to have a black candidate who was "...clean and articulate..."., all of these together reminded everyone about Bidens' decades-long history of making racist remarks and yet never seeming to pay a price for them.

11/16

Trump announces that he is running again for the presidency in 2024 and Biden uses the announcement it as an excuse to have his DOJ appoint partisan pit bull Jack Smith as Special Counsel to oversee the multiple witch hunts slapped on Trump. Bidens' AG claims that it is in the public interest to appoint a Special Counsel in order to assure both independence and accountability in particularly sensitive matters, like going after Trump. Biden approves this, since it allows prosecutors and agents to continue their Trump witch hunts expeditiously, which Biden feels can only help him in his 2024 re-election bid.

10/17

Biden defends his allowing a Special Council being appointed to co-ordinate the witch hunt pursuits of Trump, saying it will allow prosecutors and agents to continue their work and make decisions "...indisputably guided only by the facts and the law..." Trump then asks that if his, Trumps, stated interest in running for president allowed Bidens' AG to appoint a Special Counsel to investigate him, why doesn't that also mean Bidens' AG must appoint a Special Counsel to continue the criminal investigation into Bidens' son Hunter, who has been involved in far more criminal activities than Trump? Biden has no comment.

11/18

Biden attempts to dismiss accusations of his long-held racist attitude, To this end, Biden demands that reporters transcribe exactly the quote attributed to him about Obama, which was: "I mean, you got the first mainstream African-American who is articulate and bright and clean and a nice-looking guy, I mean, that's a storybook, man." The reporters glance at each other, not sure why Biden thought this would help him. Then Biden is reminded about a statement made in 2006, where he bemoaned the fact that he couldn't go into a 7-11 anywhere in Delaware without running into someone with an Indian accent working behind the counter. Incredibly, Biden has moved from Senator to Vice Presidency to president in spite of these remarks when the media would have hounded a Republican out of office for just one of them.

11/19

Bidens' attempt to buy young votes by forgiving approximately $400 billion dollars in student loan debt hits a snag. A federal judge was not amused with Biden exploiting a 9/11 era law to claim the COVID emergency gave Biden the right to steal $400 billion and hand it out to potential Democrat Party voters. In the judges' opinion, Bidens' unconstitutional action was either one of the largest delegations of legislative power to the executive branch, or one of the largest exercises of legislative power without congressional authority in the history of the United States. The judge then admonishes Biden, reminding him that America is not a country that is ruled by an all-powerful executive with a pen and a phone, but by a Constitution. Conservatives rue the day that this judge wasn't around when Obama appointed himself dictator, declaring that all he needed to rule was only a "...pen and a phone..."

11/20

In an action that he would not dare when Trump was President, the fat pajama-boy dictator of North Korea fired an intercontinental ballistic missile that landed near Japanese waters. It was his second major weapons test this month that showed a potential ability to launch nuclear strikes on the U.S. mainland. It' Harris, not Biden, who meets with the leaders of South Korea, Japan, Australia, Canada and New Zealand to discuss the launch. She quickly condemns the launch and assures these American allies that Biden will take all necessary measures to guarantee their safety, just as soon as he wakes up from his nap.

11/21

Since Biden stepped into the White House, North Koreas' fat pajama-boy dictator has fired between 60 to70 missiles of all sizes, armaments and distances, some of them falling alarmingly close to US allies. Biden is reminded that, after Trump warned FPBD that he wold blow him off the face of the planet if he conducted any missile tests towards any US allies, the FPBD fired nary a missile during the rest of Trumps' presidency. Biden is warned that his cowardly non-response to North Koreas' latest aggression will only embolden other garbage dictators around the world to take advantage of Bidens's weak spine. Trembling, Biden has no comment.

11/22

Elon Musk buys Twitter and promises it will become a true free-speech platform, so Biden sics his FTC on him. Biden is "concerned"" over recent developments at Twitter and insists that the FTC has a right to harass Musk because no CEO or company is "above the law" Biden says that Musk must follow the FTCs' revised consent decrees, "revised" since Musk bought Twitter. These "revised" orders gives Biden and his FTC new tools to "ensure compliance". Musk and all others must see these "revised consent decrees"as nothing more than a bald-faced threat to show Musk and others that they'd better not step out of line, very reminiscent of when Obama and Biden used the IRS to cripple the Tea Party.

11/23

Biden – again – brays that the American economy is strong and growing, but numbers from his own Labor Department dispute this.The Consumer Price Index (CPI) rose 0.4% from September while inflation is up 7.7% from this time last year. Food purchases climbed by 0.4% from the previous month with a 12.4% increase year-over-year. The inflation report showed that grocery store prices are continuing to rise despite Bidens false claims otherwise. The rising prices continue hamstring working class Americans struggling to make ends meet in Biden's America, with one in every five Americans doubting they'll have enough money to cover the cost of their traditional Thanksgiving meal.

11/24

Thanksgiving day in the US. About the only thing Americans can be thankful for today is that they will be able to afford at least some of their traditional Thanksgiving meal. While all are struggling with the rising cost of living in Bidens' America, he still maintains that he is getting inflation under control. Biden tries to tout his wildly misnamed $740 billion "Inflation Reduction Act", claiming it was somehow bringing down prices, even as prices continue to rise. Even die-hard Marxists like Bernie Sanders admit that Bidens' IRA won't do anything to help with inflation. As Americans put an ever-decreasing amount of food on their Thanksgiving tables, they realize this is the new reality of a holiday season in Bidens' America.

11/25

Biden announces plans to significantly tighten regulations against all causes of methane emissions in America, in Bidens' mind a key contributor to his view of a 'climate crisis.' Unfortunately, Biden is not content to stop at cutting methane emissions caused by fossil fuels. Ludicrously, Biden is targeting cows – yea, cows - yes, cows) because Biden believes that bovine flatulence, from both ends of the animal, contribute greatly to climate change by emitting methane into the atmosphere. Bidens' new measure to combat cow farts was unveiled, at great embarrassment to the US, at the United Nations Climate Change Conference. It did give the attendees there something else to laugh at besides Bidens Aviators, which he insisted on wearing even indoors.

11/26

Bidens insistence on focusing his energies on cow flatulence continues to bring howls of derision that Biden seems to be blissfully unaware of. Embarrassing for the country, true, but perhaps Americans can be thankful for one small blessing: Even though Biden is unable to come to grips with inflation, his debacle in Afghanistan, historic illegal immigration and a ruined economy, all of which Biden caused, it is at least a little reassuring that his Ensure - addled mind can focus on at least one issue, even if it's only cow farts.

11/27

A report that was written some time ago re-surfaces, is eerily prescient. In it a former Afghan ally wrote that Biden's' disastrous withdrawal plan from Afghanistan, besides leaving thousands of unnecessary dead, emboldened American enemies like Russia and China to capitalize on Bidens' weakness. The reporter predicted that Bidens' Afghan disaster would give Russia an incentive to attack Ukraine and China to attack Taiwan. Shortly after Bidens' Afghan disaster, Russia did invade the Ukraine and China began stepping up its aggression towards Taiwan, both sensing an opportunity with Biden in the White House. Finally, the reporter predicts that because of Bidens' chaotic withdrawal, former allies like Japan and South Korea would look for other allies, not being able to depend on the U.S. any longer. When reviewed today, this reporter had Bidens' incompetence and it's subsequent result pinned exactly right

11/28

In the Georgia Senate run-off race, the Democratic hopeful is hopeful that neither Biden or Harris, with their 38% approval ratings, parachute in within 100 miles of any of his campaign appearances, allowing him to keep the election as a referendum on Trump. If Harris or Biden show up, chutes unfurled, the campaign will shift to a referendum on Biden and Harris, which might cost him the election. He does invites Obama to campaign with him, but not Biden nor Harris.

11/29

With Bidens' approval, Tim Cook, the head of Apple computers and one of Bidens' biggest supporters, directs the use of his software in China to help the Communists suppress free speech and protests. When asked about the morality of this, Biden insists that Apple is a private company and Biden does not think he should get involved with private business decisions. Then Biden is asked what the difference is between Apple and Twitter, a company Biden has sent the entire weight of his administration, including the DOJ, after for some of its' "private business decisions" he doesn't agree with. Biden has no comment.

11/30

Biden sends spokesmen out to defend his two-faced handling of Twitter and Apple and their "private business decisions". Bidens' spokesmen insist that the intrusion of Biden into Twitters' business dealings is different than that of Apple because it involves possible investment by and thus possible interference from by foreign companies. Then the question is raised that if this is the benchmark, what could be more intrusive than working with a communist country to suppress free speech and political protests? Biden has no comment.

12/1

In an effort to blunt Trump and other Republicans' growing popularity in the Spanish community, Bidens' FCC allows George Sorors, a fervent Biden backer and a 'one world government' ideologue, to purchase major Spanish speaking radio stations in major American cities. This Soros-backed group will now own Spanish-language stations in cities like New York, Chicago, Dallas, Houston, Las Vegas, Los Angeles, and San Antonio. The move will help Biden target Hispanic voters with left-wing propaganda in an effort to shore up Bidens' massive decline in his approval rating among Hispanic voters.

12/2

It turns out that Bidens' claim that he averted a rail strike by coming to terms with the unions was just so much political posturing. What really happened was that union bosses forced their members to buck up and accept Bidens' deal just to get him through the midterm elections. Now it's possible that the whole thing will unravel as many of the affected unions never agreed to Bidens' plan. If it does unravel, it could mean a $2 billion-a-day economic impact on the American economy. Biden, presumably hiding in his Delaware basement, has no comment.

12/3

Speaking of Bidens' regular hiding place, the Department of Defense, Secret Service and other government records show that Biden has taken over 100 flights between his basement in Delaware and the White House, for a total of at least 185 days in his basement since he took office. This means that not only has Biden cost the taxpayers as much as 20 million dollars in taxpayer-funded airfare, he has spent over a quarter of his presidency in hiding. So much for the Aviators, rumored now he wears even in bed, making him look tough.

12/4

Going into the Midterm elections, Biden released millions of barrels of oil from the Strategic Petroleum Reserve (SPR) in a bid to lower gas prices to boost Democrats politically. With the midterm elections over and the SPR, which was established for actual emergencies, at its lowest level since 1984, it is hoped that Biden will stop siphoning emergency fuel from it. Unfazed, Bidens' new solution for the fuel crisis he created in America is to lift sanctions against Venezuela, opening the door for oil imports from this socialist dictatorship and no friend to America. This adds another country to the list of Communist countries that Biden prefers to do business with, rather than let America drill for its' own oil.

12/5

Insisting that this is not an accurate take on his actions, Biden defends his decision to enrich Communist dictatorships around the world by buying their energy, saying that he has Americas' best interests at heart. A reporter asks Biden then, if this so why did Biden shut down drilling on oil-rich federal lands the first day he occupied the White House? Also. didn't he recently tell an, environmental activist that there is no more drilling going on in America, "period", and won't be as long as he is president despite the energy crisis gripping the country? As usual, Biden is hurried from the stage by his nurses, making no comment

12/6

A new report further contradicts Bidens' claims about energy exploration in America, claiming that Biden has issued the fewest acres of federal land for drilling since the 1940's by closing off federal land and clamping down on issuing drilling permits. Biden claims his shutting down of energy drilling in America will help clean up the environment. Yet in another in an un-ending stream of hypocrisies, Biden has no problem using the oil produced from the dirtier, environment-damaging Venezuelan production rather than using the more environmentally-friendly American oil industry methods. It's clear that in going to America's enemies for their oil instead of unleashing American energy production, Biden doesn't give a damn about either the American oil industry or the environment.

12/7

Biden comes under fire for siding with radical environmentalists that want to destroy Maine's lobster industry. hey allege that lobster fishermen endanger a rare whale that can become entangled in their fishing gear. According to the lobster industry, there hasn't been a documented case of a whale being entangled in any fishing gear since

2004 and no death has ever been attributed to lobster gear. These facts apparently have to affect on Biden since Biden decides to side with the environmental extremists. Of course, ever the hypocrite, it also did not stop Biden from ordering 200 Maine lobsters flown in for a White House soiree he hosted.

12/8

Criticism of Bidens' attacks on the lobster industry intensifies. Biden is reminded that while running for president in 2020, he pledged to "… protect the livelihood and safety of the fishing community..." This was in reference to the lobster industry., but to date Biden has not taken a single action to make good on his promise. Biden cannot espouse being a president for working people while overseeing the destruction of an entire blue-collar industry, which Bidens' new whale conservation measures are doing. Lobster fishermen implore Biden to meet with Maine's congressional delegation and leaders of the lobster industry to find common sense solutions that will ensure that Maine's lobster and fishing industries and the right whales will survive for generations. So far, Biden has turned a deaf ear – or in his case, both ears – to this request.

12/9

In what might be Bidens' most insane politically motivated move yet. Biden orders the release of Victor Bout, a notorious arms merchant possibly responsible for hundreds of thousand s of deaths, to Russia in exchange for Brittney Griner, the American basketball player caught smuggling drugs into Russia. Biden claims he had no choice but to bring Griner home but leaves the other American, Paul Whelan. When asked why he had "no choice" but to bring Griner home in exchange for a murderous arms dealer, but leave Whelan there, Biden has no answer.

12/10

Criticism of Bidens' latest blunder comes swiftly from both sides. Critics on both sides point to an interview Bout did short; y after being released form prison. In it Bout reveals that he "wholeheartedly" supports Moscow's military operation in Ukraine and that if he had the opportunity and necessary skills, he would "...certainly go as a volunteer." Bout was serving a 25-year prison sentence in the United States on charges of conspiring to kill Americans, acquire and export anti-aircraft missiles and provide material support to a terrorist organization. This is the man Biden released back into the world for a leftist pothead who believes the National Anthem should not be played anymore before her basketball games; another great choice by Biden.

12/11

Biden continues his war on Elon Musk. Ever since Musk completed his purchase of Twitter and started restoring previously banned accounts – like Trump's – Biden has begun to panic over the fact that he has lost his power to control censorship on this platform. Biden and his allies now threaten to investigate Musk's purchase on the grounds that it could "... raise national security implications." On exactly what these "national security issues" might be, Biden, not surprisingly, has no comment.

12/12

After being imprisoned in Russia for nearly 10 months, Brittney Griners' return to the US included a stop at a Texas military medical facility for a routine evaluation. Biden and his State Department claim that they are now focused on ensuring that Griner and her family's well-being are "prioritized" and that all available assistance will be "...offered to them..." Critics note that Biden has given almost no money or time to the millions suffering because of him on southern border, one time even saying he has "...more important things to do..." than visit the place where his policies have wreaked such suffering and havoc. The reporter suggests if those suffering along the border were more like the constituents Biden favors like, say a black, gay, pot using female that makes disparaging remarks about America, maybe they would be "prioritized" also.

12/13

Biden throws a hissy fit because his vaccine mandate for members of the U.S. military is on the chopping block in Congress. Speaking through his press secretary, Biden slams Republicans for trying to rescind his mandate, calling it a mistake and claiming that they (the Republican) rather fight against the health of the troops than protect them. Biden continues the lie that vaccinations work and save lives, despite overwhelming, worldwide medical evidence that the COVID vaccines are little more than poor pharmaceuticals that do not prevent keep people from getting re-infected. Not content with just lying, Biden hints that he may refuse to sign any bill that reaches his desk if it contains language rescinding his mandate. People seem to have already forgotten that Bidens' voodoo-medicine vaccine mandate was responsible for kicking 8,000 troops out of the military and threatened the livelihoods of up to 60,000 more service members who also did not want to get vaccinated.

12/14

Biden continues to be the recipient of much suppressed laughter – and some not so suppressed - as once again, Biden has to be led off a stage by a young girl after a speech at a Toys for Tots event. Biden can be heard asking the youngster: "Which way do we go?" as she takes his hand and walks him in the right direction. His supporters are relieved because this 'lost' episodes wasn't as bad as his April 'shaking hands with invisible people ' incident after a speech in North Carolina. To make Bidens' embarrassing day worse, Congressman James Comer, set to take over the House Oversight Committee in January, announced that one of his first acts will be to investigate Biden's involvement with his sons' Hunter's corrupt foreign business ventures. Also, Comer makes it clear that this investigation will not be about Bidens' son alone, but also about Biden himself.

12/15

Biden declares that the new 'Protection of Marriage' Bill just passed by Congress was necessary to insure that a gay couple couldn't "... be married in the morning and thrown out of a restaurant (later) ... for being gay". Reporters try to ask Biden for an example of where this has happened recently anywhere in the in the United States. Biden ignores the question, also purposely ignoring what this bi-partisan bill unlocks; that is, an unabashed attack on every religious organization for their sincerely held religious beliefs regarding marriage. The Bill passed without an amendment proposed by Mike Lees which would have prevented the government from retaliating against religious institutions and individuals for their religious beliefs concerning marriage. Biden, as is his custom, leaves the stage without taking any questions.

12/16

Specifying that gender identification is an important part of his commitment to diversity, Biden and his officials OK the hiring of a 'non-binary' person to work as a nuclear waste official in the Department of Energy. Unfortunately this one person has now been detained twice for attempting to steal luggage in an airport. After the first incident, this solid citizen claimed that he accidentally took someone elses luggage, but the fact that he did not check any luggage on his flight debunks this. This prominent Biden employee may be confused about his sex but everyone else is pretty sure now he is a thief and a liar.

12/17

With this latest Biden embarrassment supplied by his Energy Department luggage thief, a reporter suggests that Biden should focus more on character than gender identification when evaluating employees. Biden has no comment. Besides, since Biden recent career includes lying, abandoning thousands of people, including 13 American servicemen, to die in Afghanistan, besides arming the most dangerous terrorist organizations in the world with billions of dollars of American weaponry and is rumored to repeatedly take a piece of the 'take' once his drug addled son grifts it from various world leaders while Biden family members are working with the Chinese Communist party for years, perhaps 'character' is not in the forefront of Bidens' mind, if anything is.

12/18

A video surfaces showing a migrant caravan of over 1,000 people crossing illegally into El Paso in a single night. This is the largest single group to cross at this location at one time. The Border Patrol now has over 5,000 in custody and has released hundreds more to city streets. This happened just days after Biden said he would not visit the border while in Arizona because "there are more important things going on." A reporter asks Biden, more important than visiting the area where your polices have allowed over 5 million illegal aliens and untold amounts of Fentanyl and other drugs, which have caused so much misery in America, to cross? Biden has no comment.

12/19

Blow back for Bidens' decision to swap a notorious international arms dealer for a basketball player continues, with even some of his supporters calling it "madness." Even Bidens' own DOJ thought the swap was a bad deal, given the disparity in crimes committed by Griner and Bout. Despite Bidens' denials, multiple reports suggest that Biden was given the choice by the Kremlin, but he chose to take Griner over Whelan, the other American being held there, in the trade for Bout. It is obvious that giving away one of the most dangerous men in the world for a woke basketball player will only embolden hostile countries to take more Americans hostages, a matter Biden is either unaware or unconcerned about.

12/20

Biden puts together a scheme to ignore and get around various state' laws putting restrictions on abortion. This scheme by Biden is intended to try and keep abortions – on – demand available. In his scheme, Biden intends to turn Federal facilities into abortion clinics since, Biden believes, states have no authority over what goes on in Federal facilities. Biden uses the VA as an example, like the VA for example. This might be difficult for Biden to pull off, since the VA, even though a Federal facility, has no legal authority to violate state abortion laws just because its on federal property. Once again Biden is abusing his power, trying to ram another aspect of his extreme agenda down the throats of Americans.

12/21

Bidens' attempt to sneak a law through that would allow federal facilities like the VA to perform abortions engenders immediate push back. Conservatives and even some Democrats voice their opposition, saying that the VA should remain committed to providing care for veterans and not be used as a political tool by Biden to provide taxpayer-funded abortions. This stunt by Biden is the latest subversion in a long line of actions by Biden that point to his conceited contempt for the law. Some even call Bidens' latest stunt "shameful". Accurate, but only effective if one can feel shame and Biden, demented or not, clearly can't.

12/22

Bidens' lies are being exposed so fast and so often now even some of his critics want to attribute this to Alzheimer or some other brain malfunction. Bidens' latest involves his Uncle Frank, who was awarded the Purple Heart for actions during the Battle of the Bulge, but never received the actual medal. Biden crowed that he fixed the problem when he became Vice-President, securing an actual Purple Heart medal for his uncle. Biden ends this particular tale by saying that, sadly Uncle Frank refused to accept the medal, insisting he felt guilty about receiving it while so many of his comrades died. This would be almost a tear-jerker of a a story, except Biden became Vice-President in 2008, while his uncle died in 1999.

12/23

Biden and his January 6 Committee, which consisting of a number Democrats and two Trump - hating Republicans, will allow Biden, his Justice Department and left-wing Special Counsel to bring charges against Trump "fairly", proclaiming that prosecuting him has "bipartisan support". One reporter noted that this "bipartisan" committee is made up of many of the same people who so recently initiated the Russian collusion and Ukraine impeachment hoaxes against Trump. Biden has no comment.

12/24

Biden has always claimed that climate change and the danger of carbon emissions are a deep concern of his and a major challenge for the planet. Even so, this doesn't stop Biden from allowing his Transportation Secretary taking at least 18 flights on private jets operated by the FAA, at taxpayer expense, while he lectures the rest of the populace on the damage their "carbon footprint" is doing to the country. Less one thinks these $5000/hr flights are of national importance, in September Biden

OK'd this same TS to use a private jet to travel to Canada to accept an award from a Canadian LGBTQ organization, "carbon emissions" and the American taxpayer be damned.

12/25

Biden, even though using oil from Communist countries like Russia and, Valenzuela and continuing to work with Communist China, incredibly blocks a loan for Guyana, an ally of the U.S., needed to develop its' own oil reserves in order to sell oil to, among other countries, its' ally, the U.S.: Merry Christmas, America.

12/26

Incurring Bidens' wrath, the Chief Justice steps in and issues an emergency order blocking Biden from ending Title 42, the Trump-era policy that allows for quick removal of illegal aliens caught crossing the border. Biden was set to end the program, which had the nation, particularly the border states, preparing for an unprecedented invasion of illegal aliens. Biden was told to expect as many as 14,000 illegals per day to cross the border if he rescinded the order. He was not persuaded and ordered the ending of Title 42 to proceed; hence Roberts' ruling. In a related matter, it was reported that the 19 states suing Biden over this got down on their collective knees to thank the Chief Justice and his court.

12/27

In Bidens' latest omni - spending bill that he forced through Congress, Biden included hundreds of millions of dollars to help Middle Eastern countries to secure their borders, but sadistically, not a dime of Bidens' latest spending spree was directed to help secure Americas' southern border, not a dime.

12/28

Biden jets off to St. Croix in the Virgin Islands to close out the year while his border crisis has border states and communities on the brink of ruin. Texas is dealing with a Biblical-type flood of illegal aliens pouring across the border in record numbers. Even the Democrat Mayor of the border town of El Paso declares a state of emergency after the city was overwhelmed by illegal aliens, most sleeping in the streets and under bridges after city and Border Patrol facilities were filled beyond capacity. As brutal as the street and bridge sleeping are, all is not rosy for Biden either. It turns out that, at this time of year, the weather in St. Croix can be warm and downright tepid.

12/29

A report comes out that both Biden and Harris were "very angry" that Twitter had not been more aggressive in de-platforming accounts of anyone who disagreed with them. For example, in the summer of 2021, Biden said social media companies were "killing people" for allowing what Biden called "vaccine misinformation" to be published. A reporter who published such "misinformation" was suspended hours after Biden's comments and kicked off the platform altogether the following month. Biden and Harris wanted companies like Twitter to "...do more..." in this regard, a clear implication that both wanted all of their perceived political foes be treated in this same manner.

12/30

Biden and Harris double down on their suggestion that social media outlets "do more" in silencing their critics and political opponents. Harris goes so far to say that she "expects" and "would require" that leaders in the social media sector would "...cooperate and work with..." both she and Biden. Harris says she and Biden need this help because, after all, she and Biden are "...concerned about national security, concerned about upholding and protecting our democracy..." and therefor expect the social media companies to do "...everything in their (social media) power to ensure that there is not a manipulation that is allowed or overlooked that is done with the intention of upending the security of our democracy..." Even though mangled in her usual spaghetti-soup command of language, Harris is unmistakably calling for social media companies to impose censorship on her and Bidens' critics.

12/31

Biden follows up his brilliant performance in 2021, where he led America into one of its' worst economies since 2008, with a unique encore: End-of-year reports from all financial institutions and indicators show that in 2022 Biden led America into the worst economy since 2008, even worse than the economies Trump led during the COVID pandemic. Incredibly, Biden accomplished this disaster even though he faced almost none of the handicaps Trump had to deal with during his time as President: Happy New Year, America.

2023

1/1

Biden begins the new year by suffering another major defeat, courtesy of the Supreme Court. States and business interests sued Biden and his administration over his illegal and unconstitutional federal vaccine mandate for firms with more than 100 workers. The Court struck down the mandate on a six to three vote, blasting Biden for attempting to impose an unprecedented power grab. The Court held that Biden tried to usurp Congress' authority by imposing a vaccine mandate and, further, if Congress wanted administrative agencies to impose a federal vaccine mandate, it would have drafted legislative language to do so.

1/2

After trying to illegally and unconstitutionally cancel 500 billion in student loan debt, Biden is back at it again. Now Biden is attempting to illegally increase SNAP (a government welfare program) benefits by $200 billion dollars. It is Bidens' latest attempt at transforming America into an even greater welfare state than it is now. With the "pandemic" over and businesses desperate for help, Biden continues to discourage able-bodied workers to return to work by showering them with tax-payer funded government cash.

1/3

Bidens' hypocrisy machine roars on. Biden claimed that Trump, who placed travel restrictions on China at the outbreak of the COVID "pandemic" because the virus was caused by a lab there, said Trump's travel restrictions were "denials, delays, and distractions, many of which were nakedly xenophobic." and "racist". Now Biden, worried about the potential emergence of new variants, announced new testing requirements for travelers coming to the U.S. from China. Beginning 1/5, anyone older than 2 years old arriving from China, Hong Kong or Macau will need to show a negative result from a COVID-19 test taken within two days of their flight. As far as calling Biden a xenophobe or racist, the American media is strangely quiet.

1/4

Biden ended 2022 with yet another vacation with his family at a luxury beach villa on St. Croix in the U.S. Virgin Islands. This added to the staggering amount of time, nearly 40%. that Biden has spent away from the White House during his presidency. Between his Delaware basement, Camp David, vacations in South Carolina, Massachusetts and five days in the U.S. Virgin Islands, Bidens time out of the White House amounts to a stunning 141 days. Presidents often take some time away from the office because of the stress of the job but, incredibly, Biden trips just to his Delaware basement alone now surpass the amount of time that Trump spent away from the White House at the same point in his term.

1/5

Biden adds insult to injury to taxpayers when, instead of delaying his latest vacation by a couple of days, he had the 4,155-page $1.7 trillion omnibus spending bill flown – at taxpayer expense - from Washington to the Virgin Islands for him to sign. Additionally, Biden is fighting tooth and nail to keep his 'Vaccine Mandate for the Military' in place despite a law passed last year invalidating it. Biden maintains that the law concerns only the four main branches of the military, but not for the National Guard and the Reserves: In an attempt to keep his 'pandemic' power grab in place, Biden insists that the vaccine mandate stay in place for these two branches of the military.

1/6

In one of his weirdest, pseudo 'prisoner exchange programs', Biden announces his CHNV "parole" program for illegal immigrants. In it Biden will accept 30,000 people each month from those four countries, as long as Mexico agrees to accept back 30,000 people from these four countries currently in the U.S. who did not use proper pathways into the US. The reporters looked confused, as no one understands how this new "parole" program changes anything of substance at the border. Biden is merely exchanging 30,000 "legal" aliens for 30,000 illegal ones, who wouldn't be available for 'trading' if they were not in America illegally in the first place. Reporters then ask Biden that if this new policy is in place now, how soon is he gong to start deporting the 30,000 illegals from these four countries per month that is stipulated. Looking as confused as ever, Biden has no comment.

1/7

The world is still trying to figure out what Biden, in another of his frequent un-lucid rants about infrastructure, meant when Biden said: "The rest of the countries the world is not a patch in our jeans." If we do what we want to do, we need to do." No one, and this means no one, is clear on what Biden was trying to say. Then Harris, when apprised that Ukraine is burning and Putin's army is rampaging across Europe, maintained that the most important crisis for her and Biden at the moment was was another gay rights bill that Biden needed to sign. In response to this a former aid to Thatcher posted: that Biden and Harris are "... living in the Twilight Zone.".Harris' only response is to remind all that anyone wanting to visit her or Biden will need to provide a negative COVID test, even children as young as two: Twilight Zone, indeed.

1/8

It is documented that in the first two years of Bidens' term, he opened the border to a mass invasion of illegal aliens, oversaw the disastrously executed withdrawal from Afghanistan that cost 13 American soldiers their lives and spent trillions on welfare schemes that pushed inflation to the highest level in more than 40 years and finished 2022 by using the cooperation of social; media groups to censor his critics. Now to start 2023, Biden socks American citizens with over $300 billion in tax increases, blatantly breaking his campaign promise that no American making less than $400,000 would see their taxes go up by one penny. It seems 2023 is not going to be a good year for Americans.

1/9

Incredibly, Biden is visiting the southern border – the border where his policies have produced four million+ plus illegal migrant encounters, record number of drug trafficking, record numbers of rapes, record number of sex trafficking, record number of migrant homelessness – for the first time since he became president. This cones a month to the day where Biden said he would not visit the border because "There are more important things going on". These "important things" have stopped Biden from visiting the border where Biden has created a humanitarian disaster, but they haven't stopped Biden from visiting his basement in Delaware 59 times - stopping for ice cream eight times - during the same time period.

1/10

Bidens' hypocrisy tour keeps on rolling. Biden criticized Trump for holding onto classified documents which, as President, Trump can declassify at any time. However, as vice-president, Biden had then lost control of classified documents that he had no authority to declassify. They were found in a closet at the **Penn Biden Center at the University** of Pennsylvania. Not exactly a safe place to stash America's most closely guarded secrets, particularly since the center receives $54 million in funding from Communist China. This breach in national security was discovered in early November, but buried by the media so as not to affect the mid-term elections.

1/11

Biden meets with the president of Mexico to "discuss"illegal immigration problems. Biden first commiserates with the hardships many illegals endure in their effort to enter America illegally. Then Biden assures the Mexican president that he will do all he can to make it easier for illegals to enter the US. For his part the Mexican president ends this "discussion" by thanking Biden for being the first US president "...in a long time..." that did not build "...even one meter of a wall..." Americans stifle rage because they've come to expect "discussions" like this when two monkeys try to date the same football.

1/12

Bidens' trip to the border town of El Paso turns out to be a fake-out job on the American public. The city leaders, all Democrats, cleaned out all possible illegal alien eyesores (all of which Biden created) in their city before Biden arrived, so as not to spoil any of Bidens' planned photo ops. Where they temporarily moved the thousands of homeless, the thousands of street-dwelling illegals, the thousands of illegals currently living under bridges and the thousands being abused by drugs, prostitution, sex trafficking and rape, is anyone's' guess. Critics accuse Biden of using his visit to the border as a setup for a mass illegal alien amnesty bill he hopes to ram through Congress in the near future. Biden has no comment.

1/13

Biden attempts to quiet the howls of derision for spiriting away classified government documents while damning Trump for allegedly doing the same thing. Biden starts by reassuring the America public that he "... take(s) classified documents and classified information seriously,." Then he repeats his oft-told lie about being a professor at the University of Pennsylvania, the relevance of how this excuses him for absconding with classified documents escaping everyone. Still fumbling, Biden assures the documents were safe because they were found in "... a box in a locked cabinet, or at least a closet." It apparently escapes Bidens' befuddled mind that a locked cabinet or closet is not a secure holding area for classified documents.

1/14

Biden continues to try to spin his way out of his stealing of classified documents when he was Vice-President. Biden now claims that, one, he had no idea he stole classified documents and, two, his lawyers returned the stolen property promptly. Despite the evidence, Biden claims that he was "surprised" to learn there were any government records stored in that office. What makes Bidens' crime worse that Trumps' is that Biden, as vice-president, did not have the power to declassify documents like Trump, as President, did. Unlike Trump, who has the right to posses classified documents he deems unclassified, Biden stealing the same documents is immediate ground for criminal prosecution.

1/15

While critics question if Bidens' DOJ will pursue criminal charges against him for stealing classified government documents, which he had no right to, as fervently as it is pursuing Trump for his 'theft' of classified documents – which he had a right to – Bidens' legal team discovers a second set of classified documents from Bidens' time as vice president. Even better than the first, they are discovered in a storage space in the garage of Bidens' home in Delaware. Biden tries to mollify the American people, saying this batch of classified documents are safe because they are housed in the same garage his vintage Corvette is and this garage is always locked. At this time, if Biden can look anymore the imbecile is anyone's' guess.

1/16

In honor of Martin Luther King day, the Marxist Senator from Georgia asks Biden to speak at the church where Martin Luther King served as pastor. Incredibly, Biden uses this honor to once again repeat the oft-refuted lie that he, too, was a civil rights activist in his youth. Even Bidens' most ardent supporters admit this is one of his great lies. To repeat this lie on a day honoring a true civil rights hero shows the depth of, not just any possible brain disorder, but Bidens' political opportunistic depravity.

1/17

In a bizarre example of 'your-defense-of the-crime-proves-your-crime', Biden supporters publish a speech of his filmed in 1987 where he admits that earlier in his career he lied about being a civil rights activist. In it Biden admits he never took part in any civil rights activities such as marches, protests, etc. So with Biden lying about this early in his career, then admitting he lied about it later, then his insistence on continually repeating the lie now - which he himself debunked - his supporters are left with a quandary: Is Biden a congenital liar or really suffering from something like early-onset dementia?

1/18

Biden declared war on American energy production on his first day in office when he shut down the Keystone XL pipeline. The numbers in terms of economic loss from this idiocy have now been verified. Bidens' own DOE reveals the extent of the economic damage that Biden caused when he pulled this project. A new congressional report reveals that completion of Keystone XL would have created between 16,149 and 59,000 jobs while delivering a positive economic impact of between $3.1 to $9.6 billion dollars. Biden ran for President claiming that he cared about working class Americans, but with a single stroke of a pen Biden wiped out thousands of good paying jobs for this same working class of Americans and deprived the country of a huge economic benefit.

1/19

Biden now comes under fire from his Democratic allies for his decision not to disclose the discovery of the classified documents illegally in his possession sooner. Even to them the hypocrisy of Bidens vow of 'transparency and professional management of the government' has been badly undercut, not to mention his fervor for prosecuting Trump for the same crime. Even these allies are asking why Biden didn't get the story out earlier and why he didn't get the full story out at once, instead leaking it one drip at a time. It's obvious that Biden killed the story earlier because of its' possible effect on the midterm elections, but as for the rest, Biden has no answer.

1/20

As part of Bidens' "Green New Deal", Americans will feel the pinch of billions of dollars in tax increases for fossil fuels. Bidens' backdoor plan to destroy the American oil and natural gas industry is to raise the price of gas to make it more expensive than solar and wind power. One part of Bidens' plan includes $6.5 billion dollars in new taxes on oil and natural gas drilling. This regressive tax will drive up the cost of household energy bills. The next part of Bidens' plan is to slap a massive tax increase on each barrel of oil imported into the United States. To make sure all are included in this scheme, Biden also punishes the coal industry by whacking Americans with a $1.2 billion tax on homes heated by coal power. Obviously Bidens' war on Americas' oil and gas industries has no end in sight.

1/21

Bidens' lie about not increasing taxes on working Americans is collapsing in a big way. First Biden targets the stock market and the retirement accounts of Americans by approving a new $74 billion tax that will decrease the ability of anyone whose retirement account contains stock to sell it for a profit. This will substantially reduce the value of household retirement accounts. If this wasn't enough, Biden also imposes a new, higher alternative minimum tax on business owners. What Bidens' feeble mind doesn't grasp is that a tax like this means that workers and consumers ultimately end up paying the price for business tax increases. This is because business owners pass the higher costs of doing business down in the form of lower wages and higher prices, which everyone but the feeble minded understand. So much for Bidens' promise of protecting Americas working middle-class.

1/22

More classified documents that Biden illegally had in his possession have been discovered in various other locations. If this wasn't bad enough, more light is being shed on Bidens' lies about his claim that he never discussed his son's shady foreign business dealings. A trove of his sons' emails – 185 emails in whole, and parts of 75 others – buttress claims that not only did Biden know about his sons' dealings, that Biden was part of a influencing-peddling scheme run by his son and brother. It seems they sold access to Biden in order to enrich themselves. In light of these developments, 2023 could be "The Year of the Lie" for Biden, something hard to achieve for a man who has been a serial liar for his entire career.

1/23

The Florida Attorney General is taking Biden to court over Bidens' questionable scheme he calls 'parole' to flood the country with illegal aliens. The AG argues that Bidens' abuse of the parole system is unconstitutional and violates federal immigration law. Illegal aliens being 'paroled' by Biden don't have a legal basis to be in the country under asylum law. According to the Florida AG, Bidens' move violates existing federal laws on mandatory detention. During the lead up to the court case, the AG discovered a shocking number of illegal aliens released into the country by Biden. He declares that the upcoming trial "will once again show that (Biden) is threatening Americans' safety by intentionally weakening our nation's border security." Biden has no comment.

1/24

Throughout the month, Bidens' OS has fielded a volley of questions from journalists on the investigation into Biden's mishandling of classified records, found by authorities at multiple unauthorized locations. These discoveries are ongoing even as Biden attempts to downplay the situation. Both he and his PS have said at least six times the search for classified documents "...was complete..." Maybe the seventh time will be the charm.

1/25

Under the heading of 'Nobody asked You' Biden announces his "guiding principles" in a "Blueprint for a Renters Bill of Rights,". Though not enforceable, Biden feels his blueprint is needed to underscore protections Biden feels every renter deserves. These include access to safe, quality, affordable housing, clear and fair leases and access to eviction prevention with the help of government lawyers and rent relief resources so non-paying tenants can remain sustainably housed. Biden also assures the non-payers that they can look to him and other government officials to ensure they know their rights and are protected from unlawful discrimination. Since these laws are on the books almost everywhere nationwide, the question again for Biden is; "Who asked you?"

1/26

With the COVID rent payment moratorium being lifted almost everywhere in America, Biden leaps into the fray with new 'suggestions' that make it possible for rent dodgers – some whom haven't paid rent in 3 years – can still live for free. First Biden will have the FTC examine a range of practices that affect the non-paying tenants, from the use of tenant background checks to how an applicant's source of income factors into housing decisions. It's the first time in history the FTC has issued a request for information of this type. In addition, Biden will have the CFPB coordinate enforcement efforts with the FTC to ensure that renters have accurate information in their credit reports and to investigate any company conducting background checks on tenants, which Biden thinks are unacceptable. All are waiting to see Biden publish "suggestions" that help landlords over the emotional problems they endure expecting deadbeats to pay their owed rent.

1/27

Before they can collect their collective breaths, Bidens' war on landlords escalates. Bidens' new 'suggestions' include the FHFA initiating a process to examine limits on rent increases. This is in addition to the actions announced by Biden last November that encourage financing of multifamily loans that, somehow guarantee affordable housing. In addition to these "suggestions", Biden will have HUD require public housing authorities and owners of Section 8 properties to provide at least 30 days advanced notice before terminating a lease due to nonpayment of rent. Finally, Biden places his last knife – for now – squarely in the backs of landlords by having the DOJ investigate what Biden feels is anti-competitive information sharing in rental markets, whatever the hell that means.

1/28

Reports from several news outlets detail that Biden and his family have approximately 150 SARs – Suspicious Activity Report - filed against them, as opposed to the vast majority of Americans who don't have even one. Congress has demanded an investigation of these SARs and the Biden crime family. However, the Treasury Department is blocking the release of these documents, saying that the release would hinder Bidens' effectiveness as President. This part is true: Knowing that a blatant criminal inhabits the White House would not instill confidence in his leadership for at least half the country and most of the world.

1/29

Biden starts to breathe a sigh of relief when informed that 12 classified documents were found in Pences' possession also. However, there is quite a difference between how Pence and Biden handled the matter. Pence immediately notified the FBI and made the discovery public, while Biden discovered the stolen materials one week before the midterm elections and hid this fact for over two months. When asked about this glaring discrepancy, Biden and his PS have no comment.

1/30

Biden takes a trip to Michigan to tout his "New Green Deal" which Biden thinks will encourage Americans to buy electric vehicles. To showcase his trip, Biden publishes a picture of him riding in a fully electric GMC Hummer. Perhaps because of his mental denseness, Biden does not realize the vehicle he is showcasing for "...the (American) future road trip..." can cost as much as $110,000, more than double the income for most of those same Americans.

1/31

Biden calls the Congressional filibuster "a relic of the Jim Crow era" and accused Trump of initiating voter reform laws that were 'Jim Crow on steroids'. Back in the early 2000's Biden threatened to use this "relic of Jim Crow" as a tool to keep a black woman who actually lived under Jim Crow from being placed on the Supreme Court Now today Biden wants to end this favorite tool of his in order to claim credit for putting the first Black woman on the Supreme Court. As Biden ha demonstrated many times the last two years, it's easy to flop down on both sides of an issue when you have no spine.

2/1

Bidens' open border immigration policy debacle - which has made every state a border state - comes nearer to home. Now it's the mayor of New York pleading with Biden to help him deal with the illegal immigrant problem in NYC. Because of Biden, there are currently 35,000 illegals in NYC, with 26000 of them being housed, some in $500/night hotels. The citizens of NYC are picking up the expense for this housing. With food included, the tab averages $650k per night. Now the migrants living in the $500/night hotels refuse to be moved to a shelter that the mayor opened on a Brooklyn waterfront, the immigrants calling the move "inhumane". It was just in December the mayor declared a state of emergency in NYC because "...there was simply nowhere to house the migrants..." The mayor is frustrated because so far Biden has turned a deaf ear to his pleas. The mayor could be over reacting here because, after all, Biden might just be napping.

2/2

Biden is so mentally inept that he can't even boast of his perceived successes in a coherent manner. In trying to brag about the amount of women he has on his staff, Biden Porky-Pigs his way through a number of incoherent phrases, finally finishing with: "...half the women on my staff are women..." When not being a hypocrite or lying about accomplishments he never accomplished, Biden can be counted on for malaprops which would be pure comedy genius, except sadly and even with the goofy grin, Biden is not trying to be funny

2/3

In what certainly would be considered treason in saner times, Biden allows a spy balloon from Communist China – a country that has stated America is its' avowed enemy – to fly over US military installations in Montana and take pictures. Bidens' excuse for not confronting China and shooting down the balloon is his concern about injuring the "populated areas" of Montana. This, even though in most parts of this state you can shoot a rifle in any direction and not hit a thing for fifty miles, except for an occasional tumble weed. Biden, in a blatant, gutless knee-bend to the Communists, now puts all Americans more at risk. The only silver lining in Bidens' treasonous act is that at least the tumble weeds in Montana are safe.

2/4

Biden, on his knees and mouth open towards the Communist Chinese, proclaims that the Chinese spy balloon is actually a weather balloon and not a danger to American citizens. Thus, Biden declares that the balloon will be allowed to continue its' trip across the continent. Biden admits that the balloon is maneuverable and capable of taking pictures and it is where it is only because its been blown off course. If the balloon is not for spying and is maneuverable, the question is, why can't it be 'maneuvered' out of American air space? Biden, still o his knees with open mouth, has no comment.

2/5

Bidens' contempt for the intelligence of the American public has never been more apparent than it is now. Biden postures as a tough, responsible leader for finally ordering the Communist Chinese spy balloon shot down. Of course this is only after Biden allows the balloon to fly over Alaska, parts of Canada and the entire continental U.S. for several days, collecting data. Then Biden does shoot it down, but only after it reaches the East Coast and the Communists in China received a continent load of spy data. Biden appeases his Communist friends while the only people being hurt, again, are American citizens. At least now Biden can get off his knees and close his mouth, but the imbecilic grin will probably remain.

2/6

Bidens contempt for the intelligence of the US population continues unabated. When asked if he was to blame for inflation, Biden responds: "Do I take the blame for inflation? No, because it was already there when I got here." This again begs the question: Is Biden this mentally deficient, or does he think everyone else is stupid or lacks access to a computer? A quick search shows that the inflation rate in 2020, Trumps' last year, was 1.53%. It climbed to almost 8% in just the two years Biden has been president. If there was a follow-up question from the press on Bidens' latest lie, it was not recorded.

2/7

Back in November of 2022, Biden answered questions about his obvious mental decline by promising to have a full physical exam by the end of the year, a promise echoed by his PS. January of 2023 has come and gone and Biden still hasn't taken the promised exam. It's now February and Biden uses the excuse of a 'busy and evolving travel schedule in recent weeks' as the reason for him avoiding the exam. This might be understandable, except that Biden spent almost half the month of January hiding at his multiple Delaware properties.

2/8

Bidens' second SOTU address is even more of a clown-show than his first. Bidens' bungling of words – like "conversion" instead of "confrontation" - was again on display, as was his yelling when no one, his supporters included, could figure out what he was yelling about. At one point in his yell. Biden demanded that Congress name one world leader who would exchange places with the Communist Chinese leader, leaving all completely baffled by what Biden was trying to get at. In a unprecedented moment, for a SOTU address, Congress openly laughed at some of Bidens' remarks. Biden looked confused for a moment, then broke into his famous dull-witted grin, thinking that he had inadvertently made a joke that all thought was funny. Unfortunately he hadn't and. Congress was laughing at Biden, not with him. This was a distinction Biden apparently missed.

2/9

The fallout from Bidens' SOTU speech continues. Biden is criticized for taking the moment, not to comment on the actual state of the union, but to race-bait and stoke class warfare. First Biden stupidly. laments that white parents are advantaged over parents of color because white parents, according to Biden, never have to instruct their children on how to behave when confronted by the police. Though starting by being patronizing and stupid, Biden then rants that, rather than his abysmal fairy tale economic policies being to blame, it is the successful business men in America being the reason for the country's financial problems. In two sentences and about that many minutes, Biden turns his SOTU speech into a political rant involving race-baiting and class envy, leaving the majority of anyone still watching disgusted.

2/10

In a follow-up to his SOTU debacle, Biden repeats the lie again that successful businessmen don't pay their fair share of taxes and thus exacerbate Americas' current economic woes. What Biden doesn't mention and hopes everyone in the audience is as mentally blank as he is, is that top 1% of wage earners in America pay the majority of all taxes, whereas the bottom 25% pay almost none. Once again Biden demonstrates that all he has, or maybe ever had to offer America is racial discord and class envy.

2/10

At one point Then in the same breath he brags about making it easier for energy companies to invest, but then complains hat these same companies make too much money. Then he outs himself by complaining that they're making money but are unwilling to invest because they're afraid Biden will shut them down in the future.

2/11

As expected, Biden lies so frequently now he can no longer keep them straight. After the criticism reached a crescendo about him not shooting the Chinese spy balloon down sooner, Biden claims he wanted the balloon shot down immediately after he became aware of it. Then Bidens' Defense Department reveals that Biden had know about the balloon at least five days before, when it first entered American air space over Alaska. When confronted with his lie, Biden pivots and admits he knew of the balloon for almost a week but kept it a secret so not to jeopardize an upcoming summit between America and China. It should surprise no one that at the rate that Bidens' head must swivel continually to deny his avalanche of lies, that one day it will just pop off his shoulders.

2/12

Biden is not only dumbfounding the American people but also himself when he tries to explain his lying. In another attempt to defend his catastrophic bungling of the Chinese spy balloon, Biden now claims that it was the correct decision to shoot it down only after it completed its' cross- America spy mission for the Chinese Communists. Bidens' reasoning is that it was safer to shoot the balloon down only over open water. This, after Biden lied about when he became aware of the balloon, lied about the balloon being harmless, then lied about wanting to shoot the balloon down earlier, but was stopped. Confusing? Yes. The product of a conniving, unstable mind? Perhaps, but the fear should be what Bidens' dwindling brain will produce tomorrow.

2/13

Each day now brings the capacity of Bidens' unhinged mental state more into focus. It turns out that the Chinese Communist balloon was tracked from it's initial launch from mainland China. If safely shooting the balloon down over open water was Bidens' real concern, Biden had the entire Pacific Ocean to accomplish this before the balloon made landfall in America. In fairness, in his present mental condition Biden might've been confused about the the difference between the two oceans and their locations

2/14

The backlash and criticism of Biden allowing a Chinese spy balloon to traverse the entire American landscape is not going away. This, despite Biden and the media trying to downplay it. Even Generals in the armed services say that even if Biden ignored the balloons travel across the Pacific, it could've been safely shot down when it first entered American airspace over the waters around the remote Aleutian Islands to the west of Alaska. It is the Generals' contention that if Biden was sincere in wanting to shoot the balloon down over open water and not kow-tow to the Communists, Biden had plenty of opportunity to do so. Biden has no comment.

2/15

In either their continued delusional state, or because of their unabashed contempt for the intelligence of the American citizen, Biden and Harris announce that they will pour another $956 million of American tax dollars into Central America, on top of the $3.2 billion they've already spent, in a further attempt to "curb illegal immigration". How exactly this will happen is a mystery, since the three billion American tax dollars Biden has already funneled to South America has only fueled more record illegal immigration. There is no let-up in sight, with months as recently as December and January being among the worst on record for illegals entering the US. Frustrated, the National Border Control Council (NBPC) President called out both Biden and Harris, saying that this laundering money into corrupt South America leaders hands, under the guise of illegal immigration reform, was no more than "...a political stunt." Biden and Harris have no comment.

2/16

One of the architects of Trump's successful border security policies was quoted as saying that he believed Biden and Harris sending more money to South America will make the situation worse. He believes that sending more money to Central America, while leaving the US southern border wide open, means that more cash will be available for illegal immigrants to pay their smugglers. As long as Biden and Harris keep the southern border wide open, giving American tax-payer cash to three countries in Central America will be a further accelerate to record illegal immigration by the millions, from now over one hundred countries. Biden and Harris have no comment.

2/17

In reacting to the accusations that his handling of the Chinese spy balloon has made America more vulnerable than ever, Biden and his spokespeople claim America is more safe now than it was under Trump. Contradicting this lie, a reporter points out that in 2022 alone North Korea tested 70 ballistic missiles, some of them capable of reaching the U.S. In contrast, after Trump warned North Koreas' pajama boy dictator, not a single missile was fired during the rest Trumps' presidency. This, in combination with Bidens' bungled Afghanistan withdrawal, where thousands were killed and Biden funded a top terrorist group with billions of dollars of weapons, the question has to be asked: How exactly is America safer now?

2/18

Biden takes censorship of the press – some of the press – to new levels as he asks that reporters from conservative outlets Daily Caller, New York Post and Fox News Radio be booted from Bidens' press conference, using the excuse that there weren't enough chairs available. One reporter from the NYP refused to leave the room, pointing out that there was plenty of space and chairs for everyone. Both the reporters that Biden booted and the ones allowed to remain applauded the reporter, so Biden let him stay. As usual, the briefing itself was lame, with Biden again refusing to answer any questions after delivering the remarks his nurses prepared for him. However, one reporter he attempted to exile managed one jab that angered Biden when he asked Biden if his inability to deal with China was compromised by the Biden family business relations in China. Biden scowls, mutters: "Give me a break, man," and stalks out of the room.

2/19

Biden holds a press conference where he is expected to speak on any number of items, from the Communist Chinese balloon fiasco, rising gas prices, inflation, the war in Ukraine or even the toxic gas fiasco that Biden and his Secretary of Transportation created in East Palestine. It turns out though, that with war, inflation and toxic gas to talk about, Bidens' number one concern right now is the "exorbitant" prices for tickets to concerts and sporting events, the "exorbitant" fees airlines charge parents so they can sit alongside their young children and the "exorbitant" fees charged to Americans for canceling television and telephone packages early. One can only hope that Biden gets to the bottom of this concert ticket and telephone/television pricing crisis quickly so he can attend to the less "exorbitant" problems war, inflation and toxic gas.

2/20

When asked about Bidens' reluctance to speak to the media because of his diminishing mental skills, his PS declares that Biden "... is the best communicator that we have in the White House." With the poor-to-the-point-of-being-laughable speaking skills of VP Harris – she recently called Americas' neighbor to the north "Canadia" - and her routinely delivering embarrassing word-salad speeches that leave people scratching their heads, this might be one of the few times Bidens' press secretary is actually telling the truth.

2/21

Biden and his entire administration is missing in action while the toxic chemicals released in East Palestine by the train derailment threatens the water supply for the Ohio River Basin. Biden and his Transportation Secretary waited weeks to comment on the disaster, instead spending their time complaining about there being too many 'white guys' in the construction trades. Both Biden and his SOT waited three weeks after the disaster to announce they might actually visit the site, and this only after after a major public outcry and Trump announcing he would visit the site. Even with the head of Bidens' EPA being shamed into postponing a trip to Africa with Hollywood celebrities to make a token appearance in East Palestine, Biden still won't commit to visiting the area.

2/22

After waiting weeks for Biden to NOT visit the distressed area of Est Palestine, Trump visits the area as a private citizen, bringing water, food and cleaning supplies, little of which had been brought to the area by Biden and his staff before this. Reporters note the contrast of Trump the private citizen helping the relief efforts in a distressed American community while Biden is serving the globalist agenda in Ukraine.

Trump tells the citizens of East Palestine that he will not forget them while Biden has failed them from the beginning. Some critics even venture that Biden ignored the plight of East Palestine because the surrounding counties voted 70 percent for Trump in the last election. Biden has no comment.

2/23

Almost unbelievably, if it wasn't Biden, a report leaks out that Biden and FEMA at first denied East Palestine disaster relief funds because one, the release of toxic chemicals didn't meet the traditional definition of a "disaster"and two, that East Palestine did not have enough "diversity" in the area to meet Federal standards. After Trump announced he was visiting East Palestine to bring relief supplies, FEMA reversed course and sent federal resources to the area. Critics from both sides of the aisle expressed bewilderment that Biden and his SOT would spend time ranting about such things as the racial composition of the construction industry instead of the train derailment in East Palestine. Then, again almost unbelievably, Bidens' SOT attempts to minimize the disaster by comparing it to the "thousand other train derailments" that he claims occur in the US each year. It's apparent that Bidens' own brain-derailment is infectious.

2/24

Biden, whom his doctors repeatedly claim to be in good mental and physical health, again stumbles when trying to board Air Force One. His staffers immediately blame the wind, which is not good. This means that his nurses cannot let this fit-and-healthy Biden out of his basement and in inclement weather again unless he is wearing ankle weights. In his defense, just the day before one of Bidens' staffers stumbled leaving Air Force One. It is possible Biden purposely did a 'sympathy stumble' so his staffer wouldn't feel so alone in her embarrassment … maybe.

2/25

Biden is accused of slow- walking America down the road toward World War III by continuing to funnel billions of dollars in cash and weapons to Ukraine, helping them escalate their war with Russia. Biden makes a surprise visit to Ukraine where he not only vowed to continue sending weapons and American taxpayer dollars to Ukraine for "as long as it takes." but also calls out Putin by name in an attempt to embarrass him. Taking the bait, Putin responds by reiterating a litany of anti-Western grievances that are mainstays of Russian propaganda. This bravado posturing by two idiots suffering from "little man syndrome" cannot end well.

2/26

Bidens' continued ignoring of the plight of the residents of East Palestine now reaches national attention The mayor there slams for ignoring his town while "...giving away millions of dollars..." in additional monies to Ukraine, now totaling close to $100 billion, calling it "...the biggest slap in the face...". He also criticizes Biden for waiting weeks before reaching out to him about the disaster and this only after Trump offered to do so. Still, Biden has no plans to travel to East Palestine The frustration in the area is close to reaching the boiling point as Biden repeatedly gives them the political cold shoulder. This only serves to give credence to the accusation that Bidens' ignoring of East Palestine is due to there being a large conservative voter base there that, according to the mayor; "…he (Biden) doesn't care about..."

2/27

The embarrassment of Biden and his TS continues. Having Trump visit the area of the disaster before Biden was bad enough, but now Biden and his TS continue digging themselves a deeper hole by trying to blame this disaster, incredibly, on Trump. Even Bidens' own head of the National Transportation Safety Board admitted that the braking rule ended by Trump did not include the type of train that derailed in East Palestine, meaning that rolling back the rule had nothing to do with the derailment. Further, according to the NTSB, even with ECP brakes the derailment would have occurred, the fire would have ensued, and the five vinyl chloride tank cars would still have to be vented and burned. This information was made available the same day Biden and his TS were lying to the American public about the derailment being Trumps' fault.

2/28

Biden seems to lie now every time his lips move. Now Bidens' lie about reducing the deficit is exposed by the CBO. The non-partisan agency revealed that Biden is the most reckless spender in American history. The CBOs latest 10-year forecast for the federal budget shows that Bidens' policies are on pace to add $5.45 trillion to the deficit over the next decade, $3 trillion larger than what was projected last May. Biden will add to the deficit an amount that is nearly twice the size of the entire federal budget in 2010 under Obama. This latest Biden lie is reminiscent of when Biden wrongly claimed that he lowered the national debt by $1.7 trillion, when in fact Biden grew the debt by nearly $3.7 trillion during his first 23 months in office. Biden's irresponsible spending and his lies about it are leaving the country with a massive fiscal hole that future generations will find difficult, if not impossible, to climb out of.

3/1

Biden continues to lie and tout about reducing the national debt while in office. The official numbers beg to differ, showing that the national debt was roughly $27.75 trillion when Biden took office and is approximately $31.43 trillion today. Yet Biden continues to lie about this and the trained seals in the media applaud and cheer, all the while Biden is leading them and the country over a financial cliff down to an economic hell.

3/2

Back in February Biden signed an executive order ordering the IRS to make their tax and audit procedures more "equitable". Even though Biden tries to obfuscate his real purpose, once his use of his terms 'taxing based on algorithmic equations" for "under served communities"'are dissected, it is revealed now that this EO is Bidens' order to the IRS to audit whites and Asians more extensively in order to achieve 'racial equity'. It is well documented that Biden has been an unapologetic racist throughout his career, the only difference now that he is president, Biden sees no reason to hide it.

3/3

Biden manages to anger even left-wing activists on the ground in East Palestine. Usually reliable sympathizers to Bidens' Marxist leanings, their main criticism is that Bidens' lackluster response to the area has left residents feeling like they do not matter. They point out that it has been a month now and the residents there still don't have any answers. They warn Biden that the chemicals spilled in the derailment were dangerous enough to kill animals in the area and that dead animals are warning signs that these chemicals are also deadly to humans. It's very obvious to everyone, except Biden apparently, that something is really wrong in East Palestine.

3/4

Once though not possible, Biden reaches a new low point on the human dignity scale. A mother, who lost her two sons to Fentanyl poisoning in 2020, testifies before Congress and emotionally slams Biden and his lack of response to surging fentanyl deaths in America. She points out that while the recent spy balloon crossing the country finally caught Bidens' attention, the 100,000 yearly Fentanyl poisoning deaths seem to have escaped it. Bidens' declining mental state on full display, he misses her point completely. Instead, Biden remarks that since her boys died in 2020, their poisoning is Trumps' fault, not his and then, incredible to behold with this heartbroken mother standing there, laughs. Long known to be dumb, vicious and shallow, Biden laughing at a mothers' grief on losing her sons drops him to a new, much lower level of a disgusting human being.

3/5

Reaction to Bidens' chuckling at a mothers' pain in losing her two sons' to Fentanyl poisoning is swift and harsh. Even Bidens' ardent supporters are at a loss to explain what he could've possibly found so funny. As for Trump being to blame for this tragedy, one critic pointed out that just in July and August of 2022 under Biden, federal agents seized 4,500 pounds of fentanyl. These two months compare to the 2,800 pounds seized in all of 2019 under Trump. Also under Biden, in 2021 drug overdoses reached an all-time high. Bidens' July 2022 numbers alone, 2,071 lbs of fentanyl (more than 469 million lethal doses) were seized. For this 62% increase in just two months compared to 12 months under Trump and the surging Fentanyl overdose deaths, Biden has no comment.

3/6

Fearing that his unconstitutional, illegal and immoral EO canceling all student loan debt is doomed, Biden turns his attack on private colleges and institutions. Bidens' Education Department will decide on a case-by-case basis whether to require college leaders to assume personal liability. Those decisions will be made either when an institution's program participation agreement is up for renewal or when it undergoes a change in ownership. In a press release, the department said that it will require leaders that "fail to operate in a financially responsible way" to assume personal liability for unpaid federal student loans. While not sure what this latest word salad from Biden means, it sounds like Biden, failing to get taxpayers to assume the deadbeat students debt' he is hoping to force the colleges and universities themselves to foot the bill.

3/7

Many have known for a long time, ass part of his 'Green New Deal', Biden wants to eliminate fossil fuels. It's too much to hope that Bidens feeble mind would grasp that the majority of electricity and other forms of energy are created by burning fossil fuels. Bidens' pet green energy is currently incapable of producing the level of energy needed to maintain civilization. Energy grid operators around the country are horrified that Biden doesn't have any plans for replacing fossil fuels. Some have even warned Biden that closing fossil-fuel power plants faster than renewable sources are being developed will lead only to energy shortages, blackouts and"... the bleak future America is in store for..."Biden has no comment.

3/8

Critics lampoon Biden for presenting a 'Woman of Courage' award to a man who chooses to wear a dress on International Women's Day. Bidens' critics rush to defend his choice as being natural to him, and they may have a point. For a man who can't tell the difference between Communist enemy and an ally, a spy balloon from a weather balloon, his wife from his sister, thousands left for dead and a successful withdrawal, a crippled man from a healthy man, dead woman from an empty chair and a career of not distinguishing between lies and truths, Biden not being able to tell the difference between a man and a woman is probably natural to him and the least of his pworries.

3/9

One would think that being a habitual hypocrite would tire one out, but not Biden. In yet another one Biden threatens to veto a "criminal reform" bill authored by the representatives of Washington DC. The bill would defund certain offices of the DC police department, reduce many felonies to misdemeanors, eliminate mandatory sentences and, thus, give criminals free reign in DC. The hypocrisy is these are the identical laws passed by Democratic controlled cities and states that allowed BLM and Antifa to take over and burn large sections of American cities to the ground with Harris and Bidens' tacit approval. Harris, because she set up funds to bail out the looters, Biden because he hid in his basement, coming out only after the destruction of property and lives was over. Now, without a word of apology, to the cities and lives he let his supporters burn, now Biden wants a tougher crime bill.

3/10

Nine more boxes of possible classified documents were taken from Bidens' attorneys' office, but have yet to be reviewed by the National Archives. The boxes had been shipped from the Penn Biden Center, where Biden teaches, to Bidens lawyers office and Biden disclosed this with a letter to the Archives last November. Despite having the letter and the boxes themselves for months, the NA hasn't reviewed the boxes' content to determine whether additional classified materials are inside. Since the Archives went through Trumps documents in a matter of days, why is it taking so long to review Bides' classified material? The NA has no comment.

3/11

Biden releases a sprawling 178-page new 'tax plan' that contains proposals for new taxes on wealthy Americans, including everything from how investment income is taxed to a revival of his "billionaire minimum tax" on wealth. In addition, Biden plans to raise the rate on corporate income to 28%. Biden denies that these tax increases will hurt economic growth in the years ahead and, instead, Biden assures all that it will help pay off part of the huge deficit Biden has added monstrously to since becoming president. Economists are left wondering what color the sky is in Bidens' world where massive tax increases on corporations, small business, individuals, savings and investment accounts, all at once, actually boosts an economy rather than destroys it.

3/12

Bidens' war on American energy production and fossil fuels altogether has the predictable result of soaring energy prices, sending Biden into damage control mode. Biden protests that he has done nothing to hamper domestic energy production and instead shifting the blame for high gas prices onto oil companies. Unfortunately for Biden, a leaked internal memo details that Biden and his staff acknowledge that charging energy companies lower fees for drilling permits on federal land would create "greater energy security,". Despite this, Biden still plans to raise fees on energy companies as part of his climate agenda, even though the last time fees were raised oil companies stopped bidding on for new drilling permits. At least one of Bidens' nurse should warn him, those who do not study history will most likely repeat it.

3/13

Bidens' open-border policies is a bonanza for the Mexican cartels. They are re flooding the country with deadly drugs like fentanyl and have developed a lucrative human trafficking business that's overtaken the drug trade in profits. Bidens' policies have now also emboldened the cartels to the point that they are kidnapping and murdering American citizens in broad daylight, capitalizing on the border chaos created by Biden. While the cartels continue running amok and making millions of Americans suffering, Biden continues to sit on his hands; one hand, anyway.

3/14

Shameless lying by both Biden and Harris is on the verge of becoming an epidemic, one so pervasive, documenting each occurrence is stretching the limits of journalism. Now Biden claims he became a proponent of gay marriage when he was a teenager after seeing two men kiss each other, even though there are taped speeches of his throughout his career where he decries this practice and claims that marriage should be only between a man and a woman. Then Harris follows this with a hoot of story where, as a tiny tot, asks her mother why 'conservatives' are bad people since 'to conserve' is a good thing to practice? Harris goes on to say could never reconcile this contradiction until recently. For any who believe either of these stories actually happened, there is a bridge in the Florida marshes that is for sale.

3/15

Bidens' flip-flopping on his campaign promises to 'fix' all of Trumps' so-called "errors" through Executive Orders is reaching such a crescendo that even some of his faithful supporters are beginning to get angry at Bidens schizophrenic approach to implementing policy. First Biden cancels Trumps' attempt to build a wall at the southern border, then activates it again, but calling it "repairs".rather than a "build" Then Biden canceled Trumps' policy of detaining immigrants in Mexico until they are properly processed, in favor of Bidens' "Catch and Release" plan, which only momentarily accosts illegals at the border before releasing them into the United States. Now Biden is quietly trying to re-instate Trumps' 'Stay in Mexico' immigration policy. It's no wonder that Bidens' head-spinning, flip flopping on decisions and promises has his frustrated supporter asking, in essence, 'What the hell is going on?'

3/16

Bidens' flip-flopping on both his campaign promises and stated goals continues at an increasing pace. During his campaign one of Bidens' main promises was to use EOs to cancel Trumps' policy for new drilling permits for fossil fuels in America, particularly on Federal Lands. Now Biden re-instates Trumps' policy, allowing for new drilling exploration in Alaska. Then in a bewildering, head-scratching nod to his rabid environmentalist supporters, Biden boasts that he has canceled a Trump contract to build a rode through one of their pet sanctuarys, a wild life habitat in Alaska … but 5 minutes later Biden announces that he will take bids from other contractors to build the same road. Now a lot of Biden supporters are joining the res of the world in wondering, what really is the color of the sky in Bidens' world.

3/17

Any hope Biden has for keeping his "Catch and Release" immigration policy, the one responsible for flooding America with millions of undocumented illegals, receives another blow as a Federal judge in Florida issues a ruling in a case brought by the Attorney General there. blocking the use of Bidens' "Catch and Release" policy by the Department of Homeland Security. The judge gave Biden a brutal rejection and a lecture, pointing out that the U.S.-Mexico border has become "a meaningless line in the sand" for illegal aliens entering the country. Further, the judge slammed Biden for his role in creating, what the judge called the "Biden border crisis" and gave Biden one week to appeal the ruling. So far, no comment and no appeal from Biden.

3/18

Biden decides to bail out failing, irresponsible banks like Silicon Valley Bank and Signature bank and the fallout is instant. Economists warn Americans that they are witnessing in real time the side effects of Bidens' misguided government intervention in the marketplace. Instead of allowing that same marketplace to return to regular working order, Biden continues applying his 'cures', often much worse than the original disease. The damage caused by Bidens' inflation-inducing policies and reckless, irresponsible spending now is spilling over into banking, sparking fears of another financial crisis.Biden openly brags about giving SVB a bailout, but doesn't mention the coincidences that California governor Newsome and a myriad of other Biden cronies have many millions of dollars on deposit with SVB: Yes, that coincidence. that bank; Yes, that coincidence.

3/20

Biden introduces legislation that attempts to get home appliances to comply with his 'green agenda'. Relying on one of his commissioners with the CPSC, Biden has put banning gas stoves 'on the table', using a questionable, unverified study that the stoves contribute to childhood asthma as his evidence. This is Bidens' first step in many to eventually ban all natural gas appliances in the name of fighting his mythical climate change battle. This angers leaders in the natural gas appliance industry, who warn Biden that mandates will only lead to higher costs and less efficient performance. Biden is warned that moving away from more reliable energy sources and replacing them with wind and solar, intermittent sources at best, could prove disastrous for the electric grid in America that is already overtaxed. Biden remains unconvinced and unmoved.

3/21

Bidens' war on fossil fuels takes a weird turn as a leaked memo from back in February illustrates his intent on, not only issuing constricting regulations on natural gas appliances, but also Bidens' intent to regulate refrigerators, which are mostly electric. Bidens' promise to end the use of fossil fuels as part of his environmental agenda now seems to include even electricity not generated by solar and wind power. Experts in all areas of the energy industry have repeatedly warned Bide, ad nauseun, that him killing fossil fuel energy supplies before their wind and solar replacements are fully ready to completely replace them will lead to national disasters along the lines of what has already happened in California and Texas. Biden gives no indication that he heard or understood anything.

3/22

Biden boasts that he can easily beat Trump in a potential 2024 contest, but his actions belie this braggadocio. In an attempt to knee cap Trumps' 2024 presidential bid, Biden stuffs the Manhattan D.A.'s Office with DOJ people. This includes a DOJ operative who is simultaneously running the Stormy Daniels case, a case that appears to be nothing more than another Trump witch hunt. Biden professes to know nothing about what's going on in Manhattan but Biden is clearly trying to take Trump off the board for 2024. Biden has doubts he can beat Trump in 2024, particularly if voters judge Trump's four years in office superior to the disaster that Bidens' tenure has been.

3/23

White House insiders, who insist on not being identified, report that Biden is growing increasingly frustrated with what he calls Harris' refusal to 'rise to the occasion' and her failure to ' take more off his plate", ostensibly because of her overt fear of failing. Based on the only major job she has been given, – solving the illegal immigration problem at the US southern border, has been an abysmal, historical, cataclysmic failure, it would appear her fear is justified. This has produced a strange dilemma for Biden, who has said one reason he'll run again in 2024 is to protect the country from Trump. Now Biden has to run to ostensibly protect the country from Harris, a perfect example of Tweedle Dee feeling it his duty to protect everyone from Tweedle Dum.

3/24

Bidens' mask of having no desire to be a dictator and a tyrant slips a bit when he meets Pierre Poilievre in Canada. Poilevre introduces himself to Biden as the "leader of His Majesty's Loyal Opposition". Biden, looking dazed as ever, can only mumble: after momentary confusion, "Loyal Opposition?". Poilievre responds that Canadians believe that opposition is an act of loyalty in their system. Biden laughs, grabs Poilievre's arm and remarks: "We (in America) do too, unfortunately" before moving on to meet the next person. Bidens' whimsy of being a dictator does not go unnoticed.

3/25

In his investigation of Biden and his family criminal operations, the head of the HOC finds that he can increase the number in this crime family by at least one. It appears that Hallie Biden, the widow of Bidens' son Beau, also received money directly from a business deal with a company deeply connected to the Communist Chinese. A business associate of Hunter gave Hallie $35,000 in two transactions in 2017 after he received $3 million from this company connected directly with the CCP. This was the same company that paid Hunter $6 million in 2017 to try and set up energy deals in the U.S., with 10% of the bribe gong to an unnamed "Big Guy". Another business associate of Hunters admitted in testimony before Congress that the "Big Guy" was, of course, Biden.

3/26

New polls suggest that Bidens' assertion that he could easily beat Trump in a rematch may not be a sure thing, as Americans remember the good economic times under Trump. A new McLaughlin and Associates poll found Trump leading Biden by five points in a head-to-head 2024 rematch. With the 2024 general election 20 months away, Trump also leads Biden in battleground states, where 51% of voters support Trump, while only 41 percent back Biden. Perhaps the reason Biden remains confident is that this information has not reached his basement.

3/27

Without warning, North Korea fires a ballistic missile over Japan for the first time in five years in a dangerous escalation of recent weapons tests by the Pajama Boy dictator of that country. The launch, which prompted an immediate backlash from Tokyo and Seoul, comes amid a spate of missile tests, with five launches in the past 10 days and 23 such missile test just this this year. These include both ballistic and cruise missiles tests. The world is reminded again that, after Trump informed Pajama Boy that he would blast his chubby butt into the South China Sea if he persisted with missile tests, the PBD fired nary a one the remaining years of Trumps' tenure. The world is also reminded that the PBD resumed his missile launches two months after Biden took office and has not stopped, firing as many as 8 missiles in a single day.

3/28

Biden can't help looking foolish and obtuse, even when he is trying to be humorous. At a press conference, instead of addressing the record inflation in America he has caused since he took office, Biden tells the reporters that the only reason he showed up was because he "heard there was chocolate chip ice cream." He assures assures the audience that he has a "...whole refrigerator full upstairs...," of this, one of the most expensive ice cream in the country, Expensive, indeed, with a gallon of the stuff retailing for $48 a half gallon, compared to the average price for normal ice cream of $5.56. Even this price is too much for the average American family since with Bidens' inflation, this price is up nearly 14% in just the last year. The scene is oddly reminiscent of Pelosi showing off her freezer full of the same ice cream during the COVID shutdown of households and businesses. This "let them eat cake" moment gives Americans a real glimpse of how shallow these two Marxist 'rulers' are and how monstrously dismissive they are of their 'subjects'.

3/29

In a recent interview discussing the genital mutilation of gender-confused teens, Biden was asked if he really approved of these procedures that he was advocating. Bidens' mumbling, semi-coherent answer ran along the lines of: "I don't think any state or anybody should have the right to do that. As a moral question and as a legal question, I just think it's wrong (to curtail access to gender altering medicines and procedures) ... I mean, there's a lot of, you know, you sometimes ... they try to block you from being able to access certain medicines, being able to access certain procedures, and so on... None of that should be available. I mean... my view. So I feel very, very strongly that you should have every single solitary right including, including use of your gender-identity bathrooms in public." Once again dumbfounding his audience with what might be his Ensure-deprived illiteracy, it seems clear that Biden does feels it is wrong to deny kids having irreversibly mutilating procedures, without parental permission, that will insure that they never have children of their own.

3/30

Seemingly buoyed by Trudeaus' successful crushing of his opposition during protests of Tudeaus' heavy-handed and unnecessary COVID lock downs in Canad, Biden pushes for a CBDC (Central Bank Currency System) similar to the one Canada is experimenting with. Limp-wrist ed Marxists like Biden salivate at the prospect of a CBDC because it would allow Biden to put his bony, emaciated foot on the throat of every American and every aspect of their private lives. Trudeau, a great admirer of the Communist Chinese with their stranglehold on the Chinese people and Biden, a great admirer of Truedeu seizing all the assets of his opponents, forcing them to capitulate or literally starve, made the two of them almost giddy when they met recently for a summit. A reporter noted that during this greeting both Biden and Trudeau turned their backs on the audience. This obscured seeing how Biden and Trudeau finished their handshake, but it appeared to end well below their waists.

3/31

Bidens' braggadocio of being able to beat Trump loses even more credibility as one of his main supporters, DA Bragg of New York, indicts Trump in an obvious attempt to knee cap his 2024 presidential bid. Another one of his fervent supporters, Pelosi, intimates that Trump is guilty and should be, according to the leather-faced monarch wannabe, "grateful"that he is being "allowed"a chance to prove his innocence. Someone should remind Biden, Bragg and Pelosi that in this country a man is considered innocent until proven guilty, not the other way around like it is in all the Marxist/Stalinist countries they so admire. Much to the chagrin of these three unabashed dictators-in-waiting, this is still America, at least for now.

4/1

A report posted on the Internet succinctly describes some of Bidens achievements since he has been in office. In August of 2021, Biden oversaw the biggest foreign policy debacle in American history when he screwed up the US withdrawal from Afghanistan, where his indecisive leadership and inept judgment led to the deaths of thirteen US servicemen. In July of 2022 Biden sold one million barrels of oil from the US strategic petroleum reserves to China, Americas most serious political, economic and military enemy. in the middle of an energy crisis in his own country. Then in December of 2022, recklessly released Viktor Bout, also known as the "Merchant of Death". Bout was in prison for selling weapons to terrorists and conspiring to kill Americans. One might assume that Bidens' murky mental condition is the reason he might consider these horrific blunders harmless jokes, but considering the date, the only joke is the one Biden has played on the American people the last two-plus years.

4/2

In their Louisiana and Missouri v. Biden et al, Louisiana and Missouri sue Biden over his attempt to pressure Twitter and Facebook to censor posts about COVID to suppress information about the virus that is now known to be true. These states' lawyers claim that the discovery process provided documentary proof that Biden illegally pressured social media companies to take down posts that undercut Bidens' personal narrative on COVID. Their testimony before the House Select Committee on the 'Weaponizing of the Federal Government' will expose that Bidens' coordination with social media companies and collusion with non-governmental organizations to censor speech was far more pervasive and destructive than has ever been reported so far. Biden has no comment.

4/3

Better late than never, Bloomberg reports that Biden's left-wing agenda cost American households an extra $5,200 in 2022, a staggering $433 per month. A recent study showed that not only is inflation at a 40-year-high, but also that nearly a quarter of Americans aren't getting enough to eat at times because sky-high inflation has skyrocketed the cost of living. More bad news for Biden is that economists, in predicting a recession by the end of the year, point out that Bidens' new scheme of bailing out irresponsible financial institutions is further complicating the Federal Reserve's fight against inflation. The American public is witnessing in real time how Bidens' misguided 'cure' of intervening in the marketplace has side effects much worse than the original disease.

4/4

The final tally is in on Bidens raid on Americas' Strategic Oil Supply, in place to protect the US in case of a national emergency. Reportedly Biden sold 180 million barrels of oil from Americas' emergency supply to some of Americas' worst enemies, including Russia and China. It is also reported that these. missing barrels of oil cannot be replaced until 2024 or 2025, if then. This leaves America far more vulnerable than at any time during Trumps' presidency. Biden dodges all questions on the subject.

4/5

A historic moment occurred when the Speaker of the House met with the president of Taiwan who was making a rare visit to America. It was a high-profile encounter designed to boost support for the island government and deter China's' interest in invading. Notably absent during the Taiwan Presidents' visit was Biden, a long-time Chinese Communist sympathizer and rumored business partner. Bidens' staff professed not to know where Biden was during this visit, but also ignored questions about the possibility of Biden being in his basement in Delaware, hiding.

4/6

For the second time in six months Biden receives a massive diplomatic humiliation from Saudi Arabia. Last Octobers' oil production cuts by the Saudis had followed months of intensive begging by Biden, desperate to convince Riyadh to keep oil production up. Considering this latest snub to Biden, the idea that relations between the two countries can still be called "a strategic partnership" is laughable. Bidens' famously pathetic fist bump in a face-to-face meeting with the Saudis comes to mind. It more than anything symbolizing Bidens' gross underestimation of the shift in U.S.-Saudi relations since Trump left office. Now Biden threatens "consequences" for the Saudis decision, but feebly neglects to give a hint of what they might be. In yet another accomplishment of Bidens' failed presidency, Biden has delivered a severe blow to an energy partnership between the Saudis and America that had endured for nearly 80 years.

4/7

Biden and his media allies continue to insist that Trump as President was an embarrassment on the world stage. Yet, foreign leaders appeared to respect Trump, even if they didn't like him, while Biden is being openly mocked by other countries. Recently Saudi Arabia's state-run television network lampooned Biden and Harris in a Saturday Night Live-style sketch. In one clip, Biden is seen looking confused after the conclusion of a speech, shaking hands with no one and having Harris guide him off the stage. The Saudi sketch also mocked Biden falling down the stairs while climbing into Air Force One. So much for Trump being a national embarrassment.

4/8

Incredible for almost anyone but Biden, for the umpteenth time Biden tries to blame his disastrous withdrawal from Afghanistan on Trump. One of the darkest moments of his presidency, Biden releases a a 12-page summary of his policies surrounding the withdrawal. In it Biden takes no responsibility for the disaster. Instead, once again Biden claims he was "severely constrained" by Trump's former agreement with Afghanistan on the conditions of a US withdrawal. What is left out of the report - and Biden continues to lie about - is that, while true that Trump set up the original conditions for the withdrawal, he also included a separate caveat. That is, if the Afghans broke off the peace talks, then all formerly agreed-to conditions would be moot. The Afghans did indeed break off the talks, but Biden continued to effect his own version of the withdrawal, an action that not only cost lives but left the terrorist Taliban group with billions of dollars of modern military weapons.

4/9

In perhaps Bidens' greatest show of chutzpah to date, it is revealed that Biden was allowed to contribute to the report that, shock of shocks, exonerated him and found Trump primarily to blame for Bidens' Afghanistan disaster. In summary, Biden is allowed to help write the report that finds he, Biden, blameless in a national disaster while finding Bidens' chief political opponent, Trump, at fault. Then Biden releases the report that he, Biden, helped write as proof that he, Biden, is innocent of any wrongdoing: Nice work, if you can get it.

4/10

With Bidens' political ineptness on display once again, having Trump indited has so far not worked out so well for Biden. Only a week after the indictment a new poll shows that 75% of Republicans are now more likely to vote for Trump and 48% of voters believe Biden has weaponized the DOJ, FBI, IRS, et al, Worse yet, having Trump officially viewed as a criminal has not helped Biden poll numbers either. Trump held a 4% point lead in a head-to-head comparison before the indictment and the 4% has held steady after the indictment. So much for Biden trying to knee-cap his political rival.

4/11

It is reported that Biden has created the perfect excuse to track a huge swath of his political opposition. It is now reported that under Bidens' direction, the FBI is using their National Instant Criminal Background Check System (NICS) for gun purchases for mere 'potential violations of law'. The report revealed that Biden and the FBI have been using information about citizens' income and past gun purchases as an excuse to spy on them. Not only have Biden and the FBI been using Americans' income and gun purchases to conduct warrant-less tracking, the reports show that Biden, the FBI and other federal law enforcement agencies are focusing massive amounts of resources towards spying on American citizens. Biden seems unconcerned that not only is such surveillance illegal without a proper warrant, but it also erodes public trust in him and the FBI, a trust that is already on badly cracked ice.

4/12

What is not surprising to any student of history, France – the gutless nation that the US rescued twice from the brink of oblivion – is the first European nation to throw in with the Chinese over their expected invasion of Taiwan. What is surprising is that, though France is heavily criticized by many countries and politicians for this betrayal, Biden remains silent on the subject. Then again for Biden, a long time suspected Communist Chinese sympathizer and business partner, perhaps this is not surprising at all.

4/13

Biden demonstrates again, at the same time, that both his mind is failing and his energy policy is nonsensical. On one hand he threatens to put oil companies out of business, but then begs them to produce as much oil as possible... before he puts them out of business. Bidens' energy-related closures, rather than rational, are policy-driven as left-wing ideologues now steer Bidens' ship. Bowing to the pressure of the Marxist Environmental, Social and Corporate Governance (ESG) scores, Biden has been shutting down coal plants with the promise of "green" technology that simply does not currently exist. Biden announces his 'Produce While I Destroy You' policy with his usual vacant, confused look, a look that can be seen on many Americans faces as they face an uncertain energy future

4/14

Bidens' promise to end the use of fossil fuels in order to transition America to "green energy" is putting the country's energy future in the hands of the Communist Chinese Party. The CCP is a global leader in the extraction of key resources used to create "green energy" and the manufacturing of windmills and solar panels. As the U.S. ramps up its use, the Chinese Communists are becoming dangerously intertwined in Americas' energy programs. Government officials point out the irony of Biden pushing for "green energy" at the expense of American security while enriching its' most dangerous enemy, must be lost on Biden. However, since Biden and his family have been doing business with the Communists for over a decade, the irony is not lost on Bidden at all.

4/15

More Americans are starting to panic that Biden's feckless and weak leadership is leaving the country in grave danger. A senator pointed out that Biden's disastrous withdrawal from Afghanistan sent a signal to the rest of the world that weak American leadership was back and that Americas' enemies have the green light to walk all over Biden. The senator listed as examples the Russian invasion of Ukraine and the Communist Chinese stepping up their aggression against Taiwan, as well as sending a spy balloon that brazenly violated American air space. What irked the senator was that, despite the obvious provocation by the Communists, Biden announced that his policy towards a hostile China won't change as a result of these incidents, regardless of the threat this poses for the U.S.

4/16

Biden doubles down on his policy – or lack of one – towards China. Biden again claims that China's globalization efforts to force countries around the world to bend to its' wishes, will not affect his relationship with the country his family has been working with for years. His senator critic snaps back, warning Biden that "hugs and hot cocoa" won't work when dealing with the Communists. The senator can be forgiven here: After all, hugs and hot cocoa, along with an occasional gentle pat on his head, is all Biden ever receives while ensconced in his Delaware basement.

4/17

Bidens' war on women continues. It is reported that Congress is preparing a bill that would make it illegal for men to compete in women sporting events. Biden insists that as long as the man declares that he is a woman, he has a right to compete in their events. Biden further warns that any attempt to end this destructive practice and return rational fairness to womens' sports, will be vetoed if and when it reaches his desk.

4/18

During his trip to Ireland, Biden announces to a crowd that he was "proud" of his son Hunter and, in fact, Hunter was the smartest guy he knew. This is the same Hunter who is the target of multiple criminal and Congressional investigations, whom the DOJ spent years investigating on financial crimes like money laundering and tax fraud, the same Hunter who appears to have committed an open and shut violation by lying on a federal background check form by claiming he was not addicted to drugs or alcohol when purchasing a handgun, when he clearly was. Add to this "smart" guy paying thousands of dollars to Florida and New York-based Ekaterina Moreva allegedly for escorts that he trafficked across state lines to pay for sex, it is apparent why Biden is "proud" of his "smart" son; his moral code is a direct chip off Bidens' block.

4/19

Biden delivers yet another class warfare speech where he attempts –
again - to blame Americas' economic ills on who he calls "the rich", but
Biden can't even get this right. He rails against the billionaires paying
"only" an 8% tax by spelling out the word 'eight', e-i-g-h.., leaving off
the 't'. As pathetic as this is, it can be worse. A week ago in Ireland
he tried to compliment an Irish rugby player who was instrumental in
defeating New Zealands' All Black rugby team by saying: "…hell of a
rugby player. He beat the hell out of the Black and Tans…." Unfortunately
for Biden, the 'Black and Tans' were a English militia who terrorized
the Irish in the past. Watching Bidens' mental breakdown in the U.S. is
one thing, but when he takes his mental incongruities world wide, it is
monumentally embarrassing.

4/20

Since from almost the moment Biden took office, it is glaringly apparent
that few countries respect America generally and the office of the U.S.
presidency specifically any more. With his bumbling incompetence and
clownish Aviators, Biden is fast-becoming an international joke. After
Bidens' recent mumbling, bumbling tour of Ireland, a new world order
appears to be capitalizing on his ineptitude. Saudi Arabia is striking deals
with the Iranians and Chinese, the spineless French president, of course
on his knees, continues to chase and ride on Xi Jinping's coattails, while
the president of Brazil, eager to be the next South American lapdog of
China, is calling on developing countries to replace the U.S. dollar with
their own currencies in international trade. Amazing to consider that
Americas' status in the world, held in high regard for almost 200 years,
has crumbled in just the two years since Biden took office.

4/22

Biden continues to stoke Americas' embarrassing loss of prestige around the world. It is now reported that many African nations, formerly friendly or at least neutral in their relationships with the US, have thrown in with the Chinese Communists. At the same time the Chinese Communists responded to Taiwan' President visiting Central America for 10 days by encircling the island with military planes and warships. Again embarrassing the U.S., Biden does nothing to support this American ally. Then reports surface of Russian attempting to forge closer ties with the United Arab Emirates, countries that backed America when Trump was president. In answer as to why he added these African nations, Taiwan and the United Emirates to the list of former allies he has alienated, Biden has no comment.

4/23

Polls show that 70% of Americans don't want Biden to run for a second term. Though Biden seemed flummoxed by this lack of confidence in him, he perhaps gave at least part of the reason himself when asked by a reporter if he intended to seek re-election. Biden said yes, but he was waiting for an official announcement. When asked "By whom?", Bidens' only response was to look as confused as the reporter.

4/24

When Congress officially ended the COVID state of emergency two weeks ago, Biden immediately rolled back Trumps' most effective border control measure, Title 42. This measure allowed border patrol agents to deny the oft-fake asylum requests by illegal aliens and send them back to either their own country or the country they most recently resided in. Border Patrol agents warn Biden that the impact of ending Title 42 could mean as many as 400,000 "asylum requests" by illegal aliens a month. Biden responds by having his Homeland Security office issue a memo which says, incredibly, that border agents should learn to "speed read" their way through the asylum questions they ask illegals in order to accommodate the expected monumental influx.

4/25

Rather than providing more facilities, manpower and/or money to blunt the expected 400,000/month surge in illegal immigration when Biden ends Title 42, Bidens' 'solution' to have border patrol agents learn to "speed read" asylum requests receives the expected backlash. Border agents voraciously remind Biden that, by not preparing additional facilities to house the new influx of illegals, Biden will be staring down the barrel of a humanitarian nightmare. It is apparent, though, that beyond trying to speed through the asylum claim process, Biden has no plan in place to manage the expected flood of illegals. It is ironic that the suggestion to 'speed read' as a solution for illegal immigration comes from Biden, a man who has trouble reading a teleprompter or notes - written in very large type - that are handed to him to read on a daily basis.

4/26

Biden announces his candidacy for re-election in 2024. He asks the American people to give him, Biden, a chance to "...finish the job..." he started. A quick look at just a few of Bidens 'accomplishments' include opening the southern border to millions of illegal immigrants, destroying American energy independence and produced record high levels of inflation with his inane spending policies. Additionally, Biden oversaw Americas' disastrous withdrawal from Afghanistan, insists that men play in girl sports and weaponized the justice system to go after his political opponents. Adding salt to the wound, it happens that the Consumer Confidence index reached a 9 – month low on the day Biden announced his intention to seek a second term. At this point it seems the only "job" Biden is capable of "finishing" is America itself.

4/27

Bidens' constant attempts to pit one class of Americans against another takes another turn. Often using race as a divider, Biden implements a new lending rule for banks that accomplishes the same thing. Under Bidens' new plan, home buyers with good credit will pay more for their loans in order to subsidize home buyers with poor credit. Bidens' plan will in effect pit Asian and White Americans who, as groups, have an average credit score of 745, against Black Americans whose group has an average credit score of 677. It has become obvious that Biden never misses a chance to create racial tension in America.

4/28

Bidens' plans to increase tension between the races does not go unnoticed by mortgage loan officers around the country. They tell Biden that his plan does not make sense because penalizing borrowers with larger down payments and higher credit scores will not go over well. They further inform Biden that his plan, which is racially discriminating at its' core, over complicates things in a process that is often already overwhelming with just the amount of paperwork necessary for mortgage transactions. While many in the industry strive to give consumers more affordable housing options, Biden is warned that his new rules will frustrate and confuse people and couldn't come at a worse time for an industry struggling to get back on its feet. Biden has no comment.

4/29

Bidens' visit to Ireland a week or so ago seems to have already faded from his memory. During a 'Take Your Child to Work Day' event at the White House, one child asked Biden what was the last country he visited. Biden looks hopelessly confused, mutters something about being to 89 countries and meeting with "...89 heads of state so far...", but finally confesses that he can't remember what country he just returned from. A small child in the audience prods Biden by informing him it was Ireland he just returned from. Biden breaks out in an ear-to-ear grin, looking so much like an elder patient in an assisted living facility who was just reminded by a nurse what his name is.

4/30

During his speech at the White House Correspondents' Dinner Biden made a jibe at a political foe of his, warning the audience that if they found themselves disoriented or confused, "…either you're drunk or Marjorie Taylor Greene." This from Biden, a man who routinely stumbles when performing the difficult act of walking, has to be led off of stages by nurses or young girls, holds onto curtains when attempting – but not finding – a stage exit, confuses his wife with his sister-in-law, attempts to shake hands with invisible people and addresses pithy remarks to the dead. So much for the pot calling the kettle black.

5/1

It is revealed that Biden, Big Tech companies and media outlets have been relying on so-called "objective third-party organizations" to determine whether or not information is true and if certain individuals and news companies were legitimate. Now it is reported that almost all of these watchdog groups are actually products of ideological think tanks which routinely blacklist conservatives. More disturbing is a report that Global Disinformation Index (GDI), one of the worst abusers that targets conservatives, receives funding directly from Biden and Bidens' State Department. Biden has no comment.

5/2

Bidens' continued wrestling with vindictive teleprompters provides Trump with his best re-election slogan yet. Stumbling and bumbling again through a prepared speech, Biden tries to untangle a series of phrases designed to call for his re-election. After mangling all of them Biden, frustrated, blurts out that it is Trump who should be re-elected. To be sure, a gift for Trumps' re-election bid, but that it was provided by a possible addled mind should sober any celebration.

5/3

Biden and his staff announce that he will not submit to any debates in the 2024 Democratic primary. The other candidates may debate among themselves, but Biden will not participate. Apparently Biden, acknowledging and accepting his mental depreciation, again plans on hiding in his basement during the next presidential election, just as he did in 2020, hoping for the same results. After Bidens' recent White House event when he forgot which country he just returned from, his nurses intent on keeping him hidden in his basement is prudent, if gutless.

5/4

As Bidens attempts to kick start his re-election campaign, some of his supporters are suddenly uneasy about vouching for him. The relationship between Biden and young activists is at a crossroad because according to them, Biden has fallen short on his promises. This has contributed mightily to Bidens' plunging approval ratings with 18- to 29 year-olds. For example, they cite Bidens' recent decision to approve a controversial Alaskan drilling project. Biden tries to blame Trump for this, but regardless of Bidens' attempt to pass the buck, youth voter groups express concerns that Biden seems determined to move to the political center, even at the cost of alienating this powerful voting bloc. They remind Biden that, with half of the country already opposing him, he risks his re-election chances by turning his back on the one group that supported him wholeheartedly in the last election. So far, Biden gives no indication that he is listening.

5/5

The clamor for Biden to be more responsive to the demands of younger voters continues. Multiple youth groups remind Biden that they have turned out in record numbers in recent elections and proven their mettle as organizers whose main focus is on climate, immigration, gun violence, student debt, health care and LGBTQ rights. They ask Biden that, if he is counting on them to be convincing other people to vote for him, making them wonder whether or not he is doing a great job or not is not the way to go about it. Biden has no comment.

5/6

Bidens' defense of his weaponizing the IRS to go after just 'the rich' crumbles with the re-surfacing of a video used as a IRS recruiting tool. In it, it shows IRS agents taking down, not a Wall Street broker or other member of the supposed 1%, but a small landscape business owner who failed to properly report how he paid for his vehicles. It is also reported that the 87 billion the IRS received to supposedly go after "the rich" is being used to buy duty ammunition (2.3 million), ballistic shields, (1.2 million), Smith & Wesson rifles ($474,000), duty tactical lighting; ($467,000), Barreta 1301 tactical shotguns ($427,000), tactical gear bags ($354,000), ballistic helmets ($267,000), body armor vests ($243,00) and 'various other gear for criminal investigation agents' ($1.3 million). With the IRS arming itself with enough weaponry to start a small war, it is suggested that Biden is leading the charge for authoritarian elites to get serious about their long-rumored goal of turning the Global War on Terror (GWAT) inward on American citizens.

5/7

It is reported that Bidens' primary agenda for weaponizing the IRS, to go after conservative Americans, started last year. An IRS job posting unearthed from last year asks for applicants to be willing to use firearms.

Biden made no attempt to remove the posting, which further required that aspiring agents must be willing to carry a firearm and "... must be willing to use force up to and including the use of deadly force." With the amount of armaments that the IRS has recently purchased with the largess Biden has granted them, those rich 1%'s Biden claims he is going after should be afraid... very afraid.

5/8

Biden seems hellbent on forcing radical left-wing environmentalism on working class Americans, whether they like it or not. Bidens' idiocy In this light continues to be infectious. Instead of ramping up domestic mining, Biden is turning to Communist China to supply some of the resources needed for his radical environmental green agenda. Bidens' Department of the Interior stopped a major copper and nickel mining project in northern Minnesota because it allegedly threatened waterways in the area. This project was set to become a significant domestic source of resources for electric vehicle batteries. Because of this Biden and his DOI Secretary are accused of trading away Americas' energy security for a radical climate change agenda that serves only to makes America more dependent on Communist China, Biden and his DOI guy are strangely quiet.

5/9

Biden sets yet another milestone for his presidency and it's not a good one; his 35% approval rating is not only the lowest in his term, it is the lowest in the history of any American president in his first term. Add to this Bidens' historic inflation rate, his historic illegal immigration and his historic death-laden withdrawal from Afghanistan, one can truly say Bidens' presidency is one for the history books.

5/10

Looking like butter wouldn't melt in his mouth, Biden quietly reinstates Trumps' "Remain in Mexico" policy that he canceled as part of his campaign pledge to undue most, if not all of, Trumps' immigration policy. Biden claims as coincidence that he took this action after being sued by Republican officials in Missouri and Texas to prevent the scrapping of Trumps' policy, a policy that Biden once called "inhumane". Add this to Bidens' reneging on his promise to end all construction of the border wall and ending the use of cages to house illegals, Biden - ever the hypocrite -, has quietly re-instituted most of Trumps' immigration policies.

5/11

The House Oversight and Accountability Committee reports that the Bidens' family and business associates created more than 20 companies and received more than $10 million from foreign nationals while Biden served as vice president. The HOAC also alleges that some of these payments could indicate attempts by the Biden family to sell influence and access to the then vice-president Biden. Since he began his campaign for the White House, Biden has done his best Sgt. Schultz impression, claiming: "I know nothing … NOTHING!" about his family business. This, even though the participants include his son, brother, wife and other relatives. The only way to explain this is if the door to the basement, where he has spent a good portion of his presidency, really does lock from the outside.

5/12

Biden has been sharply criticized by refugee advocates for the growing number of immigrants being held at private facilities. Biden had promised to end the private, for-profit jails but has exempted the Immigration and Customs Enforcement (ICE) agency from this effort. The result is, rather than ending these facilities, Biden has nearly doubled the number of immigrants detained in these facilities – approximately 29000 - than Trump did.

5/13

Mental denseness might be the reason why Biden misses the irony of sending $113 million more in military aid to Ukraine to help that country secure its border, while allowing record waves of illegal aliens to pour across Americas' own borders. Bidens' mental deterioration doesn't seem to be lost on the American public, though. A new poll shows that Trump would swamp Biden if the election was held today. More telling, the poll also shows that even the 18% of the American public who think Trump should be held criminally liable for any assortment of reasons, would nevertheless still vote for him today over Biden.

5/14

Despite lying for almost two-and-a-half years about the southern border being secure, Biden admits that the border has been "...in chaos..." for the entire time of his presidency. In spite of this rare display of honesty, Biden proceeds to throw more gasoline on the fire by demanding Congress pass an amnesty bill which will serve only to attract and release even more illegal aliens to and in America. It is apparent to even the most brain-dead Biden supporter that Biden has no real plan to fix the border, but instead wants more resources to process illegal aliens faster and ship them to America cities more quickly. Ever since Biden entered the Oval Office, every action he's taken immigration has led up to this current chaotic humanitarian crisis.

5/15

In yet another of his numerous attempts to pit one race against another, Biden tells Howard University graduates that the greatest threat to their future is not the historical rate of inflation he created that they are currently living under, or the global conflicts Biden is intent on involving the U.S. in, nor the humanitarian disaster his immigration policies are inflicting on their neighborhoods, or even the financial crisis Biden created that is forcing banks to close on a regular basis. No, Biden tells the students that their greatest fear should be the rise of "white supremacy" in America. His normal fear mongering, race baiting aside, Biden has a rare moment of honesty when he tells the students that: "There are those who demonize and pit people against one another. There are those who would do anything and everything, no matter how desperate or immoral, to hold onto power." A rare moment of personal reflection by Biden, and a refreshing one.

5/16

In yet another case where Biden embarrasses and humiliates America in the eyes of the world, his immigration policies force two dozen homeless veterans – that group of patriots in which some have fought and died protecting this country – to be evicted from their New York hotels to make room for illegals from the southern border. In trying to defend themselves, the hotels claim they are doing only what good capitalists do everywhere because they are only taking the tax payer funded, above-market prices Biden is willing to pay for housing his problem.

5/17

On a day Biden takes off and doesn't embarrass America on the world stage, Harris jumps in to fill the breach. She makes a trip to the wealthy Atlanta-area of Buckhead for a fundraiser. She fails to mention the Biden border crisis, of which she is the "Czar", once during a twenty minute speech to Georgia Democrats, instead focusing on abortion and complaining about January 6. Georgia Republicans put out a statement slamming Harris for attending a fundraiser while ignoring her responsibilities. It irks them that Harris is munching croissants and drinking sparkling water while Border Patrol agents and shelters on the border are overwhelmed and while cities across the country are declaring states of emergency in the wake of the worst border crisis in Americas' history. People should not be surprised by this, as they are reminded that from the day that Biden appointed her 'Border Czar', Harris has steadfastly maintained that immigration is not her responsibility. Now someone has to wake up Biden and tell him.

5/18

In a rare show of defiance, 61 Republican Congressmen pen a letter to Biden, demanding that he take a cognitive test or pull out of the 2024 presidential race. Citing their concern with his "current cognitive state and ability to serve another term as President." the Congressmen point out that, one, regardless of gender, age, or political party, all Presidents should document and demonstrate sound mental abilities and, two, a recent Harvard CAPS-Harris Poll found that 57% of voters share the Congressmen s' concerns. Biden has no comment.

5/19

At the G7 conference Biden had to be gently guided by Japanese leader Fumio Kishida, before tripping and almost falling down some stairs. Biden looked confused as his wife led him by the hand to meet his Japanese counterpart and his wife for a photo op. After shaking the Japanese leaders' hand, Biden turned to the prime minister's wife and, bizarrely, bent over with clenched fists, looking forever like a boxer getting down in his crouch. From tripping to a boxers' pose before the Japanese leaders' wife, regardless of what Bidens' intentions were, it is yet another display of the presidents infirmary, witnessed by the world.

5/20

A video of the G7 surfaces where the Japanese PM, when showing the U.S. dignitaries where to pose for photos, had to jump in to politely guide Biden to his place. This was because Biden was shuffling slowly, looking at the ground in clear confusion as to where he was supposed to stand. Now after watching Biden fend off yet again what seems to be his greatest opponent now - stairs – his friends in the media still insists that this stumbling Biden is at the peak of his mental and physical acuity. The brings to mind when some years ago the media jumped to question Trumps' health even though he walked down a ramp and didn't trip.

5/21

It is revealed that since Biden took office a large group of Republican Congressmen have sent three separate letters to Biden requesting that he submit to a cognitive exam. Biden has repeatedly failed to respond to any of the letters even though many Americans continue to question Bidens' mental and cognitive to lead the United States. In their letters the Congressmen ask why, since Biden has undergone two physical exams during his presidency, there is no indication that he has had any cognitive assessment, or if he has, the results were concealed from the public. Biden has no comment.

5/22

Bidens position on providing military aid to Ukraine takes a sudden turn. Now instead of just sending dollars, Biden commits to providing training for F16 fighter jets and, ultimately, the planes themselves. It turns out, though, that Bidens' reversal on this matter is not so sudden at all. For almost two months Biden has been quietly discussing with officials from the National Security Council, Pentagon, State Department and defense leaders from allied countries on the pros and cons of escalating the war in Ukraine. This has been, long suspected of being a major goal of Biden, even if it draws the U.S. into another war, this time with Russia. The prospect of again losing innocent lives in a pointless war hearkens a longing for the Trump years, the only years America has known peace in the last four decades.

5/23

In line with Biden painting all Trump supporters, roughly half of the people in the country, as dangerous right-wing extremists, Biden now directs his DHS group to target American citizens who exercise their Constitutional right to free speech in ways that don't align with his left-wing agenda. Surprising to some, Biden is not scared or concerned about the suspected terrorists that might be crossing his open southern border on a daily basis. No, what terrifies Biden now and keeps him awake (at least until 4:30 in the afternoon) are the soccer Moms protesting at school board meetings about the dehumanization of their children in government-run school classrooms all across the country.

5/24

Bidens' overt championing of gender-transition rights for minors has resulted in a psychological study involving 240 minor children where they were given cross-sex hormones to see what affects they would have on the minors mental health. Despite the scientific fact that those who suffer from gender dysphoria have significantly higher rates of suicide, Bidens' policies allow the study to continue. As expected, during the study 13 minors considered suicide a viable option, with 2 ending up taking their own lives His supporters tell Biden that the suicides would not have happened if only the minors had received the drugs and other 'gender-affirming care' even earlier in their lives. They assure Biden that both his gender transition policies and the study are a success, the 11 traumatized and 2 dead minors notwithstanding. Biden has no comment.

5/25

It is reported that Biden, while visiting U.S. troops stationed in Japan, once again committed stolen valor by lying about the way his son, Beau, died. He told the troops that he lost his son in Iraq. The problem with Biden repeatedly lying about this that even though his son did serve in Iraq, he died of brain cancer in 2015 in a hospital stateside, not on a Iraq battlefield. Biden has lied about the manner of his sons' death and been called out for it often, but continues to repeat the lie anyway. To be sure, lying throughout his career has never bothered Biden, but to lie about a sons' death to use it as a political prop demonstrates how empty, not just his mind, but Bidens' soul is.

5/26

Biden continues to inject his Marxist/Socialist policies into every nook and cranny of the government, including the military. It's putting the country in grave danger and Biden is furious when DeSantis calls him out on it. In a speech DeSantis insists that, under Biden, the US military has lost its way because of Bidens' insistence of forcing his diversity, equity, and inclusion (DEI) agenda on it. Based nothing more than fake science and revisionist history, Biden is forcing radical gender ideologies, Critical Race Theory (CRT) and other divisive concepts into the military. Then Biden expresses confusion as to why massive shortfalls in recruiting across the armed forces is occurring. Since this 'confuses' few if any rational people, perhaps a second can of Ensure today will make the dim bulb in his brain light up with the answer.

5/27

Giving substance to DeSantis' criticism of the damage Biden has done to the U.S. military and its' recruitment standards, it is revealed that in support of Bidens' DEI policies, the Navy has turned their recruiting efforts over to a Yeoman who performs as a drag queen to serve as their "digital ambassador". The Navy claims that this sailor, by using his drag queen persona to appeal to potential recruits on social media, was part of an effort by the Navy to connect to Gen-Z "interests and concerns." Even with drag queens now serving as recruitment officers because of Bidens' policies, he still wonders why recruiting numbers are down. Apparently the second can of Ensure didn't help.

5/28

Because of his more-apparent-than-ever mental decline, or just limp-wristed hubris, Biden demanded House Republicans pile trillions of dollars of new debt on the heads of every man, woman and child in America, all without debate. In a hysterical rant, Biden claimed unless the GOP caved in and granted him trillions in new borrowing, not only would the U.S. economy tank but the Republicans would be responsible for causing a global depression. Trying not to openly laugh at him, House Republicans called Bidens' bluff and forced him to accept cuts to his proposed spending in an effort to put America back on some sort of a path towards fiscal sanity. Bidens' bet that Americans, addicted to his excessive spending and would want more, turned out to be a bad one. A CNN poll found that 60 percent of the American people agreed with Republicans that Bidens' out-of-control spending has to end.

5/29

Even to his most ardent sycophants it is beyond dispute that Bidens' southern border policy has not only been the incentive for historical illegal immigration, but also historical human trafficking. Rather than being ashamed and embarrassed by the untold misery Biden has brought to innumerable minors being sold, abused, raped and manhandled, Biden doubles down on this abortion of human rights. Continuing his headlong rush to eliminate all of Trumps policies that had kept the border somewhat under control, Biden now sanctions the discontinuance of DNA testing of children at the border. Trump wanted the minors tested to assure that they were related to the adults that were attempting to bring them across, which eliminated most of the scourge of human trafficking. As for him resurrecting the selling, abusing, raping and manhandling of border children, Biden seems coldly indifferent, though those defending him claim that's just his senility showing through.

5/30

Bidens' sycophants continue wail in defense of Bidens' discontinuance of DNA testing of minors at the border, a current practice Trump insisted on in an effort to stop human trafficking of these minors. They point out that, first, the border is Harris' responsibility, though they are loathe to explain the disappearing act – one that even Houdini would envy – that the "Border Czar" has pulled off during her time in office. Second, they claim it unfair to hold Biden responsible since the results of his new policy, a likely major increase in child trafficking was presented to him after 4:30 in the afternoon. They are confident that once Biden wakes up and downs his morning can of Ensure, Biden will address this new abominable crisis that he has caused.

5/31

The GAO, assuming that Biden is now awake because his eyes are blinking, presents Biden with a 2022 report that shows approximately 10% of children whose DNA was tested at the border were not related to the illegal aliens claiming to be their parents or relatives. However, a national newspaper report revealed that DNA testing of border children put the family fraud number as high as 30%. Biden is informed by ICE that the DNA tests first protects children from being smuggled across the border by adults who are not their parents and, second, helps identify them. Also, on-site DNA testing has a strong deterrent effect because when faced with possible DNA testing, individuals with criminal intent often either confess about or don't attempt the child smuggling. Biden appears to be unmoved. He still insists that starting next month, border officials will no longer conduct DNA tests of border minors. With this announcement Biden finally gets the the standing ovation he has always craved, but it's from child rapists and smugglers around the world.

6/1

Biden releases a proclamation, one day before the start of Pride Month, focused on "transgender youth" and children, declaring that such young people "in over a dozen States have had their medically necessary health care banned." Biden claims that "State and local legislatures have already introduced over 600 hateful laws targeting the LGBTQI+ community.", a claim Biden cannot substantiate with facts., Biden the endorses recent legislation in California and Minnesota that allows children to access sex-change drugs and/or genital mutilation procedures even if the minor is traveling from another state. These Biden-endorsed pieces of legislation threaten to use the power of California and Minnesota state courts to take temporary emergency jurisdiction over minors who are seeking access to sex-change drugs and other procedures, even against their parents wishes,

6/3

A report surfaces that the FBI is holding a report documenting Biden taking approximately five million dollars in bribes for various political accommodations. The FBI acknowledges that they do have the Biden bribe document, but refuse the Congressional subpoena to turn it over for investigation. Instead, they offer that the document may be reviewed in their building, in a secured SCIF, as long as Congressional investigators bring no phones, recorders, cameras, notebooks, etc., - any item that would document what the Biden bribe paper actually says. Neither the Congressmen nor Biden respond.

6/4

The FBI relents and agrees to bring the report to Congress that outlines Bidens' alleged $5 million bribe-taking during his term as Vice President. This happened only after Congress subpoenaed the document, made it clear that anything short of producing the actual Biden corruption document for review would result in a contempt of Congress vote against the FBI Director. For their part, the FBI says they at first resisted the subpoena out of a concern for "...protecting the confidentiality and safety of sources and important investigative sensitivities." For their part, because the FBI cooperated a contempt vote was not necessary. For his part, Biden says nothing.

6/5

In dodging a contempt-of- Congress vote, the FBI reiterated that their slow walking of their compliance with the subpoena was only out of their concern for the possible problems which might arise. These included that using possibly unverified allegations might unfairly smear someone as guilty, taint court proceedings, harm investigations, prejudice prosecutions and/or judicial proceedings, unfairly violate privacy or reputations and create wrong impressions in the public eye. Another concern was that in complying with the subpoena they might identify CIs who provide information to law enforcement, thus placing them at risk. Strange statements coming from Bidens' FBI, since just recently they had no problem knowingly using the unverified Steele dossier to smear Trump and lie to a FISA court in order to obtain a bogus warrant to spy on Trumps' campaign, unfairly smearing him as guilty, unfairly violated his privacy and attempted to create wrong impressions of him in the public eye: Strange indeed.

6/6

Bidens' refusal to shore up the southern border forces individual states to take action in order to protect their sovereignty. Texas, under siege from the influx of illegal aliens, launched Operation Lone Star, the largest state-led border security effort in history. The Governor deploys state law enforcement and National Guard troops to its' border with Mexico. Tennessee and Nebraska have announced plans to send 100 National Guard troops and 10 state troopers to Texas to help. Florida and Mississippi vow to help Texas also, with. Florida sending 800 National Guard troops and 300 state law enforcement officers equipped with drones and boats. With the surge in fentanyl and the concurrent crime sweeping the country because of it, Biden has in effect turned every state in the Union into a border state. These states have been forced to step up and do the job of securing the border that Biden refuses to do.

6/7

Biden continues his unrelenting attack on the First Amendment in an effort to silence his political opponents. Under a thinly disguised "plan" to supposedly fight antisemitism in America, Biden has given himself unlimited power to once again silence Americans anytime they say anything Biden disagrees with. While most Americans would agree that anti-Semitic and other so-called hate speech should be discouraged, giving Biden and his lackeys the ultimate authority to determine what is improper speech should be a scary thought to all Americans. It is no accident that Bidens' latest onslaught to silence political opponents follows Elon Musk releasing the "Twitter Files," which exposed Biden colluding with Big Tech executives to monitor and censor speech and political comments Biden doesn't like.

6/8

As agreed, in order to avoid a contempt citation the FBI agrees to turn over the Biden $5 million dollar bribe-taking report to Congress. Predictably, at the same time Biden tries to distract the American public by having his DOJ indict Trump for allegedly mishandling classified documents. For Biden, another couple of historical firsts: It is the first time in American history a sitting president has his chief political rival arrested and the first time in history a sitting president has a former president arrested. Add to these Bidens' historically low poll numbers, his historical bungling of the US withdrawal from Afghanistan, his historic collapsing of the southern border, leading to a historical number of illegal aliens entering America, one might have to agree with Biden and his supporters that his presidency has so far been, in a word, historical.

6/9

Biden is asked about Saudi Arabia buying Americas' PGA golf organizations, a move that shocked much of the sports world. Questions arise about the appropriateness of America doing business with the Saudis because of their notorious connection to the 9/11 bombings in America where 3000 US citizens were killed. Many see this purchase as an attempt by the Saudis to "sports wash" their horrific human rights violations, including the murder of an American journalist. For an answer, Biden pantomimes taking a golf swing and gibberish-es: "I'm going to play for the PGA!" It is surprising, after two years of experience, reporters still expect to get a serious answer to a serious question from this brain-addled leader of America.

6/10

In what is not good news for Biden, Ronny Jackson – who served as the White House Physician for Obama and Trump.- gave a TV interview in which he said that Biden is not mentally or physically able to be president. Trumps' and Obamas' former doctor points out that Biden, continuing to have trouble talking coherently to anyone except the dead, trying to shake hands with invisible people, needing to be helped by other foreign leaders and young girls to his chair at international meetings any stage domestically, and now adding those sinister sandbags to his enemies list - along with stairs, ramps, stage exits, etc, - cannot inspire the prestige nor project the confidence and power that the American people need on the international stage. Jackson finishes the interview by calling his nurses push for Biden to run for a second term a form of malpractice. Actually most Americans, becoming more aware each day of Bidens' infirmaries, might even call it elder abuse.

6/11

Instead of Bidens and Harris' safely-distanced photo ops, Robert F. Kennedy Jr. actually visited the southern border a few days ago. Worse yet for Biden and Harris, Bidens' primary Democratic challenger did so at 2:00 AM and used his own camera to film and broadcast a huge swath of migrants illegally crossing inro the United States. Instead of repeating the idiotic Biden/Harris bromide that million of illegals crossing the American border is "good for diversity", Kennedy called out Biden and Harris, saying that the masssive illegal migration that they have encouraged is not good for either our country or the illegals and is, in his words, "unsustainable" Neither Biden nor Harris respond.

6/12

Since Biden took office more illegal aliens have entered America than the population of all but 19 states. Kennedy continues to slam Biden on this once immigration crisis that has morphed into a humanitarian one under Bidens' watch. Now an eye witness, Kennedy explains in horrifying detail how Biden is allowing the processing of illegal aliens for release into America as fast as humanly possible. Kennedy claims that the millions of illegals being allowed in by Biden are put on buses, brought to a Border Patrol station for processing and, after 4 or 5 days, released into the US on their own recognizance, most of whom are never seen or heard from again. Unlike other sycophant Democrats, Kennedy dares to call Bidens' immigration policy an "open border" policy. Biden has no comment

6/13

Accelerating Americas' slide into third world dictator status, Biden and his DOJ indict and arrest Trump on various charges. For the first time in American history, a standing president, Biden, uses the court system to try and take out his chief political rival. Sadly, close to half the country is overjoyed by Bidens' despotic move, uncaring about the enormous chasm Bidens' move digs into the soul of the Republic of the United States. One has to wonder, are Bidens' rabid supporters on the same daily diet of Ensure as Biden is, hiding in similar basements?

6/14

Bidens' border crisis and the resultant drug smuggling that Bidens' open border policies have encouraged since he took office is so bad even the Mayor of Americas' most left-wing city, San Francisco, rips Biden for not taking the problem seriously. The Mayor contends that, because of Biden, fentanyl is flooding into her city in record amounts and she demands Biden do something about it. To add fuel to this Bidens bonfire, a bipartisan group of Mayors at the U.S. Conference of Mayors draft a resolution where they demand that Biden support urgent and increased federal enforcement at the border and public health interventions to combat the national fentanyl crisis that he created. Once again ensconced safely in his basement, Biden has no comment.

6/15

It turns out that Kennedys' attacks on Biden and his immigration policy is a continuation of a previous interview where he said he would secure the border and criticized Biden, Harris and any Democrat who says it is racist to want to keep illegal aliens out of America. Kennedy makes the point that not only is it not anti-immigrant bigotry to demand an immigration system that keeps out criminals, but letting them in is what stokes bigotry. Kennedy promises that if he is elected, unlike Biden, he will enforce a secure border and expand the kind of legal immigration that "…made our country great." On health mandates, the war in Ukraine and the border, Kennedy is more in step with growing numbers of American voters, particularly dissatisfied Democrats. While Kennedys' poll number has doubled, from 12% to 24%, Bidens' languish in the high 30s.

6/16

Sine his inauguration Biden has gone all-in on forcing divisive, left-wing extremism into every nook and cranny of the federal government. Now, surprise, surprise, even his supporters are afraid Biden went too far this time. It is revealed that Biden and his Secretary of Veterans Affairs ordered American flags at some Veteran cemeteries to be replaced with the gay pride flag, beginning this month. In Mississippi, an American flag at the Biloxi National Cemetery and VA Medical Center was replaced on Memorial Day with a rainbow flag, ostensibly to honor the nation's fallen gay heroes. The move sparked a fierce backlash as Mississippi residents protested the idea that Biden had the LBGT2+ flag replace the American flag outside a veterans' cemetery. All five Mississippi Republican congressmen sent a letter demanding that the American flag be restored to its rightful position at VA facilities. Biden neither replies or comments.

6/17

Biden did nothing to discredit his reputation as a wrinkly-skin pervert when he embraced a movie actress visiting the White House. After a brief hug, Bidens' hands wanders to her chest. Startled, the woman grabbed Bidens' hands and held them away as she took a step back. This can now be added to Bidens' penchant for giving women unwanted back rubs and breathing deeply when burying his face in the hair of very young girls. Now with Bidens' insisting on wearing his Aviators both inside and outside, instead of a head of state, Biden looks more like the creepy old man in sunglasses who loiters far too long around a little girls playground, pretending to look for loose change in the grass.

6/18

Biden invites more than 1,000 male and female NCAA national championship athletes to visit the White House. It's part of the first "College Athlete Day" celebration. Incredibly, Biden forces the athletes and anyone else attending the ceremony to adhere to arcane COVID requirements that the rest of thinking Americans abandoned long ago. Biden insists that these White House guests who are not fully vaccinated wear masks at all times and maintain a 6 foot distance from others. Biden graciously does allow that fully vaccinated guests are not required to wear a mask. Biden defends his ridiculousness, claiming that he is only "following the science". In Bidens' case, this is actually true, except Bidens' "science" consists of voodoo chants, two sticks and a log.

6/19

Under Biden, China's aggressive behavior toward the United States continues to escalate. Since its inception, a central tenet of Communism has involved wiping out all religious and artistic cultural practices within a population it wishes to subjugate. For a long time now most first world countries depending on China for cheap goods, like the

United States, have turned a blind eye to such things as Chinas' current persecution of the Falun Gong. Now a new report shows that China's propaganda concerning this group has made its way into into American textbooks. Research shows that at least 10 universities are using curriculum containing propaganda attacking the Falun Gong. Yes, under the watchful eye of Biden, college campuses have become a training ground promoting Communism within the United States.

6/20

Biden unveils a new transportation goal for his administration: Hysterically, it is to build a railway from the Pacific Ocean across the Indian Ocean. Bidens' actual statement was: "We have plans to build a railroad from the Pacific all the way across the Indian Ocean..." His nurses immediately pull Biden aside to whisper two things: One, if what he meant was a railway that began at the Asian coast of the Pacific Ocean and ran all the way across the Indian Ocean, or one that begins in the Western United States and spans across two oceans and several nations, this would involve a length of track between 5000 and 10000 miles long. Second and more importantly, his nurses inform Biden that a 'train' that runs across an ocean is called a 'submarine'.

6/21

Cuba announces that it has agreed to allow China to build a spy facility on the island. This would make it possible for the Communists to eavesdrop on electronic communications across the US. Reporters wonder why Biden has no comment on the matter. True, even though a deal has been struck in principle, there doesn't seem to be any movement on building the actual facility, but still Biden has no comment. Add this to Biden allowing a Chinese spy balloon to traverse the entire U.S., collecting data, and the accusation that Biden and his family have been working for the Communists for years, is it any real wonder why Biden is silent on this new Chinese provocation? Probably not.

6/22

Biden finally responds to the charge that he accepted $5 million dollars in bribes from China by cynically challenging the American people to "...go ahead, find the money". Most Americans ignore this challenge as the majority of them believe that Bidens' biggest crime against them is his trashing their national sovereignty by leaving the southern border open to anyone, even those that wish to do harm to the United States. Since Biden took office the number of illegals that have entered America is greater than the population of 31 states. Biden is actively giving up American sovereignty while allowing drug and human smuggling, child rape and kidnapping just to consolidate power in the hands of a feeble-minded politico. Bidens' allies and supporters call him clever; the rest, maliciously narcissistic and stupid.

6/23

The media is starting to report on Bidens' radical notion that he and other leftists like Hillary and Obama thinks they should be raising the children o America. While speaking on the White House south lawn a month or so ago Biden echoed Hillarys' previous remarks on the subject, adding "There's no such thing as someone else's child, Our nation's children are all our children!" A quick refresher on this man who wants to take the place of moms and dads: While one of his sons served in the military, the other is an out-of-control meth addict whom Biden not only enabled but put in charge of national negotiations with world leaders. This weak minded emotional cripple also spawned also spawned a baby out of wedlock, a grandchild that Biden refuses to acknowledge, going so far as to deny her a place at any of Bidens' holiday tables. Yet Biden believes he is the man fit to parent Americas' children? Yeah, maybe not.

6/24

Bidens' defenders howl at the criticism of Biden being a neglectful parent and grandparent They point out that on many occasions Biden has proclaimed his pride in his meth-addled son and that he loves all six of his grandchildren. This might be true, but Biden has seven grandchildren, the seventh one he ignores being the product of his drug enabled son. Bidens' supporters offer the excuse that with so many grandchildren, it's to be expected that Biden innocently forgets how many he has. Maybe, but it's always the seventh one Biden seems to forget. Even for Biden this is a feeble excuse anyway, since the number '7' is much smaller than the number of Bidens' fingers.

6/25

Reporters wonder why Biden appears smug when commenting: "I'm very proud of my son," in reference to the guilty pleas his son accepted on three minor charges. Biden has every reason to smile. First, the plea deals his son accepted will result in no jail time. Second, Biden feels the particulars of this agreement shield him from any further investigations into the bribery and foreign influence peddling corruption charges Congress is investigating him for. Third and most important, by proclaiming that the investigation into Bidens' corruption is over, but the investigation into his sons' dealings is still ongoing, Bidens' FBI and DOJ can continue refusing to turn over to Congress any documents related to Bidens' own corruption charges: Smug, indeed.

6/26

His metal deterioration again on display, Biden reads out loud the 'end of quote' line that was at the end of a teleprompter quote he was reading to reporters. This comes just days after Biden finished a gun safety speech with the bizarre statement "God save the Queen!". It reminded Americans of a line in Bidens' State of the Union speech this year when he told Republicans: "Lots of luck in your senior year." Even his nurses, usually quick to offer feeble explanations and excuses for Bidens' many malaprops, have to throw up their hands in bewilderment. As usual, after finishing his latest speech Biden was confused about where to exit the stage and had to be led by one of his nurses; at least they can still do this properly.

6/27

Bidens' repeated claim that he knows nothing of his son's corrupt business dealings, which reaped millions for Biden and his family, took a hit with the recent release of a taped conversation between Bidens' son and Henry Zhao. In it, Bidens' son threatens Zhao with retaliation if a payment he is demanding is not received. He claims that the elder Biden – Joe himself - is sitting in on the conversation and "…if I (Bidens' son) get a call or text from anyone involved in this other than you, Zhang, or the Chairman, I will make certain that between the man sitting next to me and every person he knows and my ability to forever hold a grudge that you will regret not following my direction." It remains to be seen if the American people are willing to let this go easily, considering that it appears Biden was involved at least in one ugly extortion scheme with top officials from a foreign nation's spy agency. For his part, Biden has no comment.

6/28

One reporter attempts to catalog Bidens' lies/misstatements in a list which he publishes on social media, with varying results; Biden lies so often it's difficult to keep the list current. Just recently Biden claimed he and his administration had initiated 700,000 public projects when the number is actually 7000. Then Biden tired to take credit for a cap put on prescription drug costs for seniors he claim he started for this year when the cap doesn't take effect until 2025. Then Biden once again railed against American billionaires, claiming now they paid only 3%

in income taxes between 2010 and 2018. Apparently Bidens' nurses did not inform him that his own White House economists admit that the top 400 households in America paid an average effective tax rate of about 23% in 2018, while households earning from $50,000 to $100,000 yearly paid effective tax rates between 0% and 15%. At this pint the reporter gives up his quest for a catalog, realizing that listing Bidens' lies or his misstatements, 'misspeaks' as his nurses like to call them, could turn into a full-time job.

6/29

Any ideas Biden might have for "Father of the Year' takes another hit, again concerning the granddaughter he and his wife refuse to acknowledge. The mother of his disowned grandchild wants the girl to have Bidens' last name. The Biden family opposes this, ostensibly because "...the notoriety (of having the Biden last name) would no doubt rob the child of (a) peaceful existence." Showing that Bidens parental instincts run in the family, this mother further stated that Bidens' son, the father, has "never seen or contacted" the child and Biden senior and the first lady "remain estranged" from her. To sum up, Biden is party to the denial of paternity, then estranges himself from his grandchild, then refuses to let the child use his last name, then continues to pretend she doesn't exist. Yet, unbelievably, half of America believes Biden and his ilk should have a say in raising their children.

6/30

Bidens' paternal instincts seem to run through some members of his family. His son was successful in having the courts slash his monthly child support payments and forbidding his daughter to use 'Biden' for her last name. However, for sheer familial coldness the family member that can hold a candle with Biden is the First Lady. She authored a children's book and dedicated the work to her grandchildren. She could have left it at that, but in a seeming spiteful fit she named every grandchild by name except her out-of-wedlock granddaughter. Nor was this the only time the First Ladys' juvenile side showed. At Christmas the family hung a Christmas stocking for every grandchild except their sons' daughter, an act not lost on their disowned sibling since the Bidens also hung a stocking for their dog. Turns out that when it comes to snubbing and personally embarrassing inconvenient relatives, Bidens' dog is not the only bitch in the White House.

7/1

Bidens' mental deterioration seems to continue to infect his staff. Bidens' hypocrite environmental Czar proclaims that 25 million people around the world die each year from climate change and the use of fossil fuels. Since approximately 60 million people die around the globe each year, Biden and his flunky assert that half of all world deaths are the result of Bidens' notion of climate change. The naked stupidity of such a statement is obvious to all but Biden supporters. Even a United Nation study presented by a group of radical left-wing environmental activists predicted that approximately 38 thousand deaths – not 25 million – will be caused yearly by climate change over the next eighty years. Despite this Biden continues to use his Czars' insane proclamations to shove his anti-industry, anti-economy and anti-freedom green agenda down the throats of the American people.

7/2

Bidens' use of apocalyptic rhetoric to push his goal of eliminating fossil fuels in the U.S. does not go unnoticed. A government watchdog group, PPT, filed an ethics complaint against Bidens' climate czar for blatantly misrepresenting the science on climate change. The group points out that Biden and his czar violated their own scientific integrity policy which states that government officials must present scientific information accurately based on the best available information. The PPT points out that not only is there no scientific evidence that supports the Biden administrations' wild claims, but such statements "inevitably erodes the public's trust in its scientific and governing institutions…" On this point, the PPT is a bit late: According to several recent polls, trust in Bidens' ability to govern eroded long ago.

7/3

The Supreme Court issues a ruling blocking Bidens' student loan forgiveness program, a program even Biden admitted he had no legal or constitutional right to initiate or enforce. Yet Biden, as a fob to his constituents, feigns outrage, blames Republicans for the failure and threatens to use an arcane 1965 law to get around the SCOTUS ruling and still allow deadbeats to renege on their contractual obligations. However, this law requires a national emergency to be in place before it can be used to forestall student loan repayment. This presents no problem for Biden, however. With no national emergency in sight, Biden suggests that the law be re-written, on the fly, eliminating this requirement. It is reported that Biden, out of sight in his Delaware basement, stomps his feet and whines about the unfairness of a world that does not allow him to institute and enforce unconstitutional edicts at his whim.

7/4

More than appropriate for Independence Day, a judge hands down a big win for the First Amendment and a huge defeat for Biden. In a lawsuit filed by the Attorney Generals of Louisiana and Missouri, Biden got caught providing an enemies list for censorship in 2021 of social media users who opposed Bidens' COVID narrative. In celebration of July 4, whether intended or not, the judge issues an injunction blocking Biden and anyone in his administration from meeting with social media companies about "protected speech." In reading the injunction it becomes clear that if the allegations are true, Biden has launched the most massive attack against free speech in the history of the United

States. It will be interesting to see what reaction Biden has to this, once his nurses read the injunction to him.

7/5

A white powdery substance is found in a small packet in the West Wing of the White House, rumored to be cocaine. It's in an area where, when he's not hiding in his basement, Biden spends much of his time. The packet is immediately taken for further testing. Meanwhile Bidens' staff quickly and emphatically insists that Biden had nothing to do with and and knows nothing about the substance. However they are loath to explain why, for the first time since his inauguration, Biden is seen walking around the White House, fully awake, after 4:30 in the afternoon.

7/6

The white powder found in the White House does indeed test positive for cocaine. Bidens' staff still vehemently denies that their boss was in anyway connected with the drug and, besides, they claim Biden was at Camp David when the snort was found. Reporters ask about a story that an aged, fumbling and stumbling old man in Aviators was found in an open-air parking lot near Dulles International. He was stretched out on the trunk of a car, face up, giggling as he watched the huge airliners pass close overhead on their way to landing. Bidens' staff insist this octogenarian couldn't be Biden as he was still at Camp David. This explanation is accepted, though there are many questioning looks on the faces of the reporters,

7/7

Bidens' agenda defeats at the hands of the Supreme Court continue. In recent days the Court has struck down Bidens' illegal and unconstitutional student loan bailout plan, struck down affirmative action in college admissions and upheld the First Amendment rights of a Christian web designer not having to provide on-demand services for a homosexual wedding because it violated her religious faith. Enraged, Biden tried to whip up his supporters by smearing the Court as "not normal." It turns out that once again it is Biden who not "normal". A poll released after the Courts' activity shows that Americans approved of their decisions to uphold the First Amendment and end Biden's student loan bailout. In fact their decision to end affirmative action in college admissions was popular by a 20-point margin. To Bidens' chagrin, it turns out the Supreme Court rulings are actually representing "normal" Americans.

7/8

Republicans on the House Oversight Committee announce that they are determined to find out exactly how many illegal aliens Biden has allowed into the US via the parole process. They claim that Biden has flagrantly abused the system, using it to parole over a million aliens, who should've been inadmissible, into the United States in just over the last two years. The Republicans claim – and want Biden to either clarify or deny – that 99% of formerly inadmissible aliens who applied for an appointment through the US Customs and Border Protection agency were ultimately approved for parole. Biden has no comment.

7/9

During the daily White House press briefing, Bidens' press secretary shut down all questions concerning Bidens' continuing denial of his seventh grandchild. It appears that Biden has told all of his staff and nurses that, if asked publicly, the president only has six grandchildren, omitting the grandchild sired by his son. Biden doubles down on this order, proclaiming: "I have six grandchildren, and I'm crazy about them And I speak to them every single day; not a joke." Apparently Biden is not 'crazy' about all his grandchildren and doesn't speak to at least one of them every day. Regardless what Biden says, this is a joke, albeit a sick one.

7/10

Though the extent of Bidens' mental decline has been well-documented throughout his presidency, his latest proposal would have any shrink, even if on retainer, volunteering to give the money back. Biden and his global cooling/global warming/climate change/next fraud/hoax fanatics are insisting the only way to stop their perceived coming apocalypse is to block sunlight from hitting the earth in a bid to lower temperatures. Biden even has a name for this project. Biden calls it "Solar Radiation Modification' or 'SRM' for short. Some scientists warn that even if Bidens' fantasy would work, it also could have devastating side effects. The executive director of a solar geoengineering company said the mere existence of a White House report on SRM is "significant." This is because, even though Biden and his climate czars have produced a laundry list of astoundingly bad ideas, this one 'could take the cake'. Biden, doing his part to combat climate change, readjusts his Aviators and says nothing.

7/11

When Bidens' SRM plan is announced, what started as muffled giggles break out in guffaws when it is revealed that Biden stole the idea from an animated TV show. This explains why Biden, while touting his SRM plan, did not mention that altering the sunlight the earth receives could change global weather patterns, disrupt food supplies and do more harm than good to human health. Biden also neglects to mention that his SRM plan doesn't even address what Biden blames as the root cause of climate change, carbon emissions. Using a cartoon to battle climate change while he fumbles around, searching for his next extreme policy, is a new low even for Biden.

7/12

In a recent interview in front of a worldwide audience, Biden announces that the United States is low on 155 mm artillery ammunition rounds. Reactions from the public is swift and ranges from confused to outrage as pundits and experts alike wonder why Biden would announce any U.S. military shortage during a nationally televised interview, since it can be seen by Americas' adversaries. In Bidens' defense, in his current mental state it is possible he confused the 155 artillery rounds with what he thinks are the 155 flavors of Ben and Jerry's ice cream and this is the supply Biden is worried that America might run short of.

7/13

Bidens' carefully crafted pose as an elderly, kind, even-tempered politician takes a hit as aides report being subjected continually to Bidens' out-of-control, invective-laced tirades. It has gotten so bad that few will approach Biden alone, always being sure to take a colleague along, almost as a shield against one of Bidens' famous 'solo blasts'. Several aides recount being taken aback, assuming that such classless behavior and language are the province of the uneducated, the street thug. With Bidens' well-documented history of graduating at the bottom of his classes and penchant for nasty bullying, the surprise is that the aides are surprised at all.

7/14

A story surfaces that when visiting several cities on in a row on a political campaign tour, Biden often asks his Secret Service aides what city he is in so as not to be confused. One of Bidens' staff reported that recently Biden asked the Secret Service again about his whereabouts. Now a common enough occurrence, but this time when Biden asked the question he was standing in the White House.

7/15

Bidens' gross habit of inappropriately touching females, of all ages, now goes past creepy and approaches the outer edges of pedophilia. While visiting Finland a video shows Biden apparently try to nibble on the shoulder of a startled little girl. The incident, which took place before Biden boarded Air Force One at Helsinki-Vantaan International Airport, shows Biden leaning into a young girl and placing his mouth on her shoulder, nibbling lightly. The little girl appears frightened, but then shows incredible good taste for such a young age by turning her head away when Biden – all 81 wrinkled old years of him - tries to kiss her. In a sarcastic defense of Bidens' behavior, one wag postulates that maybe in his deteriorating mental condition, Biden now is confusing very young girls with ice cream cones.

7/16

Bidens' effort to take Trump out of the 2024 Presidential race with Jack Smiths' laughable 37-count indictment continues, but it turns out that Trump is not the only target of Bidens' weaponized Justice Department. Biden also has given the green light to his Attorney General to target and harass Trump supporters, conservatives, and pro-life activists. Not at the bottom yet, Biden gets close to it when a pastor in Philadelphia had his home raided by armed federal agents for simply praying in front of an abortion clinic. If it wasn't blatantly obvious before, Bidens' weaponizing of the justice system is now.

7/17

Throwing what has become an all-too-familiar tantrum when he doesn't get his way, Biden pushes ahead with another plan to erase student loan debt. Ignoring the Supreme Court ruling that he did not have the legal or constitutional right to do so, Biden plans on using something called the 'Higher Education Law' to write a regulation that will allow him to cancel student debt. Though not clear what the process will look like or how far it will go, Biden pushes forward anyway. It is expected to take at least several months and the resulting rule may also face legal challenges. Undeterred, Biden wanders on, not content until his vision of punishing the productive and responsible, while rewarding the unproductive and irresponsible, becomes a reality.

7/18

Biden is stunned with the House Oversight Committees' announcement that the IRS whistle blowers, who revealed the efforts that Biden and his Justice Department made to thwart the investigation into Bidens' son, would testify before the committee. It is expected that these whistle blowers will provide information to Congress about how Bidens' Justice Department refused to follow evidence that implicated Biden, tipped off his sons' attorneys, allowed the clock to run out with respect to certain charges while providing a sweetheart plea deal him. The ultimate goal of this committee is to end the apparent two-tiered justice system that allows the Biden family to operate above the law.

7/19

The House Oversight Committees' hearing into criminal activity by Biden and his family begins with it centered on the testimony of two IRS whistleblowers. They allege that the criminal probe into Hunter Biden was mishandled by the Justice Department and ended up giving preferential treatment to the younger Biden. Then the hearing ground to a halt when a Congresswoman, flashing pictures taken from Bidens' sons' laptop, asked the whistle blowers if they believed the presidents' son's involvement with prostitutes violated any federal laws, like the Mann Act. It turns out that is a question for another committee and another investigation. All in all, not a good first day for Biden.

7/20

Even when Biden takes a day off from his mumbling gaffes, there is no rest because Harris is willing and more than able to take his place. In a recent speech to college students, Harris raised eyebrows by claiming that the U.S. needs to reduce its population to help future generations have clean water and air. She stated: "When we … reduce population, more of our children can breathe clean air and drink clean water." Reducing the population to cut down on pollution has been a longstanding goal of Biden and the radical left. This harks back to Obama and his "Science Czar", who wrote a book that supported government-mandated population control. One has to look no further than China after the Communists took control. They instituted a "one-child policy," which has had disastrous consequences for that country. Apparently neither Biden nor Harris have taken that look.

7/21

Biden is taken by surprise when a Republican Senator proposes a bill to hold Biden accountable for trampling on working class Americans' First Amendment rights. His latest bill, the Free Speech Protection Act, would put Biden and his administration on notice by allowing American citizens to sue Biden and other members of the executive branch who violate their First Amendment rights. The bill would require that communications between government agencies and social media companies be regularly published in publicly available reports Biden, either stunned or jones-ing without his afternoon can of Ensure, has no comment.

7/22

Two more polls are published where the majority of Americans, including the majority of Democrat voters, feel Biden is not fit to hold office. Only a third of the Democrat voters polled believe Biden is a strong candidate.

Biden then compounds this lack of faith by announcing that, like in 2020, he will run his 2024 campaign out of his basement in Delaware. Grassroots supporters bemoan this decision, feeling it exemplifies Bidens' physical and mental weakness. However, these voters might be missing the silver lining here. Ensconced in his basement, for Biden there will be few stairs to fall down, invisible objects to trip over, doorjambs to bump his head on, invisible people to shake hands with, dead people to talk to, stages to wander around lost on, teleprompters to confound him, bicycles to fall off of and little girls for him to feel and smell. Add to this an unlimited supply of Ensure at his fingertips, Biden again hiding in his basement is probably a good thing for the Democrats and their mentally deteriorating candidate.

7/23

Some time ago Biden announced he was going to phase out gas stoves because they were, according to Bide, environmentally unfriendly. Now, not content with just gas stoves, Biden his sights on prohibiting Americans from owing gas water heaters. Biden assures American homeowners that he intends to do this in an effort, not to save the environment, but to save taxpayers billions of dollars. How Biden proposes to achieve these 'consumer savings' is unclear since electric water heaters are vastly more expensive to own and vastly more expensive to operate and repair than conventional gas ones. After hearing this, another foray into Bidens' fractured reality, the American taxpayer has to wonder if there is a natural gas leak in Bidens' basement that hasn't been attended to in awhile.

7/24

A congresswoman stuns Biden by re-introducing a bill called the ' Lead by Example Act' which was introduced earlier this year. Originally set to force members of Congress and Biden officials to receive the same health care that veterans do, this proposed iteration contains something more. It would force Biden and his agencies to set their office thermostats to 78 degrees, which is what Biden recommends the rest of the country do during the sweltering summer heat. Biden would also be required to turn over information to Congress detailing what his and his staffs' office temperatures have been since Biden took office. Bidens' DOE and EPA guidelines recommend every working-class American set their thermostats to 78 degrees in the morning, 85 degrees during the day, and crank it all the way to 88 degrees at night. Even before it is voted on, Bidens' nurses file a request for an exemption from the law. Their reasoning is purposely vague, but it has long been suspected that the temperature in Bidens' basement must be kept at a sub-60 degree level in order to preserve what is left of him.

7/25

While Biden remains somewhat preserved in his basement, he sends Harris out as a surrogate in attack-dog mode. Unfortunately for Biden, she lies or misrepresents almost every point she tries to make almost as often as he does. In a series of stump speeches, she infers that American women need regular access to abortion centers because they can control neither their bodies nor their desires, which is a lie. She says that she and Biden are fighting for a future free from discrimination and hate, while it has been documented in the courts that she and Biden have sought to discriminate and censor any and all who oppose them and have worked with social media Tech companies to make this happen. Bidens' nurses don warm weather gear and head for his basement to tell him that his attack dog is not working out so well. It is unclear if Biden, stiff but preserved, even hears them.

7/26

Either unwilling or unable to stop her, Biden – who probably hoped Harris would follow in MLKs' "I Have Dream" footsteps - allows Harris' "I Have a Nightmare' tour to continue. In another stump speech, she vows to fight for "safe communities". This from a woman who not only supported BLM while they torched and assaulted cities in the US, but also started a fund to raise bail for the few that were arrested for this criminal destruction. Then she said she would fight for paid leave, clean water and affordable childcare, amenities already existing in many American communities. Continuing on this line, she insists that she and Biden will fight so US citizens can take their laundry to the cleaners, wear clothes of their choosing, watch TV, drink coffee, eat at McDonalds and drive on the right side of the road. Harris promises that she and Biden would not stop until all of these rights were secured for all Americans.

7/27

The governor of Texas informs Biden that he will not comply with Bidens' DOJ request to remove the floating barriers in the Rio Grande River he put there to deter illegal border crossings. Further, the Governor warns Biden that he was prepared to battle him in court. Previously Biden had threatened legal action against the Governor if the barriers were not removed. The Texas governor further chastised Biden, saying that if Biden truly cared about human life, he would enforcer federal immigration laws. In the meantime, the governor warns Biden that he and his state of Texas will fully utilize its constitutional authority to deal with this crisis that Biden has created.

7/28

It is rumored that Biden has another of his famous fits when a U.S. Senator announces that he will hold up all promotions and nominations in the military until the taxpayer-funded abortion pipeline in the military is ended. Both Democrats and some Republicans criticize and try to stop the Senator but he remains steadfast. He responds to Bidens' fit, saying, one, he will continue to deter Biden from turning the military from an elite fighting force to "...just another outfit for liberal social engineering" and, two, the more Biden criticizes and mocks him, the more he's convinced0 he is doing the right thing.

7/29

After four years and intense, near-unanimous criticism, Biden finally, acknowledges his granddaughter born out of wedlock. It took reports surfacing that as many as 80% of Americans believe Bidens' disavowing of her existence for so long to be horrific before Biden caved and did the right thing. It is both sad and hard to believe that Biden and his wife are so bereft of any moral character or decency that they willingly partake in the emotional abuse of their own granddaughter until a poll – a poll – forces them to change their behavior, even if it's only because their black hearts realize it is politically unpopular

7/30

Unable to help himself, Biden cannot let his sudden, politically motivated acknowledgment of his out-of-wedlock granddaughter sift quietly into the American conscious. Incredible for anyone but them, Biden blames his and his wifes' ostracizing of their granddaughter on the child herself, saying they refused to recognize her all these years in order to protect her "privacy". Apparently the Bidens want everyone to believe that all of the interviews where they refused to acknowledge her existence, all the press briefings where they insisted they had only six grandchildren, all the book dedications where they swore their love for "all" of their grandchildren but named only six, and even the hanging of seven stockings at Christmas, but the seventh one being for their dog, all of this was done just to protect the infant girls' "privacy". If it wasn't before it should be apparent to most that Biden and his wife are very, very sick people.

7/31

Bidens' latest stab at circumventing Second Amendment rights in America takes a more subtle approach. In this one Biden blocks federal funding for any schools that have hunting and archery programs. Bidens' DOE determined that under something called the BSCA, school hunting and archery classes are precluded from receiving federal funding. This could impact millions of American children enrolled in such programs. Teachers of these classes argue that not only the skills derived from these classes help young people grow to be responsible adults, they also benefit from relationships with role models. Both arguments fall on Bidens' ever-growing deaf ears.

8/1

The most horrifying aspect of the crisis that Biden has created at the southern border is that it has highlighted the ugly fact that the US is the number one market in the world for sex-trafficked minors, the majority of which come from Mexico. It is documented that, under Biden, eighty-five thousand unaccompanied children, thousands of them under the age of five, showed up at Americas' southern border over the last two years and were "lost". One former official pointed out that, because of Biden, it is harder to adopt a cat out of a shelter than it is for a so-called 'sponsor' to show up at the border, check one of these lost kids out and take him/her home. When informed of this, Bidens' only response is to break out his famous Sgt. Shultz impression: "I see nothing... NOTHING!"

8/2

Biden and his regime are now openly working to stop Texas from blocking illegal aliens from entering the state. A video surfaces that shows Biden officials cutting holes in the wire barriers set up by Texas to block illegal immigration, allowing them further entry into the US.

Biden is determined to stop anyone from containing the damage from the disaster he has created. Bidens' excuse for cutting the wire is that since the illegal aliens had already crossed the Rio Grande and were on U.S. soil, they were protected by Federal immigration laws. According to Biden, under these laws the wire barrier put up by Texas are not permitted. Biden orders the orders the barriers removed, allowing even more illegals to enter the US, with his blessing.

8/3

Biden defends his taking down the barriers Texas erected in an effort to stop the flood of illegal immigration into the state. Biden claims that individuals who cross unlawfully into Texas and the US will be subject to something called the ' lawful pathways rule', which he insists places "...common-sense conditions on asylum eligibility..." Critics accuse Biden of creating the 'lawful pathways rule' as a jailbreak scheme that allows virtually all illegal aliens to be released into the US with little or no vetting. Biden has no comment.

8/4

Reportedly a close friend and business partner of Bidens' son will testify before Congress that Biden was routinely put on speakerphone during his sons' foreign business meetings. But before he can testify, Biden and his DOJ order the witness to report to begin serving a prison sentence he received earlier, thus making him unavailable for the Congressional hearing. After intense media backlash for his latest Stalin-esque move, Biden relents. First Trump, now this witness: If overcrowding in jails is such a problem, the strain could be eased just by releasing the political prisoners Biden has jailed.

8/5

The friend and business partner of Bidens' son testifies before Congress. He states that over the last ten years Biden joined his son on the phone as many as 20 times with various people from foreign countries while his son discussed business. However, the witness also states that Bidens' participation on these calls was relegated to mostly casual conversation, with Biden asking such questions as "How are you?' and "Hows the weather?" and even "How's the fishing?" It's good to know that, in a pinch, travelers intending to visit China, Russia or the Ukraine can call Biden on a moments notice and get tips on the weather and fishing possibilities in these vacation hot spots.

8/6

A political reporter notes that it seems more than a coincidence that every time Biden becomes immersed in a new scandal, he and and his DOJ slap Trump with new charges that seem more witch hunts than prosecutorial offenses. The reporter continues that not only do the latest indictments brought against Trump by Biden have no substance, when the reporter "….take(s) a red pen through material that is protected by the First Amendment, it reduces much of this (indictment) to a haiku…" However, Biden persists in his belief that he can arrest his way into a re-election win next year.

8/7

With all of the spurious indictments Biden fostered against Trump, it must be a major disappointment for Biden that new polls show that if the election was held today, Trump would still beat him. Before the latest indictment, Trump trailed Biden in a head-to-head election poll, 42% - 39%. After Bidens' latest courtroom clown show, polls show Trump has pulled even at 43% for both. The deadlock raises questions about what impact more indictments on the former president will do for his standing with potential voters. Biden has two more indictments ready for Trump. If past is prologue, Bidens' silly courtroom antics could indict Trump back into the White House in 2024.

8/8

At a congressional forum Gold Star families who lost loved ones spoke out about the tragedy caused by Biden disastrous exit from Afghanistan. The families demanded answers from Biden about why their loved ones were killed outside the Kabul airport nearly two years ago. One mother shared an eerily insensitive encounter with Biden shortly after her son's death. Biden told her his oft-told lie about bringing his son home also in a flag-draped coffin from the battle field. The common theme among all family members present was their disappointment in Biden for dodging accountability regarding what happened on the day their sons were killed. Even at this personally devastating moment for these parents, Biden has no comment; no accountability and no comment.

8/9

With the same imbecilic grin and thousand-mile stare, Biden debuts the term Bidenomics" as a slogan to tout his imaginary economic successes. Economists have slammed "Bidenomics" reckless spending for causing soaring inflation, a 40-year-high inflation, record drops in labor productivity, anemic economic growth, growing credit card debt, rising interest rates, insipid labor force participation, onerous regulation, falling real incomes and excess government spending, borrowing and gluttonous printing of money. On top of this, working-class Americans' disposable income is much lower under Biden due to the inflation crisis he created eroding any pay raises American workers might have received. One researcher declared that when it is distilled down to a single word, 'Bidenomics' means 'failure. For his part, Biden demands a dictionary be brought to his basement so one of his nurses can read the definition of 'success' to him again.

8/10

Biden is finally asked about Congressional testimony that had him on the phone with his son when he was discussing business deals with foreign agents. Biden snaps at the reporter, calling the question "lousy" because he, Biden, "... never talked business with anybody," The reporters in the room let out a quiet gasp: Whether Biden "talked business" or not is irrelevant By admitting that he was on the phone with these foreign agents/businessmen, Biden is admitting he lied when for months he said repeatedly that he had no connections, awareness or proximity with his sons' business dealings. In trying to defend yet another Biden lie, his supporters insist that, even if on the phone, Biden was interested only in weather and fishing tips.

8/11

Biden is stunned when the House Oversight Committee released new bank records showing $20 million in payments from oligarchs in Ukraine, Kazakhstan, and Russia into the bank accounts of various Biden family members and their associates. The memo included photographs of then Vice President Biden posing with foreign oligarchs at dinner parties after they wired money into LLCs controlled by his son. Shortly afterwards the ex-wife of the Mayor of Moscow wired $3.5 million to Bidens' son and then afterwards appeared at a dinner reception with Biden. This, coupled with his sons' admission that he was forced by Biden to hand over half his salary, makes it impossible to believe that Biden did not know and was not benefiting from the millions of dollars his son took in on these foreign lobbying schemes. Biden has no comment.

8/13

Biden suffers another setback when the Ford Motor Company announced that their commitment to fall in line behind Biden's plan to force drivers into electric vehicles is turning into a financial disaster for the company. Ford revealed that the company is projected to lose $4.5 billion on its electric vehicle division, Model E, this year alone. That's more than twice the amount the company lost on its EV division in 2022. Electric vehicles are piling up on car dealers' lots across the country with consumers sticking to more-trusted gasoline-powered equivalents. Ford went all-in on Biden and his environmental extremist supporters' effort to force Americans to switch to electric vehicles by the end of the decade. Now the company is paying the price. Biden has no comment concerning this announcement.

8/14

Biden offers a dismissive "No comment" when asked about the death toll in Hawaii, which has climbed to at least 96. During a bike ride a day earlier, Biden gave a similar unfeeling answer when asked about the tragedy, saying only that he was "...looking at it." when asked if he planned to visit the Aloha State. Biden is currently scheduled to visit Wisconsin Tuesday and travel to Camp David Thursday for meetings with the leaders of South Korea and Japan the following day. Then he plans to visit, not Hawaii, but Lake Tahoe and remain there for at least a week. On the same day as his bike ride, Biden is pictured lounging with a group of people on Rehoboth Beach, triggering outrage on social media. If Biden is aware of the criticism, his dimly-lit eyes don't show it.

8/15

Bidens' dismissive attitude of the plight of US citizens in Hawaii results in the expected outrage. His critics blast Biden for his continuing indifference to calamitous events affecting Americans. It is pointed out that his lack of empathy for the victims of the Maui fires is just the latest in a long-line of his uncaring postures, from the suffering people of East Palestine, Ohio to the suffering people in border towns. One reporter pointed out that, not unlike Nero fiddling while Rome burned, Biden was riding his bike on the beach while the people of Lahaina, Hawaii dug through the ashes of their shattered community. Even his supporters in Hawaii who campaigned and voted for Biden were angered at his seeming lack of concern. When asked about this, Biden throws fuel on the fire by replying only "No comment".

8/16

It is now suggested that the perceived story of Bidens' family corruption is backwards. Before it had been believed and reported that it was his son exploiting Bidens' name and bringing him in on deals. It turns out it really was the senior Biden using his son. It begs the question: What supposedly caring father would allow his drug-addicted son access to a fortune? Obviously enabling his son's addiction with a flood of foreign cash blows up Bidens' carefully crafted image of being a loving, concerned parent. Actually this image was already blown when it was discovered that Biden had repeatedly disavowed his out-of-wedlock granddaughter the last four years.

8/17

With Bidens' consent, the DA trying Trumps' latest indictment seeks to strip Trump of his First Amendment rights by imposing a gag order that would limit Trump's ability to defend himself from political attacks about the case while on the campaign trail. The Obama-appointed judge trying the case signaled she was supporting Bidens' efforts to muzzle his chief political rival. She also offers to speed up the trial so the DA can win a conviction of Trump at the most politically beneficial time for Biden. Trump ridicules the proceeding, calling it – as half the country seems to agree - a politically-motivated farce that Biden orchestrated to help him win re-election.

8/18

Either because of another brain-fade or outright belligerence, Biden admits that his so-called "Inflation Reduction Act" was nothing more than a scheme to impose Bidens' wildly unpopular Green New Deal on America. At a speech in New Mexico, Biden told a crowd the IRA "... has nothing to do with inflation..." but instead was targeted at energy companies for the sake of Bidens' perceived climate change crisis. Biden boasts that $368 billion of the supposed inflation fighting act was the single largest investment in climate change anywhere in the world. Meanwhile, inflation remains one of the top problems Biden has forced Americans to face for more than two years running.

8/19

In a bizarre attempt to circumvent the recent Supreme Court ruling on abortion, Biden and his HHS Secretary continue to try and exploit what they consider loopholes in the law in order to enable abortions. Bidens' HHS secretary announces that ER doctors may perform elective abortions in emergency rooms, insisting it's legal under the Emergency Medical Treatment and Labor Act (EMTALA). As interpreted by Biden, this act violates the conscience rights of medical personnel who believe that abortion is immoral. Several groups, including the the State of Texas, have filed a lawsuit to stop Biden and his HHS secretary from labeling abortions as "critical care" for pregnant women just so abortions, otherwise illegal, can be carried out in emergency rooms. One lawyer noted that trying to force doctors to take the life of an unborn child under a law that is designed to save lives is "ludicrous" Biden has no comment.

8/20

House Republicans are coming closer to exposing Biden and his familys' alleged involvement in a complex criminal corruption ring. The House Oversight Committee Chairman is going to issue a request to the National Archive and Records Administration for a number of documents directly involved in his investigations. These documents allegedly contain communications between Biden and a number of individuals seeking to gain influence in the White House in exchange for large amounts of cash. In order to disguise his identity, then-Vice President Biden allegedly used various pseudonyms such as "Robert Peters," "Robin Ware," and "JRB Ware." Sadly now, due to his diminished mental state, the pseudonym Biden uses now to hide his identity is "Joe Biden".

8/21

New polls continue to show that the number one issue in the country remains the economy. Just 38% of Americans approve of Biden's handling of the economy as inflation drives the negative mood in the public. Biden feebly keeps trying to gaslight Americans public into thinking inflation is cooling because it's 'only' been rising around three percent over the last year, a decline from the nine percent inflation in 2022. It appears Biden thinks the public too dumb to realize that the three percent increase is on top of, not instead of, the nine percent from a year ago and prices are not declining. Maybe his nurses have misled Biden into making these false claims by convincing him that the country is on the same steady diet of Ensure that he is.

8/22

When the news broke about of the devastating wildfires in Hawaii, Biden sat on the beach in Delaware. For days, when asked by the media about the fires, Biden replied "no comment", even smiling at reporters who asked the questions. It took him a week to decide to visit the island, but only after extreme political pressure. His published scheduled showed, up to that point, he had no intention of visiting the devastated area. It's lucky that Bidens' nurses read the polls to him on a daily basis. Because of this, in just the last few weeks the polls convinced Biden to acknowledge his illegitimate granddaughter and leave both beach and basement to visit the ruins in Hawaii.

8/23

In a classic example of being careful of what you ask for, it turns out that Bidens' visit actually punishes the people of Hawaii. In what was supposed to be a prepared speech Biden, in short order, says 'travedy' when trying to pronounce 'tragedy, mispronounced the names of several Hawaiian officials, ranted nonsensically about the fire, slurring his words and speaking what sounded like gibberish throughout. Biden then boasts about his relief plan for Maui, initially promised a whopping $700 to each resident, the residents of whom many had lost their homes and all worldly possessions. The fact that this pitiful amount of largess from Biden comes on the heels of his requesting another $24 billion in aid to Ukraine, again demonstrates Bidens' brain-dimmed, embarrassing lack of awareness and empathy.

8/24

In another blatant example of Biden having more in common with Americas' enemies than he does with its' citizens, Biden and his DOJ consider plea deals with the architect of the 9/11 attacks and his fellow defendants to enable them to avoid the death penalty. Biden continues the tradition started by Obama, who in May 2014 released 5 terrorists in exchange for U.S. Army Sergeant Bowe Bergdahl. Bergdahl distinguished himself by deserting his post in Afghanistan to join the enemy as a member of the Taliban. Under Trump, Bergdahl plead guilty in 2017 to charges of desertion before the enemy. Under

Biden, continuing an Obama tradition, a federal judge voids Bergdahls' conviction, calling him a hero.

8/25

It is reported that Biden and his family are huddling in an exclusive home on the shores of Lake Tahoe in Nevada amid the special counsel investigation into Bidens' son Hunter. Supposedly Biden is renting the $18 million home of a environmental activist friend for a nine-day vacation Biden needs after his arduous 6 hour trip to Hawaii to survey the fire damage there and apologize for his slow response to the devastation. Biden is joined on vacation by his wife, daughter, son Hunter and his wife and Bidens' grandchildren, except for the recently acknowledged illegitimate one. Obviously "acknowledgment" does not include vacation time with grandpa.

8/26

Reporters in Lake Tahoe, where Biden is taking nine days to recover from his grueling, 6 hour trip to Hawaii, ask Biden if he'd seen the infamous mug shot Trump took after his arrest that Biden orchestrated. In answer, Biden cackles, admits he did see it and says he thought the former president a "handsome guy", a "wonderful guy." The irony here is that with Bidens' history of lying to hide personal failures and inadequacies, plagiarizing and bullying to do the same, taking millions in graft from Americas' enemies, disavowing innocent relatives until politically expedient and continually grabbing young girls in order to sniff their hair, whose mug shot really should be on display right now?

8/27

Bidens' snarky comment about Trumps' mug shot brings to mind the last time Georgias' Fulton County issued a politically-motivated indictment of a political foe in order to brig him down. It was Martin Luther King, who was arrested on October 19, 1960, in downtown Atlanta after refusing to leave his seat at a segregated department store lunch counter. His mug shot from those decades ago is now published next to Trumps. One wonders if Biden will also declare MLK a "handsome guy" and a "wonderful man". Time will tell.

8/28

Bidens' repeated claims that he knew nothing about his familys' corrupt business dealing takes a major hit with the release of a report that outlines at least 16 times Biden lied about his involvement in his family's business dealings. It documents Bidens' lies about never speaking to his family about their business dealings with Americas' enemies, his family never receiving $1 million in payments through a third party, his son never making money in China and that his son's dealings were ethical and above board. The report contains actual transcripts of Congressional testimony, interviews and phone conversations backing up the claim that Biden did and continues to lie about being intimately involved in his family's' corrupt business dealings. Biden has no comment.

8/29

Bidens' lies are getting so extraordinary they're challenge the principles of time travel. Biden now claims he physically convinced South Carolina Senator Strom Thurmond to vote for the Civil Rights Act in 1964. The time problem with this is in 1964 Biden was just 21 years old and nowhere near the Senate seat he won at the age of 29, when he and Thurmond were contemporaries. To add more confusion to the latest Biden tall tale, an anonymous Biden staffer insists the story is absolutely true and Biden did indeed talk Thurmond into signing the CRA in 1980. That statement might have rung true except that piece of landmark legislation was signed in 1964. It seems that the time bubble Bidens' mentally debilitated brain has created for him now envelopes the entire White House staff.

8/30

Biden announces he plans to request funding for the development of a new COVID-19 vaccine, nearly a year after he declared the COVID-19 pandemic over. Biden also says he is thinking of requiring everyone in America to take it whether they previously received a vaccine or not. In an odd follow-up, Biden comments that his request to Congress for additional funds would be for a "... new vaccine that is necessary, that works." Bidens' nurses drop their heads in their hands, realizing with this latest gaffe Biden admits that some, if not all, previous vaccines were not necessary and did not work.

8/31

Even opponents of Trump now admit that after years of Bidens' presidency it appears that many of Trumps' policies were more effective. Unemployment was down, the economy was exploding upwards, business-strangling regulations were being relaxed and even foreign investors, for the first time in years, were racing to pour money into the surging American economy. Now under Biden, inflation remains high, the economy is stagnant and foreign investment has slowed considerably. When removing the number of people just returning to old jobs held previous to COVID, employment in new jobs remains low. Bidens' only 'solution' to the economic and social disasters he has created is, sadly, to use the intelligence agencies to keep the man who was president when America was thriving from becoming president again.

9/1

In his ever-increasing thirst for power, Biden is out to crush anyone who disagrees with him. Not content in taking out his political rivals in a Banana Republic-style, Biden has his DOJ sue Elon Musk. Biden is suing Musk for not hiring refugees, illegal aliens and asylum seekers to work on sensitive projects at his SpaceX company. Musk contends that his SpaceX company relies on highly trained, highly educated technicians and scientists, skills few if any illegal aliens have. Biden scoffs, insisting that in those pictures of thousands of illegal aliens huddled under bridges in southern states there are computer and scheduling programmers, mechanical, thermal and quality control engineers, just waiting for a job at SpaceX. Since Musk continues to deny these worthy applicants a job, the lawsuit continues.

9/2

Despite howls of laughter from all sides, Biden doubles-down on his insistence that Musk hire all the highly trained illegal alien techs and scientists just waiting for him at the border. Biden contends that Musks' SpaceX job postings are racist because they say that only U.S. citizens and lawful permanent residents can apply for openings. Biden insists that all illegal aliens, including asylum seekers and refugees, are protected from such hiring discrimination. It's as if Biden believes that every day the coyotes – the professional human traffic smugglers working at the southern border – are bringing in hundreds of illegal aliens skilled in logistics, parts management, antenna design, ordinance, drafting and even soldering skills that Musk can use but is denying opportunities to. Biden and his DOJ push forward with their lawsuit.

9/3

Critics now contend Bidens' current lawsuit against Musk is political revenge for Musk buying Twitter and turning it into a true free-speech platform, defying Biden and his administration. Under the previous Twitter management the Biden and the FBI had a cozy relationship that allowed them to pressure the platform to censor conservatives. A federal lawsuit brought by the states of Missouri and Louisiana revealed a widespread operation by Biden and his staff to coordinate with compliant Twitter employees to remove posts critical of Biden. Also, during the 2020 election, Twitter helped Bidens' presidential aspirations in the final weeks of the campaign by censoring the New York Posts' story about the contents of Hunter Biden's laptop. Bidens' current lawsuit against Musk is more about personal revenge than any employment opportunity concerns Biden has for for illegal aliens.

9/4

Reports surface suggesting that Biden is intent on using his revenge lawsuit against Musk to make an example of him. It was recently learned that Musk fought a motion by special counsel Jack Smith. Who is currently prosecuting Trump, for access to Trump's Twitter account and to prevent Musk from informing Trump that the government snooped around in his account. Smith then went to an Obama-appointed judge and won the right to impose a $350,000 fine on Musk because of his resistance. It's clear that, with this lawsuit, Biden wants Americans to know that there is a price to pay for going against his wishes. Bidens' message is that if he can crush the world's richest man for disagreeing with him, what chance do normal, everyday Americans who disagree with Biden have?

9/5

Biden is again questioned about his continued reneging on his promise to visit East Palestine, Ohio. Biden was criticized for not visiting East Palestine immediately following the train derailment there. He has yet to travel to the area, though he promised to do so back in March. His new excuse is that he hasn't "been able to break away." This comment is particularly derisive because not only has Biden spent approximately 40% of his tenure on vacation, Biden just recently returned from a nine day vacation in Lake Tahoe. After spending nearly the majority of his presidency on vacation, Biden is asked exactly what he has to "break away" from. Biden has no comment, possibly because he is still on vacation.

9/6

Both Senate Republicans and Democrats fire off two letters in opposition of of Bidens' recent nationwide crackdown on hunting and archery programs in schools. The letters state that Biden and his DOE misinterpreted legislation regarding funding for such programs and called on Biden to restore funding. The letters, signed by both Democrats and Republicans. remind Biden of the important role these programs can play in students' lives. The letters explain that archery is an inclusive extracurricular activity that empowers students from all backgrounds to learn a sport and compete. Hunting safety classes teach safety, wildlife management, landowner relations and personal responsibility. Despite these pleas, Biden has no comment.

9/7

In response to a request by Trump's attorneys to delay one of his trials, Biden and the judge overseeing the case refuse, saying that Trump should not be granted any more leeway than the Boston marathon bomber or those involved in the 9/11 bombing received. The extraordinary amount of hubris it takes to lump Trumps' questioning of the 2020 election results in with terrorists who murdered American citizens is staggering. It would be embarrassing to most, but again, this is Biden.

9/8

Bidens' giggling enjoyment and his sycophants cheering of Trumps' long-longed for mug shot is short-lived. It turns out Trump, ever the entrepreneur, has used the picture to raise close to 10 million dollars. From t-shirts to coffee mugs. Trump is selling the image on all types of merchandise. Now Biden and his supporters threaten possible legal action, They weirdly claim that Trump is violating copyright laws since the mug shot is ostensibly owned by the Fulton County DA who issued it. Petty, yes, but not unexpected from the brain-slow bully Biden has been throughout his career.

9/9

Panic is starting to surge in Democratic ranks as many are sounding the alarm that Bidens' failure to keep immigration under control has dangerous political consequences, now and in the future. Local leaders in New York, long considered a Democratic stronghold, warn Biden that issues like mass immigration not only disrupts the lives of New Yorkers, but also the party's grip on the state. Even the press outlets in New York publish articles warning Biden of this very thing. They're afraid that the Democratic Party may face another reckoning like it did when it was was unexpectedly disrupted by GOP contenders in the 2022 midterm elections. Biden has no comment.

9//10

Biden takes another ominous step in his bid for complete censorship of all who disagree with him. Bidens' latest move is to have the US Special Operations Command (USSOCOM) hire a social media surveillance company, Acrete AI, to combat what Biden deems to be "misinformation." Biden and the USSOCOM grant a contract to Acrete AI to employ their app, Argus Social, which is designed precisely for what Biden wants: To identify "misinformation'" at an embryonic stage before those narratives "...evolve and gain traction..." and censor it. Critics vehemently point out that this partnership is a dangerous step forward in Bidens' censorship program. Ignoring the critics, Biden pops open another can of Ensure and settles back, enjoying this new powerful step.

9/11

Bidens' feud with Texas heats up since its governor continues to bus illegal aliens to 'blue' or liberal Democratic-controlled states and their sanctuary cities. First, Biden and his staff orders the governor to remove the barriers he placed in the Rio Grand River in an effort to stop the massive illegal immigration going on there. Then Biden announces his intention to misuse an immigration policy that keeps immigrants scheduled for deportation close to the border in order to stop the governor from shipping any more illegals out of state. In answer, the governor immediately appealed the ruling, saying he was willing to take the case to the Supreme Court if needed. He vows to increase the number of illegals bused out of state if Biden keeps up this type of harassment. Biden has no comment.

9/12

Biden continues to embarrass himself and America on the world stage. In front of the audience gathered for the G7 summit, Biden delivers a rambling, incoherent speech, slurring disjointedly between unconnected topics and using fragmented sentences in a confusing attempt at a theme. Then in the middle of this brilliant discourse, Biden loses his train of thought, mumbles some more, then looking weary, he tells this audience comprised of world leaders that he "... didn't know what they were going to do, but he was goring to bed." His nurses jump in and end the charade before too many questions can be asked. Biden, looking more like an elderly game show contestant than the leader of the free world, is mercifully lead off the stage.

9/13

Outrage is voiced at Bidens' decision to carry out a prisoner exchange with Iran. In Bidens' deal, 5 Iranian prisoners will be exchanged for 5 American detainees, but Biden also unfreezes 6 billion dollars of Iranian funds. Biden insists that the money will be used only for humanitarian purposes and not to further Irans' goal of building a nuclear bomb. However, Iran counters by telling Biden and the US that the money belongs to Iran and the ayatollahs will spend it anyway they like. Dumbfounded, dazed and confused, Biden again is completely outmaneuvered by an enemy of America.

9/14

Biden does not respond to a request for comment about the backlash concerning his $6 billion dollar ransom payment to Iran. Critics contend that Biden's' ransom payment deal will only encourage enemies of the U.S. to take more Americans hostage and demonstrates again Bidens' weak-kneed approach when negotiating with Americas' enemies. Bidens' only defense, though weak, could be that his critics leap too quickly to accuse Biden of a treasonous intent when it can be explained simply by Bidens' well-documented, willful stupidity.

9/15

As Bidens' ransom payoff to Iran becomes more publicized, criticisms from all sides mount. Some Congressmen claim that Bidens' billion dollar capitulation to the ayatollahs puts Iran in a better position to develop a nuclear weapon, fund terrorists, embolden Americas' adversaries and put Americans' safety and security at risk. All demands for answers from Biden fall on deaf ears, literally. What angers most, though, is the belief that Biden purposely chose to fund Irans' pursuit of a nuclear weapon on 9/11, the anniversary of the infamous terrorist attacks on America. In doing so Biden raises a snarky middle finger to all patriotic

Americans, a practice started by Obama years ago, Actually, the sight of the raised appendage brought relief to Bidens' supporters. For the longest time they were afraid that Biden was spending too much time in his basement with that finger, like Obama, shoved squarely up his rear end.

9/16

The anger over Bidens' insulting 9/11 billion dollar 'gift' to Iran is not dissipating. This, despite Biden lying about informing Congress to the steps taken in the deal and his assurances that additional briefings are already scheduled, neither of which are true. Biden again comically asserts that Iran can use his ransom payments only for humanitarian purposes. Critics world wide laugh at this, knowing that the ayatollahs are more disposed to using the money to fund more attacks on Israel, more attacks on American troops in the region, not to mention building and selling more missiles and drones to Russia, rather than build a childrens' hospital. What sticks most in the craw of the critics is the 'coincidence' of Biden sending his gift to the terrorists on the exact anniversary of the worst terrorist attack in history, one that left in excess of 3000 American dead on American soil. Of all of Bidens' anti-American actions, this is considered his most shameful.

9/17

Bidens' nurses are besides themselves trying to keep Bidens' penchant for lying under control. Recently Biden lies several times in one short speech. In it, Biden boasts that he courageously visited Ground Zero the day after the bombing to witness that tragedy first hand … only he didn't. With his nurses eyes growing wider, Biden then spins a tale of how he was in Pittsburgh to personally witness a bridge collapse there and how he empathized with the suffering residents … only he wasn't and didn't. His nurses move in to stop him, but before they can reach the podium Biden, fake tears welling, relates how serendipitous, how almost spiritual it was that his grandfather died in the same hospital that he was born in only a few days later. Touching, except his grandfather died a year before Biden was born and in another state. Mercifully his nurses reach Biden, cut the mike, make some semi-coherent excuses to the crowd and hustle this oatmeal-brained, duplicitous 'leader of the free world' off the stage.

9/18

Bidens' nurses and staff attempt to play down his rapid fire spate of lies in his last speech. Unfortunately Bidens' lying has become so commonplace there are fact checkers poised now at every speech or briefing he gives. Those who witnessed his latest gaffe fest had the Internet buzzing overtime. They immediately found that Biden lied about being at ground zero the next day after the bombing, lied about personally witnessing a bridge collapse in Pittsburgh and lied about his grandfather dying in the same hospital within a few days of Biden being born there. Bidens' nurses defend him, saying that all the stories have a ring of truth to them, it's just that Biden sometimes is confused about the dates and times of the actual events. Biden, still looking confused about the present time and his whereabouts, has no comment.

9/19

Bidens' critics do not accept his nurses' explanation defense that Bidens' continual lying is a product of a healthy mind confused only by a few dates and times. They remind the nurses about other Biden 'confusions', like his boast of driving an 18-wheel truck when it was a school bus, his visit to a hate-crime ravaged mosque which never took place or his conversation with a Amtrak employee who had died a year before the supposed conversation. Add to this Bidens' repeatedly 'confusing' the difference between Americas' debt and deficit, his penchant of stumbling over unseen objects and talking to and trying to shake hands with persons also unseen, one thing is clear: Unless covered head-to-toe in bubble wrap, Biden should never be let out of his basement, not to mention anywhere near to the leadership of the free world.

9/20

Biden and his staff are mocked after a F-35 fighter jet, which the pilot ejected from, goes missing in South Carolina. Even with what is supposed to be the most technically advanced air corps in the world, Biden pathetically has to ask for ordinary citizens, perhaps those out for a Sunday stroll or walking their dogs, to help in locating the plane. As far as the military is concerned, many of them believe that if Biden wasn't so focused on pushing his radical left-wing policy of gender identity and awareness, the proper use of pronouns, the kicking out of unvaccinated soldiers or using drag queens as recruiting agents, perhaps said military could focus on slightly more important aspects of their job, like locating a 80 million downed aircraft.

9/21

Biden emphatically denies that there is anything to the impeachment inquiry launched by the House over a week ago. Hedging bets, though, Biden moves into damage control before the inquiry reaches full steam, begging the media to save him. Biden issues a memo to all the major news outlets, demanding that they "...ramp up their scrutiny" of House Republicans "... for opening an impeachment inquiry based on lies." Biden sends the memo to major media outlets, claiming there is "... no evidence that (Biden) did anything wrong..." In the memo Biden demands that the media target Republicans for not only uncovering mountains of evidence that incriminate both him and his family, but having the audacity to actually try to hold Biden accountable for it.

9/22

Bidens' memo requesting media censorship of Republican-exposed evidence of his and his familys' corruption doesn't seem to be sitting well with some of Bidens' 'media allies. For a long time they tried to keep a lid on the alarming evidence uncovered about Biden and his crime family, but the House Oversight's extensive findings of corruption made the story too big to ignore. As an aside, Bidens' memo was laughably titled "It's Time For The Media To Do More To Scrutinize House Republicans' Demonstrably False Claims That They're Basing Impeachment Stunt On." If there was ever a question about Biden graduating at the bottom of his class, giving a title to a memo that is longer than the memo itself should remove all doubt. If Bidens' nurses ever do cover him in bubble wrap when he leaves his basement, they should pull the wrap a bit tighter. This way it might keep Biden from punishing anymore word processors or text editors he comes in contact with.

9/23

Gas prices again surge across the country and Biden is again excoriated for giving away American fuel supplies to China. Since his first day in office Bidens' declared war on American energy production has crippled domestic fossil fuel production and made America more dependent on foreign producers, many who are either sworn or tacit enemies of the US. Not only has Biden bolstered Chinas' fossil fuel supply, he has bolstered Chinas' struggling economy by buying the wind turbines and solar panels for his 'Green Energy Plan' for America' from them. It seems that in his "Bidenomics", Biden grin-fully feels the best way to handle Americas' current economic woes is to let inflation rage, cripple domestic energy production and prop up possibly Americas' most dangerous foreign enemy: Good plan, this "Bidenomics"

9/24

The two-faced irony in Bidens' 'Green Plan for America'' is that by restricting American oil production Biden is causing far more damage to Earth, the planet he whines he cares so much about. This is because the same amount of oil is being extracted from the earth, but by countries like Iran, China, Russia and Venezuela, whose methods of fossil fuel extraction are far more harmful to the planet than those used in the U.S. The extraction methods used in America are far cleaner and more environmentally friendly. This is probably all lost on Biden since, one, hypocrisy is a hallmark of his career and, two, with his diminished mental capacity, it is doubtful Biden even knows what irony is.

9/25

Trump takes credit for Bidens' hastily announced plans to meet with striking United Auto Workers (UAW) union members, since Biden decided to go only because he, Trump, previously announced his trip to the state. Up until then Biden had no plans to visit the auto workers. Trump and his team assert that Bidens trip to Michigan is nothing more than a cheap photo op. Two things are certain: One, if Trump had not said anything, Biden would be giving UAW workers in Michigan the 'East Palestine' treatment' or the 'Maui' treatment; two, despite Bidens' repeated denials, it is apparent that Trump still lives rent free in what is left of Bidens' mind.

9/26

Because Trumps' announced plans to visit Michigan caught Biden by surprise, the logistics surrounding Bidens' hastily announced visit to Michigan to try to beat Trump were described as "chaotic" and "a mess." It seems that Bidens' panicked itinerary to visit the striking auto workers was a product if his confused mind. First, members of the UAW on one picket line were told that Biden would be coming to their location, only to hear later that that plan was scrapped. Speculation spread that Biden would go to whatever picket line was closest to the airport, even though this would force him to confront his ever-present enemy, airplane stairs. Because of this there was a rumor that the trip might be canceled altogether. Biden vehemently denied this, claiming that for the sake of the striking workers, he would once again face his nemesis head-on, if somewhat carefully.

9/27

Reports of Bidens' chaotic trip to support the striking UAW workers keep coming in. It turns out that even the press corps looking to cover the president's visit were unsure where exactly to go or where Biden was to appear. Meanwhile, Bidens' press secretary continues to deny that Bidens' last minute Michigan trip, coincidentally booked only after Trump announced his plans to visit, had anything to do with Trump. With each adamant denial, Bidens' press secretary' voice gets more nasally strident, making it clear that, though in danger of being overbooked, Trump also lives rent free in her head.

9/28

Biden tries to draw a tricky distinction when he joined the striking autoworkers. Biden insists his joining the workers did not signal that he was supportive of any specific requests that the UAW might be making, nor was he involved in negotiations. Then Biden quite clumsily makes a speech to the workers where he declares that "…the middle class built this country (and) the unions built the middle class" and implores the strikers to "… keep going…" because they have "…earned a hell of a lot more than you're getting paid now." By declaring his non-involvement in negotiating, but then openly negotiating, Biden gives the strikers a glimpse of the quixotic world the mentally feeble Biden inhabits daily. It's the one where the back part of his brain has no idea what the front part is doing.

9/29

Biden signs legislation that reverses his previous decision to defund school hunting an fishing courses nationwide. Biden had intentionally misinterpreted the Elementary and Secondary Education Act, signed into law decades ago, as an excuse to shut down any education course in America involving guns. This latest attempt by Biden to grab Americas' guns raised the ire of even his Democratic allies. It was they who were responsible for passing legislation insisting that Biden continue to support such programs Having no moral center, Biden quickly capitulates. For cover, Bidens' staff announce that Biden "...supports a legislative solution to ensure ESEA funding can be used for valuable school enrichment programs, such as hunter safety and archery..." Once thought impossible, Biden proves that, yes, having no backbone can occasionally cause the right thing being done, even if for the wrong reasons.

9/30

Bidens' continues to lie about being unaware of his sons' business dealings, influence pedaling with foreign companies and receiving money from China. Unfortunately for Biden, bank records furnished to Congress show that two wires from a Chinese equity firm, totaling in excess of $250,000, were addressed directly to Biden's basement house in Delaware, the same house where Biden illegally stashed classified documents. The only way Biden could be telling the truth about not knowing about the bribe is if the UPS driver just dropped the money-laundered package on Bidens' porch. It is possible then that the bribe never made its' way o the basement.

10/1

Bidens' lying about not being aware of his sons' Hunters' business dealings takes another huge hit. It is revealed that it was in Bidens' basement where his son made threats to a Chinese energy conglomerate official, claiming that he was sitting next to his father. Then a picture surfaces showing Biden having a cup of coffee with his son and this same Chinese official, where afterwards Biden wrote college recommendation letters for this mans' son and daughter. If after having a $250000 dollar bribe addressed to him, sitting next to his son while he threatens a Chinese official with his fathers' influence, sharing a cup of coffee with the same and writing letters of recommendation for the Chinese officials' kids, can still leave Biden "unaware" of his son's dealings, critics ask Biden what would it take for him to become "aware" of them? Biden has no comment.

10/2

Bidens' carefully media-crafted image as a loving father who helped his son overcome his struggles with addiction, is starting to unravel. Some in the media now take a 180-degree turn in their opinion and think that maybe Biden failed as a father by enabling his son's problems. Congressional investigators uncover evidence that Biden turned a blind eye to his sons' wild drug, alcohol, and prostitute-fueled lifestyle, particularly during Obamas' presidency when Bidens' access as VP seemed to be up for sale. With what the investigators found, it seems impossible that Biden did not know his son was pedaling his access and funding his destructive lifestyle with the proceeds. Yet, rather than seeing his son get the help he badly needed, Biden instead lined his familys' pockets with money from foreign oligarchs. Worse yet, Bidens' son claims that his Dad demanded half of any money he grifted. It is apparent now, to even the most strident Biden supporter, that lining the family's pockets was a higher priority for Biden than his sons' health.

10/3

Bidens' attempt to control every aspect of every Americans' life, even to the smallest detail, reaches a new low. Biden now wants to regulate

– wait for it – pool pumps. Biden and his DOE want to establish higher energy efficiency standards for pool pump motors that manufacturers will have to comply with starting in September 2025. Yes, with inflation still running rampant, Ukraine trying to draw the US into WW lll, with hundreds of Americans dying from fentanyl poisoning and thousands of illegals crossing into the US daily because of his open-border policies, Biden and what's left of his marshmallow brain is focused on pool pumps. Yet again – and embarrassingly so – not a great look for the supposed leader of the free world.

10/4

A report surfaces that Biden allegedly ordered the FBI to make unannounced "knock and talk" visits to the homes of hundreds of thousands of supporters of former president Trump. Generally a "knock-and-talk" visit involves knocking on a door, speaking with the occupants and asking for permission to search the residence. It is is considered a consensual encounter, but in this case, if true, it is fairly certain that this tactic is being used by the bully Biden as a form of intimidation. Biden, his staff, the FBI and the DOJ were all contacted and asked to either verify or deny the allegation. So far, Biden and all have no comment.

10/5

It seems that finally Bidens' broken brain realizes that the illegal immigration catastrophe he created is one of the main reasons for his unpopularity. In an effort to stop his plummeting poll numbers, Biden announces he is constructing a new piece of wall at the southern border. Then, after receiving immediate and overwhelming flack from his Marxist pro - illegal immigration allies the schizophrenic Biden orders a "pause" in the wall construction. Then in another head-spinning minute, Biden declares that due to a ruling enacted by his voodoo doll of excuses, Trump, his hands are tied and that this piece of the wall must be built. Yet, after these flip-flops and blaming Trump, Biden still wants credit for "addressing" the illegal immigration border crisis…, the one he created. Completely baffled, all sides seek some clarification and, at the same time, rush to buy aspirin at the White House Commissary. They might get the aspirin, but since it's after 4:30 in the afternoon, any 'clarification' from Biden will have to wait until tomorrow.

10/6

Bidens' Marxist pro-illegal immigration supporters are furious at his decision to continue the construction of any piece of a wall on Americas' southern border. They remind Biden of his vehement campaign promise to stop all border wall construction immediately and forever. Biden attempts to waffle again but his DHS informs Biden that he must carry out Trumps pledge to build at least 20 more miles of the wall or risk running afoul of the law. While Biden can use Trump as an excuse for this continuing construction, Biden has no scapegoat for using his executive order power to waive 26 federal laws, some of them environmental in nature, to allow this border wall construction. Bidens' Marxist supporters are still furious with him, but Biden is nowhere to be found, presumably ensconced safely in his Delaware basement.

10/7

In less than a month after Bidens' 6 billion dollar ransom gift to Iran, Hamas, a terrorist group funded mainly by Iran, stormed from the blockaded Gaza Strip into nearby Israeli towns, killing hundreds and abducting others in an unprecedented attack during a major Jewish holiday. In an assault of startling breadth, Hamas gunmen suddenly had enough funds to bankroll them rolling into as many as 22 locations outside the Gaza Strip. This included towns and other communities as far as 15 miles from the Gaza border, where they gunned down civilians and soldiers and took hostages. It is apparent that because of Bidens' insistence on funding Iran, the main sponsor of Hamas, that some of the blood shed now in Israel is on Bidens' hands.

10/8

Biden, vehemently denying that he is in any way responsible for the current bloodshed in Israel, claims that the murderous leaders of Iran still assure him that the 6 billion dollars Biden gifted them a few weeks ago is being used only for "humanitarian" endeavors, like building hospitals and schools. As usual looking vacant and confused, Bidens' oatmeal brain probably can't conceive the fact that what the murderous Iranian and Hamas terrorists consider "humanitarian", particularly when it comes to their mission of killing all Jews, might be slightly different than what the term means to most civilized people.

10/9

Biden is reminded that Trump warned him weeks ago that his six billion dollar gift to Iran would "…finance terrorism all across the Middle East." Biden, almost whining, still insists that there is no evidence that the $6 billion dollars he gifted Iran helped finance the current attacks on Israel. Besides Biden, seeming quite miffed, assures all that the ayatollahs would not dare to use the money to fund terrorism because Biden, in his biggest little-boy voice, told them not to. Then Biden is reminded that immediately after he told the killers that the money could be used only for medicine, food and other humanitarian purposes, the Iranian President told him, in effect, to pound sand because the Iranian government would decide how and what the $6 billion would be spent on. After this critique, Biden is caught hands clenched, stomping his feet. His nurses quickly assures the American public that Biden is remaining calm and resolute, that his stomping fit was not a reaction to any current criticism, but because his morning dose of Ensure went down the wrong pipe.

10/10

Bidens' incompetence in responding to the crisis in Israel would be mind-boggling if it was anyone other than Biden. First he didn't, or his nurses didn't, bother to wake up/wake him up until 8 hours after Hamas attacked Israel. Then Bidens' first command decision was that he would make no command decision about the crisis. His supporters of course defend Biden, saying they were sure Biden was delaying speaking about the crisis until he received a full briefing. This would've been fine, except Biden spent the day hosting a barbecue for friends and family, complete with a live band. In the best tradition of another dictator, Nero, Biden was flipping burgers and literally listening to fiddles while Israel burned.

10/11

After a weekend of BBQs and refusing to speak to the press concerning Israel, when Biden does speak he only embarrasses himself further. First, Biden shows up over an hour late. Then Biden confirms that at least 14 Americans have died and more have been taken hostage, but he has no strategy to save them. Biden speaks for 11 minutes, does not address the accusation of what part his $6 billion dollar gift to Iran played in the massacre and quickly leaves the stage without taking any questions. Rather than being reassuring, the only thing Biden accomplishes in those 11 minutes is once again display to the world how weak and irresponsible he is.

10/12

Both conservative and liberal reporters display frustration over Biden evading questions about his $6 billion dollar gift to Iran helping fund the massacre in Israel. Biden still maintains that Iran couldn't possibly use the money to pay terrorists because the money is still sitting on pallets, untouched. Incredulous that Biden thinks them this stupid, the reporters point out that while those specific dollars haven't been spent, having the new $6 billion in their account allows the Iranians to use $6 billion from others areas of their economy to fund their terrorist proxies. Biden ignores this point and, instead, brags that he can freeze the new funds whenever appropriate. When asked, by the still-unbelieving reporters, d what could be a more appropriate time to freeze the funds than right after the massacre, Biden has no comment. The reporters leave looking, like Biden always looks, dazed and confused.

10/13

Bidens' bumbling, fumbling response to the war in Gaza reminds Americans of his many foreign policy flubs, going all the way back to Bidens' ham-fisted withdrawal from Afghanistan which got 13 Americans murdered. It turns out that Bidens' floundering in the polls is dragging his entire party down. Now 57% of Americans think that Republicans would do a better job protecting the country from terrorism and foreign threats, compared to just 35% for Democrats. This is the biggest margin in favor of Republicans on the issue since 2002. This backs into another recent poll where 53% of Americans think Republicans would do a better job on the economy, compared to just 39% for Biden and the Democrats. Amazingly, or maybe not so amazingly, Biden seems blissfully unaware of the effect his nonchalant incompetence is having on his own party.

10/14

Biden continues to brand his economic policies as 'Bidenomics', leaving economists to wonder why Biden would brand an economy in his name when the economy is in such poor shape. Despite Biden constantly insisting the American economy is fine, since Biden took office, overall prices are still up nearly 17%, including a 20% increase in food prices and a 63% increase in gas prices. Poll after poll show that most voters believe Biden is hurting the economy more than he is helping it. Despite

Bidens' histrionics, voters need to see and feel an economy in their own personal bank accounts and, until they do, the general view of Bidens' incompetence in handling the economy won't change, no matter how often or how loud Biden yells about the economy being fine.

10/15

Biden visits Philadelphia, purportedly to yell again about how great the economy is doing under his watch. Knowing his penchant for hurting himself, this time his nurses erect a small stage with only a few steps for Biden to transverse. Intent on disappointing them, Biden puts on another clown show. Trying to show a non-existent vigor, he starts to jog to the stage, but stops after only a couple of steps, out of breath. Then he trips twice trying to mount the baby steps, having to catch the rail to keep from falling. Doing this while still wearing his clownish Aviator sunglasses, Biden looks much less a vigorous old man than one that more than ever should be covered head-to-toe in bubble wrap whenever he leaves his basement.

10/16

Trump responds to Biden recently attacking in the media. He makes the same point that many political experts and economists have already made, that Bidens' claim that the $6 billion he handed Iran would be used only for humanitarian purposes demonstrates either Bidens' naivete or stupidity. Trump reiterates the obvious, that even if Iran doesn't use those specific 'dollars-on-the-pallet' monies, Bidens' gift allows the mullahs to use $ 6 billion dollars from somewhere else in their budget to fund their goal of murdering all Jews. Trump also compares the success of his foreign policy to Bidens' failed one. To mention a few, Trump defeated ISIS, negotiated Middle East peace deals and was the first president in 40 years not to start any new wars; this, while Biden, among other failures, has brought the U.S. to the brink of three different world wars in the Middle East, Ukraine, and Taiwan. To all of this, Biden has no comment.

10/17

A report comes out that Biden has given many millions to an organization named 'United Nations Relief & Works Agency, or UNRWA. This, even though it is widely known that the facilitates of this, purported Palestinian refugee agency have been repeatedly used by Hamas terrorists for military purposes. These include staging grounds, weapons depots, hideouts and shielding Hamas military assets. Since the UNRWA, a United Nations organization, has provide support and safe harbor to terrorists in Gaza, it is considered a branch of Hamas. Despite this, Biden plans to unfreeze over $360 million US tax dollars for the UNRWA that Trump froze during his presidency, specifically because of this groups' support of Hamas. Incredibly – and unknown to most Americans – during his presidency, Biden has knowingly given a total of $730 million to this Hamas proxy.

10/18

In yet another schizophrenic foreign policy flourish, Biden visits Israel to pledge American support in its' war with Hamas, only to turn around and allow the U.N. To lift sanctions on Iran's capability to purchase and supply missiles to enemies of the U.S. and Israel. Now Iran, the sponsor of Hamas and other terrorist organizations around the world, will be able to procure and sell missiles and drones to whoever it wishes Pundits remark about Bidens' schizoid nature, noting that it was just a week ago Biden said he was "heartbroken" about the images of the worst massacre of Jews since the Holocaust, but now is comfortable handing another gift to the sponsor nation of the murderers. Bidens' bumbling, haphazard approach to world affairs, while providing much derisive humor around the globe these past couple of years, will now more than likely will lead directly to innocent people being killed.

10/19

In what seems to be his generous and never-ending support of Iran, Biden still says nothing as the UN prepares. to lift sanctions on Iran's capability to purchase and supply arms to terrorist groups around the world. The U.N.'s embargo against Iran ends next week. Reporters note Bidens' schizophrenic foreign policy once again, since it was just a week ago Biden gave a speech saying he was "heartbroken" about the images of the Hamas massacre of Jews, what he called "...the worst since the Holocaust...". Now Biden will allow the sanctions to end, handing yet another gift to Iran and a shot in the arm to Hamas in its' war with Israel.

10/20

Biden gives a speech from the White House, ostensibly to address the war in Israel and the Americans killed or taken hostage there. Instead, Biden spends the majority of his speech talking about the need for billions of more tax dollars for Ukraine and the threat of Islamic-phobia he claims is sweeping the country, Biden mentions only in passing the Americans killed and taken hostage in Israel. To add insult to injury, Biden asks Congress for another 100 million to be sent to … yes, Gaza. Addressing the shocked looks on reporters faces, Biden politely assures all that safeguards are in place to assure that none of the funds will be used by Hamas or any other terrorist groups. In response, reporters politely ask Biden not to piss down their backs and tell them it's rain.

10/21

Reporters half-jokingly point out that with Bidens' $6 billion dollar gift to Iran, his $730 million dollar gift to the the Hamas proxy UNRWA his attempt to lift the embargo on Irans' ability to purchase war weapons and, now his proposed $100 million dollar gift to Hamas for "humanitarian needs", the number one state sponsor in terrorism in the world is actually Biden, second only maybe to Iran. This is a unique accomplishment for a president of the United States and really not much of a joke.

10/22

Biden suffers a major defeat in his attempt to rig elections when a U.S. District Judge in Georgia smacked down Bidens' attempt to undermine election integrity in Georgia. Lawmakers there passed election integrity measures in 2021 that required voter identification on absentee ballots, banned ballot harvesting, and limited the use of drop boxes among other common-sense changes. Biden had called the new election integrity laws in Georgia "outrageous" and "an atrocity" while smearing the requirement of having a valid ID to vote as "racist" and "Jim Crow in the 21st century." The judge upheld the law anyway, writing that Biden his DOJ had not demonstrated tat the new Georgia law discriminated against black voters in any way.

10/23

It turns out that when Biden was in Israel recently he re-told the lie about Golda Meir considering him the American ambassador to Israel during the Yom Kipper war of 1973. Just on the face of it it is laughable to think that Meir would voluntarily ask an inexperienced young senator to be her liaison. Biden did meet the Israeli Prime Minister during the war, but his only contribution was to advise Meir to adopt a ceasefire immediately, advice which she considered bone-head and rejected out of hand. Even Bidens' ardent supporters beg him to stop re-telling this lie since it invokes so much ridicule from all sides. With his pathology, though, Biden can't help himself.

10/24

Biden double-downs on his lie about his meeting with Golda Meir, insisting that when they met Meir called him 'Mr. Ambassador" and asked Biden if he would like to take a photograph with her. Someone reminds Biden that in a version of this story earlier this year, Biden claimed the Prime Minister refereed to him only as 'son' or 'senator', but never 'Mr. Ambassador'. Bidens' confusion might be understandable since it was around this same time that he bragged about his foreign policy expertise, claiming he knew "... as much about American foreign policy as anybody living, including Dr. Kissinger..." because "That's what I've done (foreign policy) my whole life — for the last 270 years." Even though Biden has the thousand-mile stare, slurs his words and stumbles around like your everyday centenarian, reporters check their notes to reassure themselves that Biden is only 80 years old.

10/25

Bidens' trip to Israel might have been a political stunt to make the 80-year-old appear Presidential, but like Bidens' botched withdrawal from Afghanistan - where he got thirteen US soldiers killed – this visit put more American soldiers lives in harms way. Bidens' White House social media account published a picture of Biden shaking hands with members of a U.S. Army Special Forces unit, which often conduct classified, covert operations. Even though it's well-established policy to blur the faces of the soldiers in order to protect them, Biden and his staff do not do this. The blunder revealed their identities to Hamas and other terrorist groups, putting their lives immediately in danger. Biden seems blissfully unaware that his bumbling incompetence has put more American lives at risk again.

10/26

Biden is roundly criticized for his inept handling of his politically-motivated photo op that put at least four American soldiers lives in danger. Four soldiers were shown in the photo meeting Biden, but their faces weren't blurred out to protect their identities as is the usual policy. Some dismayed reporters asks, is Biden and his White House careless in endangering these mens' lives, or just stupid? Biden and his staff attempt to assuage the public by assuring Americans that the post was taken down in less than an hour. This is true, but not before it received several hundred thousand views. How many of these were by Americas' enemies is anyones' guess.

10/27

Biden sends a message to the Iranian Supreme Leader Ayatollah Ali Khamene, warning him against any more targeting of U.S. personnel in the Middle East, a day after a spate of attacks – at least 12 in Iraq and 4 in Syria - on American forces in the region. Of course Iran's leaders, both abroad and here in the UN, ignore Bidens' request for a response, After recently funding Irans' animalistic, terrorist ambitions with billions of gifted dollars, it takes someone with a debilitated brain like Biden to be surprised when the animals not only use it against him, but also ignore him.

10/28

American households continue to experience price increases for goods and services anywhere from 15% to 40% in their daily lives. They have long suspected the various inflation rates that Biden cites, from 3% to 8%, as proof that his 'Bidenomics' is working, are more a product of Bidens' slight of hand than actual productive policies. It's now revealed that this is true. One trick that Biden employs is using different product groups to track the CPI every time, which skews inflation numbers significantly. Not astonishingly,. some website that conduct their own analysis of Americas' economy shows that the actual inflation rate since Biden took office is a colossal 23.94%. This is much more in line with what everyday Americans have been experiencing in their everyday lives.

10/29

A recent report informs Biden that, so far this year, 169 terrorists on Americas' terrorist watch list have been arrested at the southern border, a tenfold increase from the number arrested all of last year. The report also documents that close to a quarter million people tried to illegally enter the US just in August of this year. In response, Biden and his CBP come up with a new slogan aimed directly at all who want to enter the country illegally: "Just Don't Do It" This is reminiscent of Nancy Reagans' famously simplistic "Just Say No" slogan as her answer to the raging drug problems of the '80s. It appears that Biden will be about as successful as Nancy was: After noting the quarter million illegal crossing attempts in August and listening very carefully to Bidens' new slogan, 269000 individuals attempted to cross the border illegally in September.

10/30

Almost lost in the report detailing the illegal alien arrests at the border in August and September was the fact that of all the millions of illegals Biden has allowed to enter the country since his inauguration, less than 6000 have appeared before an immigration judge. This means that of the millions of illegals Biden has released into the US since he took office, 99.7 percent of those illegal aliens have not been removed or even had a hearing. Biden has no comment.

10/31

A video released by the White House shows Biden with visiting youngsters on Halloween. The purpose of the video was a photo op to show Biden in a favorable light, handing out Halloween candy and interacting with young people like a vibrant, doting grandpa. Instead it showed a doddering old man, shuffling on stage and fumbling with the candy until he drops it. Bidens' staff immediately jumps into spin mode, claiming Biden dropped the candy, not because he is feeble, but only because a little girls' dinosaur costume frightened him. If this dinosaur-costumed girl, so tiny that her mother had to carry her, really did frighten Biden, think of what his physical reaction will be when he sits across from Putin or Xi.

11/1

With Bidens' double talking, first claiming Israel as an ally, but then sending millions of dollars to the Palestinians, doing nothing to ameliorate the chaos, violent anti-Semitic protests grow across America. Bidens' press secretary is asked a simple question: Since Biden declared that elderly people who pray peacefully in front of abortion clinics and parents who show up at school board meetings to protest the Marxist sexualization of their children are domestic terrorists, shouldn't the college professors, students and other Palestinian supporters who demand that all Jews throats be cut, shouldn't they also be considered domestic terrorists? Both Biden and his press secretary, strangely quiet, have no comment.

11/2

The latest Gallup poll shows Biden's approval number plunging to 37 percent, down from 41 percent a month ago. With 63 percent of Americans disapproving of the job Biden is doing as president. Bidens' approval within just within his own Democratic party sank by 11 points in the same time frame. A troubling sign for Biden – and the nation – is the poll found that a major cause of Biden's falling poll numbers with Democrats was due to their irritation with Biden for what they perceived as him not supporting Hamas and Palestine, the criminals, as much as he supported Israel, the victims. As hard as it is to fathom, in the wake of the Hamas slaughter of innocents, a poll showed that 49 percent of Democrats support the Palestinians. It must be comforting for Biden to know that he is part of such a moral-based party.

11/3

A portion of recently released archives from the time Biden spent as Vice-President reveal that Hunter Biden's firm Rosemont Seneca exchanged more than 1,000 emails with his father. The documents were released as part of a lawsuit which requested a wide range of records from Biden's time as vice president during the Obama administration. These latest releases show that the line between Bidens' sons private business dealings and Biden himself was often blurred, more evidence that no daylight existed between Hunter Biden's foreign business dealings and his father during the time Biden served as VP for Obama.

11/4

Poll after poll bring nothing but bad news for Biden. One conducted in September but released only recently, shows that two-thirds of Democrats want a different candidate than Biden in 2024. More discouraging for Biden, 82 percent of those voters didn't care who that alternative was. Biden's age is one factor driving the dissatisfaction with the idea of Biden running for re-election. 60 percent of Democratic voters believe Biden's age could prevent him from beating Trump in 2024. The constant stream of videos showing a bewildered and confused Biden unable to walk on his own, or looking to shake hands with people who aren't there, or the terrified look whenever confronted by stairs, make concerns about Biden's age and mental competence unavoidable

11/5

From his basement fantasy land, Biden issues an EO in a legislative attempt to stave off what he sees as the inevitable demise of humanity at the hands of roaming, hunter-killer robots created by AI. Biden believes his standards will guide the development of AI. These include requirements to "develop standards, tools and tests to help ensure that AI systems are safe, secure, and trustworthy," and to make sure all relevant data about AI models is shared with the US government. Leave it to Biden and his basement brain to think he can, with a stroke of his pen, save the world from the scary netherworld of AI science, killer robots be damned.

11/6

The blatant hypocrisy of Biden and his Marxist colleagues is reaching points both comedic and tragic. Since his election, Biden has allowed millions of illegals to flood states he considered political enemies in an effort to trash their thriving economies and install hordes of new Democrat voters. In the past Marxist states like California and New York have applauded Biden for his 'humanitarian' empathy. However, now that 125000 of these illegals – or "newly arrived individuals" which is the latest euphemism for them – have made their way to New York City, both the Marxist state governor and the Marxist mayor of New York Citys' have cried 'uncle'. They claim that even this number of illegals, minuscule when compared to the millions Biden has flooded the southern states with, presents them with a problem so large they demand that Biden send help. Even with their fervent support of Biden on the wane,. Biden has no comment.

11/7

Biden receives another setback in his effort to flood America in what he hopes will be Democratic voting illegals. Biden had ordered his staff to cut the wire barriers the state of Texas had erected in an effort to curtail illegal immigration in the stale. The Texas Attorney General and its' Public Policy Foundation sued Biden over his brazen attempt to destroy their state. This led to to U.S. District Judge issuing a temporary restraining order, blocking Biden from from destroying the barrier. The judge scolded Biden, saying that the "public interest" of Texas "... demands effective measures to prevent the illegal entry of aliens at the Mexican border..." and that destroying the wire would "... facilitate rather than prevent unlawful conduct." Biden, in full pout, whines that he will appeal the judges' ruling.

11/8

Biden, content to allow millions of illegals to flood into America, is now being criticized by some of his most ardent supporters. Two in that camp, the governor of New York and the mayor of New York City, now call out Biden for his "ineffectual and economically crushing mishandling" of the illegal alien border crisis. The governor openly complains that the border "... is too open right now ..." and that too many of the illegals are ending up in New York by "...simply saying they need asylum." The governor still claims that it's in the DNA of New York to welcome immigrants, but "... there has to be some limits in place." The mayor of New York City went further, telling Biden at a public meeting: "Never in my life have I had a problem that I did not see an ending to. I don't see an ending to this. I don't see an ending to this. This issue will destroy New York City; destroy New York City."Biden, ever the empathetic, says nothing.

11/9

Biden keeps his unbroken streak of 'stepping in it' with the latest rebuff from the American car buying public. Biden and his EPA issued a mandate that would require two-thirds of all new vehicles produced and sold by US auto manufacturers to be electric by 2032. Biden has poured hundreds of billions of American taxpayer dollars into subsidies for these EVs, trying to bribe working-class Americans into buying these vastly more expensive vehicles that few can reasonably afford. Even with subsidies, the average cost of a electric vehicle in America is $76000, as compared to the $49000 a comparable gas powered one costs. Because of this, Bidens' massive EV push is falling flat as consumers turn their back on electric vehicles. This adds yet another defeat to Bidens' juvenile vision of 'greening' America.

11/10

Bad news for his vision of 'greening' America continues to haunt Biden. Two of the US top auto makers, Ford and GM, announce they are backing off their EV goals despite the billions Biden has awarded them in grants. They cite the sluggish US economy – another gift from Biden – and lack of consumer demand for these expensive vehicles. Worst for Biden, any hope of support from foreign manufactures like Mercedes-Benz and Honda were doused when they both announced they too were slowing their plans for electrification, citing that the current EV industry isn't financially viable or sustainable for automakers. This fact evidently is lost in Bidens' economically- challenged mind. Bidens' only defense is that if he had his full mental capacity, like it's rumored he did a few decades ago, perhaps he would not have pursued such foolery.

11/11

Bidens' pleas for auto makers to keep pursuing his electrification plan for America automobiles seems to fall on deaf ears. GM announced that it is scaling back its' goal of producing 400,000 electric vehicles by the middle of 2024 because of demand and profitability problems. Both Ford and GM tell Biden that both of them expects their EV divisions will lose more than $4 billion this year alone. Pouring more salt in Bidens' open "greening" wound, Honda and GM announced that they were scrapping plans for a joint EV factory they had agreed to partner on. The billions of American tax dollars Biden has given to automakers as EV bribe's pale in comparison to the many billions they stand to lose pursuing Bidens' foolish, economically unsustainable 'green' vision'.

11/12

Bidens' support of Ukraines' escalating war with Russia seems to be turning into another one of Bidens' foreign policy fiascoes. Since February 2022, Biden has funneled over $130 billion in taxpayer money and weapons to Ukraine. There is decreasing support in America to Bidens' continued funding of this war. And increasing support for some sort of a peace deal. It is increasingly apparent that Biden is risking nuclear war with Russia over a country that has little strategic value to the United States. On top of this, with Biden risking going to war to secure the Ukrainian border while leaving Americas' southern border an open sore, complete with rape, drugs and human trafficking, the irony is almost too much to bare.

11/13

American support for Bidens' Ukraine war takes another hit when a report surfaces concerning an interview from former Israeli Prime Minister Naftali Bennet. In it, Bennet reveals that Ukraine and Russia were on the verge of ending the war but Biden and his globalist allies wanted to keep the war going, thinking they could defeat the Russian army and bring down Putin. Now, despite America emptying its arsenal and going further into debt, the Ukrainians admit they are losing the war, saying that they don't have the men or the weapons necessary to win. To top this off, just as critics of the war predicted, the corrupt Ukrainian government is stealing the money pouring into their country from America and its' allies. To top off this corruption, now Biden and his Congressional cronies want to muscle a slush fund that includes another $61 billion for Ukraine through Congress. It is apparent that the

American people are learning the Ukraine war is another Biden foreign policy failure and a graft-filled one to boot.

11/14

A video of Biden attending a solemn wreath-laying ceremony at the Tomb of The Unknown Soldier in Arlington is going viral. In it Biden seems extremely disoriented and confused. Biden stood there for quite some time, staring at the ground, before he turned from the wreath to walk away. However, he hesitated, stumbled a bit and then seeming confused by where he was. turned to the service member standing there for directions. The service member directed Biden to get back in line next to the vice president, where he stood for the remainder of the ceremony. After the video went viral, many viewers took to social media calling the scene "embarrassing" and "pathetic.". As one onlooker sarcastically wrote: "Our enemies must be shaking in their boots."

11/15

Bad news keeps rolling in on Biden. A poll recently conducted by Bloomberg and Morning Consult indicates that Trump is leading Biden 47% to 43% in Arizona, Georgia, Michigan, Nevada, North Carolina, Pennsylvania, and Wisconsin. The poll also showed that it's Bidens' languishing economy that is the main issue powering Trump's lead in those states. A majority of swing state voters said that the economy was better off under Trump, with 49% of voters saying they trusted his work on the economy compared to 35% for Biden. More tone deaf than usual, Biden keeps touting his "Bidenomics" economic agenda even though voters aren't buying his spin on his economic failures. In fact, twice as many voters in swing states insist that Bidenomics is bad for the economy. Evidently this startling fact has not penetrated Bidens' basement wall.

11/16

Bidens' collapse in the polls has even his ardent supporters wringing their hands. As a group they whine that Trump, a guy that is getting indicted in four different states on 90-plus different criminal counts and supposedly led an insurrection against the country, is not only close but actually pulling ahead in Marxist-blue states where Biden should be up big. For the polls to be even this close, let alone show Trump winning, is a reflection on how bad the voters view the Democrat Party brand as a whole and the stumbling, fumbling Biden in particular.

11/17

Rumors continue to surface regarding Bidens' problems with the Secret Service, from his lack of respect for the agents and their jobs to his 2-year-old German Shepard biting more than a dozen of them. The worse, though, is the rumor that Biden likes to swim nude in front of the agents, even the female ones. There seems to be some truth to this, if only evidenced by the number of female agents requiring medical leave. They claim that not only will they never be able to forget the sight, but even when they close their eyes the image of the nude, wrinkled, age-spotted stumbling Biden is burned on the back of their eyelids.

11/18

With accusations of Biden lying about the border crisis, his business dealings with China, the economy, inflation, et al, his dwindling number of supporters once again rise to his defense. They insist that in his present mental condition it is possible that Biden does not understand the words he's speaking. They ask, since Bidens' nurses are writing his speeches which Biden then, when he can get the words out, repeats verbatim, can Biden really be accused of lying? Buffoonery, maybe, cognitively disoriented, maybe, but lying? Reporters are left to ponder this conundrum.

11/19

A number of Osama Bin Ladens' letters surface on TikTok. Bidens' Marxists supporters believe all of them are authentic and poignant, except for one. In this one Bin Laden states that he wants Obama to be assassinated so the buffoonish Vice-President Biden can take his place. From a monsters lips to god's ears, Biden supporters insist this one letter, among all the other Bin Laden letter is fake.

11/20

Several days ago Biden and the president of Mexico met face to face to discuss the mutual concerns of their respective countries They discussed topics like the Mexican cartels, global warming, climate change and their respective fentanyl epidemics. Amazingly, though, Biden and his counterpart barely mention the humanitarian catastrophe at their common border. On his return from his meeting with Biden, Mexicos' president announces that he will reject all efforts by the state of Texas to return illegals, saying that he will accept only illegals repatriated by Biden. Knowing that since he became president Biden has returned less than .05% of the reported 5-to-10 million illegals that have crossed the border, it is apparent that the suffering there suits both the Mexican president and Bidens' common political goals.

11/21

In a comical example of the pot calling the kettle black, Bidens' communications director produced a dossier attacking the underlying arguments for Congress opening the impeachment inquiry on Biden. With Bidens' approval, he lambastes House Republicans for "…lurching toward impeachment over allegations that are not only unfounded but, in virtually all cases, have been actively disproven…" and "…only serve to generate confusion, put false premises in people's feeds and obscure the truth." Even with his ever-fading grasp on reality, is it possible that

Biden has already forgotten this is exactly what he and his Congressional allies did to Trump, not once, but twice? First Psaki, then Harris, then Bidens' transportation secretary, then his current PS and now Bidens' communication director? There can no question about it now, Bidens' brain dilapidation is contagious.

11/22

Poll after poll continue to show that an ever-growing number of Americans feel Biden is both mentally and physically unfit to be president. Those perceptions continue to be fueled by high-profile moments, including his fall at an Air Force Academy graduation, staircase stumbles boarding Air Force One, the revelation he uses a medical device to aid breathing during sleep (including daytime naps in his basement) and dozens of unceasing, almost daily verbal gaffes. Taken together, they have fanned uneasiness among even Bidens' most ardent supporters that the man who has cast himself as the bulwark against Trump's return is just one illness or injury away from plunging his campaign into disaster.

11/23

During his career Biden has developed a well-documented, gross public fascination for very young girls that are regularly caught on film. These videos show Bidens' strange interactions with the young ones; whispering in their ears, touching their shoulders, sniffing their hair and smiling – scenes creepy enough to make normal adults gag. In what all can only hope is his nadir, Biden noticed a little girl in the audience at a Thanksgiving celebration in Virginia. The girl was wearing Mickey Mouse ears. Biden approached the girl, told her he loved the MM ears, then asked: "How old are you? 17?" The tyke responded: "6," to the 81-year-old Biden. It seemed odd that Biden would guess such a large number for such a young girl. Reporters were confused, until a local informed them that the age of consent in Virginia is 15. On this day, this one day in particular, the young tyke could be thankful there were other adults around.

11/24

The video of Bidens' creepy interaction with the 6-year old in Virginia goes viral. It prompts eerie memories of a similar event that took place in the same state in 2021. Then Biden was attending an event for military personnel in Hampton. In the middle of his speech, Biden stops and points to a family being honored who had a elementary-school aged daughter. Looking at the girl, Biden says: "I love those barrettes in your hair, she looks like she's 19 years old." After a pause, Biden continued, saying that the little girl is "… sitting there with her – like a little lady with her legs crossed." Any other citizen exhibiting such overt tendencies, especially over many years, would be a candidate for at least an ankle monitor. For now, the preteen girls in Virginia have to be thankful that the age of consent in their state is 15.

11/25

Bidens' nurses have created a safety net of small accommodations to mitigate his almost-daily mental and physical gaffes. They not only include using a lower set of stairs for boarding Air Force One, but Secret Service agents and staff are instructed to use flashlights and verbal warnings to guide Biden on and off various stages. As for his mental lapses, Bidens' nurses will try to enforce a 'No more Impromptu Meetings' policy. They hope this will keep Biden from embarrassing himself like he did earlier this year. It was when Bidens' staff brought their kids to visit the White House on 'Take Your Child to Work" day. There Biden took part in an impromptu question-and-answer session where he first forgot that he had just visited Ireland. Then, right after saying that he spoke to his grandchildren everyday, Biden struggled to recall where exactly his grandchildren lived.

11/26

Despite Bidens' constant bragging about his accomplishments while president, American voters still express their dissatisfaction with his job performance. In addition, no matter how much or how often Biden dismisses concerns about his age, voters are worried. Polls continue to show that even a majority of Democrats are worried about Biden's age and ability to carry out the country's most important job. Biden is reminded that it was just two months ago a Wall Street Journal poll showed that 73% of voters said Biden was too old to run for reelection, while only 47% of voters thought Trump's age was an impediment to him running again. Biden has no comment.

11/27

His narcissistic hubris on display once again, Biden essentially tells the U.S. Supreme Court to pound sand. This after the highest court in the land told Biden decisively last month that his unilateral plan to cancel hundreds of billions in student loan debt, at taxpayer expense, was an egregious unconstitutional overreach of his office. That same day the ruling came down, Biden announced that he would unilaterally forgive the debt, anyway. SCOTUS decided not to respond because it became apparent that Bidens' rumored early-onset Alzheimers kicked in, apparently leaving Biden confused. He released a statement, probably versed by his nurses, stating that he "…will not let Republican elected officials succeed in denying hardworking Americans the relief they need." SCOTUS couldn't respond because, one, none of them are elected officials and, two, like everyone else they had no idea who or what Biden was talking about.

11/28

In a backhanded, secretive move to solve his problem of trashing of American cities with his illegal alien infestation, Biden proposes to trash Americas' national parks and other public lands by housing the illegals there. Regardless of the massive "You've got to be kidding!" reaction from most Americans, Biden is moving forward with using national park land to establish migrant housing encampment. In the letter published by several Congressmen that originally exposed Bidens' demented plan, they also questioned the legality of housing people on national park land. One again, Bidens' blatant hypocrisy is mind-numbing. On one hand Biden claims to be an environmentalist, to the point of adding mountains of new environmental regulations while in office that did little more than strangle Americas' free-market system. Yet, he is willing to trash this same environment if it helps him mitigate the illegal immigration debacle he created.

11/29

Thanks to the Congressmens' letter exposing Bidens' secret plan to use national parks and other public lands to house illegals is no longer a secret. Republicans in the House are opening an investigation into Biden flagrantly ignoring environmental regulations in order to try to do this. They sent a letter to Bidens' environmental quality chief, criticizing her and Biden for brushing aside environmental laws to lease public lands for housing illegal aliens. Their rebuke reminded both she and Biden that, regardless of personal or political beliefs on illegal immigration policy, there is common ground among Americans in keeping their treasured national parks out of the debate. The letter also noted that national parks exist for visitors to experience the wonder, the joy of nature and learn more about the great history of America, not to serve as housing projects to solve political messes that Biden creates.

11/30

The total number of illegal aliens Biden smuggled into New York this year is estimated to be 100,000, adding to the several hundred thousand already there. Instead of resisting Bidens' horrendous illegal immigrant wave, the mayor of New York slashed monies from New York's $110 billion budget to cover the cost of the $7 billion gap in next years budget for housing and providing services for the mob of illegals Biden sent there. To plug the holes, New York's police force was reduced to its lowest level since the 1980s and education programs, already on life support, were further gutted. The prediction made by some New York city officials, that Biden's endless stream of illegal aliens would "destroy" their city has now materialized.

12/1

In his nearly three-years as president, Biden's foreign policy record has been as dismal as his domestic one. Part of Bidens' many problems is his misplaced priorities. Instead of beefing up Americas defense capability in a material way, Biden is spending a large part of the military budget on his Diversity, Equality, Inclusion and Accessibility initiatives, sometimes just known as 'DEIA'. In addition to what Biden spent in 2022 and 2023 on DEIA initiatives, Biden is planning to spend an additional $114 million on these initiatives in 2024, bringing the total Biden has spent on these largely useless 'feel good' programs to over a quarter of a billion dollars. While Russia continues its' campaign against the Ukraine, the fat pajama boy dictator of North Korea is firing missiles, China is committing genocide on the Uyghrs and Arab militants in Gaza are beheading babies and throwing them in ovens, Biden is focusing on making sure gays in the US military feel 'included'.

12/2

The media rushes to cover up a new, major Biden scandal when a Republican lawmaker blows the whistle on this Communist Chinese operation in America that Biden has known about for some time. By accident, a secret Chinese-owned bio lab was discovered tucked away in an industrial park in Reedley, California, just outside of Fresno. The bio lab was uncovered by a random building code inspector who found Chinese citizens in lab coats inside the building, working in an area filled with laboratory equipment, freezers and vials that allegedly contained viruses including COVID, HIV, malaria, and rubella. The shock here was that Biden, his CDC and FBI refused to investigate the secret Communist Chinese bio lab when it was first brought to their respective attentions. It wasn't until the local Congressman got on the case that the CDC was forced to send a team to investigate and that wasn't until months later. Despite reports, witnesses and 8X10 glossies of the operation, Biden still does not acknowledge the presence of the Communist lab.

12/3

As more information is revealed, it becomes apparent that Biden, his CDC and FBI tried to turn a blind eye to the bombshell discovery of Communist China potentially operating a number of bio weapons labs in the U.S. At first and eerily similar to the Chinese spy balloon, Biden and his cohorts are unwilling to handle this serious threat to national security from China, even when it's right under their collective noses. The whistle blowers who found the lab said that when they called the CDC to report what they found, the CDC just hung up. Next they called the FBI, but the FBI said they couldn't respond because, of all the moronic excuses, there were no ties to WMD weapons. The whistle blowers called the White House last, only to be informed that since it was after 4:30 in the afternoon, they would have better luck calling tomorrow.

12/4

With inflation remaining one of the top issues facing voters in 2024. Biden steps out to assure the country that, because of his policies, inflation is over and the cost of goods is under control. As usual, Biden is being purposefully deceptive. The rate of inflation has slowed, but that doesn't mean that prices have fallen, only that prices aren't increasing as fast which means inflation isn't "over".When confronted by this, another Biden untruth, Biden tries to switch tracks, but only exposes again his ignorance in elementary school economics. Bidens' new tact is to try to convince Americans that any inflation they might think they see has nothing to do with Bidens' trillions of dollars in wasteful spending, but because business owners are engaging in "price gouging." It's obvious that the difference between Bidens' rampaging inflation rate slowing and costs actually coming down will forever escape Bidens' feeble brain, as most things do these days.

12/5

Unable or unwilling to stop showcasing his ignorance, Biden doubles down on his attacks on American businessmen, insisting they cut their prices even though their costs keep rising. In a speech Biden proclaims that any corporation "…that has not brought their prices back down, even as inflation has come down… it's time to stop the price gouging, give the American consumer a break." It is more apparent than ever that the only time the American consumer will get a break now is when this, dangerous incompetent leaves office.

2/6

In a move missed by most because most thought it must be a comic parody, Biden announces he is going to use the Defense Production Act to enforce his climate change agenda. People at first laughed at Biden the clown because the DPA was put in place during the Cold War in case there was an escalation of tensions between the US and Russia. Mirth turned to concern when all realized that Biden is a very unhappy clown, willing to use a vital tool of national security to advance one of his dangerous anti-science agendas. So rather than keeping his attention on national and international matters like inflation, the wars in Ukraine and Gaza, the illegal immigration and contingent fentanyl overdose epidemic in America, all of which he is responsible for, Biden instead declares war on the sky.

12/7

As part of his declaration of war on the heavens, Biden insists that all Americans must limit their future lifestyles, including forgoing air travel and the consumption of products produced by carbon-emitting offenders, such as beef. It is quickly pointed out that while Biden insists on Americans sacrificing, his Special Envoy for Climate visited Dubai recently for the global climate change conference known as COP28. Not only did his envoy travel on one of the 1000 private jets – the worst carbon emitting method of travel - that delivered attendees to the conference, wile there they dined on sumptuous restaurant fare, including beef. Biden has no comment on yet another one of his glaring hypocrisies.

12/8

While Bidens' barking seals applaud his declaration of war on the sky and Mother Nature, Biden gets pole-axed by the president of the American Gas Association. She points out that the increased use of natural gas has been responsible for 60% of the electrical grid's CO2 emissions reductions. Also, this vital tool for emissions reductions and energy system resilience should not be unfairly undermined through Bidens' misuse of the Defense Production Act. She finishes by telling Biden that there are many sensible climate measures that he keeps ignoring and, if Biden was serious about reducing carbon emissions, he would not be so aggressively anti-natural gas. Biden, never one to be confused by scientific fact, says nothing.

12/9

At a recent rally Trump is reminded of Bidens' boast that he would like to take him "... behind the gym...." in order to teach him manners. Trump laughs it off. First, Biden would have to find the gym. Next his nurses would have to lead Biden behind it, making sure the path was clear of pebbles and sticks so Biden wouldn't trip. Then the nurses would have to stand behind Biden and move his arms back and forth for him if he wanted to punch Trump. Trump laughs along with the crowd because fighting Biden, a man who is physically challenged eating a bowl of jello, would be like fighting Mr. Magoo; much more mirth than actual violence.

12/10

While Biden assures the rest of world that America is committed to his "green agenda", the assurances are being made under a shadow cast by Trump. The Socialist/Marxist countries are worried that Americans will award a second term to the Republican, the man who yanked the US out of the Paris Agreement and dialed back economy-crippling "green" regulations. They were particularly incensed when Trump canceled tax payer funds committed by Obama supposedly to help poor countries "... bearing the brunt of global warming..." even though it was learned that some of these "poor countries", like Somalia, were using the funds to stockpile their war chests. These same garbage countries warn Biden that a Trump victory would threaten his and US credibility in any future climate talks. Biden, his eyes bleary from being awake for almost 4 hours, says nothing.

12/11

Poll after poll keep rocking Bidens' confidence about seeking a second term. They continue to show that voters are concerned that Bidens' rapid cognitive and physical decline is on display virtually every time he appears in public, even if only for a brief minute. They also show that 77% of Americans are growing concerned about his ability to effectively carry out his duties as President. While it's to be expected that 89% of Republicans agree Biden is too old to hold office again, the bad news for Biden is that 69% of his fellow Democrats feel the same way.

12/12

In an embarrassing twist, Sammy 'The Bull' Gravano, an ex-Gambino crime family mobster, expressed shock at what Bidens' FBI and DOJ allowed Biden and his family to get away with from their alleged foreign influence-peddling scheme. Saying he couldn't understand how the country is "…listening to these things and no action is being taken…" the 'Bull' goes on to state that he had friends who served"… 22 lifetime sentences for this kind of stuff." If he could feel shame, Biden would be embarrassed that a mobster, who allegedly took part in multiple murders himself, could be shocked by the criminal activity of someone who is supposedly the president of the United States. That is, if Biden could feel shame.

12/13

Trump holds a rally where he declares that, if re-elected, he will be a "dictator" on day one for the purpose of closing the border and eliminating Bidens' edicts that are crushing Americas' fossil fuel industry. Trump goes on to assure his audience that after that first day government operations will return to normal and that he is "… not a dictator." Biden immediately takes Trumps' quote out of context, warning America that to elect Trump would be the same as electing a dictator. Hilariously, this comes from Biden, a man who unilaterally imposed vaccine and mask mandate on the country, unconstitutionally and illegally ordered all student loans be forgiven and banned evictions for non-paying tenants during the government COVID over-reaction hoax, all with no voter or

Congressional approval. With even the Supreme Court informing him he had no Constitutional authority for any of his actions, Biden calling Trump a 'dictator' is a defining case of a a mentally confused pot calling the kettle black.

12/14

Bidens' image as a king or dictator in enlarged significantly when reports surface of some of Bidens' shenanigans that the mainstream media, if not hiding, have kept in the shadows before now. Now documents are surfacing showing that Biden threatened to use anti-trust lawsuits to break up any social media company that did not or refused to censor conservatives and any others who disagreed with Bidens' views on his wars, his "green agenda", climate change, immigration and COVID policies. It is now apparent that Bidens' 'confused black kettle' has been rolling around DC for some time.

12/15

Another 'misplaced' report surfaces that is essentially a slap in the face to Bidens' goal of destroy fossil fuel production in the US. Last November Sultan Al-Jaber, the minister of industry and advanced technology for the United Arab Emirates, stated that there is "no science" showing a fossil fuel phaseout is needed to reach the unrealistic goals of the Paris Accords. In an effort to save face, Biden and his 'climate czar' Kerry 'suggest' that the Sultan walk back his statement. With conflicts raging in all parts of the world, one has to wonder if Bidens' special envoys' implied threat to a high-ranking official of a wealthy country could put American lives at risk. Actually, a more immediate threat to lives is Bidens' war on coal and other fossil fuels. If Biden, his czar and his global elitists succeed in this, scientific facts show that many millions could freeze in coming winters.

12/16

Biden continues to brag that his "Bidenomics" has had a positive effect on the countrys' debt and deficit. Of course Biden hopes no one notices that he has had the advantage of a 43% increase in federal tax receipts from 2020 to 2022, thanks to Trumps' 2017 Tax Cuts and Jobs Act. In 2020, federal income tax revenues were $3.4 trillion. In 2022, they increased to a record $4.8 trillion. Thanks to Trump, revenues from both individual income taxes and corporate income taxes were the highest they have ever been. Individual income tax revenues were over $2 trillion in 2021 and 2022 for the first time, which was a 64 percent increase in 2022 over 2020. Looking ever the fool, Biden's constant whining that business doesn't pay its fair share takes an embarrassing hit when it's reported that revenues from corporate income taxes in 2022 were over $400 billion for the first time - an increase of almost 100% percent over 2020, thanks to Trump. When asked about the largess his 'Bidenomics' budget received courtesy of Trump, Biden has no comment.

12/17

Biden is furthered embarrassed when a report from economist shows that if he had returned to the 2019 pre-COVID spending levels and rejected the trillions of dollars in excess spending that has characterized his first two years, Biden could have come much closer to a balanced budget for 2022. Adjusting the 2019 spending for inflation and given the remarkable increase in revenues thanks to Trump, the deficit in 2022 would have been only $194 billion instead of $1.3 trillion. Worse than missing a chance to almost-balance the budget, the CBOs' baseline projection is that the annual deficit will be over $1 trillion dollars through 2029 and, thanks to Biden, then will go over $2 trillion dollars for the years spanning 2030-2033. Despite Bidens' insistent, grossly misplaced braggadocio, the only thing Biden and his 'Bidenomics' is good for is driving America over an economic cliff.

12/18

Bidens' political revenge pettiness showcases again when he orders the cancellation of a $885 million contract to Elon Musk's Starlink service. This service was to provide high-speed internet to 35 states and nearly 700,000 Americans living in rural areas. Bidens' decision comes after several failed attempts by Biden to force Musk to use his social media X platform to censor conservatives and all others who disagree and/or are critical of Bidens' policies. Leaving all those Americans stranded with no Internet access is an example of yet another personal political harassment of Musk ordered by Biden, all while pouting in his basement.

12/19

Biden releases a bizarre video supposedly showcasing Christmas spirit in the White House. In it, dancers clad in freakish outfits twist and swirl through the halls of the White House in what is supposed to be the Bidens' interpretation of the Nutcracker Suite. What made it worse for Biden was that his video was compared to Trumps' wife Melanias' Christmas video. Critics commented on how, unlike the Bidens, Melanias' video was tasteful, seasonal and appealed to most everyone, while they called the Biden video tacky and tasteless. They point out that nowhere in the video is a semblance of Christmas spirit, nowhere is any sign of Christmas tradition and nowhere is there even any recognizable interpretation of the fabled Nutcracker. What the critics missed, in their obvious disdain, was that Bidens' tacky, tasteless video did showcase a summary of Bidens' first three years in office … nowhere.

12/20

Biden continues to try to force Americans to buy electric vehicles. Bidens' EPA proposed a rule that would require that two-thirds of all new vehicles sold in America be electric by 2032. They expect to accomplish this by setting the most stringent tailpipe emissions standards in history in a bid to end the use of gasoline-powered vehicles. However Congress, including several Democrats, pass the CARS Act which stopped Biden and his EPA from issuing any regulations that require the use of specific engine technologies or restrict the sales of new cars based on their engines. Biden, though in an enraged pout over this rejection, had no comment.

12/21

Despite Bidens' bluff and bluster about his 'Bidenomics', his 'green agenda' and his declared war on Mother Nature, polls continue to show Trump leading Biden both nationally and in the battleground states that will likely decide the 2024 election. Some anonymous sources suggest even Obama feels that Democrats could lose in 2024 if Biden is the nominee. Currently Biden has a 34% approval rating, an all-time low since he was elected nearly three years ago. Biden continues to downplay the polls showing him losing to Trump, saying simply: "You're reading the wrong polls..." This might be true simply because no one can be certain which polls Bidens' nurses are reading to him on a daily basis.

12/22

The CDCs' latest report reveals that drug overdose deaths in America surged from approximately 60,000 a year to over 100,000 a year – and have stayed there – since almost the first day of Bidens' reign. Mexican drug cartels are capitalizing on Bidens' wide-open southern border policy to flood the country with fentanyl, the leading cause of death for Americans 18 to 45. Even Bidens' DEA admitted that last year federal authorities seized enough fentanyl to kill every person in the US several times over. Since Biden took office, drugs seizures are up 94%., but doesn't include all the fentanyl Biden has allowed into the the country. Even with this drug evidence, the human trafficking and the fact 14,000 illegals attempted to cross into the US in a single day last week, Biden steadfastly insists that the southern border is secure. Hopefully soon Bidens' nurses will read some of this evidence to him, or at least something other than the comics, regardless of how big a 'Hagar the Horrible" fan Biden is.

12/23

Fallout continues for Biden from last months' report from New York Citys' Democratic mayor that the Biden's border policies are responsible for the billion budget gap in the mayors' budget for next year. Bidens' policies are responsible for flooding NYC with an additional 100,000 illegal aliens. Accommodating them and the resultant $7 billion budget gap they cause will mean disrupting city services New Yorkers rely on daily. The mayor, placing the blame squarely on Biden, urges legal residents of the city to mobilize, go to D.C, "…the source of our discontent…", to emphasize to Biden that what is happening to New York City is not fair, legal or just. Coming from a former staunch supporter of Biden, this might be a portent of a future where many former allies desert Biden, viewing him now as a doddering, fumbling sinking ship.

12/24

Shortly after entering office, Biden issued a tumultuous amount of Executive Orders, mainly to undo all the work Trump had done previously for the American economy. Lost in the maze of paperwork was a Biden environmental edict known as his "30/30" plan to "protect" the American environment. Currently about 13% of US land is under direct federal control. Bidens' plan is to use the 1906 Antiquities Act to grab an additional 17% of Americans' private property by 2030 (hence the '30/30 name) and turn it over to Biden and the Federal Government. Closer scrutiny now reveals that, since the 1906 Act pertains only to land already under Federal control, Bidens' plan to use it to appropriate more

American land from its citizens is nothing more than a egregious land grab of private property.

12/25

A firestorm of criticism quickly against Biden for, once again, shamelessly bastardizing the Constitution and American law by trying to use a 1906 law to justify stealing private property from American citizens In response, Biden reassures the public that it will be the National Forest Service, not he, that will manage any new private property Biden acquires. What is missed by almost all in the fine print is that Biden is allowing BLM – the same BLM that burned down and occupied major portions of American cities, that destroyed thousand of businesses and assaulted innocent people – that same BLM - is who Biden is putting in charge of 'co-stewarding' these new lands with the NFS. After this announcement, the public is left with the same glazed, faraway look in their eyes that Biden wears everyday.

12/26

Bidens' decision to appoint BLM as stewards of any new private property he appropriates dumb strikes the majority of American people. Noting BLMs' previous handiwork with and penchant for fire, it is rumored that even Smokey the Bear, fearing for his and his forests' safety, filed a petition against Biden. Still puzzled, concerned citizens note that, unless Biden needs innocent people on these stolen lands to be assaulted and their businesses destroyed and burned to the ground, it is unclear what exactly BLMs' role will be in their new stewardship.

12/27

Reports in the media show that the same worries that plagued Americans for most of the past year still resonate now. Three-fourths of Americans believe Biden is too old to serve another four years, that they are worried that inflation is still too high, crime is surging, and that Biden is leading them into World War III. Making it worse, Democrats who run so-called sanctuary cities and states have had enough of Biden's border crisis and are starting to turn on him. Even voters between the ages of 18 and 34 say they are as likely to vote for Trump as they are for Biden, a sharp drop from the margins Biden enjoyed over Trump in 2020. It is evident that with a goofy grin and a can of Esure firmly in hand, Biden's problems are not going away any time soon.

12/28

Beyond harassing Trump, Biden expands his weaponizing of his presidency by declaring war on the nation's largest Christian university, Grand Canyon University (GCU). Through his FTC, Biden is going after GCU for alleged deceptive telemarketing practices and the misrepresentation of costs. Biden and his FTC promise to "aggressively pursue" anyone who tries to take advantage of students, yet says nothing about the thousands of Christian students who are consistently harassed and alienated everyday on college campuses across the nation. It's impossible to separate this attack on GCU from the reality that Bidens' lust to fine, sanction, censor and imprison Americans is focused almost solely on conservatives.

12/29

Biden is accused of purposely making the immigration crisis worse for political gain. Sounding absurd, even for Biden, officers in the field contend that Biden is raping the American taxpayer for the benefit of the illegals. A Pinal County Sheriff disclosed that Biden is making illegally entering America a lucrative proposition. According to him, Biden is providing every illegal alien a cell phone, a plane ticket to whatever city in America they want to go to and a $5,000 Visa gift card. As outrageous as this sounds, both Biden and his "border czar" Harris have yet to address these allegations: An absurd accusation, maybe, but taxpaying legal American citizen are waiting for an answer.

12/30

Economists as a group blame Bidens' "Bidenomics" policies as the reason that inflation continues unabated and the economy limps along at a 1.9% growth rate. Though this has been steadily reported for over a year, Biden still champions this shark-skin policy and plans to use it as a reason for his re-election. This, despite a report by economists alerting Biden that many Americans on the brink of retirement will have to work an additional 10 years. This, to make up for the money they've lost in their 401ks and pensions in just the three years Biden has been president. Regardless of this new, brutal burden Biden has inflicted on the American taxpayer, he refuses to alter his 'Bidenomic' policies. In his defense, again, it's not certain that his nurses have read these reports to Biden.

12/31

Bidens' fear of Trump reaches laughable heights as he approves of his lackeys on the Colorado Supreme court prohibiting Trump from appearing on the states' 2024 primary ballot. Backlash was immediate, both state and nationwide. The Colorado Republican Party immediately filed an appeal to the Supreme Court arguing that this unprecedented decision stood to strip away democracy, not only in Colorado, but in America as well. The CSC, exhibiting gutlessness from both sides, offered to stay its decision if Trump begged them to do so. Facing such pressure, the states' faux Marxist Secretary of State backed down and, with tail at least temporarily between her States' legs, announced that Trumps' name would appear on the March 5 Colorado primary ballot

2024

1/1

Bidens' panic over consistently trailing Trump in poll after poll reaches a new high when a new poll finds that Biden's support with black voters – one of his main constituencies - has dropped from 87% to 63%. In response, Biden rehashes the old trope that Trump is Hitler, Trump supporters are Nazis, Trump is a threat to American democracy, etc., etc. New in Bidens tirade, however, is his dog-whistle insinuation to his violence-prone supporters - like BLM - that Trump must be 'dealt' with. in order to save America. This is the group that recently burned down major portions of American cities, assaulting police officers and other innocents. Biden falls just short of advocating the assassination of Trump, but CNN reports that younger aides on Biden's re-election campaign have been overheard discussing their anticipation of when Biden would go "full Hitler" on Trump. For his part, Biden does nothing to deescalate this threat of violence against his political opponent.

1/2

The battle between Biden trying to destroy the state of Texas with illegal immigrants and Texas' attempt to protect itself from Biden, rages on. Previously Biden had ordered the buoys Texas had installed in the middle of the Rio Grande river to inhibit illegal crossings to be removed. Then Texas installed miles of razor wire in another attempt to accomplish the same: Biden ordered the wire cut down. Texas sued Biden to stop the wire cutting and a judge agrees, saying cutting the wire illegally destroys state property and undermines the security of Texas citizens. Biden has asks the Supreme Court to allow the wire cutting to continue, but a federal appeals court ordered Biden to stop cutting the razor wire while court proceedings play out. Furious at a states' attempt to protect itself, Biden and his DOJ file an emergency application, asking the Supreme Court to overturn that decision, removing all impediments for illegals trying to cross the border into Texas.

1/3

Bidens' disingenuous attitude to the southern border crisis reaches another height when he shamelessly tries to shoehorn desired funding for "immigration reform" into a Bill requesting aid for the Ukraine in its' battle with Russia. Passage was stalled when alert Republicans notice that Biden was requesting funds, not to stop illegal immigration, but to process more illegal immigrants through his 'catch and release' policy. From Bidens' decision to rescind Trumps' 'Remain in Mexico' policy to the widespread abuse of the parole and asylum systems, Biden has undermined security everywhere at the border. There is a direct cause-and-effect between Bidens' reckless immigration policies and the record 300,000 illegal immigrants encountered at the border just last month. In comparison, during the Trump years, illegal immigrant encounters dropped as low as 300/month.

1/4

It is reported that the Islamic State recently took credit for setting off two bombs in Iran that killed nearly 100 people and wounded hundreds of others at a memorial ceremony. What was strange, despite the acknowledgment of the IS responsibility in the matter, was that protesters of the explosions were waving "Death to Israel' and 'Death to America' placards. Stranger still, Biden sent condolences to Irans' top officials, the same officials who have vowed to wipe both Israel and America off the map. Is it any wonder the world, witnessing a man grovel before another who promises to kill him, sees Biden as nothing more than a weak-kneed fool?

1/5

Biden continues to be tone deaf – or, in his case, really deaf – to the concerns of the majority of Americans who understand his excessive government spending is the major cause of the country's inflation and their suffering. So deaf that, amidst this suffering Biden has inflicted on the American public with his "Bidenomics", he is proposing to hand government employees their largest pay increase in more than 40 years. In refusing to tighten his belt in the middle of exploding deficits and the runaway inflation he caused, Bidens' uncaring attitude towards the struggles everyday Americans endure trying to make ends meet goes beyond deaf, to deaf and dumb.

1/6

Instead of downplaying his proposed obscene largess to government workers, Biden defends this taxpayer-supplied charity. Biden insists that government workers are underpaid when compared to their counterparts in the private sector. Whether lying or just ignorant, Bidens' claim isn't true. The U.S. Office of Personnel Management released data that showed that in 2023 government workers made an average yearly salary of $98,943. This included workers in the Washington, D.C area. This special class of employee, many of them Biden supporters, averaged over $125,000 per year. If his soggy brain was capable of receiving anything, Biden would've received a reality check when the Bureau of Labor Statistics released data showing that the median yearly salary for working-class Americans is roughly $58,000, or one-half of their public sector counterparts. Obviously government workers are living the good life on the taxpayers' dimes, thanks to their sugar-daddy Biden.

1/7

Bidens' insistence that government workers are underpaid creates a backlash that has business analysts looking at exactly what government employees are being paid and exactly how much of a pay increase Biden is giving them. It turns out that the civilian workers in the federal government will see their paychecks increase by an average of 5.2% this year, coming on top of a a 4.6% raise Biden gave them last year. At that time this was the largest increase in government employees' pay in two decades. Adding to this, government employees in San Francisco and other Democrat-controlled cities will receive additional increases. Some wonder about the coincidence that the last time government employees received a 9% boost in their pay was under Jimmy Carter, considered the worst president in American history, until now.

1/8

Biden' attempt to subvert pro-life states like Arkansas by using taxpayer dollars to fund the travel, meals and lodging expenses of military service members' out-of-state travel for abortions. Not only does Bidens' policy violate federal law, it forces commanding officers to approve such abortion leave. Now it is reported that one top military leader has resigned his commission over Bidens' policy, citing religious objections to complying. In an angry letter sent to Biden, the Governor of Arkansas put the blame for the officers' resignation squarely on Bidens' shoulders, chastising him for forcing this man to choose between his faith and his commitment of service to his country. Biden has no comment.

1/9

It is reported that last week Biden asked the president of Mexico for help in controlling their common border and the 300,000/month illegal aliens attempting to cross into the US. Mexicos' president agreed, as along as Biden agreed to, one, send $20 billion in "aid" to Mexico and other Latin American countries; two, give work visas to 10 million illegal Hispanics currently in the U.S. and, three, end economic sanctions against Venezuela and Cuba. In effect, the clown president of Mexico demanded that Biden subsidize countries that are flooding America illegally with their citizens, make U.S. citizens out of all illegals currently residing illegally in America and make friends with Communist countries that are enemies of America. If there is still any doubt in any American as to how weak and foolish Biden appears to the rest of the world, this paper-mache, tin pot, perfumed "leader" of Mexico just put an end to it.

1/10

It leaks out that Biden has been secretly holding closed-door meetings at the White House with his top donors to alleviate their concerns about his age and energy going into the 2024 election. When asked about these secret meetings, Bidens' campaign manager insisted that, instead of a liability, Bidens age and, indirectly, his decreased mental faculties, are his "… superpower(s) because of his experience." Many might think it strange to call tripping over unseen objects, befuddled by stage curtains, talking to and trying to shake hands with invisible and/or dead people, challenged and terrified by any type of stairs, groping women and grabbing adolescent girls to sniff their hair, all as "super powers".If this is really the case, if one does find himself in trouble, it would still be best to turn on the Bat Signal, using Biden only as a very, very, very distant second choice.

1/11

While seniors still struggle handling the costs merely for their daily staples during Bidens' inflationary surge, it seems Biden still doesn't care. Instead of addressing the cost of living crisis, Biden has been using monies from Medicare to fund his "Green New Deal" priorities like subsidizing electric vehicles, which doesn't help the elderly one wit. Right now one in seven Americans over the age of 65 rely solely on Social Security payments to support themselves, while a survey in 2022 found that 45 percent of America's elderly used charitable food banks or applied for government food stamps in order to sustain themselves. The one accomplishment Biden can own, but really shouldn't brag about, is that this number has more than doubled since he took office.

1/12

Biden and his staff chafe under the accusation that they don't care about the elderly in America. Biden openly brags that the new drug negotiation regulations he inserted into his hilariously-named 'Inflation Reduction Act' supposedly "saved" approximately $280 billion for senior citizens. However, this was due only to Biden forcing pharmaceutical firms to take it in the shorts by accepting much lower Medicare reimbursements. The awful truth is that almost all of the money Biden "saved" for seniors was used to subsidize some of Bidens' more bizarre climate agenda items: Biden has yet to explain how subsidizing Teslas for wealthy suburbanites in California improves the health of retirees in Wisconsin.

1/13

It was only a couple of months ago when Biden announced his support for Israel to do whatever they thought necessary to destroy the October 7 terrorists and secure Israels' safety. However, after being booed and heckled by pro - Hamas activists in the middle of a speech, Biden insists that he "…understand(s) their passion..." and reassures the terrorist supporters that he has been working with the Israeli government to "...get (them) out of Gaza, and doing all I can to do it." Nowhere in Bidens' speech does he denounce the anti-Semitic portion of his base that supports the murderous, raping, baby-killing Hamas terrorists. Biden keeps inching closer to publicly embracing Hamas. For its' part, Israel has no immediate comment, as if expecting Bidens' gutless wavering.

1/14

In an unprecedented, historical backstabbing move, Biden announces that the US will no longer support the independence of Taiwan, for decades one of Americas' most valued allies. Taiwanese voters rebuffed China by giving their Democratic Progressive Party's (DPP) presidential candidate a third presidential term, ignoring the Communist countrys' demand to oust him. Where Trump called to congratulate the Taiwanese President after his last election, Biden snubs him, saying only: "We (America) do not support independence..." Critics call Biden spineless, but are reminded, correctly, that before that particular moniker can be affixed to him, Biden would have to have had a spine in the first place.

1/15

Biden defends his double-cross of Taiwan by insisting that his abandoning a treasured ally was just a continuation of a policy started in 1979 when Carter, another gutless admirer of the Communist Chinese, switched US diplomatic recognition from independent Taiwan to Communist China. The difference is that Carter spent most of his career on his hands and knees, exposed, fawning over China while it was just last fall that Biden promised Taiwan that US forces would defend it in case of a Chinese invasion. Of course asking Biden to keep promises is like asking a monkey not to eat an extra banana: Expecting a positive reaction is fruitless and the monkey just ends up annoyed.

1/16

Amidst mounting criticism of Biden deserting long-standing ally Taiwan, Biden insists that, though he will not support a formal declaration of independence by Taiwan, he will maintain 'unofficial relations' with the self-governed island. Biden promises to send an unofficial delegation to Taiwan and looks forward to working with their leaders to advance their (the US and Taiwan) longstanding unofficial relationship. Biden then hedges his bets by adding that he will do so "… as long as it is consistent with the U.S. 'One China' policy.", the policy that favors China and does not recognize Taiwan's' independence. Once again in trying to appease both slave and slave master, Biden comes across like a blithering, moral-less idiot.

1/17

Recently a staggering 10,000 migrants crossed illegally into Eagle Pass, Texas, in just 24 hours. Even more staggering is that the population of Eagle Pass in under 29,000. For perspective, using the same per capita rates, this is the same as if 1.5 million illegals appeared in a single day in Los Angeles or 3 million showed up in a day in New York City. Biden looks confused when hearing these numbers so while Biden is eating breakfast his nurses attempt to explain this higher math by scratching figures on the back of the Denny's' children coloring place mat Biden has before him. They give up shortly, though, after Biden becomes transfixed trying to solve the maze.

1/18

Bidens' two-tier approach to justice is on full display as he continues to prosecute and jail innocent bystanders for what Biden calls the 1/6/21 "insurrection". This, while self-proclaimed "trans rights" and other activists have turned storming state capitol buildings into a political routine. It has escalated to the point where a group of pro-Hamas supporters held a protest at the White House that quickly got out of hand and turned into a near riot. Videos clearly shows these supporters of Hamas scaling the White House fence in an attempt to invade the grounds, forcing White House staff to be relocated during the incident. Unlike the reporting during the 1/6/21 incident, Bidens' media allies make almost no mention of the Hamas riot. Ever the hypocrite, Biden doesn't call for the arrest and/or prosecution of these insurrectionists, nor does Biden demand the FBI raid their homes and toss them in jail like he did to the 1/6/21 participants. Bidens' media friends try to cover for him, but this time they don't have a leg to stand on: All of Bidens' actions this time took place before 4:30 in the afternoon.

1/19

In a recent interview, Jill Biden acknowledged how proud she was of her husband and how committed she was to helping Biden do whatever it takes to carry out his legacy, a legacy so far consisting of open borders, pro-abortion and pro-war. She states that Biden "…is the right man or the right person for the job at this moment in history." and that Biden was wise, had wisdom and experience and knows every leader on the world stage by name. This is hard to believe since it wasn't that long ago that Biden not only forgot her name but confused her with her sister. Any other woman would be embarrassed about her husband forgetting her name. Apparently, along with his cognitive troubles, Bidens' lack of shame is also contagious.

1/20

Biden and his Secretary of State (SoS) roll out the red carpet for Liu Jianchao, China's leading envoy, who also is the architect of Chinas' global scheme to kidnap and silence anti-Communist dissidents. Liu's "Operation Foxhunt" includes setting up actual Chinese police stations' in places like New York to find and extort dissidents. Jianchaos' trip to the US was capped by a reception at the State Department the day after he met Biden's deputy national security adviser. It also included a visit to the prestigious Council on Foreign Relations in Manhattan, a reception with a billionaire Wall Street investor and an audience with the UN Secretary General. This red carpet treatment of this Communist sparked outrage among human rights and dissident groups whose friends and family members have been targeted by this man and his "Operation Foxhunt". Biden, glassy stare intact, has no comment.

1/21

On this anniversary of Bidens' third year in office, America takes stock in all the damage Biden has done to her in such a short time.

The beginning of the damage goes back to Bidens' very first days in office when he proudly canceled and reversed Trumps' 'Stay in Mexico' policy. This paved the way for an unfettered invasion of an estimated 10 million additional illegals into the US. This alone destroyed the day-to-day lives of millions of American citizens, both at the southern border and in major cities across the country. Then, as a favor to his Chinese business partners, Biden reversed Trumps' ban on the Chinese software Tik-Tok, allowing the Communists to establish both a foothold and a spy-hold into the lives of untold millions of Americas youth. Even some of Bidens' ardent supporters begrudgingly admit that Trump was right and it would "…have been a heck of a lot easier (to take action on these problems back then) than trying to take action (now)…" Biden has no comment. His sell-out of Taiwan to a monstrous, Communist in-human rights violator like China and his pandering, kneeling capitulation to terrorist groups like Iran and Hamas has made Biden a world-wide laughing stock, for sale to any grifting bidder willing to pour his ill-gotten gains down Bidens' pants.

1/22

Highlighting the disasters caused by Bidens' unilateral reversal of Trumps' policies reminds all of another, more deadly decision Biden made at that same time: Biden removed the Houthis, a satellite terrorist group of Iran, from the terror watch list where Trump had placed them. This allowed Iran to arm their murdering proxy terrorists. Now Iran is sending them into the commercial trading waters of the Red Sea, attacking ships and American military outposts in the area. Bidens' only response is a few, paltry missile strikes that seem to hit nothing but a couple of camels out in the open desert in their rear ends. Biden refuses to do little more than this 'camel-butt' attack, his staff insisting that further retaliation would only escalate matters in the Middle East. As a result, the Houthis belligerently continue their attacks unscathed, even if their camels are not.

1/23

After Trumps' overwhelming victory in the Iowa caucus, Biden records a message taunting him, boasting that he is the only one ever to beat Trump and he, Biden, is "...looking forward to doing it again" Many pundits quickly point out that Biden's promo only added to the growing concerns about his age and mental acuity. In it Biden is sitting at a table far too small for him, slumped forward, blank stare and frozen grin on his face. Rather than a world leader, Biden looks more like a greatly aged elder, sitting at the little kids table at Thanksgiving, letting his grandchildren take turns feeding him.

1/24

Biden had promised that retaliatory strikes would increase against the Houthis if American lives were at stake. Now two Navy Seals are reported lost and presumed dead in a confrontation with this terrorist group, but other than a few more 'camel-butt' strikes, Biden still refuses to retaliate. It reminds voters of Obamas' famous "Red Line in the Sand" proclamation, the one he warned Middle East terrorists not to cross during his presidency. Problem was, every time terrorists pushed across that line, Obama gutlessly moved it. Now Obamas' protege Biden is seen shuffling across the White House lawn, ignoring shouted questions about the two dead Navy Seal, dragging his own red line behind him.

1/25

In an unprecedented and somewhat historical move, the Supreme Court sides with Biden and grants him the authority to cut down and remove any razor wire or other impediments that the state of Texas has erected. Texas did this in an attempt to protect itself from the catastrophic illegal alien invasion that Biden has authorized since the first days of his presidency. What might be historical is that the wire was erected on private property. What Biden has said and the Supreme Court has now enshrined, is that if Biden wants millions of illegals to cross into the US, bringing with them terrorists, drug and human trafficking and any number of un-vaccinated diseases, the private property rights of American citizens do not, can not and will not deter him.

1/26

The Border Patrol Union releases a statement slamming the Supreme Courts' latest ruling which allows Biden to create yet another incentive for more illegals to cross the border and enter the US. The Union points out that with this ruling, Biden can now allow even more gang members and criminals to infiltrate the United States. Their statement also reveals that Border Patrol agents fully support what Texas is trying to accomplish in the absence of true border security policies from Biden. As expected, Biden has no comment.

1/27

Biden laughably cites the impacts on energy costs, America's energy security and his concern for the environment as excuses for him stopping all Liquefied Natural Gas exports from Texas to Americas' allies across the globe. The Texas Land Commissioner immediately, vehemently responds, accusing Bidens' of stopping the Texas exports as retaliation against Texas for standing up to Biden over the border crisis. The Texas Railroad Commissioner also chimed in, pointing out that if Biden is serious about "restoring global order", the exporting of` LNG is one of the keys. Besides being extremely profitable for both Texas and America, selling LNG will help make America energy dominant again, like it was under Trump. Biden has no comment.

1/28

The Texas Railroad Commissioner continues her harsh criticism of Biden. She calls his move to stop Texas from selling LNG at home and to our allies "... reckless, irresponsible and unacceptable." She openly derides Bidens' "concern for the environment" excuse for stopping these sales, saying that Bidens' embargo on LNG helps neither the environment nor hard-working Americans and our allies. In a final swipe at Bidens' stupidity, she correctly asserts that the only one Bidens' asinine embargo on Texas helps is Putin and Russia, a major exporter of LNG, one of Americas' worst sworn enemies and now the main supplier of LNG to Americas European allies.

1/29

A video from several days ago resurfaces that should be embarrassing for Biden. In it, one of Bidens' ardent CNN supporters advises Biden to remain hidden in his basement, like he did in 2020, if he wants to be re-elected. The reason for this advice was that in Bidens' present mental and physical condition he "...doesn't inspire confidence..." Rather, the reporter feels that the people who have benefited from Bidens' policies should be the ones speaking on his behalf. Actually, this shouldn't be hard to do. If one doesn't count all the government employees that received outlandish raises while private citizens struggled to buy food, the environment and global cooling/global warming/climate change hoaxers that received billion for projects that have and will always be failed taxpayer-money sumps, the thousands of BLM and Antifa animals that burned and looted their way through America while Biden and Harris worked hard to free them, the hundreds of hospitals that ripped off hard-working Americans for billions by reporting faked COVID deaths, the millions of slime ball tenants across the country that Biden allowed to stick their landlords with years of unpaid rent and utility bills, the 10 million new illegal citizens with Biden-provided cell phones and $1000 gift cards now live off the backs of the legal ones, the millions of entitled brats that are passing off their irresponsible stupidity - known colloquially as student loans – to those whose only crime is that they got off their asses and made something of themselves, the hundreds of thousands of criminals that can loot and assault without fear of consequences and, finally, the tens of millions of grifters who have joined the welfare rolls since Biden became president, where his trillion dollar giveaway programs provide them with housing, food, cars, education, clothing, laptop computers, and cellphones – all free to them but a backbreaking burden for responsible Americans - then it shouldn't be too difficult to find the two citizens that have actually found some honest, productive benefit in Bidens' policies.

1/30

Biden has allowed over 150 attacks on US personnel in the Middle East since the Hamas massacre in Israel on 10/6/23 and done near-to-nothing in response. Bidens' excuse this time for his cowardice is allowing American soldiers to be Middle East punching bags, is that doing nothing is better than doing something that the terrorist animals might interpret as Biden escalating the conflict. Now 3 American soldiers are dead and more than 30 wounded. With even more American blood on his hands that could have been avoided, Bidens' only response is that he "…will hold all those responsible to account at a time and in a manner of (my) our choosing." Apparently not learning from the 13 servicemen he got murdered in Afghanistan in another event that could've been avoided, how much more American blood has to be shed before Biden, Aviators in place, finally crawls his wrinkled rump out of his basement and at least feigns leadership.

1/31

The killing of three Americans and the injuring of 34 others in Jordan seems to rouse Biden from his self-induced foreign policy coma, but only slightly. Speaking of the young dead, Biden delivers a flowery speech, saying they: "...embodied the very best of our nation..." and promises to "...hold those responsible for the attack to account..." Then Bidens' lack of guts slips through, as he admits that he is unsure of when, where or how this "account(ing)" will take place because "...facts are still being gathered..." One fact is certain: Bidens' spineless dealings with Iran supposedly come from his fear of "escalating" the conflict in the Middle East. Another fact is that last year Biden gifted Iran and their ayatollahs approximately 20 billion dollars. Now the whole world can be assured that these murderers will have no problem using Bidens' gift to "escalate" the conflict, spilling more American blood.

2/1

A report surfaces that Biden relaxed U.S. enforcement of oil sanctions against Iran through October of 2023, even after its' involvement in the 10/7 massacre in Israel. This allowed the murderous ayatollahs to refill their coffers to the tune of 1.4 million barrels of oil per day, up 80% from the limit Trump put on the terrorist nation during his presidency. The Iranian surge in oil exports under Biden has brought Iran an additional $32 billion dollars. This means that, along with the 20 billion of "humanitarian" aid and the 6 billion "ransom" he paid, Biden unilaterally has funded the country that has sworn to wipe both Israel and the US off the map, to the tune of roughly 60 billion dollars just since last year. Biden has no comment.

2/2

Bidens' recent grovelling before Iran causes one reporter to note an interesting pattern. China repeatedly bullies Taiwan and Biden sides with the Communists against a supposed ally. Several Marxist/ Communist countries in South America demand cash to help them with their "immigration" problem and Biden sends them millions. Palestine rails that its' sole purpose is to wipe both Israel and America off the map and Biden sends them $200 million in "humanitarian" aid. At the behest of Iran, Biden takes the Houthis off the terror watch list, where

Trump had placed them, and Iran returns the favor by arming this terrorist group and sets them off to attack American ships and military installations. An interesting and quite sick pattern indeed, to which Biden has no comment.

2/3

The publishing of Bidens' uncontrollable urge to acquiesce to every despicable dictator and Communist leader in the world exposes another Biden hypocrisy, this one mind-bending. Biden is currently demanding that Congress fund a many-billion dollar aid package for Ukraine in its' war with Russia. At the same time Bidens' embargo on Texas selling NLG world wide has served to enrich Russia NLG exports to the tune of billions of dollars. This head-shaking approach means that Biden, on the one hand, is demanding billions of tax payer dollars to help Ukraine fight Russia while simultaneously making it possible for Russia to rake in billions of dollars in windfall profits which it can use to continue to finance its' war with Ukraine. In short, Biden is asking taxpayers to finance one country defending itself against one of Americas' foremost enemies while at the same time directly financing that enemy; mind-bending, indeed.

2/4

Bidens' constant grovelling before every dictator, Communist leader and religious sociopath in the world has presented his wife with an on-going, seemingly never-ending task; that is, sewing knee pads in all of Bidens' pants. However, she has yet to solve the problem of Bidens' pants belt coming loose every time he kneels in front of this motley assortment of human garbage and tyrants; she is considering suspenders.

2/5

Bidens' deteriorating mental condition is on display once again. This time Biden hilariously blames the high cost of groceries and other essentials on grocery store owners themselves. Biden blames them for "ripping people off", using terms his nurses obviously wrote for him, like "greedflation" and "shrinkflation". Biden insists that Americans are tired of being "played for suckers" by these greedy grocery store owners. Yes, it's not the untold trillions Biden has added to the debt and deficit, not Bidens' war on energy companies which has caused the price of fuel and everything else to skyrocket, not Bidens' gutless submission to terrorists who disrupt commercial supply lines to the US … no, it's the local grocer to blame for the average 25% inflation Americans have endured the last three years. As it turns out, the only one playing the American people for suckers the last three years is Biden.

2/6

Bidens' border crisis reaches a new level of disgust when a group of illegal aliens attack two police officers in New York City. Five of the group are arrested immediately, but are just as quickly released with no bail by the Biden-approved District Attorney, the same one Biden has sicced on Trump. As one of the illegal animals is leaving the court room, smile on his face, he gives a one finger salute to the camera. Coincidentally, concerning Bidens' open border policy, this is the same salute Biden has been giving the American people for the last three years.

2/7

The director of investigations for the Immigration Reform Law Institute lambastes Biden, saying that it is ironic that Biden claims his administration is '... the most transparent in history...' when Biden has repeatedly attempted to change immigration laws without congressional authorization and then tries to hide the evidence of his misdeeds from the American public. The directors' conclusion is that it's obvious Biden is determined to keep the southern border as porous as possible.

2/8

After a months-long investigation into Bidens' improper retention of classified documents related to national security, the Special Counsel responsible said he would not bring criminal charges against Biden, describing Biden as a "...sympathetic, well-meaning, elderly man with a poor memory." The Special Council further stated in the report that it would be difficult to convince a jury to convict Biden of a "...serious felony that requires a mental state of willfulness." It is the first time in American judicial history anyone can recall that a possible criminal involved in a possible criminal act of treason is forgiven due to mental incompetence.

2/9

Supporters of Biden initiate a rabid defense of Biden in light of the Special Prosecutor dropping all national security treason charges against Biden because of his mental instability. Their defense takes an unexpected direct hit when the SP reports that Bidens' memory "...appeared to have significant limitations." Further, in reviewing Bidens' conversations with his ghostwriter as far back as 2017, the SP found Bidens' comments "painfully slow" with Biden struggling to remember such things as when he was vice-president and when his term began or ended. What Bidens' media friends either missed or chose to ignore, is that Bidens' cognitive disabilities were on full display in 2017, three years before he began his stumbling tour as president.

2/10

As Bidens' supporters continue to accuse the SP of performing a "political hit" in regards to his report on Bidens' mental instabilities, the SP clarifies his concerns about Bidens' current mental acuity. He points out that regrettably Biden did not remember, even within several years, when his son Beau died. Also, Bidens' memory appeared hazy when describing the Afghanistan debate that was once so important to him. In addition, the SP said Biden had real problems with Obamas' ambassador to Afghanistan, even though as recent as November Biden had written a glowing review of the man. In short, the SP said that based on "... direct interactions with and observations of (Biden), he is someone (with) whom many jurors will want to identify (with) reasonable doubt,.." Because of all this, the SP felt it was fruitless to proceed criminally against the mentally confused president.

2/11

In an attempt at damage control over the Special Prosecutors' report, Bidens' personal attorney goes to both the Special Council and Bidens' Attorney General to register Bidens' complaints over what he viewed to be pejorative and unnecessary digs at his memory. Accusations are made that the SP is a Republican activist, but this seems unlikely since he was appointed by Bidens' AG and acolyte Merrick Garland. Recent polls show Bidens' mental acuity continues to be a concern for voters. A large majority of Americans feel Biden is not mentally and physically capable of serving another term. Bidens' supporters still assert that Biden is not feeble and is capable of being commander in chief, though what they base this opinion on is becoming increasingly unclear.

2/12

It responding to the Special Prosecutors' analysis of her husbands' memory, it is rumored that Bidens' wife wrote a letter to donors where she questioned whether the SPs' comments were politically motivated. The letter reportedly caused the most money in donations to pour into Bidens' re-election campaign to date. It is gratifying and truly refreshing to know that in this age of political cynicism the Marxist supporters of Biden, who are so often portrayed as myopic, shallow people, are so joyfully willing to open their hearts, their minds and their pocketbooks to help the mentally feeble.

2/13

Democratic strategists shake their heads in disbelief when Biden declines to sit for the traditional presidential Super Bowl interview for the second year in a row, This signals that his nurses have little confidence in him, with good reason. A recent report by a SP said that it would be pointless to prosecute Biden for any "…serious felony that requires a mental state of willfulness." In response, Biden tries to holds a fiery press conference defending his memory and mental capability, but it does not go well. Biden confuses the president of Egypt with the president of Mexico, which serves only to remind his audience of another press conference Biden held a few days ago. In that one Biden bragged about reassuring Francois Mitterrand that "America is back!" at the G7 conference he attended. This would be quite a trick since the French President died in 1996, 25 years before Bidens' supposed meeting with him. It's now evident, even back when Biden supposedly had all his mental faculties in place, Biden still saw dead people.

2/14

Many pundits believe Biden will dodge not only any debates against Trump but even his own Democrat challengers because, as one pundit put it, "...he can't stand up for 90 minutes without devolving into an embarrassing Grandpa Simpson-like display." As if to add credence to this criticism, instead of sitting for the traditional in-person Super bowl interview, Biden releases a video he made a couple of days ago.

In it Biden parenthetically asks Super Bowl shoppers if they noticed paying the same price for products that were now in smaller packages. With a vapid stare, Biden proudly calls this practice "Shrinkflation" and demands the big consumer brands put a stop to it. It is hard to take him seriously, though. In the video Biden, flapping his hands feebly, looks less like a leader than a feeble old man, ranting to a bewildered stock boy: "These potato chips don't feel fresh!" as he squeezes the air out of the bag.

2/15

Accusations of Biden supporting a two-tier justice system grow louder in the media. Critics claim that Biden and his DOJ are eager to send peaceful Christians, caught' praying in front of abortion clinics, to as much as eleven years in federal prison while this same DOJ gave BLM rioters who torched businesses and beat up innocent bystanders an average of little more than two years behind bars. Biden denies his DOJ practices a two-tier justice system, but the Associated Press verified that BLM defendants who actually pleaded guilty and/or were convicted of federal crimes - including rioting, arson and conspiracy – received only minimum sentences. Biden has no comment.

2/16

Biden finally decides to visit East Palestine, Ohio, more than a year after a fiery train derailment spilled toxic chemicals there, turning the city into a bio-hazard. More embarrassing for Biden, Trump the private citizen visited the city within days of the accident, bringing food and water to its' residents. Biden, widely criticized for not visiting East Palestine sooner, is accused now of doing so only because his 2024 campaign is in trouble. Trump continues to slam Biden for ignoring the city during the crisis, saying that Biden visiting East Palestine now for a political photo op is an insult to those who live and work there.

2/17

In a recent interview Russias' Communist dictator Putin admitted that he would rather see Biden as president of the US than Trump. Some of Bidens' supporters disavow Putins' endorsement, but in a recent interview Biden claimed that nine heads of state have privately told him that he must win re-election because they feel democracy will be threatened if Trump wins. Biden does not name which nine heads of state these were, but it doesn't matter. Few (if any) countries in the world have the same Democratic Republic model as America., where individual rights are held sacrosanct over the rights of the state. Biden, in his infinite mental numbness, takes it as compliment that Putin and other Marxist/collectivist leaders prefer him as president. In contrast, Trump says he takes it as "a great compliment" that the Communist leader wants Biden in the White House instead of him.

2/18

While Biden continues to rant publicly about Trump, according to at least one of Bidens' left-leaning support publication, Biden becomes even more unhinged in private. According to this publication, Biden regularly curses Trump privately, calling Trump a "sick f**k" and a "f**king a**hole". Regardless of his bluster of having no fear of his political rival, it is apparent that Trump has taken up permanent residence in what is left of Bidens' graying mind.

2/19

Nancy Pelosi, who is 84 and struggling with her own mental problems, is asked if she thinks Biden, who exhibits senile behavior daily, is fit to run for a second term and be president again. She replies yes, Biden is fit to be president because he is "wise" and "capable". Of course asking Pelosi about Bidens' fitness is like asking the neighbor whom has never returned the lawn mower he borrowed, if neighbors lending tools to neighbors is a good idea.

2/20

In a desperate attempt to blunt the ever-increasing criticism of Bidens' age and mental deterioration, Biden sycophants claim his age is actually a "superpower". That is, since Biden is so old he grew up in the era of Lyndon Johnson's Great Society he can use it as a model for his own "successful" policies. This, even though the policies initiated during Johnsons' Great Society have morphed into mostly catastrophic failures. Biden's own 'successes' include record-high inflation, a disastrous foreign policy, an illegal alien crisis that has reached even northern Democrat strongholds and, as a result, historically bad approval numbers for a sitting president. The only difference between Biden and Johnson is that Bidens' successes have morphed into catastrophes while he's still in office.

2/21

Despite his nurses best efforts to protect him from his greatest foe, Biden again trips twice more on stairs while attempting to board Air Force One. This happens even after 'baby stairs' - shorter, less challenging stairs – were set up for Biden by his nurses in the hope that this would help him defeat this relentless nemesis. This follows another near tumble by Biden in Philadelphia a few days ago where Biden stumbles again while ascending another short flight of stairs. Instead of focusing on his idiotic claim that global warming is the greatest threat America faces, for his own safety Biden should focus on his greatest enemy, that being anything with a riser.

2/22

Biden continues to trail Trump badly in all national polls, the major reasons being record inflation and the approximately 10 million illegal aliens he has allowed to enter to enter the US during his tenure. With an election looming in a few months, Biden reaches perhaps the high-point of his multiple hypocrisies: Biden hints that he might re-institute the very Trump immigration policies that were so successful in curbing illegal immigration, the ones he canceled almost immediately upon becoming president. Receiving instantaneous backlash from his illegal immigration activist supporters, Biden back pedals a bit and claims he is only "thinking" about doing this. Of course with Bidens' mental vagaries, what constitutes "thinking" by Biden is any ones' guess.

2/23I

In what has become all-too-familiar and all-too-sad, Biden is filmed shuffling slowly, almost painfully across a tarmac towards Air Force One, clutching Nancy Pelosis' hand for support. It's actually hard to tell which octogenarian is supporting which. In viewing their slow, struggling walk, they look less like Democratic party stalwarts and more like two elder-lies heading for their assisted-living lunch, snickering that since there are two of them no one will be able to stop them from cutting the line to get to the bread pudding first.

2/24

Biden issues a rambling accusation that the Republicans in Congress "are worse" than the racist US senators he served with in the 1960s, just because of their reluctance to support more funding for Ukraine's' war with Russia. Speaking at a fundraiser, Biden says that in his time in the Senate he served with real racists, but "…these guys (Republicans) are worse.". Calling Congressmen racists because of their reluctance to war-fund is idiotic, is idiotic even for Biden, with all due respect to idiots. Tying this reluctance to fund wars to some dark behavior of some Americans 60 years ago is a pathetically obvious dog whistle for Bidens' brain-challenged supporters, again with all due respect to dogs.

2/25

In what cab be described only as a panic move, Biden attempts to blame his allowing 10 million illegal aliens to enter the country during his three years as president, hilariously, on Trump. Biden claims his "comprehensive immigration reform" package failed passing in Congress because of Trumps' criticism of it. Biden claims that without this legislation, he is powerless to shut down illegal border crossings. What Biden and his allies in the media hope no one notices is that Biden already has the power to shut down the border. It is the same power Trump used to reduce border crossings attempts to 100 a day, as opposed to Bidens' 10000-a-day incidents now. Biden is asked, instead of asking for new legislative powers, why doesn't he use the authority he already has? Biden has no comment.

2/26

One merely has to look to see what is hidden in the weeds of Bidens' "comprehensive immigration reform" bill to understand Bidens' near-hysterical demand that it be passed. It turns out that it is just another attempt by Biden to massively increase the size of government. Bidens' "reform" awards billions to Bidens' Homeland Security Office, not to stop the 10000 daily illegal immigrant incidents, but to streamline the processing of the illegals. Another part of the bill Biden is attempting to hide is that it gives Biden the right to allow 5000 illegals a day, or close to 2 million a year, to legally enter the US without restrictions. According to Bidens' bill, only after the two million number is reached is Biden, allowed to close the border'. The reality is that Biden doesn't need this new law to shut down the border, but Biden does need it to legally, massively grow the government and allow 2 million more illegals to enter the country 'legally' each year

2/28

Bidens' excuse that he needs Republican support granting him more authority before he can shut down the border gets blown out of the water by reporters. They find that Biden already has this authority, outlined in detail in Section 212(f) of the Immigration and Nationality Act. Here it clearly states that Biden (or any President) has broad leeway to block entry of certain immigrants if it would be "detrimental" to the national interest of the United States. Clearly 10 million additional illegal aliens, some surely on the terror watch list and most draining American taxpayer money, would be considered "detrimental" to Americas' national interest to anyone with half a brain. Unfortunately, this "half brain" qualification gives Biden an out.

2/29

Following his annual physical, his doctor announces that Biden is "fit for duty" and that Biden is "...a healthy, active, robust 81-year-old male, who remains fit to successfully execute the duties of the Presidency." This is a man who has trouble walking, does not know his left from his right, continually sees and attempts to shake hands with dead people, grabs little girls to sniff their hair, gets lost if left unattended on a stage, cannot remember the names of current world leaders, confuses his wife with other women and can't even mange 'kiddie' stairs without help. To declare that such a mental and physical discombobulation passed a physical examination and is deemed "fit", is all the proof needed that Obama and his Obamacare have truly crippled the American medical profession.

3/1

After years of being criticized for not going, Biden announces that he will visit Texas, one of the hardest hit states suffering from the illegal immigration disaster Biden has caused. Biden picks Brownsville to visit and this is not an accident. Instead of the thousands and thousands of illegal incidents other areas of Texas suffer from daily, Brownsville averages between 6 and 12 incidents a day.This means that Biden can show up for his photo op and the cameras won't be catching the hordes of thousands of illegal aliens crossing the border or the mobs of illegals jammed in detention facilities. When Texas tries to protect itself, Biden blocks them, saying that immigration is a federal matter. Then when Texas asks Biden for help in fixing the horrible mess he created, Biden then says that immigration is a state matter. Bidens' two-faced approach to the Texas problem only proves what Americans have known all along: Biden wants the border open to millions of illegals, even if it means his poll numbers against Trump continue to sink.

3/2

In a panicked attempt to shore up his declining numbers among young voters, Biden announces the cancellation of $1.2 billion dollars in student loan debt, even though he was smacked down by the Supreme Court last year when he attempted the same stunt. Since that defeat, Biden has canceled a total of $138 million in student loans in smaller chunks in order to avoid another court challenge. By ignoring the Supreme Court and canceling some student loan debt, Biden keeps the hope alive for the rest of the borrowers that more dictatorial proclamations will be coming to erase their debts also. Biden has no empathy at all for the rest of the Americans Biden considers expendable, the ones who paid their own debts and now have to pay the debts of these Biden - loyal student grifters.

3/3

In another bizarre move to placate his radical left supporters, Biden and his assistant AG of the DOJ Civil Rights Division sue states that criminalize HIV infected people who knowingly infect other people with the virus. Biden and his AAG claim that the purpose of the lawsuit is to insure that people with HIV are not targeted because of their disability. Again, either because of his mental denseness or because his nurses did not read these statutes to him correctly, these state laws do not discriminate against anyone that has the virus, but only those who willfully infect others with it. Whether maliciously stupid or just too dumb to understand this distinction, Biden and his AAG push forward with the lawsuits.

3/4

Bidens' attempt to protect the HIV-infected who willfully infect others with the disease from facing criminal prosecution is roundly and soundly criticized. Everyone is reminded that it was Biden who attempted to use OSHA to strong-arm every single business in the country with 50 or more employees to force their workers to get the COVID vaccine. That was one thing, but facilitating the spread of HIV under the cover of 'fairness' is something else. The idea that intentionally spreading HIV is somehow protected under the Americans with Disabilities Act is ludicrous. It is no wonder that a large part of the American population is starting to realize that Biden and his staff have pushed past any dementia/senility boundary and are rapidly approaching psychosis.

3/5

Much to the chagrin of Biden, in a 9-0 vote the Supreme Court rules that no state can prevent a Presidential candidate from appearing on it's ballot just because they don't like him, a stunt that Colorado and several other states attempted to do to Trump. The Marxist judges in these states attempted to use a 150 year-old sedition law to accomplish this lawlessness. This law was enacted at the end of the Civil War to prevent Confederate soldiers from attaining political office in the newly reunited America. The fact that these blatantly political state judges attempted blatantly to interfere in a Federal election should be cause for censure, or at least a rebuke. Biden has no comment.3

3/6

As expected, Biden supporters suffer an emotional breakdown following the Supreme Courts' ruling on the attempted election interference by the judges in Colorado and other states. Bidens' supporters immediately call for the abolition of the Supreme Court, followed by demanding that the Electoral College and Congress – Congress - also be abolished. This would leave Biden as sole ruler and dictator, a dream Bidens' Marxist supporters have had since the days of Trotsky. As a last ditch attempt to get their demands met, Biden and his supporters clench their fists and puff their cheeks, swearing to hold their breathes until they get their way. Unfortunately, since it's after 4;30 in the afternoon, Bidens' vacuous stare makes it difficult to determine if holding his breath is making him suffers at all.

3/7

Biden and his Federal regulators finalize a rule to cap most credit card late fees at $8. This is part of a broader plan by Biden to eliminate what he feels are junk fees. The new rules apply to large credit card issuers, those with more than 1 million accounts. This new rule is Bidens' latest feeble attempts to show American families – as he did when he unconstitutionally forgave student debt or when he demanded that businesses arbitrarily lower prices - that Biden knows better than the market what will help families hurting from the high cost of the inflation death-spiral he caused.

3/8

Biden delivers another disastrous SOTU speech. Hopped up on Ensure, Biden rants and raves, first making spurious comparison between the economy now and economy during COVID, then insults the Supreme Court justices and, as usual, finished by blaming American conservatives for all of Americas' current problems. The low point comes when Biden is vociferously challenged by a member of Congress to say aloud the name of the the young girl recently killed by an illegal alien Bidens' policies allowed into the US. Biden accepts the challenge, but then embarrasses himself and the entire country by butchering the young girls' name. Bidens' humiliated supporters attempt to use exhaustion, or even senility as an excuse, but Bidens' reputation as a thoughtless, shallow bully remains intact.

3/9

Mispronouncing Laken Rileys' name during his SOTU speech was not even Bidens' most insulting gaffe of the evening. After acknowledging that the young lady was killed by one of his illegals, Biden tries to mitigate her murder by rhetorically asking, albeit in broken English:: "But how many thousands of people being killed by legals?" The screeching, ranting, bad grammar, juvenile insults and garbled rhetoric is by now expected of Biden. What is not expected is how Biden could be so clueless with his snide remark equivocating the poor girls brutal murder by an illegal to murders committed by "legals"s. How brain-dead does one have to be not to realize how much hurt this thoughtless remark would cause Lakens' grieving parents. Of course with Biden 'brain dead' is a relative term, but still.

3/10

Only a day after Bidens' supporters use Bidens' rambling, ugly, SOTU address to "prove" his mental fitness, Biden gaffes his way through a campaign event at a Middle school in Pennsylvania. First Biden mistakenly refers to the events that happened at the White House on January 6 as taking place on July 6. Then in a rare moment of honesty, Biden declares that he has "...added more to the national debt than any president in his term in all of history...". Biden supporters, heads in hands, groan at this true, though inadvertent admission. Not yet finished, Biden wraps up his speech by urging Pennsylvanians to: "Send me to Congress!", evidently unaware of the office he is running for. The one silver lining for Bidens' supporters after yet another public disaster, Biden did not trip while leaving the stage.

3/11

Bidens' crudely insensitive remarks during his SOTU speech, including mispronouncing Laken Rileys' name, draws a sharp response from the murdered girls' mother. In a post to the media she slams Biden, insisting that, even if feeble and pathetic, Biden should be able to pronounce her daughters' name correctly. One would think that Lakens' mother was owed at least an apology from Biden. Biden did apologize, but not to Lakens' mother for mispronouncing her name or mitigating her murder. Instead Biden apologizes to his supporters, his rabid Marxist base and to illegal aliens everywhere for using the word "illegal" rather than"undocumented" when describing the murdering animal who brutally took Lakens' life. Bidens' hollow, misplaced apology, delivered with his usual glassy-eyed look, leaves most in America stunned at Bidens' callousness.

3/12

Once the callousness of Bidens' insipid apology sets in, the public reaction is immediate, calling on Biden to apologize for his cruel, thoughtless apology. Remarkably, except for anyone who has minimal functioning brain cells, Biden doubles down and insists that he was misunderstood, that he did not apologize at all and saw no reason why he should.

Biden does not regret insulting the murdered girl by mispronouncing her name or minimizing her "illegal" murder by equivocating it with "legal" murders. Rather, Biden declares his only regret is not using the term "undocumented" to describe the murderous illegal scum. It's astonishing that all Biden got out of this thoughtless, insensitive incident that caused so much heartbreak to the murdered girls' family, was that he misused a word. Astonishing, even for those who, for years, have watched Bidens' brain disintegrate into the consistency of oatmeal.

3/13

Still not backing down, Biden sends his deputy press secretary out to reporters to make it clear he did not and has no intention of apologizing to the murdered girls parents for abusing her with his 'non-apology/ apology'. Probably out of habit of having to explain everything to Biden multiple times, the press secretary denies four times to the press that Biden apologized. First, she says: "I want to be really clear ... the president absolutely did not apologize.", then "There was no apology anywhere in that conversation ...", then again "He (Biden) did not apologize...." and finally "He (Biden) used a different word." It might have escaped the notice of Bidens' PS, but not the public: In her desperate attempt to protect Biden, she issued one more denial than St. Peter did when Pilates' goons showed up to hang Christ.

3/14

A group of House Republicans fired off a pointed letter to Biden, calling on him to immediately terminate a program of his that has flown more than 320,000 migrants into the U.S. from all parts of the world. The letter expressed the grave concerns over Biden actions to fly these illegal immigrants from Latin American airports to 43 cities across the United States, insisting these secret flights only compound the already horrific crisis at the southern border. The letter further demands that not only Biden provide Congress and the American people with information as to where these illegal immigrants have been deposited, but also to terminate this practice immediately. Rumored again to be hiding in his basement in Delaware, Biden has no comment.

3/15

Fallout continues from Biden and his impeached DHS Secretary exploiting something called the "CBP One app" to sneak unvetted illegals into America n by the hundreds of thousands. Outraged Congressmen promise they will not stand idly by and watch as Biden recklessly unravels national security and endangers American lives. The letter demands that Biden answer such questions as what prompted him to fly illegal immigrants into the United States, what airports were illegal immigrants flown into, what dates did these flights occur, what nations were these illegal immigrants flown from, how much American taxpayer-money was used to subsidize these flights and who in hell is responsible for overseeing this program? Not surprising, Biden refuses to answer.

3/16

Biden receives another slap down when a Federal judge issues a preliminary injunction stopping Biden from diverting money away from border wall construction that Congress appropriated back in 2019. The judge scolds Biden, saying that he "... acted completely improperly by refusing to spend the money that Congress appropriated for border wall construction, and even attempting to redirect those funds," The judge continues to scolds Biden, saying that his actions demonstrate his obvious agenda of open borders at any price. The judge heatedly reminds Biden that these specific funds appropriated by Congress can be used only for the construction of physical barriers, such as additional walls, fencing, buoys, etc. The Texas AG praises the judge for reigning in this rouge executive who has dictatorial ambitions. Meanwhile Biden remains in his basement today, sulking, reportedly sipping on his third can of Ensure.

3/17

In response to the judges' ruling, Biden comically or delusionally – or both - insists that the U.S. southern border is safe and he has done more than any other president in history to secure that border. The truth is that Biden has issued over 90 executive orders since taking office that have gutted immigration enforcement and opened the border. This has resulted, since Biden became president, in between seven and ten million illegal aliens flooding into the country, overrunning cities and communities Instead of trying to fix the problem, Biden fought any state that tried border wall construction. Biden took Texas to court twice to stop that state from carrying out immigration enforcement. At every turn Biden has taken the side of open border activists and resisted all efforts to stop illegal aliens from marching into the US.

3/18

Bidens' fear-mongering about the supposed threat of Christian Nationalism takes a radical, sick leap even for him. In something only a half-functioning brain could conjure up, Biden wants voters to believe that the country is on the cusp of becoming a theocratic dictatorship. It is reported that Biden uses a website that characterized Christians as a "threat" to justify his position. Once this information is made public Biden, ever the coward, issues a disclaimer that states he does not vouch for the accuracy, legality, or content of this website, the one he used. This allows Biden to cite radical sources that specifically target Christians, while disavowing said sources in advance, just in case there is blow back; a coward indeed.

3/19

Biden continues to stun friends and foes alike with one incomprehensible brain-dead move after another. Now in the midst of Israels' fight with the rat-terrorist group Hamas, Biden grants a four-month waiver of US sanctions on Iran, allowing this country, the one directly funding Hamas, access to another $10 billion dollars. Bidens' contempt for the intelligence of the average American shows when Biden assures all that this new money can be used "for humanitarian purposes only" and not a penny of it will be used to fund terrorists. Biden waits, with watery eyes, to see if anyone in America calls him on his latest scam. If no one calls, Biden will take this as a sign and will follow up this scam by announcing he has a piece of property to sell, cheap, located at 1600 Pennsylvania Avenue in Washington DC.

3/20

Still denying that there is any "direct evidences" that Iran bankrolls Hamas, the Houghtis and other terrorist groups, Biden allows 70 billion more "New Money"dollars to flow to Iran to be used "only" for humanitarian purposes. This brings Bidens' recent funding total to the terrorist country to 80 billion dollars. His critics continue to raise concerns that Iran will misuse the funds to finance terrorist activities. Bidens' only hope in pulling off this 'New Money for Iran' scam is if the American public is so stupid it doesn't realize that by using this 80 billion of 'new' money for humanitarian purposes, Iran is free to use 80 billion of their 'old money' to finance Hamas and any other group bent on terrorist destruction. With so many calling Biden on his latest scam, he gives up on his plan to fund his retirement and funeral by selling the White House. Instead Biden will continue selling political influence to the Communist Chinese to fund his late-in-life expenditures.

3/21

Biden and his wife defend one of their top aides accused of sexual harassment. Nearly a dozen current and former colleagues of this man have alleged a long-running history of bullying and verbal sexual harassment, including his public speculation on the genital sizes of staffers. These staffers told the New York Post that they came forward in hopes that this Biden aid would be held accountable, but fear nothing will be done because of his closeness to the first lady. Her office would not directly answer these allegations. Instead it released a statement claiming that this aid is "... generous, conscientious (and) brilliant..." and he has "... always been quite intentional and purposeful in making sure colleagues at every level feel valued and appreciated..." Of course this skirts the obvious question of exactly how he makes them feel "valued and appreciated".

3/22

Many thought Biden insane when, in order to 'socialize' some of his LGBTQ supporters perverse agenda, Biden did not object to grown men showering with underage girls. Now Bidens' need to "socialize" reaches a whole new level with his proposal to relocate grizzly bears to the federally-managed North Cascades National Park. Biden is doing this despite vehement objections from local residents. Grizzly bears are the fiercest Apex predators in North America and Biden wants to release them in a park that borders rural communities and ranches. Biden claims that moving the dangerous predators to the park would provide "...greater management flexibility should conflict situations (like bears eating the ranchers animals) arise," Using the same reasoning he did when allowing grown men to shower with underage girls, Biden and his agencies assure all that moving the bears would be "...consistent with the overall goal of... promoting social tolerance and human safety." Insane, indeed.

3/23

Dozens of local residents in northern Washington continue to voice strong opposition to Bidens' plan to release grizzly bears in a federally-managed forest area near their communities. More than 200 local residents attended a public comment session, citing their concerns for the safety of their lives and property if the predators move out of the park and into their neighboring communities. Biden reassures the nervous residents that his own personal research in this matter has convinced him this cannot and will not happen. Biden cannot understand their apprehension since his research has shown him that bears walk upright, wear hats and ties and are only agitated if they come across an unattended picnic basket. Reporters wonder if Bidens' 'research bears' are named Yogi and Boo-Boo, but Bidens' nurses don't allow any questions.

3/24

Still outraged at Bidens' grizzly bear "socialization plan", residents in northern Washington demand to know what Bidens' plan is for dealing with Yogi and Boo-Boo when the introduction of these predators cause the inevitable human attacks, crop loss and livestock depredation. They also ask Biden how much will they be expected to lose before they can defend themselves with deadly force from these predators Biden is introducing into their backyards. Instead of answering these questions, Biden heatedly and repeatedly denies that the old Hanna Barbera cartoon is the basis for his grizzly bear research. Suspicions remain however when, along with the grizzly bears, Biden requests that a goodly supply of "pic-a-nik" baskets also be relocated to various areas in the park.

3/25

Americans have been stranded in Haiti since its' collapse two weeks ago. Biden finally announces his plan to rescue Americans stuck in Haiti, but it turns out to be no plan at all. Port-au-Prince, where most Americans are stranded, is shut down so Biden and his State Department arrange a charter flight for them in Cap-Haitien, on the other side of the country. This means Biden expects stranded Americans to travel over 100 miles through the violence to reach the extraction point. Showing the same empathy Biden displayed when he got thirteen soldiers killed in Afghanistan, Biden and his SD inform the Americans that they should travel to the extraction site in Cap-Haitien at their "own risk." As a final slap in their faces, before any American who survives the trip to Cap-Haitien can board any flight to safety, they must sign a promissory note agreeing to reimburse Biden for the cost of the flight.

3/26

More than 100 migrants burst though razor wire and violently attempt to overpower Texas National guardsmen at the southern border. When asked for a reaction, Biden blamed the Texas governors' strict anti-illegal immigration policies for the incident, insinuating that if the Governor made it easier for illegals to enter the country, there would be no need for such confrontations. Combined with the new report that in February there were 189,922 migrant encounters at the southern border - the highest for a month ever recorded. - the mental gymnastics it takes for Biden to blame a problem he created on the man trying his best to solve it, is astonishing even for someone with oatmeal for a brain.

3/27

In an interview with an American reporter, the president of Mexico reiterates his blackmail demands for Biden if he wants help in fixing the chaos at the border between their two countries. This punk president again proposes/demands that Biden pay $20 billion a year to "poor countries" in Latin America and the Caribbean, lift sanctions on Venezuela, end the Cuban embargo and legalize millions of illegal aliens living in the U.S. Instead of offering a counter-proposal, like taking the 30 million or so illegals living in America now and dumping them back into Mexico, Biden stays hiding in his basement, his hands shaking so bad he can barely hold onto his morning can of Ensure.

3/28

Biden has has long extolled his relationship with "his friend", the president of Mexico. Biden often marvels at this mans' longevity as head of his country, even though rumor has it that it is the ties this supposed Mexican 'icon' has with the drug cartels in his country that are the main reason for his longevity. The Mexican president denies this, claiming his popularity is because of his giving nature, his willingness to shower his countrymen with 'free' gifts. As an example of his generosity, this punk gives out the cell phone number of an American reporter who is writing a piece critical of him, making her a target for any cartel gangsters' reprisal. Even with this threat to an American citizen, direct or otherwise, Biden hides and says nothing.

3/29

A retired U.S. Air Force General gives an interview claiming that Haiti has become "...a 'Mad Max' hellscape..." and predicted that members of the gangs battling for control of the country could eventually make their way to the U.S. because of Bidens' open border policies. He points out that millions of fighting-age men have already been allowed into America from every terror group around the world because of Biden. Biden has no comment and continues to either feign ignorance or outright ignore the growing danger his immigration policies, or the lack of them, pose for America.

3/30

A former senior adviser to the DHS warns that none of the illegal aliens coming into the country under Biden are being vetted, regardless which country they're coning from. Many of these countries, like Iran, China, and Russia, don't have systems that keep track of people and refuse to share information about the people that are coming into the U.S. This advisor also notes that since Biden and many of his elitist supporters are not worried about this since they are protected by their government-provided security details. Finally this advisor warns that a bleak future awaits many American cities because of Biden's illegal immigration failures and because he and many of his associates see no "reverse gear" on Biden. In response to these allegations, Biden has no comment.

3/31

Biden outrages Catholics and Christians worldwide by declaring that Easter Sunday this year is officially "Transgender Day of Visibility". Many took Bidens' proclamation to mean that he was using his presidency to wage war on their beliefs. Bidens' nurses defend him, pointing out that Biden has proclaimed 3/31 to be TDoV every year of his presidency and that it was just a co-incidence that the date fell on Easter Sunday this year. TDoV last fell on Easter Sunday in 2013 during Obamas'' term in office, but even he didn't issue a proclamation turning Easter Sunday into TDoV. By proclaiming Easter Sunday as officially TDoV, without mentioning the holiday held sacred by hundreds of millions of people for thousands of years, Biden effectively spits on their religious beliefs.

4/1

If Biden hoped his Transgender Proclamation on Easter would set off a firestorm of controversy with whom Biden calls "right wing extremists", he is mistaken. While some religious groups express outrage, most mock and humiliate Biden. They ask that when Biden speaks of "right-wing extremists"who disprove of child mutilation, is he aware that most European countries have shut down their gender clinics and banned hormone treatments on children? Ironically and tragically, Biden has placed himself to the left of all these Socialist countries that both he and Obama have insisted for decades that America should emulate. It's a little sick - actually, a lot sick – that Biden applauds these Socialist countries for their political and economic systems, but not when they stop mutilating their children.

4/2

Perhaps because of the mockery Biden is enduring at home, or because European allies continue to distance themselves from a man they realize is a nutcase, Biden denies that he made any such proclamation about Easter being "Transgender Visibility Day", saying simply "I didn't do that." This prompts two questions from politicians on both sides of the isle:.One, is Biden lying again, or is he really unaware of what is going on in his name? Then, two, if Biden isn't lying and is truly unaware of what is going on in his administration, who is really running the country?

4/3

Biden continues to deny that he was responsible for the "Transgender Day of Visibility" proclamation. Actually, two points stand as his defense: One, since said proclamation was written in decent, coherent English and contained neither garbled grammar or fictitious, narcissistic exploits from Bidens' past, it is possible that it was ghost-written by one of his nurses. Two, reporters are reminded that when dealing with Biden, don't immediately attribute to malice what can be explained by stupidity and incompetence.

4/4

Bidens' denial of his participation in the "Transgender Day of Visibility" proclamation rings a little hollow. Biden defends the proclamation – the one he had nothing to do with – insisting it in no way was meant to insult the Christian holiday held dear by millions around the world. However, Boro Fondo, a group of Biden activists, was planning a "Trans Day of Vengeance" on Easter Sunday, the same day of Bidens' proclamation, the one he had nothing to do with. Push back was so fierce from Christian and Catholic groups that Boro Fondo canceled the event, due to it being "sim-characterized" as a day of violence by "right wing news sites". A little advice here for Biden and Boro Fondo: If they really didn't want their event to be "sim-characterized" as a day of violence, perhaps it wasn't the best idea to use the word "vengeance" in its' title.

4/5

It is evident that Biden, who ran on the promise of being "Conciliator in Chief" is actually more of 'Panderer in Chief'. As he falls farther and farther behind Trump in the polls, Biden shamelessly attempts to buy votes. First he announces that he and Harris are establishing a "anti Muslim" hate crime committee to pander to all the Muslim votes Biden feels he recently lost in Michigan. Then Biden seeks to shore up evaporating support from young people by granting clemency for those convicted of pot possession. In addition, Biden has cannabis reclassified under the Controlled Substances Act from a Class 1 to a Class 3 drug, drastically reducing the penalty for possession. Yes, what the youth of America, already some of the most poorly educated in the world and who recently lost two more years of education due to COVID, need right now is more and easier access to pot.

4/6

Bidens' pandering for votes is not slowing down. First Biden announces that he is allocating $442 billion dollars to various states for 'infrastructure initiatives. Of course he says it's just a coincidence that 12 states where residents will benefit the most from the money are won by Trump in 2020. Then Biden establishes a 'anti-Muslim hate' committee to woo Muslim voters, even though Jews suffer more than 60% of all hate crimes in America. Added to his already - promised easier access to pot for Americas' youth and regardless of all his failures, Biden has definitely earned the title of "Panderer in Chief".

4/7

A report is published about the protester Bidens' praetorian guard dragged out of his State of the Union address and arrested back in March. It turns out that the protester was Steve Nikoui, the father of Marine Lance Cpl. Kareem Nikoui, one of the 13 service members Biden got killed in an ISIS suicide bombing during Biden's botched withdrawal from Afghanistan. Mr. Nikouis' crime was shouting "Remember Abbey Gate! U.S. Marines!" at Biden before being led away in cuffs. Abbey Gate is the entrance to the Kabul International Airport in Afghanistan where the bomb was detonated that killed the 13 American servicemen, Nikouis' son among them. A trial date for this 'outrageous behavior' by Mr. Nikoui has not yet been set

4/8

The arrest of Steve Nikoui brings back for many the painful memories of Bidens' botched withdrawal from Afghanistan. Among his multiple screw-ups, Biden had to redeploy Marines to the Kabul airport after he forgot to evacuate thousands of American citizens trapped behind Taliban lines. It also reminded people of Bidens' behavior when the remains of Nikouis' son and 12 other U.S. service members killed in Bidens' screw-up were returned to their families at Dover AFB in Delaware. There Biden paid his respects to the flag-draped coffins by continually checking his watch during the ceremony. To this day, Biden has never spoken the names of these fallen heroes in public.

4/9

The incredible amount of blood that is already on Bidens' hands is being increased yearly by the 100,000+ deaths caused by fentanyl, a drug Bidens' open border policies are allowing to be trafficked across the southern border. The leading cause of death for Americans between the ages of 18 and 49, fentanyl has shattered the lives of countless working-class American families. Recently a number of mothers who have lost their sons to this poison slammed Biden for turning the border over to the cartels and allowing them to push enough of this drug into the US to kill every American citizen several times over. When again confronted with this heartbreaking tragedy of his making, Biden stumbles away to his basement to hide.

4/10

In yet another speech, Biden again repeats the lie about traveling 17000 miles with Xi Ping, the Communist dictator. Biden has told this story at least 21 times during his presidency, despite it being widely debunked even by some of his supporters. In the fall of 2022 a Washington newspaper gave Biden a "bottomless Pinocchio" rating for this storys' lack of veracity and the number of times Biden has lied about it. In a sorry attempt to give credence, media supporters of Biden went back through his entire career and added up all the trips he has taken to China, even throwing in trips Chinese politicians made to visit him, but could come up with no more than 6000 miles. Despite this the American public probably has not heard this lie for the last time.

4/11

In a recent interview a Fox News correspondent admitted that when she interviewed Biden in 2021 the interview was scripted, word for word. Her bosses at Fox instructed her to repeat every word exactly as they had written it and she was not to deviate from the script one iota. Every question was scripted and gone over dozens of times by editors and executives, all in an effort to protect Biden. She was even instructed on what she could ask and how she could ask it, with no follow-ups. She said that this encounter with Biden made her sad because she saw it as a form of elder abuse, the way Biden needed to be propped up. It made her ask herself, when someone is struggling as badly as Biden, does anyone close to him, including his wife, really care about Biden as a person? When the only concern of those close to Biden is holding onto power, the answer is obvious.

4/12

In a CNN interview Robert Kennedy talks about specific instances where Biden attempted to censor him. Though Biden continues to deny any personal involvement in this, Kennedy points out that if Biden didn't want the censorship to happen, he could have stopped it, but didn't. Freedom of Information requests and court cases have shown that Biden and his staff were actively involved in attempts to censor him. Upon hearing this, one CNN host attempts to run cover for Biden. She maintains Biden didn't set out to specifically censor Kennedy or his political critics and/or rivals, that all Biden was involved in was "...encouraging social media sites to monitor and take down false information..." Besides, according to her, there was no provable evidence that Biden was personally involved in these censorship antics. Kennedy, grinning, delivers a long, pointed rebuttal, but in essence it comes down to 'If it looks like a pig, smells like a pig and grunts like a pig, it's a pig'.

4/13

In trying to have it both ways, Biden sends his press secretary out to the media to assure everyone that he condemns the protesters who shouted "Death to America" and "Death to Israel" during a rally in Michigan nearly a week ago. However, in a naked attempt to appeal to the large Muslim population there, Biden waited a week to personally condemn the protesters. The Governor of Michigan and the Muslim Congresswoman representing the state, both avid supporters of Biden, also remained silent at the time. In the past Biden and these two have been quick to immediately condemn any speech or written article criticizing anything Muslim as being "Islamophobia". In this case where shouts of "Death to America" can be heard, Biden and these two great patriots remain silent.

4/14

Biden puts his unabashed attempt to curry the ever-fading youth vote on steroids. Biden tries again to cancel student loan debts for up to 25 million borrowers, despite the Supreme Court ruling Bidens' first try at this unconstitutional. Bidens' new plan draws on a different legal justification, which Biden hopes will be able to survive all court challenges. If the plan holds, Biden will write down the student loan balances, some partially and some wholly, for the majority of student debt holders. This might sound appealing to this particular grifter class of Biden supporters, but there are consequences. By canceling debt payments Biden is forgoing future revenue, which adds to Americas' annual deficit and its' total national debt. In his demented version of 'Back to the Future', now Biden expects innocent, hard-working future taxpayers to foot the bill for his mistakes.

4/15

After almost a week and facing pressure from both sides of the aisle, Biden finally says that he does not want the votes of those caught on video chanting "Death to America" during a recent anti-Israel rally in Michigan. Bidens' reluctance to denounce this "Death to America" crowd sooner stems from his cynical view that he will need the votes of this flagrantly anti-America crowd come November. It seems Americans should be alarmed knowing that its' leader is willing, for the sake of a few votes. to indulge those that wish to bring death to their country,

4/16

As Bidens' poll numbers continue to drop, California governor Gavin Newsome holds a pres conference where he reminds Biden that the president could ".Send me in, coach! ", implying he is willing to do anything to secure Bidens' re-election. There is some symbiosis here. Biden has made a career out of congenitally lying about his career exploits regardless how often they are debunked. Newsome, much younger than Biden, repeatedly brags of how well he has run California, even as the state devolves into a crime ridden, illegal alien and homeless mess right before all Californians eyes. One of Newsomes' best lies is how he played baseball for Santa Clara University even though the school, the coaches and even the players have repeatedly and angrily debunked this. I f Biden really needs to 'send someone in', he'd be hard pressed to pick a better lying surrogate.

4/17

Again it is reported in the media that Biden has openly and purposely allowed roughly ten million illegals from all over the world to enter the US during his presidency. Now that his re-election is in jeopardy, Biden again pivots to claiming that he is powerless to stop this crisis he created and implores Congress again to pass his fake "Comprehensive

Border Security" bill. Trump rightly points out that Bidens' bill does little to secure the border but will give Biden the legal authority to bring in 5000 more illegals every day. This would amount close to 2,000,000 additional 'legal illegals' every year, which Trump contends is Bidens' real purpose behind his so-called border security bill. These new legal-illegals, on top of the millions of illegals Biden has already allowed to enter the country, will only exacerbate the problems Biden has caused with this historical invasion of the U.S.

4/18

In Bidens' attempt to keep the border crisis out of the headlines while running for re-election, Biden continues to lie about needing Congressional approval before he can fix the crisis at the southern border. Point of fact, Trump used Executive Orders to put immigration policies immediately in place in an attempt to keep America safe. On the other hand, Biden used the same EO authority every President has to rescind all of Trumps' polices, making America immediately unsafe. Now when asked why he doesn't use the same EO authority to close the border as he did to open it, all Biden can do is slip on his ridiculous Aviators, grab the podium with shaking hands feeble hands and say, in effect "No hablo Ingles". Meanwhile illegal aliens from around the world know that Biden has rolled out the welcome mat for them, criminal and non-criminal alike.

4/19

The problems Biden created because of his open-border policy has come home to every corner of the country, the latest being South Dakota. The Governor there has rebuked Biden for months now because Bidens' open-border policies are bringing crime and drugs to her state. She has raised the alarm that Mexican drug cartels are operating in some, if not all, of the 9 Indian reservations in her state. They operate with impunity because Indian Reservations are considered Federal property and, by law the Governor and her state law enforcement officers cannot intervene. Her only recourse is to demand that Biden address the problem, but so far Biden has shown no inclination to do so. So while rape, murder, arson and drug trafficking crime rates soar on the South Dakota Indian Reservations, Biden sits on his hands in his Delaware basement, fretting over his own latest crisis, that of who is going to replace Pat Sajak as host of 'Wheel of Fortune'.

4/20

During Bidens' visit to a war memorial near his hometown in Scranton, Biden spins a yarn about how his uncle was eaten by cannibals during World War ll after his plane was shot down. Even before the guffaws die down, Bidens' Press Secretary acknowledged that while Bidens' uncle (whom Biden likes to call "Uncle Bosie,") did die in a plane crash in WWII, he was not eaten by cannibals as Biden suggests. When asked why Biden would lie about an incident so easy to verify, his PS explained that he didn't lie, that Biden was just having an "emotional moment". This is an interesting term: When your job is covering for a habitual liar like Biden, perhaps calling his lies "emotional moments" makes them more palpable.

4/22

The Supreme Court hears a challenge to Biden and his staff using a decades-old law to charge hundreds of Trump supporters with obstructing an official proceeding on 1/6/21. This law, passed in the wake of the Enron financial scandal, is a felony carrying a 20-year prison sentence. The law refers only to the destruction of documents and evidence, but Biden and his prosecutors have twisted it to mean obstructing the Electoral College vote. In their decision, the Justices made it clear they would have no truck with this incredible stretching of the law by Biden. The Justices embarrass Biden openly in court, forcing them to re-trench. In response, Biden again clenches his fists and threatens to hold his breath, but the Justices ignore him.

4/23

The the Supreme Court reports more problems with Bidens' prosecutors and their witch-hunt trials of Trump and his supporters. Chief among them is the one the Justices pointed out right from the beginning: That is, it was evident Biden was using his twisted interpretation of this law to prosecute only conservatives and political rivals, Trump being Bidens' obvious focal point. By contrast, the Justices point to the liberal protesters disrupting Supreme Court hearings and a liberal Congressman pulling a fire alarm to prevent Congress from voting on a bill. They ask, in effect, are Biden and his attorneys going to prosecute them also? In summation the Justices rule that this law applies only to the altering or destruction of documents. Since none of the people arrested on January 6th were accused of altering evidence, they cannot be prosecuted under the law Biden and his crowd arrested them for. Biden and his lawyers, speechless and embarrassed, both now clench their fists and threaten to hold their breaths, but the Justices ignore them.

4/24

Trump made a headline-drawing visit to a New York bodega during a break in the witch-hunt trial Biden arranged for him in Manhattan. Biden attempts to copy it by making a heavily choreographed stop at a Sheetz, a gas station chain famous for its friendly customer service and its popular made-to-order food. The stop didn't go as Biden hoped. While Trump was enthusiastically greeted and cheered on his visit, Biden was pretty much ignored at his except for two people requesting selfies. In fact, it is rumored that when the Sheetz hostess was asked if she was impressed by the presidents' visit, she said that she didn't remember any president visiting, just some doddery elder, supported at the elbows, who shuffled through her place and didn't leave a tip.

4/25

Perhaps because of the cool reception for him at Sheetz, as soon as the last photo op of Biden was taken there, Biden and his EOEC sue this beloved family-owned business for racial discrimination. Biden is suing the company for, of all things, using criminal background checks in their hiring practices. Biden claims that this disproportionately impacts black, American Indian and multiracial applicants. The fact that these groups have substantially larger criminal records than other groups is tossed off by Biden as coincidence. Biden is asked about the classlessness of using Sheetz for a photo op, then turning around and suing them. Biden replies: "I didn't do that. Why would I do that? I love their Big Mac… where would I...", then trails off. Confused again of where he was at and what he is being asked about, the rest of Bidens' reply is muffled as he is quickly surrounded by his nurses.

4/26

Bidens' classless, tasteless lawsuit against Sheetz moves on, even though both Biden and his EOEC admit that there is no intentional discrimination going on at the company. Biden is using what his EOEC calls 'Disparate Impact Theory' to continue the suit This so-called "theory" holds companies liable for discrimination even when it's an unintentional result of policy. The actual numbers that spurred this action makes Biden look like a clown. They reveal that Biden is suing Sheetz because in their hiring, the company rejected 14.5% of black applicants for failing a criminal background check while only 8% of white applicants were denied for the same reason. This means that what Biden is offering Sheetz is if they find 57% more white applicants with criminal records, interviews and rejects them, then equity will be achieved and Biden will drop the lawsuit. A clown indeed; a sad clown to be sure, but still a clown.

4/27

Biden agrees to a softball interview with Howard Stern, one where Stern would steer the president into a clearing that would reflect only Bidens' pho-greatness as a leader and a down-home, regular guy. Unfortunately the hapless Biden steers the interview off the rails and into darkness. First Biden lies about how many people he saved as a lifeguard, both while growing up and later in college. Then Biden says that women were constantly sending him "salacious pictures" when he was in the Senate, but he turned all the pictures over to the Secret Service. This likely another lie since e Senators don't rate Secret Service protection. Then Biden lies about leading the desegregation effort in his neighborhood while still a child. Expanding on this false hood, Biden claims he was arrested while or because – Biden is not quite sure - he was standing on a porch with a black family. Bidens' final whopper is that he was state runner-up scoring champ in football, an achievement Biden says was made possible because he has such "soft hands".The second part of this lie might be verifiable. If one could gather together all the young girls Biden has grabbed to fondle and sniff their hair, and all the women and Hollywood starlets he's groped, one could ask them how soft Bidens' hands are.

4/28

Lost in the thunderous daily noise created by Bidens' failed immigration, foreign and economic policies, many voters missed Biden signing an expansion of the Title IX law several days ago. Title IX is the law that prohibits sex-based discrimination at any school which accepts Federal monies. Bidens' expansion makes it illegal to call teachers and students by any pronoun other than the one they choose. It also makes it illegal to bar any student or teacher from using the locker room or bathroom of their choice, regardless of their biological gender. Five states have already sued Biden over these new rules while officials in other states, stopping short of filing lawsuits, say they will not enforce these new rules that mandate compliance with Bidens' radically perverse gender ideology.

4/29

Gender mutilation activists are furious with Biden, insisting that his new Title IX proclamation does not go far enough in protecting so-called "gender affirming rights". They demand that Bidens' proclamation include making it illegal to bar men from participating in womens' sports. Biden does not weigh in on this demand, leaving it instead to the various schools to address this demand. Biden punts on this issue despite recent reports of girls being badly injured by men playing against them. Bidens' gutlessness in this exposes his fear of offending the gender – mutilation crowd that is part of his core constituent base and guarantees more injuries for young girls playing sports in America.

4/30

Another bad day for Biden that he brings on himself. First, after just signing off on a $61 billion aid package to Ukraine, the Ukrainians do the one thing Biden asked them not to, bomb another oil facility in Russia. This puts Biden in a tough position. His crime family has long-standing 'business' connections with Ukraine, but Biden needs Russian oil to offset the shortages he caused in here in America by constantly attacking its' fossil fuel industries. Before Biden can deal with this 'Sophies Choice', social media personality Farha Khalidi now admits that Biden paid her to spread "political propaganda" on her platforms while not telling her hundreds of thousands of followers what she was up to. Biden, already caught coercing major social media platforms to censor conservatives, is now caught paying other media outlets to spread his personal propaganda. On this bad day, Bidens' doddering, braggadocio behavior might engender sympathy from some, but it's hard to feel sorry for a fool, even an old fool, whose wounds are so often self-inflicted.

5/1

A news website reveals that Biden's nurses no longer trust him to walk by himself. From now on they will surround Biden as he shuffles from place to place, ostensibly to keep Biden from falling. It turns out the real reason for this new entourage is to hide Bidens' impaired gait from prying news cameras. Facing re-election, the last thing Bidens' nurses want is a video showing Biden, not as the capable leader of the free world, but rather as an impaired elder on his way to a diner, shuffling as fast as he can so not to miss the early-bird special.

5/2

More and more commentators notice that Biden's physical and mental decline "... puts the entire country at risk." and has turned America into a laughingstock on the world stage. Now Biden is having trouble distinguishing which of his stories are self-deprecating and which are true insults. Biden recounts a trip he took recently to Scranton. While there Biden asserts he was met by a "...seven years old, eight years old..." child who greeted Biden by giving him the middle finger salute. Biden said that, while surprised, that this particular salute "... happens all the time." One wag remarks that having youngsters greet Biden in this manner might actually be inspiring. At a time when most young people embrace Bidens' liberal Marxist ideology, the fact that kids giving Biden the middle finger "happens all the time" might be a positive sign for the future of America.

5/3

Biden is again accused of flying close to a half million illegals into the U.S. and depositing them in at least 40 American cities. Instead of answering his accusers, Biden tacitly admits this is true by informing reporters that he is also planning to fly Palestinians into the U.S. with few vetting process in place, all on the taxpayers' dime. Biden is asked how can flying hundreds of thousands of illegals and others who might have terrorist connections, be in the best interest of the U.S. Biden dodges the question, instead saying he believes this situation is a win-win for everyone: The illegals get a free flight to a location of their choosing where they can free-load off the American taxpayer, the Palestinians, terrorists included, can do the same and Biden gets the biggest 'win', a boatload of frequent flier miles on his credit card.

5/4

It seems that a couple of days ago Biden gave a speech in which he railed against his supposed allies in the media because they aren't writing enough puff pieces about how well he is doing in the polls, regardless that the majority of them show Biden consistently trailing Trump. Biden contends that in the last 23 national polls his nurses have read to him, he has been ahead in 10 of them, Trump only in 8, the rest tied. Because of these numbers, Biden believes the momentum is clearly in his favor. Biden demands that his leftist media friends do something about the negative articles that show him trailing Trump. Unfortunately, 24 hours after Biden delivered his marching orders, reality intruded. Polls from Arizona, Georgia, Michigan, Nevada, North Carolina, Pennsylvania and Wisconsin showed Trump not only increasing his lead, but leading Biden in six of the seven so-called 'swing states'.

5/5

Since his first day in office, Bidens' attack on small businesses in America has continued unabated, with Biden is using every opportunity to force feed his Marxist crap down their throats. A recent ruling by Bidens' Equal Opportunity Employment Commission (EOEC) is another example of this. This new law perverts the intended meaning of of a bill passed by Congress in 2022, the 'Pregnant Workers Fairness Act'. This bill was enacted to accommodate pregnant women in the workplace. Biden and his EOEC insist the this original law should now include employer accommodations for both abortion and birth control for their employees. Critics blast Biden, accusing him of not following the intent of the original law, but instead using his EOEC to advance his personal abortion agenda. Since Bidens' EOEC has no comment, it is assumed they are hiding in Bidens' basement with him.

5/6

Biden complains to his nurses about being plagued by pro-Hamas protesters, upset by the names they're calling him, like "Genocide Joe". Yet in a classic case of 'chickens coming home to roost', the groups funding the terrorist protesters are some of the same ones funding Bidens' reelection. They include such donors as Soros, Rockefeller and Pritzker. It is rumored that the protests at Columbia and other universities were organized by groups like Jewish Voice for Peace and IfNotNow, both supported by the Tides Foundation which, it turns out is seeded by Soros and previously by the Gates Foundation. While this leaves Biden stuck in a very uncomfortable middle, it does explain a recent secret report issued by his nurses. It confirms that lately they have found Biden at his desk, often slapping himself hard across the face while yelling: "Stop hitting me, stop hitting me!"

5/7

For the first time since he became president Biden decides to address the crisis at the southern border by allocating additional funds to the area. Everyone wonders what Bidens' first move with the funds be: Will it be to curb the flow of thousands of illegals crashing the border on a daily basis? Will it be an effort to stop the flow of fentanyl, the drug that's crossing the border and killing 100,000 Americans a year? Then again, will it be used to stop the sex trafficking and rapes of minors? All significant, disturbing problems … but no. Biden proposes that a much better use of the new money is to use it adopt shelter dogs abandoned close to the border and train them to be 'comfort animals' for Border Patrol agents. These are the same agents who are routinely denied by Biden requested funds to help stop the daily flow of thousands of illegals, the flow of fentanyl and the sex trafficking and rapes of minors. Having to contend with these horrendous problems for years with neither support or relief from Biden, it is doubtful that his dogs will bring much comfort to these agents.

5/8

With the elections season approaching, Biden gets more bad news when Democrats join Republicans and both point their fingers at Biden for being responsible for "the worst border security crisis in the nation's history." 13 members of Bidens' own party joined Republicans in voting for something called H.RES.1112, a resolution "...denouncing the Bidens' immigration policies..." and calling for stronger border security measures. Several of the Democrats told reporters they joined the Republicans in this matter because Biden has failed to secure the southern border and stop the violent drug cartels pumping fentanyl and other drugs into America. In considering this mutiny by his own Democrats and their biting criticism, Biden pushes his Aviators back up higher on his nose, refusing to comment.

5/9

Biden continues trying to blackmail school districts across the country to accept the new civil rights regulations he signed in the last couple of weeks. Those regulations made it a crime to call teachers and students by anything other than their chosen pronoun and also made it a crime to keep students or teachers out of any locker room or bathroom they wanted to use, regardless of their biological sex. Bidens' new law clashes directly with many States' laws on this matter. Bidens' answer is blackmail, threatening any state or school district that does not enforce his ruling with forfeiting any federal funding it receives. Bidens' trademark bullying may not work so easily this time: In four separate lawsuits, filed in federal courts in Alabama, Louisiana, Texas and Kentucky, AGs in more than a dozen states are trying to block the regulations from going to effect in August as Biden has planned.

5/10

Acknowledging his failed economic and foreign policies, Biden tries to force abortion into being the main issue in the upcoming election. To his dismay, his nurses show him a poll that demonstrates his strategy is not working. In this poll, abortion was far down the list, with Americans voting overwhelmingly that Bidens' record inflation is number one concern. One would expect this since Biden grew the inflation rate of 1.4% - what Trump left him - a staggering 600%, to its' historic high of 9%. This would be a major problem for most, but not Biden. He schedules an interview on CNN, where he lies in an attempt to rewrite history, claiming that inflation was already at 9% when he took office. Incredibly, Biden wants voters to believe that those who documented the gift 1.4% rate that Trump left him - economists from here and all over the world, financial institutions, the Wall Street Journal and other financial publications, the Bureau of Labor Statistics, the Bureau Of Economic Analysis and even Bidens' own Commerce Department – are all the ones who are lying, not him.

5/11

It turns out that in his CNN interview, the lie Biden told about the inflation rate differences between his and Trumps' term was not the only one. Perhaps the latest polls showing Biden trailing Trump badly across the nation, including swing states, panicked him. Whatever it was, Biden spouted lies and twisted truths at a spectacular rate, even for him. Besides the inflation rate, Biden lied about the number of jobs he created, about the tax rate that "the rich" in America pay and even the number of civilians killed by Israel in Gaza. One website that popped up shortly after Bidens' interview listed 15 lies that Biden told in the

17 minutes the interview lasted. While maybe hard to believe, this fact is corroborated by the record number of nation-wide, fact-checking machines that reportedly short-circuited by the interviews' end.

5/12

Biden supporters are furious at their perceived mockery of Bidens' "15 lies in 17 minutes" CNN interview being splashed across social media. One story that Biden tells they swear is true is what happened at a recent state dinner attended by leaders from all over the world. While he is at the dinner, Biden swears that "… 80% of them (world leaders) say 'you gotta win. My democracy is at stake.'" In truth, this did happen. What Biden leaves out, or perhaps was never aware of, is that while Biden was napping during dinner - his head almost in his soup dish - someone snuck up from behind and pinned a 'Donald Trump' name tag on his jacket.

5/13

Biden shows a new depth in his bullying crudeness by turning Mothers Day into an attack on Trump. Biden approves of an ad that shows a clip of Trump talking about his America First border security policies, carefully edited to give the false impression that Trump wants to break up illegal alien families in the U.S. If Biden played the entire video it would show that Trump was only making arrangements for the children to be cared for separately at the border so they wouldn't have not be incarcerated while their parents were waiting for their hearing. Bidens' ad angers Trump. His spokesman responds by noting what "...a sad, miserable, cowardly existence (Biden must have) to make such a disgusting ad on such a joyous day." True, and what is also true is that even on Mothers Day, Trump continues to live rent free in what's left of Bidens' mind.

5/14

Biden supporters are left dumbfounded by the 80 to 100 thousand people that reportedly attend a Trump rally in New Jersey, many of them camping out overnight just to see him. What makes it worse for Biden, New Jersey is historically a Democratic stronghold. Reporters contrast Trumps' event with the fundraiser Biden recently attended. There some local officials, a few supporters and a group of anti-Israel protesters were all that showed up. One wag noted that Biden, outside of his staff, some politicians and protesters, couldn't draw enough people to fill a "broom closet". True, but on the bright side, it wouldn't have to be a very big closet.

5/15

Internal DHS data, acquired only because it was subpoenaed, confirms the rumor that Biden has flown hundreds of thousands of migrants into 45+ U.S. cities using his "CHNV" mass parole program. This program allows Biden to legally import 30,000 immigrants per month each from Cuba, Haiti, Nicaragua and Venezuela as long as an equal number of illegals from these countries that are in the U.S. already are deported back into Mexico. According to CBP data, Biden has flown at least 404,000 migrants into the U.S. via this program since Biden started it back in January of 2023. This same data reflects, contrary to his promises, that to date Biden has deported few if any illegals from these four countries back to Mexico.

5/16

Though most can make no sense of Bidens' semi-coherent ramblings, at times what he doesn't say can be just as revealing. A bill aimed at booting illegal immigrants out of the U.S. if they assault police officers passed the House of Representatives, but only by a 265 to 148 vote. 148 Democrats, all of whom support Biden, voted to allow criminals, already in the U.S. illegally, to remain in the country even after they assault police officers. The fact that Biden has no comment on his partys' resolute demand that violent illegals who have assaulted police officers be allowed to remain speaks louder than any mumbling collection of letters and sounds Biden might drool.

5/17

A diary allegedly belonging to one of Bidens' daughters surfaced some time ago. In it she detailed a troubled youth caused by, among other things, being exposed to events that "over - sexualized" her. One of these events was Biden taking what she describes as "probably inappropriate" showers with her. The entire Biden family disputes the authenticity of the diary, saying there is no proof that it belongs to Bidens' daughter. Their denials take a hit when a recording surfaces of Bidens' daughter asking the person who now has her diary to return it because it belongs to her. Several times on the recording she confirms that the diary "is mine"and threatens to get the Secret Service involved. It seems that neither the authenticity nor the owner of the diary is a subject of dispute, even if what's written on the inside is.

5/18

While Biden watches, the House passes a two-part resolution, one which condemns all violence against all law enforcement, the second criticizing jurisdictions that call for defundng police departments. Consistent with their vote to allow criminal illegals who attack police officers in America to stay in America, 61 of Bidens Democratic allies vote against the measure. The Democrat vote comes just after the FBI released new statistics showing that assaults against law enforcement reached a ten-year-high in 2023, with 79,000 recorded attacks. Astonishing no one, Biden says nothing, letting both anti-law enforcement votes by his Congressional supporters fly by without comment, perhaps because they didn't pass close enough to his basement window.

5/19

Bidens' VP Harris took time out from her busy schedule of not securing Americas' southern border to participate in a conversation with something called the 'Asian Pacific American Institute for Congressional Studies Legislative Leadership Conference Summit'.In response to questions about her career, she gives one of her infamous word-salad speeches. She finishes by instructing the participants that when in their careers the they confront doors that are closed to them by people that "...don't look like them...", they "…need to kick that (expletive) door down." Bidens' VP, always classy, felt it necessary to drop the F-bomb to emphasize her personal career advice that has carried her to the heights of her success: When kicking these supposed obstacles down – even metaphysically - it's always easier to do it from an upright position

5/20

Biden arrives in Atlanta to deliver what many expect will be an awkward, race-pandering commencement speech at Morehouse College. The awkwardness for Biden started long before he made it to the college. Unlike Trump, who is regularly greeted by tens of thousands of people wherever he appears, literally no one showed up to greet Biden. This did not go unnoticed by onlookers. One reporter remarked that the only people on the sidewalk as Bidens' motorcade passed were only those that wanted to cross the street. Another jibed that while Trump recently attracted a reported overwhelming crowd of 100,000 in New Jersey, Biden attracted an overwhelming crowd of four in Atlanta. One researcher from the RNC even waxed quasi- philosophical, asking: "If a presidential motorcade passes through town but absolutely nobody cares – did it really pass through town?" Since Biden eventually did make it to Morehouse, evidently it did.

5/21

Black voters react strongly to Bidens' commencements address at Morehouse, but not in a positive way for Biden. Many students accuse Biden of race-baiting in a desperate effort to shore up his rapidly-waning support among black voters, which has plummeted 27% since Biden took office. Many students expressed the feeling that it was "very obvious" that they were being used to score political points. Some of the students and teachers even turned their backs on Biden during the ceremony in silent protest of how Biden has treated American Blacks during his time in office. Many students felt insulted by Bidens' race-baiting speech that portrayed all minorities as victims incapable of competing without Bidens' help, and all whites as oppressors. They also found it ironic that Biden, a "… BLM-style race hustler that promotes anti-American racial division, discrimination and segregation..." thought it appropriate that he should be the one to lecture the Morehouse students on racism.

5/22

Outrage at Bidens' race-baiting commencement speech at Morehouse College continues. The part of the speech that inflames critics the most is the section where Biden implied that absolutely nothing, including democracy, would be waiting for the graduates since "... black men are being killed (everyday) in the street (of America)" Bidens' gross attempt to tie the graduates' future to what happened to George Floyd does not go unnoticed. What Biden carefully omitted from his race-baiting is that while it's true in America black men are being killed in the streets, they are being killed mostly by other black men and have been for years. In 2019, the year before George Floyd was killed, there were 2,906 black murder cases where the race of the killer was known. The racial breakdown was 246 white, 86 'other' and a astounding 2,574 black, meaning that close to 90% of those American Blacks killed that year were murdered, not by whites or the police, but by other American Blacks. Whatever Bidens' goal is in his relentless race-baiting of the American voter, regardless of color, truth is not one of them.

5/23

Taiwan – a country that before Biden was one of Americas' staunchest allies - elects an anti-Chinese Communist as its' new President. In response, Communist China unleashes a two-day exercise involving its' army, navy and rocket forces. The drills completely encircle the island and are conducted, according to a Communist spokesman, to "…serve as a strong punishment for the separatist acts of Taiwan independence' forces…" and as a "…stern warning against the interference and provocation by external forces." In response, the new President of Taiwan vows to "…defend the values of democracy and safeguard peace and stability in the region." What is just as telling in his statement is what Taiwans' President did not say. In the past Taiwan could call on the U.S. for support. However, after Biden announced he would not interfere with the Communists' "One China" policy, which includes the annexation of Taiwan, the Taiwanese people have come to realize that with Biden they are on their own.

5/24

While Biden sits on his hands, a special maliciousness about Chinas' attack on Taiwan becomes apparent. This is the height of the fishing season, a major industry in Taiwan. By choosing this time of year to surround the tiny island with their ships, China has grossly impacted the fishing industry of the island. Not only are the Communists preventing Taiwanese fishermen access to the water, the presence of their ships force the islands' normally large population of fish to scatter to other areas of the sea. This essentially ruins Taiwans' fishing industry for the season. As for this Communist excursion being a warning against interference by Taiwans' allies, other countries may come to Taiwans' aid, but like what most former allies have learned since Biden became president, there is a good chance it won't be America.

5/25

Reaction to Bidens' race-baiting speech at Morehous College still simmers in the media. It causes voters to reconsider a series of polls taken in the last few months. One found that Trumps' support among Black voters had risen to 23%, compared to the 4% support he had in the 2020 election. Another poll found that approximately 30% of American Black men polled across seven swing states are backing Trumps' bid to return to the White House. At the same time Biden's support among black k voters has plummeted to 63%, close to a 30-point decline from the 92% that Biden won in 2020. More and more American Black voters feel that Trump relates better than Biden to their community, a voting block Biden felt his race-baiting had locked down.

5/26

Trump calls out Biden for his catastrophic failure in attempting to force Americans to buy electric vehicles. Biden stubbornly holds onto this dream despite three years of consistent reports showing that the vast majority of Americans don't want these vehicles even if they could afford them, which most cannot. Of the 4 million vehicles purchased last year, 98% were not EVs. Then Biden and his transportation secretary are asked what happened to the half million new charging stations, paid for with $7.5 billion of Americans' taxpayer monies on the promise they would be completed by 2030. To date, a total of eight – eight - stations have been finished. Both Biden and his incompetent TS have no comment.

5/27

On this Memorial Day Biden lays the traditional wreath at the Tomb of the Unknown Soldier. It seems that paying respects to Americas' heroes is too much for Biden as he is caught napping during the ceremony. His nurses defend Biden, saying that Biden wasn't sleeping, but just resting his eyes for an extended period of time. Unfortunately this latest antic by Biden conjures up memories of when Biden attended the casket arrival at Dover of the 13 soldiers he got killed in Afghanistan. During that ceremony Biden was caught several times checking his watch, as if he wanted to be anywhere except standing next to his 13 flag-draped coffins. To this day Bidens' nurses insist that Bidens' critics got it all wrong. They maintain Biden was not checking his watch as if worried about missing the next re-run of Matlock. No, they say Biden was merely having trouble shutting off his watch alarm, which beeps incessantly whenever it's time for Bidens' next can of Ensure.

5/28

Biden continues to ignore reality. EV sales are plummeting all over the world. Manufacturers from Tesla on down are curtailing production and laying off employees due to the lack of demand for these over-priced, expensive-to maintain vehicles. Companies that build batteries and other parts for these vehicles are slowing down or outright canceling future investments in the technology. Despite this Biden bubble-brains a demand that in 6 years 50% of all new cars sold in America must be electric. This requires a 400% increase each year for the next 6 years, for cars that most don't want now. Biden and his TS might be forgiven their stupidity that makes them world-wide laughingstocks, though: These numbers are rather large and do exceed the total number of both mens' fingers and toes.

5/29

Because of the Freedom of Information Act, new documents are released regarding Bidens' organizing the raid in August, 2022, of Trumps Mar-A-Lago residence. Biden said that the raid was only for searching for classified documents he accused Trump of stealing. A look at the actual warrant shows it contained an OK from Biden for the FBI to use "deadly force" if necessary against Trump, his wife and any guests at Mar-A-Lago. Biden defends this action, asserting that the threat to use deadly force is in all search warrants he signs off on. Biden can't explain, though the FBIs' savage ransacking of Trumps' house, including his wife Melanias' lingerie drawer. Noting the FBIs' history, this part of the raid can be explained: The agents anger probably came from hoping, but failing to find anything in Melanias' underwear drawer that was their size.

5/30

Trump is found guilty in the first of four sham trials Biden has arranged for him. The bastardizing of the American legal system by Biden is now on full display. First a gag order is placed on Trump, but not on the jury, leaving them free to talk to friends, family and consume all sorts of media coverage, all of which could have influenced their decisions. Then Trump is never informed of what specific crime he's being charged with until the case is over and jury instructions are issued. Then in the instructions, the judge presents the jurors with a smorgasbord of of crimes to choose from. He reassures the jurors that a unanimous verdict is not required, as long as least one juror thinks Trump is guilty of at least one of each of the array of crime choices presented to them. This Banana-Republic stunt of a verdict will be tossed out on appeal, but Biden doesn't care. If an appeals court tosses the conviction next year, but the guilty verdict helps Biden win in November, then Bidens' plan will have worked.

5/31

Since Biden spends the majority of his time these days hiding in his basement, Washington media is surprised when he decides to hold a presser to talk about Trumps' felony conviction. Biden graciously allows that Trump will be given the opportunity to appeal the kangaroo-court conviction Biden arranged for him, but admonishes Trump, saying that it was "reckless" and "dangerous" to call this obviously rigged trial, rigged. As Biden was leaving, a reporter shouted: "Donald Trump refers to himself as a political prisoner and blames you directly. What's your response to that, sir?" The president paused and lurched his head in a Exorcist-type turn towards the reporter. Then slowly pulling his gums back, Biden grimaced a smile that reporters called "disturbing" and "creepy" for almost a full, disturbing 10 seconds before walking away with no comment.

6/1

As polls continue to show that the sham conviction Trump received in New York did not diminish his nationwide lead, panic begins to set in for Biden. He repeatedly and loudly defends Trumps' conviction and accuses Trump of being reckless and dangerous for denouncing the kangaroo-court verdict he was handed. This comes from Biden, a man who brags about his influence pedaling in Ukraine, defends his sons' drug-infused dealings with Americas' enemies, has boasted about disregarding several Supreme Court rulings against him and has openly mocked the Justices on national TV in his SOTU broadcasts. Bidens' panic is understandable since he received word today that his plan to derail Trump with phony convictions is not working: In just 10 hours after the kangaroo guilty verdict, Trump received 39 million dollars in new donations, so many that his website that handles donations crashed.

6/2

Bidens' fragile mental state seems to be on the verge of derangement when he announces a peace agreement he has proffered to Hamas over the objections of Americas' supposed ally, Israel. In it Biden promises the gangster terrorists that Israel will initiate an immediate ceasefire, leave Gaza and provide relief aid to the Palestinians, all with only a promise by the thugs to release Israeli hostages sometime in the future. Israel immediately disavows Bidens' proposal, telling Biden that any agreement involving a cease fire and withdrawal from Gaza until

Hamas is destroyed is a "non-starter" Much to Bidens' embarrassment, the Israelis are not the only ones to tell Biden to pound sand. It turns out that the Hamas terrorists don't want to accept Bidens' "peace deal" either. This just confirms what Hamas has long been accused of, that these miscreants welcome the bloodshed they bring on their own people and wish it to continue.

6/3

To no ones bewilderment except Biden, Trumps' new donations reach a reported $300 million in just the 4 days since Biden and his henchmens' kangaroo verdict in New York. Biden attempts his best 'Peter 'Denying Christ' impression, first denying that Trump was treated unfairly and, as such, shouldn't dispute his conviction because no one is "above the law". Then he denies that Trump has anything to be mad about since he can always appeal his conviction. Thirdly, Biden pleads that since this was a State case and not a Federal one, he denies having any involvement in the matter. Reporters start to laugh, but then quiet immediately upon hearing a distant noise: It's not a cock crowing, but the sound of Trumps' donation website ginning back to life.

6/4

Biden announces that he might sign an executive order shortly that will "shut down the southern border", something that Trump did essentially 3 years ago. Biting their lips in an attempt to hide their derisive laughter, reporters hear Biden tell them that his "shutdown" will still enable him to allow 2500 illegals to cross the border daily, meaning that by the first week in November Biden will see to it that another 400,000 illegals cross the border. Add to this the approximate 25000 each month Biden is flying into the U.S. via his CHNV Mass Parole program, by election day in November Bidens' "shutdown" will add another 500,000 illegals to the 10+ million Biden has already allowed in: Quite a shutdown, indeed.

6/5

Biden signs an Executive Order on immigration, piling hypocrisy upon hypocrisy. Biden had claimed he had no such power to close the border this first 3 ½ years in office, so let 10 to 11 million illegals enter the country. Now Biden uses his EO power to shut down the border, his order is the same one he tried to get Congress to pass recently. They refused because Bidens' "shutdown" plan was no plan at all. It still allowed over 1 million illegals to enter the county yearly, permits all children to still cross the border and these are in addition to the ones Biden flies into the country on a monthly basis. Then Biden accuses Republicans of being at fault for the border crisis when on his first day in office Biden himself stripped all the border protections Trump had put in place. Biden continues to be a man of stumbling, bumbling hypocrisy and lies.

6/6

Lost in the war of words Biden has launched on Trump since the Manhattan trial is that the gag order, preventing Trump from speaking about the trial, is still in place despite the trial being over. Further, the DA Bragg, after eating an entire lunch by himself that was catered for his staff, insists that the gag order remain in place indefinitely for the foreseeable future. There is no such gag order for Biden, Stormy Daniels or Cohen. This trio has hit all manner of media, all proclaiming their innocence, all with disparaging, insulting comments about Trump and all righteously proclaiming that "justice was served". One has to wonder what the odds are of these three - one a convicted thief and grifting liar, one a sleazy porn star and then, Biden – all in the same line of work, being brought together through the confluence of this trial.

6/7

Bidens' pandering is rapidly approaching the psychotic and it seems that polls are the driving force behind Bidens' madness. When a recent poll showed that the majority of voters believe Trump did a much better job with the economy, Biden flooded states that he lost in 2020 with billions of tax-payer dollars, with no constraints on how the money could be spent. When another poll showed Biden losing support among Muslim supporters of Hamas, Biden switches his support from Israel to the terrorist group, now claiming both parties equally responsible for the bloodshed. In essence, Biden is morally equating the Jews butchered on 10/7 with the Hamas animals who did the butchering. With Bidens' incessant backstabbing of allies, backtracking and flip-flopping his positions wherever the latest polls direct him to go, no one should be surprised one of these days, during one of his famous word-salad speeches, Bidens' head just pops.

6/8

Despite Bidens' continued denials, it has been documented that he emptied a large part the U.S. arsenal to arm Ukraine in its' losing war against Russia. Now, provocatively, Biden gives the go-ahead for Ukraine to carry out military strikes against Russia using those very weapons from the U.S. arsenal. Biden claims he doesn't want World War III with Russia but his continual green lighting of Americas' increased involvement in Ukraines' war runs the risk of doing exactly that. Further confusing the entire world, this is a stance that is polar opposite of when Biden told Ukraine that it must end it's war with Russia – the one Biden keeps escalating - before it could be considered for membership in NATO. Yet another example of Bidens' head-shaking attempt to simultaneously support both sides of a dangerous issues, clearly Bidens' head is ready to pop.

6/9

One of Bidens' ugliest agenda items since the beginning of his presidency is his determination to make his Marxist/Socialist race warfare policy the guiding principle in every walk of American life and force his anti-life principles down the throats of every American. Bidens' latest target is the VA where, under the guise of DEI, he is implementing race-based training programs that explicitly exclude white veterans. Bidens' VA communications official issued a statement which said that discrimination against white veterans is not new, that the VA began "a lot of our racial equity work" in the spring of 2021 after Biden issued his executive order on DEI for the military. He, like Biden, dismissed push back from critics of these blatantly racist programs, arguing that in the military, "treating everybody the same might not be enough." This is pure racism and, being a life-long racist himself, pure Biden.

6/10

The irony of Biden demanding that DEI be forced into Americas' military is not lost on anyone. The Obamas' created the myth of "institutionalized" racism that is, according to them, ".. in the DNA..." of every white person in America, just as a matter of being born white. Since then Biden and others of his racist ilk have used the moniker 'institutionalized racism' as a dog-whistle in order to attract black voters. The Obamas chided whites who protested being called racists, saying that since racism was in their DNA it was probable they were unaware of their "unconscious bias". The irony is that now their protege Biden, following their lead, is the first to openly, officially and consciously institutionalize racism in America., using the Veterans Administration as a starting point.

6/11

Biden travels to Normandy for the 80th anniversary of D-Day, the greatest military success in American history. Biden and the French president were set to greet and congratulate the veterans of that historical day. For most this is a somber, respectively muted remembrance and appreciation for those brave men, but not for Biden. Just as the ceremony is about to begin, Biden bizarrely begins to look around aimlessly, then squats down and freezes in place, fists clenched, looking for all the world like one of the gargoyles that perch on nearby French cathedrals. In front of shocked onlookers but before anyone can move, Bidens' wife shuffles him off the stage, leaving the French president to greet the D-Day heroes by himself. This is another humiliating, world-wide embarrassment for America, courtesy of Biden.

6/12

Bidens' perceived weakness on the world stage and his disastrous open-border policy has started to bring the pigeons home to to roost. Eight individuals from Tajikistan with suspected ties to ISIS, who crossed into the U.S. from the southern border, are detained in Los Angeles, Philadelphia and New York City. According to Biden, the suspects were allowed to enter the U.S. after being vetted and no national security issues were uncovered. Once in the country, though, authorities uncovered information indicating these eight had some ties or affiliation with ISIS so now the suspects have been detained. To add to this, at the same time the terrorists that snuck across the border are detained, four Russian warships arrive in Cuba. This is the, the first time Russias' military has visited the island in force since the disastrous Cuban Missile Crisis back in the early '60s. Needless to say, a very bad day for Biden.

6/13

Russia at first reassures Biden that there is no cause to worry about the four Russian warships that have arrived in Cuba, but then scolds Biden for appearing to ignore all diplomatic signals from Moscow until its' army or navy takes action. In response Bidens' National Security Advisor tells him that there is no evidence that Russia was transferring any missiles to Cuba, but this action can be seen as a Russian show of force as tensions rise over the Ukraine and Americas' involvement there. Biden too assures the American people that there is nothing to worry about and he will stay vigilant. Yes, as long as he is not being attacked by a flight of stairs, assaulted by creepy, scary teleprompters or crouching down like a frozen Gargoyle in France, Biden will remain vigilant.

6/14

A video catches a group of world leaders, including Biden, at the G7 conference with eyes skyward to review a parachute exhibition put on for their behalf. While the rest are looking upwards, Biden wanders away by himself. Critics claim Biden was going on a 'walk-about' in a nearby forest, while supporters say Biden was merely walking away in order to congratulate a parachutist who completed his jump. Either way, Biden stands frozen, goofy grin on his face. Then the Italian Prime Minister, looking more like an assisted-living nurse, hurries over to retrieve Biden, turn him around and lead him back to the group, goofy grin and all. Onlookers wonder how Biden could still smile after such an embarrassment until it is revealed that the Prime Minister promised Biden that, if he was good and returned to the group without being fussy, she would get him an ice cream.

6/15

Biden signs a 10-year security pact with Ukraine, guaranteeing a supply of weapons, intelligence support, a 50 billion dollar loan to rebuild the country and technology needed to win Ukraines' current war with Russia and to deter any new one. However, after signing Biden declines to attend a peace summit in Switzerland comprised of 90 countries around the world, all committed to finding a peaceful resolution to the conflict. Despite the beseeching of the Ukrainian president, Biden instead chooses to travel to LA to party with such intellectual heavyweights as George Clooney, Julia Roberts and Barbara Streisand. As if to emphasize how little he thinks of the peace conference, Biden sends VP Harris, famous world-wide for her incomprehensible word-salad rants, to take his place. To add insult to those already injured – and to the dismayed anger of the 90 countries in attendance – Biden sends Harris to the peace summit without providing an interpreter.

6/16

While Biden parties with Hollywood celebrities, the peace summit in Switzerland ends with 78 of the 90 participating countries calling for the "territorial integrity" of Ukraine to be the basis for any peace agreement between that country and Russia. Several countries in attendance that do business with Russia refused to join in the resolution. Many delegates were seen leaving the summit on unsteady legs, eyes wide and slapping the sides of their heads as if trying to restore their hearing. At first thought caused by consternation over the countries that refused to participate in the resolution, it was later learned that Bidens' VP Harris gave a speech. Based on her past speeches, this might've been the main reason for the discombobulation of the delegates rather than any concern over the countries that did not wish to participate.

6/17

If polls are to be believed, Bidens' hopes that a guilty verdict in Trumps sham Manhattan trial would sink Trump take another hit. The Marist poll has been one of the most favorable pollsters for Biden, consistently reporting Biden leading Trump in all of its' national surveys. Now this same poll shows Biden trailing Trump 45% to 47% in Pennsylvania, a state key to Bidens' re-election. Panicked and realizing he can't run on his failed domestic, foreign and economic policies, Biden now plans to make abortion rights the key issue of his campaign. Believing this is the only issue he can win on, Bidens' campaign will hold more than 30 events across America, hoping to force abortion into being the key and only issue in the upcoming election. In order to accomplish this, Biden wishes himself good luck in making the American people not notice his inflated prices that make ends harder for them to meet everyday, the invasion of illegals his immigration policies have unleashed, destroying their cities, or the brink of World War lll his foreign policies have brought America to the brink of.

6/18

A video from Bidens' Los Angeles fundraiser is surfing on social media. It shows that at the end of the gala Biden stops and freezes as he starts to leave the stage, just as he did several times at the recent G7 Summit. Biden stays standing, stock still, until Obama takes him by the wrist, puts his hand on his back and escorts Biden off the stage. Bidens' nurses insist that he was not lost, but just standing in one place all that time in order to soak up the applause form the audience. They could not explain why Biden stayed frozen in place and did not exit the stage with the others until Obama helps him.

6/19

Since Biden assured Ukraine that it would have Americas' unwavering support regardless how long it continued its' war with Russia, the Ukrainian government has resorted to harsh tactics against anyone in the U.S. criticizing the war. American journalist Gonzalo Lira died in a Ukrainian prison after criticizing the country's government and the Bidens' involvement in the war. Now it is revealed that prominent conservatives, journalists and Republican politicians opposing pouring more American taxpayer money into the war have turned up on an online enemies list. A U.S. Senator and a Congressman join to send a letter to Biden and his Secretary of State, demanding answers about their role in generating this enemies list comprised of U.S. citizens. Both Biden and his SoS have no comment.

6/20

In another thumb-in-the-eye to Biden, Putin announces he will visit Hanoi this week. There Putin will meet Vietnam's new president, To Lam, and other leaders during his two-day visit, highlighting Communist-ruled Vietnam's loyalty to Russia. This is a particular slap in the face to Biden since just last year Biden had supposedly upgraded relations with Hanoi, making the U.S. Vietnam's top trading partner. Biden reacts harshly, with one of his spokesmen declaring that no country should give Putin a platform to promote his Ukraine war and "... normalize his atrocities." Perhaps one of Bidens' nurses should remind Biden of the old saw, that if you lie with dogs there's a good chance you get up with fleas. Then again, judging from his career, Biden doesn't seem to much mind the pesky critters.

6/21

Biden listens to a Trump speech where the former President says that Bidens' foreign policy blunders over the last three years have made

America "... a laughingstock around the world." Biden heatedly denies this, but looking at Bidens' foreign policy blunders just the last three weeks justifies Trumps' claim. First Biden offers Hamas a "peace proposal" that is essentially a 'get-out-of-jail-free' card', This is a "peace deal" that not only back stabs Americas' ally, Israel, it is one that even the terrorists won't accept. Then Russia sails warships into Cuba, a stone throw away from U.S. shores, with Biden saying nary a word. Then while many of the worlds' countries meet in Sweden for a peace summit to end the war in Ukraine Biden primarily financed, he decides not to attend that meeting, instead attending a celebrity-studded party in Hollywood. Biden finishes his three-week foreign policy debacle by having to witness Russia re-establish "loyalty ties" with Vietnam and North Korea, more enemies of the U.S. Biden: a laughingstock dragging America behind him.

6/22

The blood on Bidens' hands caused by illegal aliens he has let cross the border keeps growing. Last week an illegal – who had crossed the southern border four times – was arrested for the rape and murder of Rachel Morin, a mother of 5. This is not an isolated incident. Under Biden there have been many cases of illegal aliens committing heinous crimes in the U.S., including the rape and murder of a 13-year-old girl in Queens, New York, the murder of a 12-year-old girl in Houston, Texas and the recent rape and murder of Laken Riley, the young lady made famous by Biden, in an attempt to show empathy, slurred her name and eventually mispronounced it at his latest SOTU address. Bidens' open-border policies have led to a surge of violent crimes committed by illegals who were never properly vetted In Rachel Morins' case, it is already the second murder in Harford County by an illegal alien from El Salvador in just two years. Biden and Mayorkas, the Tweedledee and Tweedledum in the proliferation of illegal immigration, raise bloodied right hands and still swear the border is secure.

6/23

Bidens' head of DHS, Mayorkas, is raked over the social media coals by Rachel Morin's mother for referring to her murdered daughter only as some "individual" instead of using her name or mentioning that she was a mother of five. She goes further, accusing Bidens' DHS Secretary of making a purely political speech and, by Biden and Mayorkas not using her daughters name or acknowledging that she was a mother "... depersonalizes her and makes her an object." She also angrily revealed that, showing their typical lack of class and human dignity, neither Biden nor Mayorkas or anyone from their staffs has reached out to her and her grieving family since her daughter's alleged killer was arrested.

6/24

Bidens' critics list the striking similarities between Laken Riley and Rachel Morris' murders and their murderers. Both Laken and Rachel were ambushed, raped and murdered while running or hiking. The two pieces of illegal trash that committed these crimes had crossed and re-crossed Bidens' open southern border, unvetted, several times. Rachels' killer was wanted for murder in El Salvador and assault in California before making his way to Maryland to kill her. Lakens' murderer had been arrested several times in the U.S., but released each time without being deported before making his way to Georgia and killing her The other similarity in the two cases is that, though supposedly expressing empathy with and sympathy for the victims and their families, neither Biden or Mayorkas could be bothered with learning the names of the two young women they helped murder.

6/25

Before the country can fully absorb the shock of Lakens' and Rachels' murders, the blood on Bidens' hands from vicious crimes committed by his illegals is moving up to his elbows. This time it is in New York where a criminal from Ecuador who entered the country through Eagle Pass, Texas, ambushed two 13 year-olds in a field after they left their school. He forced them them into nearby woods at knife point and tied them up before sexually assaulting the girl. Fortunately a dozen citizens or so who lived in the neighborhood recognized the man, tackled and held him until the police arrived to make the arrest. The victims' name was not released, giving Biden, Mayorkas and their staffs no chance to forget her, too.

6/26

The bloodletting by Bidens' illegals reaches a fever pitch. As a direct result of Bidens' immigration policies, two more animals that crossed the southern border illegally kidnapped, raped, strangled and then tossed the body of 12-year old Jocelyn Nongaray in a drainage ditch in Houston. Both animals had immigration violation holds on their court records, but instead of deporting them, ICE fit the pair with ankle monitors and turned them loose. More disheartening, simple security cameras around the city recorded the animals as they approached Jocelyn, escorted her in and out of a convenience store and then towards the bridge where they raped and killed her. After all, if your everyday, simple 7-11 security camera can follow these criminal animals, what does Biden have his ICE agents monitoring? A soccer game? The local doughnut shop to see when the morning rush wait lines are gone? The reluctance to deport and the simultaneous reluctance to monitor illegal alien criminals is perhaps the most damning indictment of Bidens' now-murderous open border policies.

6/27

It's another day and Biden reaches another low moral point, two of them in fact. First, polls – the only items that frighten Biden into action – reflect that high fuel prices are a major concern for American voters. Bidens' solution is to once again drop to his knees and beg Americas' worst enemies - Russia, Iran, China, Venezuela – to produce additional fuel supplies. Biden hopes this will keep gas prices low for the American voter in the run-up to November elections. Astonishingly, Biden doesn't know or doesn't care that his largess will fund the atrocities these monster countries are currently committing all over the world. Next, Biden is asked why he has not personally reached out to the family of Jocelyn Nongaray, the 12 year-old murdered by two of his illegals. Bidens' nurses insist he has, but all that can be found is a canned "Our hearts go out to..." speech one of them delivered. Perhaps none of his nurses explained to Biden that "reaching out" and touching the backside of his basement window is not the same as "reaching out" to a family mortally aggrieved because of his immigration policies.

6/28

Trump and Biden hold their first debate and it goes downhill quickly for Biden. Within 20 minutes he is slurring his speech into word - salad answers and then freezing in place, mouth open, staring blankly as if trying to remember where he was. After one such answer, Trump quipped: "I didn't understand one word of what he just said, but I don't think he (Biden) does either." This greatly accelerated Bidens' slide. Sadly, the height of Bidens' intellectual responses to Trump is only to repeat: "He's lying, he's lying!" over and over – and over –again. In the cultural and moral morass America is currently in, Biden can still be re-elected. Nevertheless, any sentient being still voting for Biden after watching his latest debacle has to know they are voting for a physically, mentally fragile octogenarian bully who should have willingly gone to pasture a long time ago.

6/29

Despite calls, even from Democrats, for him to bow out after his disastrous debate performance, a defiant Biden vowed to stay in the race and beat Trump come November. In his speech, Biden acknowledged that he is not young, doesn't walk as well as he used to, doesn't speak or debate well, but insists he still knows right from wrong and "...how to do this job." Even while giving this speech and waving his arms in his in his best Stalin-esque style, Biden still appears frail and this doesn't do much to reassure his audience. What Biden does do is leave all wondering how he plans to "get the job (of being president) done" while not walking, talking or speaking well. Biden leaves the stage, again with assistance from his wife, without addressing this dilemma.

6/30

Despite his embarrassing debate performance and other recent stumbles, Biden tries to reassure Americans that he is the same virile, scrappy "Lunch Bucket Joe" he's always been. However, most Americans remain unconvinced. In fact, going back to the BLM and Antifa riots which Biden refused to censure until the burning embers had died down and bodies were carted off, back to the 13 servicemen he got killed with his botched withdrawal from Afghanistan, back to the thousands Biden helped kill in the Middle East by his continued re-funding of Iran, enabling it to re-fund their terrorist proxies, back to the hundreds of thousands of Americans that have died during Bidens' tenure due to the fentanyl poison he has allowed to cross the southern border and the rash of women raped and murdered by illegal criminals crossing that same border, maybe "Lunch Bucket Joe" is no longer a proper nickname. Based on his performance up until now, the 3 ½ year juncture of his term, a better moniker for Biden might be "Blood Bucket Joe".

... and the saga continues.

(This page intentionally left blank for the reader to record any and all punctuation, grammar, spelling and other errors he/she wishes to note. However, if the critique spans more than a single page, the reader is on the hook for any additional paper.)